APPROACHES TO THE BIBLE:
THE OLD TESTAMENT

PRENTICE-HALL INTERNATIONAL, INC., *London*
PRENTICE-HALL OF AUSTRALIA, PTY., LTD., *Sydney*
PRENTICE-HALL OF CANADA, LTD., *Toronto*
PRENTICE-HALL FRANCE, S.A.R.L., *Paris*
PRENTICE-HALL OF JAPAN, INC., *Tokyo*
PRENTICE-HALL DE MEXICO, S.A., *Mexico City*

REVEREND ALDO J. TOS

APPROACHES TO THE BIBLE:
THE OLD TESTAMENT

PRENTICE-HALL, INC.

Englewood Cliffs, N. J.

1 9 6 3

Nihil Obstat:

Myles M. Bourke, S.S.L., S.T.D.
Censor Librorum

Imprimatur:

✠ Francis Cardinal Spellman
Archbishop of New York
January 16, 1963

The *Nihil Obstat* and *Imprimatur* are official
declarations that a book or pamphlet is free
of doctrinal or moral error. No implication is
contained therein that those who have granted
the *Nihil Obstat* and *Imprimatur* agree with
the contents, opinions or statements expressed.

Third Printing . . . . . November 1963

© 1963 by PRENTICE-HALL, INC., *Englewood Cliffs, N. J.*

LIBRARY OF CONGRESS CATALOG CARD NO.: 63-9966

PRINTED IN THE UNITED STATES OF AMERICA   C

TO

THE FACULTY AND STUDENTS

OF

MARIST COLLEGE

POUGHKEEPSIE, N. Y.

PREFACE

THE CHURCH is in the midst of a great Biblical revival. This return to the Bible may be part of the general enthusiasm to get back to essentials in many areas, and particularly in Religion. At any rate, there is definitely a "new spring" in the Church, and it is increasingly evident that the members of the Mystical Body, guided by the directives of the Magisterium, are eager to go to the true sources of the Christian Life, the Bible and the Liturgy.

It is providential that there should be a return to the Bible at the same time that the Christians of the world, Catholic and Protestant, are moved by the spirit of ecumenism. Even admitting the difficulties present in a Biblically-oriented dialogue among Christians, it is evident that the Scriptures are a divinely-given basis for such dialogue.

The purpose of this book is to present a systematic introductory study which attempts to foster an intelligent and vital Christian approach to the Bible, especially the Old Testament. Cardinal Bea, who played a significant role during the first session of the Second Vatican Council, has said that "all true Catholicism is and should be based on the Word of God in Scripture. Scripture should be the source of spiritual life for every Catholic and especially for every priest. . . . The Church has, especially during the last fifty years, insisted on a Biblical orientation for Catholics." It is hoped that this work will aid in the attainment of a fruitful understanding of the Plan of God which is revealed in the History of Salvation. For the Christian the Bible must be viewed and studied in the context of the living and worshipping Church. It must be understood in the perspective of the salvation-history which began with Creation and will end at the Parousia, the Second Coming of Jesus the Lord.

Biblical scholarship has made much progress in the last few decades.

As a result, some opinions which have been held for many years have been abandoned, and others, based on more recent theological, historical, and archaeological studies, have been advanced. This is to be expected in an area that has been apologetically defensive, if not dormant, since the Reformation. Doubtless, the Church has great devotion to the past, particularly to the age of its infancy which was the period of the Fathers. But it has had to warn us about the dangers of *antiquarianism,* which would try to make the limits of the past the exclusive rule of orthodoxy and worship, as though the veracity or validity of an opinion were necessarily proportionate to its antiquity.

Evidently, a book of this type owes much to the work of others. Scholars will find nothing new in it. The footnotes and bibliography show how much this work owes to the dedicated Biblical scholars of our age; such references are also tokens of gratitude for their labors. It is hoped that the citations will be an aid to further study on the part of readers. Particular thanks are due to those who read the manuscript and made valuable suggestions. I am grateful to Monsignor Patrick W. Skehan, S.T.D. of the Department of Semitic and Egyptian Languages at The Catholic University of America, Washington, D.C., for his sustained interest and encouragement and also for contributing the section on the contents of the Dead Sea Scrolls. I am greatly indebted to my former teacher Monsignor Myles M. Bourke, S.T.D., S.S.L., Professor of Sacred Scripture, St. Joseph's Seminary, Yonkers, N. Y. for years of friendship which have included much scholarly assistance.

Finally: I should like to thank the Reverend Gerard DiSenso for his painstaking criticism of the structure of the work; the Marist Brothers for their help in compiling the index; the School Sisters of Notre Dame of Our Lady of Mount Carmel School and the Sisters of Saint Dominic of Our Lady of Lourdes High School, Poughkeepsie, N. Y. for their patient proof-reading; Mrs. Donald Thomas for her secretarial assistance; and Miss Elizabeth DiStefano for the innumerable hours spent in typing the manuscript.

ACKNOWLEDGMENTS

Grateful acknowledgment is hereby made to the following publishers for permission to quote from copyrighted material.

Benziger Brothers, New York, N. Y., for *The Mass of the Roman Rite* by Joseph A. Jungmann, S.J., 1951, 1955.

The Bruce Publishing Company, Milwaukee, Wisconsin, for *The History of Israel,* by Giuseppe Ricciotti, 1955, and *The Two-Edged Sword* by John L. McKenzie, S.J., 1956.

The Catholic Biblical Quarterly for "Sin in Paradise" by Louis F. Hartmann, C.Ss.R., XX (January, 1958), 26-40.

Desclée Company, New York, N. Y., for *Guide to the Bible* by A. Robert and A. Tricot (eds.), 2d ed., 1960.

Fides Publishers Association, Notre Dame, Indiana, for *Themes of Theology: God Among Men* by Bernard Murchland (ed.), 1960.

Grail Publications, St. Meinrad, Indiana, for *Rome and The Study of Scripture,* 1958.

Harper & Row, Publishers, New York, N. Y., for *Our Bible and the Ancient Manuscripts* by Frederic Kenyon, rev. ed., 1958.

Hawthorn Books Inc., New York, N. Y., for *The Origins of Man* by Nicholas Corte, 1958.

The Johns Hopkins Press, Baltimore, Md., for *Archaeology and the Religion of Israel* by William F. Albright, 1956, and *From the Stone Age to Christianity* by William F. Albright, 1957.

P. J. Kenedy & Sons, New York, N. Y., for *The Bible, Word of God in Words of Men* by Jean Levie, S.J., 1961.

The Liturgical Press, Collegeville, Minn., for *History of the Old Testament* by Paul Heinisch, 1952.

National Catholic Welfare Conference, Washington, D.C. for the encyclicals *Mystici Corporis* and *Humani Generis,* and the address *The Proofs for the Existence of God,* by Pope Pius XII.

Thomas Nelson & Sons, New York, N. Y., for *A Catholic Commentary on Holy Scripture* by Dom Bernard Orchard (ed.), 1953, and *Atlas of the Bible* by L. H. Grollenberg, 1956.

The Newman Press, Westminster, Md., for *Ancient Christian Writers Series,* vols. 1 and 2, 1946, and *The Christian Approach to the Bible* by Celestin Charlier, 1958, and *The Book of Psalms* by Edward J. Kissane, 1953, and *From Shadows to Reality* by Jean Daniélou, 1960.

Paulist Press, New York, N. Y., for *The Book of Exodus* by Roland E. Murphy, O.Carm., 1960, and *The Book of Josue* by Joseph J. DeVault, S.J., 1960.

Penguin Books Ltd., Harmondsworth, Middlesex, England, and Baltimore, Md., for *Archaeology of Palestine* by William F. Albright, rev. ed., 1960.

The Pope Speaks, Washington, D.C. for the address of Pope Pius XII, "The Dignity of Woman," III (Spring, 1957), 367-75, and that of Pope John XXIII, "At the Lateran Basilica," V (Summer, 1959), 281-88.

Prentice-Hall, Inc., Englewood Cliffs, N. J., for *Ideas and Men: The Story of Western Thought* by Crane Brinton, 1950, and *Understanding the Old Testament* by Bernhard W. Anderson, 1957.

Henry Regnery Company, Chicago, Illinois, for *The Lord of History* by Jean Daniélou, S.J., 1958.

Sheed & Ward Inc., New York, N. Y., for *The Bible in the Church* by Bruce Vawter, C.M., 1959.

Student Christian Movement Press Limited, London, England, and Alec R. Allenson, Inc., Naperville, Illinois, for *Ten Years of Discovery in the Wilderness of Judaea* by J. T. Milik, 1959.

The Thomist, Washington, D.C., for "Catholic Biblical Scholarship and College Theology," by Carroll Stuhlmueller, C.P., XXIII (October, 1960), 533-63.

University of Notre Dame Press, Notre Dame, Ind., for *The Meaning of Sacred Scripture* by Louis Bouyer, 1958, and *The Bible and the Liturgy* by Jean Daniélou, 1956.

The Westminster Press, Philadelphia, Pa., for *History of Israel* by John Bright, 1959.

Weston College Press, Weston, Mass., for *Foreword to the Old Testament Books* by Frederick L. Moriarty, S.J., 1954.

Proceedings of the Catholic Theological Society of America, Yonkers, N. Y., for "In Many Fragmentary and Varying Utterances: The Use of Messianic Prophecy in Apologetics," by Bruce Vawter, C.M., 1959, pp. 97-119.

*   *   *   *   *

Quotations from the First Eight Books, the Sapiential Books, the Prophetic Books of the Old Testament, and the Books of the New Testament are from Confraternity of Christian Doctrine translation and are used with the permission of the Confraternity of Christian Doctrine, Washington, D.C. Other Biblical quotations are from the Douay Version.

CONTENTS

PREFACE   vii
ACKNOWLEDGMENTS   ix
LIST OF ILLUSTRATIONS   xvii
LIST OF TABLES   xix
THE BOOKS OF THE BIBLE AND THEIR ABBREVIATIONS . .   xxi

1. THE CHURCH, THE BIBLE, AND THE CHRISTIAN   1

   Introduction   1
   Bible and Tradition   2
   Historical Survey   4
   Revelation and Christian Faith   16

2. BIBLICAL THEOLOGY AND SALVATION–HISTORY   19

   Introduction   19
   Biblical Theology   19
   Salvation–History: The Plan of God   20
      Creation: Cosmic and Human   20
      Preparation in the Old Testament   21
      Fulfillment in Christ   22
      Continuation in the Church   23
      Achievement in Heaven   25

3. THE NATURE OF BIBLICAL INSPIRATION   27

   Introduction   27
   False Notions   28
   Correct Notions   29
   Nature of Instrumental Causality   30
   Spoken Word to Written Word   32

4. BIBLICAL LITERARY FORMS 35

    Introduction 35
    Meaning of Literary Forms 36
    Kinds of Literary Forms 37
        Poetic 37
        Apocalyptic 37
        Historical 39

5. INTRODUCTION TO THE PENTATEUCH 42

    Meaning of the Name 42
    Purpose and Literary Category 43
    The Traditions 44
        Yahwist 44
        Elohist 44
        Deuteronomic 44
        Priestly 45
    Basic Unity of the Pentateuch 45
    Thesis of the Pentateuch 46
    Outline of the Books 47

6. THE BOOK OF GENESIS 49

    The Purpose of Genesis 49
    Genesis and Science 49
    Anthropomorphism 50
    Semitic Cosmogony 51
    The Creation of the Universe 53
        Monotheism versus Polytheism 53
        The Two Accounts of Creation 54
        The Days of Creation 55
    The Origin of Mankind 55
    Genesis and Evolution 58
    The Fall: Original Sin 59
    The Promise of Salvation 62
    The Role of Cain and Abel 63
    The Genealogies 64
    The Flood and Noe 66
    The Tower of Babel 67
    The Patriarchal Period 68
    Abraham, Isaac, and Jacob 69
    Joseph the Magnanimous 74

7. THE BOOK OF EXODUS 77

The Name 77
Importance of the Exodus 77
Evidence for the Event 78
Literary Form of the Book 78
Bondage in Egypt 79
Moses 80
Meaning of "Yahweh" 80
The Plagues 81
Number Who Left Egypt 82
Date of the Exodus 83
The Crossing of the Sea 84
The Manna and the Quails 85
Mt. Sinai 86
The Covenant 87
The Ten Commandments 88
Prohibition of Images 90
The Golden Calf 90
The Character of Moses 90
The Exodus and the Christian 91
    Typology 92
    The Books of the New Testament 93
    Christian Patrology 94
    The Liturgy 96

8. THE BOOK OF LEVITICUS 101

The Name 101
Style 101
Historical Background 101
Sacrifices 103
Feasts in Israel 104
Day of Atonement 105
The "Lex Talionis" 106
Leviticus and Christians 106

9. THE BOOK OF NUMBERS 107

The Name 107
Origin and Purpose 107
The Shekinah 107
The Sin of Moses 108
The Talking Donkey 108

10. THE BOOK OF DEUTERONOMY 111

    The Name 111
    Origin and Spirit 111
    The Choice of Israel 112
    The Shema 113
    The Hebrew Credo 113
    Command Concerning Pagan Places of Worship 114
    The Herem 115

11. FROM THE DESERT TO THE PROMISED LAND
    (1250–1030 B.C.) 116

    Introduction 116
    The Book of Josue 117
    The Crossing of the Jordan 118
    The Battle of Jericho 118
    The Battle of Hai 118
    The Sun at Gabaon and Moon at Aialon 119
    Conquest of Canaan 120
    Aftermath 120
    The Book of Judges 121

12. THE UNITED MONARCHY IN PALESTINE
    (1030–931 B.C.) 123

    Introduction 123
    The Sources 124
        Books of Samuel 124
        Books of Kings 125
        Books of Chronicles 126
    Saul: First King of Israel 126
    David 128
        Note on the Dynastic Oracle 130
    Solomon 130

13. THE SCHISM: KINGDOMS OF ISRAEL AND JUDA
    (931–587 B.C.) 134

    Introduction 134
    Characteristics of the kingdoms 135
    Brief History of the kingdoms 135

     Kingdom of Israel (931–721 B.C.) 135
          PROPHETS IN ISRAEL: elia and eliseus .... 137'
           amos: prophet of the god of justice 142
           osee: prophet of the god of love 143
     Kingdom of Juda (931–587) 145
           isaia: prophet of the holiness of god 151
           jeremia: prophet of the new covenant 157

14. THE BABYLONIAN EXILE (587–538 B.C.) 161

    Introduction 161
    Social Conditions 162
    Religious Revival 163
           ezechiel: prophet of the exile 164

15. RETURN FROM EXILE AND PERSIAN PERIOD
    (538–333 B.C.) 169

    Introduction 169
    Ezra and Nehemia 170
    The Persian Period 171
        Situation 171
        The Language 172
        The Bible 173

16. THE HELLENISTIC PERIOD AND MACCABEAN RULE
    (333–63 B.C.) 174

    Introduction 174
    Alexander the Great 174
    The Ptolemaic and Seleucid Dynasties 175
    The Process of Hellenization 176
    The Book of Daniel 177
    The Books of Maccabees 179
    The Maccabean Revolt 180
    Aftermath 181

17. THE ROMAN PERIOD (63 B.C.–) 183

    Introduction 183
    Herod the Great: His Rule and Its Consequences 184

18. PARTIES AND SECTS 187

    Introduction 187

    The Scribes 187
    The Sanhedrin 188
    The Pharisees 189
    The Sadducees 189
    The Essenes 190

19. THE PROPHETS AND MESSIANISM 192

    Introduction 192
    Meaning of "Prophet" 192
    Kinds of Prophets 193
    Requirements for a Prophet 194
    The Work of the Prophets 196
    The Teaching of the Prophets 196
    Summary of Biblical Messianism 200
    The Prophet and the Christian 202

20. MESSIANISM AND APOLOGETICS 205

    Introduction 205
    Comments about Texts 208
        Malachia 3, 1 208
        Isaia 7, 14 208
        Michea 5, 2 209
        Isaia 35 5-6 209
        Zacharia 9, 9 210
        Isaia 53, 12 210
        Psalm 21, 17-19; 68, 22 211
        Genesis 3, 15 212
        Daniel 7, 13-14 212

21. INTRODUCTION TO THE WISDOM LITERATURE 214

    Introduction 214
    Sages of Israel 215
    The Wisdom Books 216
    The Literary Form: Mashal 218
    The Book of Job 219
    Proverbs 221
    Ecclesiastes 222
    The Theme of Wisdom Personified 223

22. INTRODUCTION TO THE PSALTER 227

   Name and Contents 227
   Authorship and Dates of the Psalms 228
   Literary Genres (Forms) 230
      Hymns 232
         PSALMS OF SION 232
         PSALMS OF THE KINGDOM OF GOD 232
      Supplications (Psalms of Lamentation) 233
         INDIVIDUAL SUPPLICATIONS 233
         COMMUNAL (COLLECTIVE) SUPPLICATIONS 234
      Thanksgiving 234
      Variant Genres and Combinations 234
      Royal Psalms and Messianic Psalms 235
   Psalms in the Worship of Israel 237
   A Note Concerning the Hallel 238
   Teachings in the Psalms 239
   Religious Value of the Psalms 240

23. THE DEAD SEA SCROLLS 242

   Diary Related to the Findings 242
   The Age of the Manuscripts 248
   The Contents of the Scrolls 249
   Some Conclusions 253

APPENDICES

   I. MANUSCRIPTS AND VERSIONS OF THE BIBLE 256

   Introduction 256
   Hebrew Manuscripts 257
   The Septuagint Translation (LXX) 257
   Other Translations 259
   Latin Versions 259

   II. ENGLISH TRANSLATIONS OF THE BIBLE 261

   III. READINGS IN THE BOOKS OF THE OLD TESTAMENT .. 263

BIBLIOGRAPHY 266

   Editions of the Bible 266
   Documents of the Magisterium 266

Basic Reference Books 266
General Works 266
The Bible and Christians 268
Biblical Theology 268
Salvation–History 269
Biblical Inspiration and Literary Forms 270
Biblical History 270
Documents Related to the Old Testament 270
Biblical Archaeology 270
Biblical Geography 271
The Pentateuch 271
The Prophets and Messianism 272
The Wisdom Literature 272
The Psalms 273
The Dead Sea Scrolls 273
Periodicals 274

ILLUSTRATIONS

1. SALVATION–HISTORY: THE PLAN OF GOD   26

2. SEMITIC COSMOGONY   52

3. THE ANCIENT NEAR EAST   70

4. THE ROUTE OF THE EXODUS   86

5. THE TEMPLE AND PALACE OF SOLOMON   132

6. MAP OF PALESTINE FROM THE TIME OF SAUL
   TO THE BABYLONIAN EXILE   133

7. THE DEAD SEA AREA   244

TABLES

1. BIBLICAL HISTORY—BOOKS OF THE OLD
    TESTAMENT—SECULAR HISTORY 34

2. THE PLAGUES IN THE TRADITIONS 81

3. THE CATHOLIC AND NON-CATHOLIC DIVISIONS OF
    THE COMMANDMENTS 89

4. TYPOLOGY OF THE EXODUS IN PATRISTIC WRITINGS.. 97

5. THE LITURGY OF THE PASCHAL MYSTERY 98-99

6. THE KINGDOMS OF JUDA AND ISRAEL 159

THE BOOKS OF THE BIBLE
AND THEIR ABBREVIATIONS

THE OLD TESTAMENT

ABDIA	Abd	JUDITH	Jdt
AGGAI	Ag	3 KINGS	3 Kgs
AMOS	Am	4 KINGS	4 Kgs
BARUCH	Bar	LAMENTATIONS	Lam
CANTICLE OF CANTICLES	Ct	LEVITICUS	Lv
1 CHRONICLES	1 Chr	1 MACCABEES	1 Mc
(PARALIPOMENON)		2 MACCABEES	2 Mc
2 CHRONICLES	2 Chr	MALACHIA	Mal
(PARALIPOMENON)		MICHEA	Mi
DANIEL	Dn	NAHUM	Na
DEUTERONOMY	Dt	NEHEMIA	Neh
ECCLESIASTES	Eccl	NUMBERS	Nu
ESTHER	Est	OSEE	Os
EXODUS	Ex	PROVERBS	Prv
EZECHIEL	Ez	PSALMS	Ps (s)
EZRA	Ezr	RUTH	Ru
GENESIS	Gn	1 SAMUEL	1 Sm
HABACUC	Hb	2 SAMUEL	2 Sm
ISAIA	Is	SIRACH	Sir
JEREMIA	Jer	(ECCLESIASTICUS)	
JOB	Jb	SOPHONIA	So
JOEL	Jl	TOBIA	Tb
JONA	Jon	WISDOM	Wis
JOSUE	Jos	ZACHARIA	Za
JUDGES	Jgs		

THE NEW TESTAMENT

ACTS OF THE APOSTLES	Acts	LUKE	Lk
APOCALYPSE	Ap	MARK	Mk
COLOSSIANS	Col	MATTHEW	Mt
1 CORINTHIANS	1 Cor	1 PETER	1 Pt
2 CORINTHIANS	2 Cor	2 PETER	2 Pt
EPHESIANS	Eph	PHILEMON	Phlm
GALATIANS	Gal	PHILIPPIANS	Phil
HEBREWS	Heb	ROMANS	Rom
JAMES	Jas	1 THESSALONIANS	1 Thes
1 JOHN (Epistle)	1 Jn	2 THESSALONIANS	2 Thes
2 JOHN (Epistle)	2 Jn	1 TIMOTHY	1 Tm
3 JOHN (Epistle)	3 Jn	2 TIMOTHY	2 Tm
JOHN (Gospel)	Jn	TITUS	Ti
JUDE	Jude		

APPROACHES TO THE BIBLE:

THE OLD TESTAMENT

one

THE CHURCH, THE BIBLE,
AND THE CHRISTIAN

INTRODUCTION

THE BIBLE is the Book. It has resulted from the accumulation of a whole library of books, composed by many authors over a span of more than a thousand years. For both Christians and Jews it is the Book, set apart from all other books because it is sacred as no other book is sacred—in its origins, in its contents, and in the reverence which it demands of those who approach it. The Church in the Liturgy gives great homage to the Bible, carrying it in procession, incensing it, kissing it, giving it the place of honor on the altar; all because the Bible is *the Book* of the Church, the Word of God and the inspired history of His Acts.

If Catholics are returning to a study of the Bible and if their piety is becoming more Biblically oriented, it is not merely because of some transitory curiosity. Neither is it because of the literary appeal that the Bible has. The reason would seem to be that we are beginning to understand better that the Word of God has an irreplaceable part in our lives of Faith. The present interest in the Holy Scriptures must ultimately be attributed to the Holy Spirit who is rousing in the Church a hunger for the Bible. This is part of the fulfillment of the ancient prophecy: "I will send forth a famine into the land; not a famine of bread, nor a thirst of water, but of hearing the Word of the Lord" (Amos 8,11).

The present revival is drawing more and more attention to the role that Sacred Scripture should play in our lives as members of the Church. Once again the Book is beginning to be understood as the inspired record of the living and personal intervention of God in the lives of His creatures. If Christians can be convinced that God Himself truly speaks to us through the

1

pages of the Bible, they will begin to better understand the history of salvation and the intimate relations between the Bible and the Church. Just as the Word of God cannot be a substitute for the Church, so the teaching of the Church is not a substitute for the Word of God, but a development and interpretation of that Word. God entrusted the Scriptures to the Church; it is in the Church, by the light of Faith, that we are to read and meditate upon them.

BIBLE AND TRADITION

It is sometimes said that, inasmuch as Scripture is used in Catholic teaching only to confirm the tradition of the Church, it is at best something superfluous in the life of the Church. This is to forget that it was to the Church that the active ministry of the Word of God was committed in a tradition that is not something static and lifeless, but living. The relation of the Church and the Bible is usually expressed in the phrase, "the Bible and Tradition", the former referring to the inspired written documents, the latter to the beliefs that have been handed down by word of mouth and are found in the documents of the Fathers of the Church as well as in the declarations of the Church. This phrase has tended to give the impression that there are two parallel sources of religious truth. It is most important that we understand the matter correctly. We must not imagine that the Bible and Tradition are "like two distinct reservoirs receiving the waters of divine truth from distinct and separate springs. There is in a sense but one source of revealed truth, viz., divine Tradition, by which is meant the body of revealed truth handed down from the Apostles through the ages and contained in the doctrine, teaching and practice of the Catholic Church".[1] It is the Church that gives life to the letter of Scripture. It is only in the life of the Church, the People of God, that the Bible becomes "living and effectual, and more piercing than any two-edged sword" (Heb 4,12).

The "source of Christianity is, indeed, the Word of God, but that Word of God is the Bible and Tradition. . . . Tradition and Scripture are not two independent sources which complete one another as two separable parts of a whole. . . . To the Christian of antiquity, the Bible is so inseparable from Tradition as to be, in fact, a part of it: it is its essential element, its nucleus, so to say. But on the other hand, if it were to be torn from the living whole which is constituted by the many factors of Tradition, guarded and transmitted by the conscience of the Church, always watchful, always active—then the Bible would indeed become incomprehensible. . . . For the Catholic, then, the Bible and Tradition does not mean the Bible plus a foreign element without which it would remain incomplete. It means the living environment,

[1] William Leonard and Dom Bernard Orchard, "The Place of the Bible in the Church," *A Catholic Commentary on Holy Scripture*, Dom Bernard Orchard, ed. (New York: Thomas Nelson and Sons, 1953), p. 1.

its native light. It is the Bible and nothing but the Bible, but it is the whole Bible, not in its letter only, but with the Spirit which dictated it and which does not cease to inspire the reading of it." [2]

Theologically, it is not and cannot be a question of the Bible *or* the Church, or the Church versus the Bible. In terms of exact theology, it is the *Bible in the Church.* The exercise of authority over the Bible by the Church arises from the very nature of the Church, which is the living voice of Jesus, Son of God, in the world by virtue of the Spirit of Truth which forever abides with it according to the promise: "I will ask the Father and he will give you another Advocate to dwell with you, forever, the Spirit of truth whom the world can not receive because it neither sees him nor knows him. But you shall know him, because he will dwell with you, and be in you" (Jn 14,16-17).

Many do not know the Bible. While no one would maintain that the reading of the Bible is necessary for salvation, surely no one can deny that it is spiritually profitable. It is through a knowledge of the revealed Word of God that we come to a better appreciation of His Plan of Salvation for ourselves and for the world. St. Paul taught this when he said that the Scriptures are able "to instruct us unto salvation by the faith which is Christ Jesus" (2 Tim 3,15). St. Jerome, a great Biblical scholar and Doctor of the Church, said that "To ignore the Scripture is to ignore Christ." He also said: "If there is anything in this life which sustains a wise man and induces him to maintain his serenity amidst the tribulations and adversities of the world, it is in the first place, I consider, the meditation and knowledge of the Scriptures". [3]

Throughout the history of the Church there have been some periods when the Bible was a forgotten or neglected Book, but it cannot be said that this unnatural situation was the result of the expressed official teaching of the Church. It is true, as we shall see later, that at times local ecclesiastical councils or personages and even Ecumenical Councils issued decrees concerning the reading of the Bible. But contrary to the heated discussion of antagonists

[2] Louis Bouyer, *The Meaning of Sacred Scripture,* trans. Mary Perkins Ryan (Notre Dame: University of Notre Dame Press, 1958), p. 2. The relationship of Scripture and Tradition is the subject of much contemporary study and research. See the following for information concerning several approaches to this important subject: Paul Auvray, "Scripture and Tradition in the Hebrew Community," *Theology Digest,* VI (Winter, 1958), 31-32; Walter J. Burghardt, S.J., "The Catholic Concept of Tradition," *Proceedings of the Catholic Theological Society of America* (1951), pp. 42-76; G. Dejaifve, "Scripture, Tradition, and the Church," *Theology Digest,* VI (Spring, 1958), 67-72; Joseph R. Geiselmann, "Scripture and Tradition in Catholic Theology," *Theology Digest,* VI (Spring, 1958), 73-78; Josef Pieper, "The Concept of Tradition," *Theology Digest,* VIII (Winter, 1960), 3-7; George Tavard, A.A., "Tradition and Scripture," *Worship,* XXXV (May, 1961), 375-78; and, John L. Murphy, "Unwritten Traditions at Trent," *The American Ecclesiastical Review,* CXLVI, (April, 1962), 233-63.

[3] Quoted in Pope Pius XII, *Divino Afflante Spiritu,* 57, in *Rome and the Study of Scripture* (St. Meinrad, Ind.: Grail Publications, 1958); all references to the encyclical will be given as DAS with the paragraph number found in this edition of documents. An extensive commentary on the encyclical is in Jean Levie, S.J., *The Bible, Word of God in Words of Men,* trans. S. H. Treman (New York: P. J. Kenedy & Sons, 1961), pp. 133-90.

in many of the "Church versus the Bible" polemics, it cannot be proved that the decrees were meant as absolute, universal condemnations of the reading of the Bible by the members of the Church.

HISTORICAL SURVEY

A reading of the Gospels will reveal that Jesus often made use of the Scriptures in His teaching as well as in His discussions with the people of Palestine (v.gr Mt 13,14; 15,8; 22,32; Lk 4,16-22; Jn 5,39). Following His example, the apostles and evangelists made frequent use of the Old Testament in their preaching as evidenced, for example, by the sermons which are found in the Acts of the Apostles (Acts 2;3;4;10;13). Moreover, the other documents of the New Testament, the Epistles and the Apocalypse, are full of references to the books of the Bible which, of course, mean the Old Testament.

During the early Christian centuries, the members of the Church were instructed directly from the Bible, which now included both the Old and the New Testaments. One has only to thumb through the documents of early Christianity, particularly those of the Fathers of the Church, to see how much the Bible was the "staple food" of the clergy and the laity. St. Clement, writing to the Corinthians toward the end of the first century, took it for granted that his readers knew the Word of God: "Surely, you are acquainted, beloved, and well acquainted, with the Sacred Scriptures, and have explored the oracles of God; and therefore we write these things merely to serve as a reminder".[4]

Later, St. Jerome (347-420) gave the following advice to one of his friends: "Read assiduously and learn as much as you can. Let sleep find you holding your Bible, and when your head nods let it be resting on the sacred page".[5] St. John Chrysostom (345-407) suggested that every household, rich or poor, should have a copy of the New Testament—and it was to be used. This testifies to the fact that copies of the books of the Bible were available and that Catholics were encouraged to read them.

"There is no evidence that the Church showed herself hostile to Bible reading in those centuries, and, if we speak particularly of vernacular versions, we have the striking fact that in Egypt between the second half of the third century and the end of the sixth century Holy Scripture was read in four or five different dialects of Coptic. . . . Thus, before the end of the great patristic age (broadly A.D. 500-600) several versions had established themselves in the East." [6]

Public reading of Scripture was held in high regard in the Church from the very beginning. As a matter of fact, during the first few centuries the Bible

---

[4] *First Epistle to the Corinthians,* 53 in *Ancient Christian Writers,* Johannes Quasten and Joseph C. Plumpe, eds. (Westminster, Md.: The Newman Bookshop, 1946, I, 41.
[5] *Letter to Paula,* quoted in Leonard and Orchard, *op. cit.,* p. 3.
[6] Leonard and Orchard, *op. cit.,* p. 5.

was the only book used in liturgical actions. It was in the worship of the Liturgy that the people were instructed with the Word of God which formed the readings and chants. The development of the Fore-Mass, the Liturgy of the Word, often called the Mass of the Catechumens, was influenced by the practice of the synagogue with whose services the Apostles and the early Christians were acquainted—readings from Scripture, psalm singing, and explanations of the readings. The Christian people, literate and illiterate, were instructed and nourished by the Bible which was read or sung during the first part of the Mass. As time went on, particularly by the end of the first millenium of Christianity, this ceased to be the general rule. There were many factors which helped to cause a change in what had been the traditional way in which the members of the Church and the Word were brought together.

The language of the liturgy was the language of the people both in the West and in the East. Gradually, changes occurred and new languages developed. Soon the liturgical language which was retained from ancient times became incomprehensible to the people. In the West, some attempts were made to remedy the situation by issuing vernacular editions of the Scripture lessons used during the Liturgy of the Mass; in the East, there were shifts made to the current vernacular of the people which affected the whole Liturgical action of the Mass.

By the time of the Carolingian empire in the eighth century, the "Mass Liturgy so far as understanding its language was concerned, became a clerical reserve. A new kind of *disciplina arcani* or discipline of the secret developed, a concealment of things holy, not from the heathen—there were none—but from the Christian people themselves".[7] Gradually, perhaps imperceptively and even unintentionally, a divorce was taking place which would have severe repercussions in the worship-life of Christians. "The line of separation between altar and people, between clergy and laity, between those whose duty it was to perform the sacramental action and those who formed the celebrating congregation—a separation which was always taken for granted as essential to the Church's constitution, and which was never really forgotten—was now made into a broad line of demarcation, not to say a wall of division." [8]

The incomprehensibility of the liturgical language was not the only thing which caused the separation between the congregation and the Altar with its double nourishment, Eucharist and Bible. A study of all the factors would require a separate book. Hence, only a few will be mentioned: (1) the rise of certain interpretations of the Mass which were highly allegorical and which resulted in the people doing nothing except following the actions of the priest which were interpreted so as to recall the sufferings and death of Christ; (2) the emphasis on the Mass as a "sacred mystery" performed in silence

---

[7] Joseph Jungmann, S.J., *The Mass of the Roman Rite,* trans. Francis A. Brunner, C.SS.R. (2 vols.; New York: Benziger Brothers, Inc., 1951), I, 81.
[8] *Ibid.,* p. 83; see also pp. 391-409.

with little if any direct concern for the people who were present; (3) certain forms of private devotions which emphasized "looking at the Host" rather than taking an active part in the Mass; (4) the social, intellectual, religious, and moral problems during the Dark Ages. Briefly, since the Word and the Liturgy are intimately related, a misunderstanding of the latter, and a lack of active participation in it, result in the loss of the context which gives life and meaning to the former.

During the Middle Ages, particularly after the rise of the Universities, the Bible was the center of theological discussion among scholars and students. A look at the voluminous works produced during those years is enough to convince one of the truth of this statement.[9] However, the common man did not have such personal contact with the Bible. Although it is true, as is often remarked, that the stained glass windows of the many churches and cathedrals built at the time were the "Bible of the poor and the illiterate," it is also true that many were blind to the full meaning of such a "Bible." Contact with the Word of God through stained glass and pictures is hardly adequate compensation for the loss of a direct, personal contact with the inspired text itself, particularly in the context of the Liturgy.

As time went on, other factors contributed to a loss of personal contact with the Bible on the part of the members of the Church. The late Middle Ages witnessed the rise of the spirit of the Renaissance with its humanistic orientation and its emphasis on homocentrism. It is true that the Renaissance led to a multiplication of copies of the Latin Vulgate (the translation made by St. Jerome during the fourth century), to an interest in the original languages of the Scriptures, and to some attempts at producing vernacular translations of the Bible. But the period of the Renaissance also witnessed a moral crisis and the development of a rationalism which were the result of the "gradual divorce which had been growing for some time between thought and action, between the individual and society, between man and God. The whole structure of Christian integrity was crumbling. The decline of the Bible, the lack of active participation in the liturgy, the excesses of Nominalism, the moral corruption of Churchmen—these were just the fruits of that collapse." [10]

Evidently, the milieu was hardly one in which the Christian life could always be lived with utmost fidelity. There were "islands" of great Christian life and learning and also individuals who were heroic saints. Yet, surely, the picture was generally not a bright one. Under the circumstances a decline of the Scriptures in the lives of the Christian people was inevitable. That decline continued until the sixteenth century when the Protestant Revolt hit western Europe.

---

[9] St. Thomas Aquinas, *Summa Theologiae;* also Etienne Gilson, *History of Christian Philosophy* (New York: Random House, 1955).

[10] Celestin Charlier, *The Christian Approach to the Bible,* trans. Hubert J. Richards and Brenden Peters (Westminster, Md.: The Newman Press, 1958), p. 13.

The assaults of Martin Luther (1483-1546), Philip Melanchthon (1497-1560), John Calvin (1509-64), John Knox (1505-72), Ulrich Zwingli (1484-1531) and others were directed not only against evident abuses in clerical and lay circles of the Church, but also against the very structure of the Church itself, which the reformers maintained was far from being the society intended by Jesus Christ. These men and their followers rejected the Catholic Church and thus brought about a major rupture in the historical unfolding of the Christian message. The Bible was removed from the current of Christian Tradition; it was torn from its environment which was the Church. The Book became man's only source of faith and spiritual life, and private interpretation was substituted for the teachings of the Magisterium of the Church.

The Protestants made a great deal of the issue of the vernacular Bible. "With the Bible available in the vernacular, the priest no longer had the monopoly he had enjoyed when only a Latin version existed. The reformers, Wycliffe, Hus, Luther, Calvin, all made possible the wide circulation of the Bible in their native tongues. The printing press by the sixteenth century had begun to make something like mass production of Bibles possible. Any reader could now lay his hands on a Bible. The Bible was thus to be the real, the incontrovertible authority, God's words, not man's." [11] Martin Luther produced a German translation (1522) which is deservedly considered a classic of the times. England witnessed the vernacular edition of the Scriptures by William Tyndale (1525), Miles Coverdale (1535), and the *Great Bible* (1539-41).

The cry of the Reformers was: "The Bible in the language of the people!" Admittedly this was something desirable, but they spoke as if they had invented the idea. As we have seen, the centuries preceding the sixteenth were not always favorable for living the full Christian life, and necessarily, for reading the Scriptures. But, it would be an historial fallacy to say that those ages did not see any attempts at vernacular translations.

The credit for the earliest attempt to achieve an English vernacular translation of the Bible must go to the Anglo-Saxons. Less than a century after St. Augustine arrived from Rome to Christianize England (597), Caedmon, the first English poet whose name is known, produced a paraphrase of combined parts of the Bible (670). This work is the native beginning of English literature. In 709, Aldhelm, an English bishop, translated the Psalms; thus, he holds the honor of being the first translator of the Bible into English. Bede, the author of the important work, *History of the English Church,* translated

---

[11] Craine Brinton, *Ideas and Men. The Story of Western Thought* (Englewood Cliffs, N. J.: Prentice-Hall, Inc., 1950), pp. 310-11. For an excellent study of the theological principles involved in the Reformation see Louis Bouyer, *The Spirit and Forms of Protestantism,* trans. A. V. Littledale (Westminster, Md.: The Newman Press, 1956); chapter VI, "The Sovereign Authority of Scripture," pp. 116-35, contains insights which will help to evaluate Martin Luther's insistence on the role of the Bible in the life of the Christian.

the Gospel of St. John in 735, and in 990 Aelfric, the archbishop of Canterbury, translated a considerable portion of the Old Testament into English. From the tenth century to the eve of the break with Rome caused by Henry VIII· in the sixteenth century there were other translations produced, all with ecclesiastical approval. It is, therefore, unfair to cite the condemnation of the translation of John Wycliffe, a heretic, as evidence that the Church forbade the production of all translations of the Bible in English. The actual words of the Synod of Oxford which condemned the work of Wycliffe in 1408 are: "We decree and ordain that no man hereafter by his own authority translate any text of Sacred Scripture into English or any other tongue, by way of a book, booklet or tract, nor read any such book, booklet or tract now lately composed in the time of John Wycliffe aforesaid, or since, either in part or in whole, publicly or privately, under pain of major excommunication, *until that translation be approved by the Ordinary of the place or, if the case demand it, by a Provincial Council.* He that acts contrary to this shall likewise be punished as a promoter of heresy and error." The words of the Synod are strong but they must be read in their historical context which was that of insurgent heretical movements.[12]

A misunderstanding of the reasons behind an ecclesiastical decree or an insufficient knowledge of the decree itself often leads to unwarranted conclusions.

Little is known about attempts to produce vernacular Bibles on the continent of Europe before the fifteenth century. There are extant copies of translations made in France and Germany. There are about 3,600 German manuscripts of the Bible or of parts of the Bible which were produced before the invention of printing by Johann Gutenberg of Mainz (1398-1468). "The earliest vernacular Bibles were not connected with the Reformation controversy. A German Bible was printed at Strassburg by Mentelin in 1466, and eighteen others besides Psalters and other separate books appeared before the publication of the first part of Luther's translation in 1522, an Italian Bible was printed in Venice in 1471, and a Dutch one in 1477. A French Bible was printed at Lyons about 1478, and another about 1487. Even in England the greater part of the Bible narrative was available in Caxton's version of the Golden Legend, printed in 1483. But with the outbreak of the Reformation, Bible translation took on a new and controversial aspect."[13]

The calamity caused by the Protestant Revolt was enormous. As far as the Bible was concerned, the Church saw the disastrous consequences of the principles of the Revolt's leaders and it acted quickly by drawing up a series

---

[12] See Philip Hughes, *A History of the Church* (New York: Sheed & Ward, 1947), III, 309-12; Henry Bettenson, *Documents of the Christian Church* (New York: Oxford University Press, 1947), pp. 245-56.

[13] Frederic Kenyon, *Our Bible and the Ancient Manuscripts,* rev. ed. (New York: Harper & Row, Publishers, 1958), p. 283. See also Patrick W. Skehan, "The Translations into the Vernacular," in A. Robert and A. Tricot (eds.), *Guide to the Bible,* trans. Edward P. Arbez, S.S. and Martin R. P. McGuire, 2nd ed. (New York: Desclee Company, 1960), I, 665-72.

of protective measures at the Council of Trent (1545-63). Like previous ecclesiastical decisions, the decrees of the Council did not forbid the reading of vernacular translations of the Bible without qualification; only editions of the Bible which were not approved by competent authority *(sine licentia superiorum ecclesiasticorum)* were forbidden. Actually, the decrees were moderate and intended only to protect the Bible, which from the beginning of Christianity had always been considered the Book of the Church. However, there were unfortunate results. The decrees served as a sort of springboard for individuals who then, as now, "leap into every intellectual struggle with the bludgeon of reaction, anxious to prove themselves more Catholic than the Pope by translating a contemporary discipline into essential policy".[14] There were some who spread the idea that the decrees of the Council forbade all reading of the Bible. Consequently, an unfortunate distrust of private Bible reading began to spread. Excessive caution became a characteristic of many Catholics who were convinced that "Catholics must not read the Bible!" A companion to such distrust often was a lack of understanding of and active participation in the Liturgy, which is the context that reveals much of the life and spirit of the letter of the Bible.

During the seventeenth and eighteenth centuries Catholics became less and less attached to the Bible. The situation was further complicated by the subsequent rise and spread of Rationalism, Naturalism, and Deism, which did much to destroy the true concept of God and the supernatural.[15] Man was soon left to his fallible, erring self. These philosophies were joined by revolutionary ideas in the fields of science. Soon the conviction grew that science alone could give a complete report and explanation of the whole of reality. Dichotomies were established: the natural versus the supernatural; reason versus faith; science versus religion.

The Bible was subjected to attacks of historical and literary criticism which was strongly influenced by the works of men like Baruch (Benedict) Spinoza (1632-77) and Francois Voltaire (1694-1777); the pantheistic ideas of the former and the anti-religious views of the latter went far in aiding those who promoted disbelief in the Bible.

The nineteenth century was heir to all the currents of thought and critical attacks of previous centuries. It was also the age during which the theory of evolution made its appearance and soon became not only the shibboleth of the positive sciences, but also the moving spirit of the approaches to practically all facets of human life—philosophy, religion, literature, etc. Innumerable books and articles were published by critico-literary authors like the

---

[14] From *The Bible in the Church* by Bruce Vawter, C.M., © Sheed & Ward, Inc., 1959, p. 35.

[15] *Rationalism* teaches that reason is self-sufficient to know all things and does not need help from any supposed revelation from God; *Naturalism* refers to the view that all facts and events have only natural causes and significance; *Deism* accepts the existence of God but denies His omnipresence, providence, and revelation.

Protestants K. H. Graf (1815-69) and Julius Wellhausen (1844-1918), and two writers who left the Church, Ernest Renan (1823-92) and Alfred Loisy (1857-1940).

Many of the Biblical commentaries and books written by Protestants in the late nineteenth and early twentieth centuries were produced by men who were philosophical and theological skeptics. Yet, it was also at this time that Biblical criticism among Protestants made some positive contributions because of the attention paid to the study of the oriental background of the Scriptural books, the development of philology, and a clearer understanding of Semitic languages.

The critics, particularly those who belonged to the Graf-Wellhausen group, emphasized the point that the Bible was nothing more than a "scissor and paste product", the result of the combination of fragments and documents taken from a variety of sources, often pagan. It was at this time that there was a great deal of discussion concerning the "Documentary Hypothesis of the Pentateuch," which held that the first five books of the Bible were in no way connected with Moses but were the result of the union of four distinct documents—referred to as the Yahwist, Elohist, Deuteronomic, and Priestly Sources.[16]

Although Wellhausen was the principal exponent of this approach to the Bible, particularly the Pentateuch, the roots of the movement are found in the works of two Catholic authors, Richard Simon (1638-1712), sometimes called the "father of modern critical study of the Old Testament," and Jean Astruc (1684-1766) who tried to produce a better understanding of sources and literary forms found in the Bible. Simon and Astruc saw that the Church had nothing to fear from critical work. They saw that only solid scholarship could offset the terrible intellectual and spiritual crisis which the writings of Spinoza and Voltaire were projecting in Europe with their rationalistic literary criticism of the Scriptures. Unfortunately, these Catholic authors became the objects of bitter denunciations on the part of many of their contemporaries. The French bishop and orator, Jacques Bossuet (1627-1704) denounced Simon, whose works, he said, were not only undistinguished in their scholarship, but filled with immense evil for the faithful members of the Church. As a result of the attacks, Catholic critical study of the Bible came to a halt and it was left to non-Catholics to pursue this line of work.

Many of the features of Simon's historico-literary method have been accepted by both Catholic and Protestant interpreters of the Bible. He was a

---

[16] The following works contain a good coverage of the material related to the views of the critics: J. Coppens, *The Old Testament and the Critics* (Paterson, N. J.: St. Anthony Guild Press, 1942); R. A. Dyson and R. A. F. MacKenzie, "Higher Criticism," *A Catholic Commentary on Holy Scripture,* pp. 61-66; A. Vincent, "Interpretation: From the Beginning of the Nineteenth Century to the Present Time," *Guide to the Bible,* I, 713-22. Giuseppe Ricciotti, *The Life of Christ,* trans. Alba I. Zizzamia (Milwaukee: The Bruce Publishing Company, 1947), pp. 179-216, is a very good summary of the rationalistic interpretations of the life of Jesus.

scholar three centuries ahead of his time. Many of his writings seem quite modern when they are read in the light of recent advances, particularly the documents of the Church in the last few decades.[17]

During the critical years of the nineteenth century, Catholic authors did not always measure up to the needs of the age. "A Catholic reaction resulted in biographies which emphasized chronological facts, historical details and geographical data. These books betray a troublesome concern to insist (and perhaps, over insist) upon the supernatural. Unfortunately, these great Catholic biographies tended to overlook the individual viewpoints of the various evangelists and disregard their particular theological themes and their doctrinal content. Apologetical arguments saw the Old Testament fulfilled in the New Testament by means of dates, numbers, places and people, rather than by means of great doctrinal truths, such as poverty, humility, expiatory sufferings, transcendence and corporate solidarity."[18]

The attacks made on the Bible by the critics plus the factors mentioned throughout this introduction, were complicated by other unhappy circumstances. First, there was the influence of an anti-intellectualism on the part of some Catholics, the aftermath of the conflict with the eighteenth century rationalists. Even the reforms of the great and scholarly Pope Leo XIII, which spurred Catholic activity in the fields of Scripture, theology, patrology, philosophy, and history, did not succeed in removing such influence from the Catholic scene. Second, the Modernist heresy began to gain ground and even infiltrate into Catholic institutions of higher learning. This heresy reduced religion to feeling; religion was not something supernatural but merely the natural product of an emotional need; the Bible was only a human document and those who believe that God is its author manifest excessive simplicity and ignorance.[19] Third, attitudes concerning the Bible were influenced by the fact that ideas concerning the nature of inspiration and revelation were not too clear. "The closing years of the nineteenth century were a time of fog and whirlwind, or of hysterical fright and rash conclusions."[20]

The reaction of the Church came quickly. In the sixteenth century, the Council of Trent met the needs of its age by issuing decrees intended to protect the Bible from misunderstanding and misuse; now the Church acted with similar protective measures. The Council of the Vatican (1869-70) repeated the teaching of Trent concerning the Bible, particularly the Canon

---

[17] Very little has been published about Richard Simon. The best source now available for information about him is Jean Steinmann, *Richard Simon et les origines de l'exegese biblique* (Bruges: Desclee de Brouwer, 1960). A summary of the book is in the review by Bishop John J. Whealon, *The Catholic Biblical Quarterly*, XXIV (January, 1962), 70-72.

[18] Carroll Stuhlmueller, C.P., "Catholic Biblical Scholarship and College Theology," *The Thomist*, XXIII (October, 1960), 538.

[19] For a summary of Modernism see the article in Pietro Parente, *Dictionary of Dogmatic Theology*, trans. Emmanuel Doronzo (Milwaukee: The Bruce Publishing Company, 1951) pp. 190-1, and also *The Church Teaches* (St. Louis: B. Herder Book Co., 1955), pp. 52-55.

[20] Stuhlmueller, *op. cit.,* p. 539.

of Scripture, and further insisted that Biblical interpretation must be mindful of the teachings of the Fathers of the Church; Pope Leo XIII issued an encyclical on Sacred·Scripture, *Providentissimus Deus* (1893), to encourage Biblical scholars and to guide them, in general, in the approaches to the Bible; the Biblical Commission was established (1902) to formulate rules and issue decrees concerning Biblical matters; the *Biblical Institute* was founded in Rome (1909) to prepare future professors of Scripture; Pope Benedict XV wrote another encyclical on the study of the Bible, *Spiritus Paraclitus* (1920). Catholics were encouraged to come to grips with the problems raised by the various critics. The literature of the time shows that they were so faithful to this encouragement that they sometimes lost sight of the Bible as a source of doctrine and spiritual nourishment. An extreme form of conservatism developed because some did not see the beneficial contributions that scientific and literary researches could bring to the study and understanding of the Bible.

The last thirty years have witnessed a refreshing spirit in Catholic studies on the Bible. Much credit for this is due to the patient, often silent, work of a French Dominican priest-scholar, Pére Marie-Joseph Lagrange (1855-1938), who established the *École Biblique* at Jerusalem (1890) where he labored almost to the time of his death. He also founded the *Revue Biblique* (1892), which has the reputation of being the best Catholic Biblical periodical in the world. Through his labors, which rested on an absolute loyalty and devotion to the Church and made use of all the tools of critical investigation, Catholic Biblical scholarship attained prestige and international respect.[21]

In 1936, the Biblical movement in the United States received a great impetus through the formation of The Catholic Biblical Association of America. Its aims are to "devote itself to the scientific study of the Bible and to such branches of learning as are connected with it, in conformity with the spirit and the instructions of the Catholic Church . . . cooperate with the Hierarchy and in particular with the Episcopal Committee of the Confraternity of Christian Doctrine in expounding and defending the teachings of the Church regarding the Bible and in promoting a greater love for and a deeper knowledge of the Sacred Scriptures . . . promote a better mutual acquaintance among the Catholic Biblical scholars of America and to provide them with encouragement and support in their special fields of study." [22] Since 1939 the Association has published *The Catholic Biblical Quarterly,* a scholarly periodical which presents the best Biblical articles in the English language.

The present interest in the Bible among Catholics is due in great measure to the vision and work of Pope Pius XII who in 1943 wrote the encyclical

---

[21] A good collection of articles about Pére Lagrange is in Richard T. Murphy, O.P. (ed.), *Pére Lagrange and the Scriptures* (Milwaukee: The Bruce Publishing Company, 1946). See also the summary of Lagrange's life and work in Barnabas M. Ahern, C.P., "Gathering the Fragments: Pére Lagrange," *Worship, XXXVI* (March, 1962), 242-48.
[22] An historical sketch of The Association and also its Constitution are contained in the Supplement to *The Catholic Biblical Quarterly,* XXII (January, 1960), 3-8.

Divino Afflante Spiritu which is considered the modern Magna Carta of the Biblical Movement. It was his belief that "our times also can contribute something towards the deeper and more accurate interpretation of Sacred Scripture." The Pope noted that the "conditions of biblical studies and their subsidiary sciences have greatly changed within the last fifty years," and, consequently, much help has been received for the "more correct and fuller understanding of the Sacred Books." Anticipating the criticism of those who view with alarm the contemporary Catholic developments in the field of Scripture, Pius XII declared that "all moreover should abhor that intemperate zeal which imagines that whatever is new should for that very reason be opposed or suspected." He reminded those who study and write on Biblical matters, as well as their fellow Catholics, that much remains to be done because "in the immense matter contained in the Sacred Books—legislative, historical, sapiential and prophetical—there are but a few texts whose sense has been defined by the authority of the Church . . . and there remain therefore many things, and of the greatest importance, in the discussion and exposition of which the skill and genius of Catholic commentators may and ought to be freely exercised, so that each may contribute his part to the advantage of all, to the continued progress of the sacred doctrine and to the defense and honor of the Church. This true liberty of the children of God . . . is the condition and source of all lasting fruit and of all solid progress in Catholic doctrine." [23]

Since the appearance of *Divino Afflante Spiritu* there have been other official documents from the Holy See which serve as guides in the development and advancement of Biblical studies. Among these have been the letter from the Biblical Commission to Cardinal Suhard of Paris regarding the study of the first 11 chapters of the Book of Genesis (January 16, 1948); the encyclical *Humani Generis* (1950), which expressed caution concerning the interpretation of the Scriptures, particularly in what regards the origin of man; the Monitum (Admonition) of the Holy Office on June 20, 1961, which acknowledges the "praiseworthy enthusiasm for Biblical studies" but cautions against views which doubt "the genuine historical and objective truth of the Sacred Scriptures" and urges "due discretion and reverence" in the study of the Bible. [24]

---

[23] DAS, 47-48.
[24] The pertinent passages from *Humani Generis* are in *Rome and the Study of Scripture,* p. 113. See Jean DeFraine, S.J., "The Encyclical 'Humani Generis' and Sacred Scripture," *Theology Digest,* II (Autumn, 1954), 155-58; also Jacques Dupont, O.S.B., "The Force of the Decrees of the Biblical Commission," *Theology Digest,* V (Winter, 1957), 38, and Edward Siegman, C.SS.P., "The Decrees of the Pontifical Biblical Commission: A Recent Clarification," *The Catholic Biblical Quarterly,* XVIII (January, 1956), 23-29. Comments about the reactions to the Monitum of June 20, 1961 are in Bruce Vawter, C.M., "The Wayward Press," *America,* CV (August 6, 1961), 591-92 and W. L. Moran, S.J., "Father Kennedy's Exegesis of the Holy Office Monitum," *The American Ecclesiastical Review,* CXLVI (March, 1962), 174-80. See the following article for a survey of aspects of the Biblical controversy in the United States: William S. Schnierla, "Roma Locuta . . . ?" *St. Vladimir's Seminary Quarterly Review,* VI (Summer, 1962), 79-92; reprinted in *Cross Currents,* XII (Fall, 1962), 407-21.

The work of scholars, guided by the expressed wishes of the Church, has done much to restore the Bible to its privileged position as the "most precious source of doctrine on faith and morals." [25] Once again the Book is looked upon not merely as a source for quotations or edifying stories but as the history, slow and progressive, of revelation and salvation. It is understood more and more as the inspired repository of the Message of Salvation.

The new era of Biblical study opened just as the Liturgical Movement was beginning to gain momentum. The same year that saw the publication of *Divino Afflante Spiritu* (1943) also witnessed the encyclical *Mystici Corporis,* which presents the teaching concerning the Church as the Mystical Body of Christ. Its contents clarified the nature of the Church as a living organism whose head is Christ who communicates His life to us His members. The contents of this encyclical are the basic motivating forces of the Liturgical Movement which also received encouragement and direction in the important encyclical on the Sacred Liturgy, *Mediator Dei* (1947). The Liturgical Movement has helped Catholics to see themselves not only as "spectators" of the Mass but as "active participators" in the Sacred Action which is the worship of Christ and His members. Centuries ago Christians were divorced from the Altar and, consequently, from the Bible. Now the closer union of Altar and People heralds a return to the Word of God. An intelligent use of the Missal, and other forms of participation legislated in the documents of the Holy See which continue to be sent to the Catholic world have caused an increased desire to know more about the texts which are found in the daily and Sunday Masses. This desire leads Christians to the Bible itself.

Pope Pius XII wrote: "No pains, no energy is to be spared in making it possible for the faithful to perceive ever more plainly the meaning of the Scriptures as intended by the Holy Spirit who inspired it and as expressed by the sacred writer." [26] Our present Holy Father, Pope John XXIII, has expressed his mind also: "Even though all the cares and interests of the pastoral ministry are dear to Us, and We realize the importance of each and every one, the thing We feel most of all is an obligation to keep on stirring up an enthusiasm everywhere for every expression of the Divine Book, which God meant to cast light on the whole path of life from infancy to the most advanced years. . . . Unfortunately, in all ages, there are always a few dark clouds, arising from certain notions that have little to do with true science, cluttering up the horizon whenever men attempt to see the Gospel in all its clear and radiant splendor. This is the task that is called to mind by the Book laid upon the altar: to teach true doctrine, proper discipline of life, and the ways in which man can rise toward God". [27]

[25] DAS, 1.
[26] *In cotidianis precibus* (March 24, 1945), *Rome and the Study of Scripture,* p. 109.
[27] Discourse at the Lateran Basilica (November 23, 1958), *The Pope Speaks,* V (Summer, 1959), 285.

The solid progress of the Catholic Biblical movement depends upon the laborious work of many scholars, "the resolute laborers in the vineyard of the Lord," as Pius XII called them. Since there are many unsolved problems there

> is no reason why the Catholic commentator, inspired by an active and ardent love of his subject and sincerely devoted to Holy Mother Church, should in any way be deterred from grappling again and again with these difficult problems, hitherto unsolved, not only that he may refute the objections of the adversaries, but also may attempt to find a satisfactory solution, which will be in full accord with the doctrine of the Church, in particular with the traditional teaching regarding the inerrancy of Sacred Scripture, and which will at the same time satisfy the indubitable conclusions of profane sciences.
>
> Let all the other sons of the Church bear in mind that the efforts of these resolute laborers in the vineyard of the Lord should be judged not only with equity and justice, but also with the greatest charity; all moreover should abhor that intemperate zeal which imagines that whatever is new should for that very reason be opposed or suspected. . . .
>
> There remain therefore many things, and of the greatest importance, in the discussion and exposition of which the skill and genius of Catholic commentators may and ought to be freely exercised, so that each may contribute his part to the advantage of all, to the continued progress of the sacred doctrine and to the defense and honor of the Church.
>
> This true liberty of the children of God, which adheres faithfully to the teaching of the Church and accepts and uses gratefully the contributions of profane science, this liberty, upheld and sustained in every way by the confidence of all, is the condition and source of all lasting fruit and of all solid progress in Catholic doctrine.[28]

Catholics must never take their understanding of the Faith for granted. We must strive to develop our intellectual grasp and make sure that it is really Catholic doctrine which we affirm and not merely some inadequate or incomplete childhood memories. The latter often are nothing more than the modes of expression which parents or teachers used to instruct the young. Much harm can result from a die-hard devotion to some fact or view which is in no way essential to the Faith. Loyalty to the accidentals of religion, which are at times useful and praiseworthy, is not necessarily the guarantee of orthodoxy in matters of doctrine. "A mind clinging fiercely to all the formulas of the manuals of its youth, without ever agreeing to rethink them in accordance with advances in the religious sciences, is not mature and, if it belongs to one who has pastoral or administrative responsibilities, may dam-

[28] DAS, 46-48.

age and weaken the faith or peace in the faith of well-intentioned scholars." [29] It is the Church which our Lord "has appointed guardian and interpreter of the whole deposit of divinely revealed truth." [30] It is to the Church that the Bible has been entrusted, and it is in the Church that all persons have the guarantee of intellectual security and the correct understanding of the revelation contained in the Message of Salvation.

Those devoted to the Biblical movement must have absolute allegiance to the Church. This loyalty must be motivated by the firm belief that Jesus and the Church form one Mystical Body. It is Jesus who rules, governs, and guides the Church directly and personally; He does this in a visible manner through His Vicar, the Holy Father, and the bishops.

REVELATION AND CHRISTIAN FAITH

God speaks to man in two ways. In the first place, He reveals Himself on the natural level in creation and in the conscience of the individual (Rom 1, 18-21; Acts 14, 14-17; 17, 22-29). But it is difficult for everyone to hear, see and follow God who reveals Himself in these ways. There is a danger that individuals will "miss the point" of the message or will pervert it altogether, as can be seen in many superstitious and immoral practices among the pagans of ancient times and even in our own day. Furthermore, God reveals Himself on the supernatural level, by means of divine Revelation in which He chooses certain individuals to whom He entrusts His message and whom He commissions to communicate it to others. He accompanies His message with signs, at times, miracles, so that His messengers will have proof to offer concerning the divine origin of the words they speak.

Through history God has spoken at various times, in various ways, and through various individuals. He finally spoke in His Son, Jesus—the Word made flesh. "God, who at sundry times and in divers manners spoke in times past to the fathers by the prophets, last of all in these days has spoken to us by His son, whom He appointed heir of all things" (Heb 1,1-2).

The supernatural Revelation is to be transmitted from age to age until the end of the world. Therefore, it must be preserved faithfully and entrusted to each succeeding generation without any admixture of error. The message of God is directed toward the salvation of man by means of a liberation from sin and error. The message must be true and each generation must be certain that it receives the "truth that will make men free" (Jn 8,32).

God has not only acted by revealing Himself and His Word; He also has

---

[29] Levie, *op. cit.,* p. 197.

[30] *Humani Generis,* 22 (Washington, D. C.: National Catholic Welfare Conference, 1950), p. 11. See also the addresses of Pope Pius XII, "The Teaching Authority of the Church," and "The Church and Its Power of Sanctifying and Ruling," *Pope Pius XII and Theological Studies* (St. Meinrad, Ind.: Grail Publications, 1957), pp. 45-68.

fashioned a People who will be the depository of the truth. His Word will always be with His People; all men will know where to turn to hear the Word because the People will be the visible sign of His invisible presence. The People will be the sacrament and the sign of God before the world. The People of Israel was the Chosen Race throughout almost two millennia. It was the depository of God's revealed message and the means through which the Word was preserved and transmitted in the centuries during which God was acting to prepare the whole world for the great advent of His Son.

Then in the "fullness of time" Jesus came, the definitive Revelation arrived, a new People was formed and the last age of the world began. Now, all men were called to the "one shepherd, one flock," to the Church which is the "pillar and the mainstay of truth" (I Tim 3,15). The Church is the great Sacrament in the world, and all who seek the truth will find it there, all who desire the life will receive it there. The Church is the great Sign and witness of God's presence among His people.

To accept all this, to believe that God still speaks and acts in our age requires Faith. This is not something which is unreasonable, a travesty committed against man's highest faculty, the mind. It is not a shackling of the spirit of inquiry; it is not something which we do blindly and foolishly. Faith is the response of man to the call of God expressed in His message, His Word. Faith is the acceptance of all that God says because He is Truth who can "neither deceive nor be deceived." But, Faith is not just an act of the mind, it is the response of a human person confronted by a Person and a Message. *It is the total commitment of the person to the Word of God, to Christ. The whole being is involved in the act of Faith—the mind, the will, the heart.* This response is not something merely human and natural; it relies on a supernatural gift from God Himself.[31] Moreover, the response also relies on certain conditions which dispose a person to make the act of Faith and to persevere in belief:

1. There must be no obstacle within the person which prevents a personal relationship with Christ. The person who does not want to

---

[31] The following are recommended for an understanding of the nature and role of Faith in the life of the Christian: Bruce Vawter, C.M., "The Biblical Idea of Faith," *Worship,* XXXIV (August, 1960), 443-50; Romano Guardini, *The Life of Faith,* trans. John Chapin (Westminster, Md.: The Newman Press, 1961); Eugene Joly, *What is Faith?* trans. Dom Illtyd Trethowan (New York: Hawthorn Books, Publishers, 1958); Jean Mouroux, *I Believe, The Personal Structure of Faith,* trans. Michael Turner (New York: Sheed & Ward, 1959); Franz X. Arnold, "The Aim of Religious Education: Faith as the Assent of the Mind and Commitment of the Whole Person," *Lumen Vitae,* XI (October-December, 1956), 571-82; Roger Poelman, "Faith, An Inward Growth," *Lumen Vitae,* XI (October-December, 1956), 583-94; Joseph Dheilly, "Faith Nourished by the Study of the Bible," *Lumen Vitae,* IX (April-June, 1954), 235-48; see also the articles by Charles Davis, "Faith and Reason," Romano Guardini, "Faith and Doubt," Jean Levie, S.J., "Faith and Intellectual Sincerity," and Alan Richardson, "Faith and Presuppositions," in John J. Heany, S.J. (ed.), *Faith, Reason and the Gospels* (Westminster, Md.: The Newman Press, 1961), pp. 5-88.

believe cannot be made to believe. The human will is so free that
not even God can force it to act in a way contrary to its own
choosing.

2. The relationship with God must be not only personal but communal.
    To believe in God is "to do whatever he tells you" (Jn 2,5). God's
    Word is in His People; to believe means to become a member of
    that People, a member of the Church, the Mystical Body of Christ.
    It is in the Church that Christ continues to act so that men will
    have life.

3. There must be love for Christ. This love is the bond which preserves
    and strengthens the relationship between the person who believes
    and the one in whom he believes, between the Catholic and the
    Word. The individual who deliberately remains aloof and distant
    from the source of life—Christ who acts in the Sacraments in the
    Church—is a person whose love is weakening and who will soon
    find that he believes less and less, and soon, not at all.

Christianity is not just some rational form of theism. Unfortunately, this
is the impression created by some forms of apologetics which give the idea
that a person can reason to the Faith. All that valid apologetics can hope to
do is show that the Christian Faith is reasonable. It cannot be proved by
reason.[32]

These truths must be understood if the true nature of the Bible in the life
of the Christian is to be grasped. God speaks and acts in the Church, His
People, of which we are members. The Bible has been entrusted to the Community, the Church; it is the Church that guarantees the divine origin of the
Scriptures and protects them so that they can be passed on through the ages.
The Church with its divinely entrusted solicitude for the Holy Book protects
it, so that the People will possess it and understand it without fear or perversion
of the truth.

[32] "Sacred Doctrine also makes use of human reason, not, indeed, to prove faith (for thereby
the merit of faith would come to an end), but to make clear other things that are set forth
in this doctrine. Since, therefore, grace does not destroy nature, but perfects it, natural reason
should minister to faith as the natural inclination of the will ministers to charity." St. Thomas
Aquinas, *Summa Theologiae,* 1, q.1, a.8, ad 2. See also Bernard Haering, C.SS.R., "The
Christian Message and Apologetics and the Modern Mentality," *Lumen Vitae,* XVI (September,
1961), 425-34.

two

BIBLICAL THEOLOGY AND
SALVATION-HISTORY

I. INTRODUCTION

ONE OF THE AIMS of the Biblical movement, directed and encouraged by the Magisterium of the Church, is to make Christians more conscious of the Divine Plan which is unfolding in history. Pope Pius XII spoke of the Bible as the "most precious source of doctrine on faith and morals." It is the task of all who are members of Christ to study the Bible in the Church in order to arrive at an understanding of the implications of the Holy Father's statement.

The Bible is more than a "storage chest" in which *proof texts* are sought for the beliefs and practices of the Church. To see the Scriptures only as a collection of single texts which substantiate the various items which we Catholics believe to be part of the revelation of God is an insufficient view. Such an approach tends to emphasize *parts* instead of the *whole* and as a result tends to an underestimation of the role that the Word of God plays in the economy of salvation. For this reason, there is an increasing awareness on the part of many in the Church that the whole plan found in the Revelation communicated by God has to be seen if believers are to understand properly the individual elements found in it.

II. BIBLICAL THEOLOGY

Is it possible to form a synthesis that will help Christians understand the Plan of God as well as their role in it? This is the question that faces all believers, and particularly the Biblical theologians. Their task is to apply Christian minds, enlightened by Faith, to the individual books of the Bible and derive from them those testimonies which will then be formed into a complete system. This is a difficult task, requiring not only a professional competence in the various sciences that are necessary for the understanding of the Biblical writing as intended by the inspired author, but also a thorough grasp of all the doctrine taught by the Church throughout its existence.

Biblical theology seeks to show the relation of the parts to the whole in the plan of God; it seeks to understand the individual acts of God in relation to the message which He has communicated to the Church. The themes found in the Word of God have to be studied in order to achieve the construction of an intelligible whole, a coherent unity which will be meaningful to believers. Persons, events, and words in the Old Testament have to be studied and seen in relation to the persons, events, and words of the New Testament. All things have to be seen in relation to the Person of Christ who is the central figure and fact in the *heilsgeschichte*, sacred-history.

The nature of God and His plan of salvation are revealed in the acts which He performs throughout history. He has acted in the past and has established a bond, a covenant, with men; He continues to act for His people. The acts of the past are the buttress of the believer's hope; the realization of what God has done makes us more conscious of the meaning of what He continues to do. Salvation-history is the account of the intervention of God in our world, drawing mankind to Himself, communicating His divine life, and bringing about His universal reign.

Biblical theology has much to do before it achieves the great synthesis that it seeks. But it has already been successful in pointing out the importance of the *whole* instead of merely the *parts* in salvation-history.

III. SALVATION-HISTORY: THE PLAN OF GOD

God has revealed Himself; men experience His presence. Through His acts, men can come to an understanding of His existence and presence among them. "Since the creation of the world his invisible attributes are clearly seen—his everlasting power also and divinity—being understood through the things that are made" (Rom 1,20).

God has acted during the various stages of salvation-history and the Bible reveals both the stages and the Divine Acts.[1]

1. CREATION: COSMIC AND HUMAN

The early chapters of the book of Genesis present the theological teachings concerning the act of creation and the rebellion of man against God. By means of a series of stories, the inspired writings teach the consequences of

---

[1] See the following for an introductory study of Salvation-History and its general divisions: Marcel Van Caster, S.J., "The Substance of the Christian Message: The Mystery of Salvation," *Lumen Vitae*, X (October-December, 1955), 495-508.

Original Sin—jealousy and murder (Cain and Abel), sin and punishment (Noe and the Flood), pride and dissension (Tower of Babel).

2. PREPARATION IN THE OLD TESTAMENT

A. *God Chose a Man*

During the nineteenth century B.C. God chose a pagan named Abram, and asked a great act of faith of him. Abram left his home; he became the "father of many people." He is the father of all who believe: "The men of faith are the real sons of Abraham. . . . Therefore the men of faith shall be blessed with faithful Abraham" (Gal 3,7-9).

During the thirteenth century B.C. God chose another man, Moses, to liberate the Hebrews who were in captivity in Egypt.

B. *God Chose a People*

The events of the Passover and Exodus reveal the presence of God among His people. He made a Covenant with the Hebrews at Mt. Sinai: "If you hearken to my voice and keep my covenant, you shall be my special possession, dearer to me than all other people, though all the earth is mine. You shall be to me a kingdom of priests, a holy nation" (Ex 19,5-6).

Once the people had been formed into a unit, they could be taught about God—that He is one and holy, that He is the Lord, Yahweh. They could be taught that His love is a demanding one as well as a jealous one; He will not tolerate any form of allegiance to the gods of the pagans. His love is also merciful and forgiving toward those who repent sincerely for their misdeeds and infidelities.

C. *God Chose a Home for His People*

The Hebrews conquered the land of Canaan; about 150 years were necessary to accomplish the feat (1200-1050 B.C.). God gave them a king and a kingdom: Saul, David, and Solomon (1030-931 B.C.). The Glory of the Lord dwelled in the majestic Temple of Jerusalem.

The period of prosperity led to the neglect of God. Rivalries and dissensions tore the fabric of the kingdom and finally led to a schism after the death of Solomon. The northern kingdom was known as Israel, the southern one, Juda.

In time God chose men to speak in His name. They were known as Prophets; it was their task to remind the people of the covenant-obligations (750-587 B.C.).

Infidelities continued, and worship was even given to other gods. Punishment came when the Babylonian armies swept through the land and destroyed Jerusalem and its Temple. Many of the people were brought into exile in Babylon (587-38 B.C.).

D. *A Religious Community Was Fashioned*

The years that followed the Exile saw the formation of the true spirit of the Chosen People. The Temple was rebuilt and the community prayed and meditated as it waited in the hope of seeing the fulfillment of the promises of the Lord in the coming of the Messiah (538-6 B.C.).

A more interior type of piety developed. Thoughts turned to an Israel that was more than something limited to the flesh. There were glimpses of a spiritual Israel that would include all people, not just the Jews. Narrow parochialism slowly began to give way to spiritual universalism through the influence of the post-Exilic prophets and writings. But the task was difficult because the presence of foreign armies in Palestine caused many of the people to retain a strong spirit of nationalism; they thought of liberation and the Messianic kingdom in political terms.

During the period of Roman occupation, after 63 B.C., many assumed that the Savior would come, overthrow the rule of Rome and establish a Jewish empire that would never end. This contributed to the great tragedy which was the rejection of the Savior when He did come: "He came unto his own, and his own received him not" (Jn 1,11). Only a remnant remained faithful to the true ideals.

The poor of the Lord, the *anawim,* prepared for the fulfillment of the promises; they firmly believed in the Lord and trusted in His Word. They accepted Him when He came: Mary, His mother, praised God for remembering the promise which He made "toward our fathers, toward Abraham and his descendants forever . . ." (Lk 1,54); Zachary saw that God was accomplishing the "oath that He swore to Abraham our father" (Lk 1,73); Simeon gave thanks because he saw the "light of revelation for the Gentiles and the glory of your people Israel" (Lk 2,32); Anna "spoke of him to all who were awaiting the redemption of Jerusalem" (Lk 2,38).

3. FULFILLMENT IN CHRIST

A. *Jesus is the Lord*

Jesus is the center of the Mystery of Salvation; He is "our hope of glory" (Col 1,27). He came, not to put aside the Law and the Prophets, but to fulfill them (Mt 5,17). He came as the fulfillment of the promises of the Old Testament. The *types, signs,* and *symbols* were fulfilled in a manner which surpassed the dreams and expectations of all the people; the lamb, the manna, and the temple were but dim realities when seen in relation to Him who is the Lamb of God, the living Bread from Heaven, and the Temple in which dwells the fullness of divinity. The people of the Old Covenant were the symbol of the people of the New Covenant; the Old had been the shadow, the New is the reality.

B. *The Church is the Kingdom*

The great work which occupied the public life of Jesus was the establishment of the kingdom of God, the Church. He chose men to be apostles and appointed Peter as their head; He bestowed power and authority to teach, rule, and sanctify men. He completed His earthly work on the Cross; there the New Covenant replaced the Old Law; through His Resurrection and Ascension He was glorified, and sent the Holy Spirit.[2]

4. CONTINUATION IN THE CHURCH

A. *The Mystery of Salvation Penetrates the Members of Christ*

The Chosen People had been the flock of God (Ez 34; Ps 99,3); the Church is the flock of Christ (Jn 10,1-17). It is the "flock which he won for himself at the price of his own blood" (Acts 20,28). The people of the Old Covenant had been called to be a "kingdom of priests, a holy nation" (Ex 19,6). St. Peter told Christians: "You, however, are a chosen race, a royal priesthood, a holy nation, a purchased people. . . . You who in times past were not a people, but are now the People of God; who had not obtained mercy, but now have obtained mercy" (I Pt 2,9-10).

During the liturgy of the Paschal Vigil we pray: "Grant that all the peoples of the world may become children of Abraham, and share the dignity of Israel." [3]

B. *The Church is the Mystical Body of Christ*

Jesus is present and active in the world in a body composed of human beings, a body that is alive with His Spirit. "It was possible for Him personally, immediately to impart these graces to men; but He wished to do so only through a visible Church that would be formed by the union of men, and thus through that Church every man would perform a work of collaboration with Him in dispensing the graces of Redemption." [4]

St. Paul's favorite expression for the Church is "the body of Christ." He taught Christians that "just as in one body we have many members, yet all the members have not the same function, so we, the many, are one body in Christ, but severally members one of another" (Rom 12,4-5). He revealed what should be the sentiments of all Christians who are committed to Christ when he said: "I rejoice now in the sufferings I bear for your sake; and what is lacking of the sufferings of Christ I fill up in my flesh for his body, which is the Church" (Col 1,24).[5]

Christ is the head of the body which is the Church: "Grow up in all things

---

[2] These points are developed briefly by Pope Pius XII in *Mystici Corporis*, 32-41 (New York: The America Press, n.d.), pp. 16-20.

[3] Prayer after the second lesson of the Paschal Vigil.

[4] *Mystici Corporis*, 16, 68-69.

in him who is the head, Christ. For from him the whole body . . . derives its increase to the building up of itself in love" (Eph 4,15-16). Membership in the Church accomplishes union with Christ and from Him comes divine life. The members of Christ are the heirs of the promise made to Abraham. It is the Plan of God that the "blessing of Abraham might come to the Gentiles through Christ Jesus, that through faith we might receive the promise of the Spirit" (Gal 3,14).

"The Church is Jesus Christ diffused and communicated; it is Jesus Christ whole, it is Jesus Christ perfect man, Jesus Christ in His fullness" (Bossuet).

C. *The Sacraments Are the Acts of Christ*

The Sacraments are the continuation of the *mirabilia Dei,* the wonderful acts of God performed during the period of the Old Testament. "There is, then, a sacred history of successive individual acts of creative power; the election of Abraham, the exodus from Egypt, the kingdom of David, the incarnation of Christ, and his resurrection, the sacraments of the Church, and the Last Judgement." [6]

The Sacraments are the acts of the Lord, the Risen Christ, accomplished by the Church. "When the Sacraments of the Church are administered by external rite, it is He who produces their effect in souls. He nourishes the redeemed with His own flesh and blood, and thus calms the soul's turbulent passions; He gives increase of grace and is preparing future glory for souls and bodies. All these treasures of His Divine goodness He is said to disburse to the members of His Mystical Body, not merely because He, who is the Eucharistic Victim on earth and the glorified Victim in Heaven, lets His wounds and prayers plead our cause before the Eternal Father, but because He selects, He determines, He distributes every single grace to every single person." [7]

D. *The Commandments Are Part of Our Response to the Love of God*

The great Commandment for Christians is the one that is summed up in the Law of Charity. "You shall love the Lord your God with your whole heart, and with your whole soul, and with your whole mind" (Mt 22,37; Dt 6,5). The Commandments of the Decalogue are part of our response to the love that God shows through the acts which He performs on our behalf. They are prohibitions which in reality are explicit determinations of the Commandment of Love.

---

[5] For an excellent study of the theology of St. Paul see William Grossouw, *In Christ,* trans. Martin W. Schoenberg, O.S.C. (Westminster, Md.: The Newman Press, 1952), also L. Cerfaux, *Christ in the Theology of St. Paul,* trans. Geoffrey Webb and Adrian Walker (New York: Herder and Herder, 1959), and by the same author, *The Church in the Theology of St. Paul,* trans. Geoffrey Webb and Adrian Walker (New York: Herder and Herder, 1959).

[6] Jean Daniélou, S.J., *The Lord of History,* trans. Nigel Abercrombie (Chicago: Henry Regnery, 1958), p. 139.

[7] *Mystici Corporis,* 63-64.

These concrete determinations of the Commandments of God represent the extreme limit beyond which love is excluded. Cut off from their biblical foundation and presented as a closed system of obligations which are imposed upon the Christian, the Ten Commandments are a form of intolerable legalism. The heart of Christianity is the Sermon on the Mount, not a litany of actions which merely protect love or keep it barely alive. In the context of the Sermon on the Mount the Commandments appear not as the separate articles of a code, but animated by the spirit that is their common soul. In this way all danger of considering them the sufficient conditions for salvation is avoided. What salvation requires is the sincere desire to go beyond that point of departure the Commandments represent to the perfection we are called to, a perfection which is comparable to a mathematical limit that we can attain only by constantly striving after it, or more exactly, by becoming polarized by it.[8]

5. ACHIEVEMENT IN HEAVEN

The Church, the Mystical Body of Christ, is the New Israel, marching through history toward the promised land of heaven. The Old Israel made its way through the desert toward the land of Canaan under the leadership of God's representatives, Moses, Aaron, and Josue; the New Israel is guided by the divinely appointed leaders in the person of Peter, his successors, and all those appointed to rule, teach, and sanctify the flock of God.

The Plan of God will be fulfilled at the Second Coming of Christ, the *Parousia*. The period between the Ascension of Jesus and His return at the end of the world is the period of the Church; it is the missionary period during which the Good News of Salvation, the Gospel, must be brought to all nations and peoples.

The Church is the present stage in the History of Salvation; it is the preparation for the Parousia and the heavenly Jerusalem:

And I saw the holy city, New Jerusalem, coming down out of heaven from God, made ready as a bride adorned for her husband. And I heard a loud voice from the throne saying, "Behold the dwelling of God with men, and he will dwell with them. And they will be his people, and God himself will be with them as their God. And God will wipe away every tear from their eyes. And death shall be no more; neither shall there be mourning, nor crying, nor pain any more, for the former things have passed away.

Ap 21,2-4

[8] Bernard Murchland (ed.), *Themes of Theology: God Among Men* (Notre Dame: Fides Publishers Association, 1960), p. 48. See Gerard Gilleman, S.J., "Biblical Revelation of the Primacy of Charity," *Lumen Vitae*, XVI (March, 1961), 9-26, and by the same author, *The Primacy of Charity in Moral Theology* (Westminster, Md.; The Newman Press, 1959). An outstanding contemporary work which presents a rich approach to moral theology is Bernard Häring, *The Law of Christ*, trans. Edwin G. Kaiser, C.PP.S. (Westminster, Md.: The Newman Press, 1961).

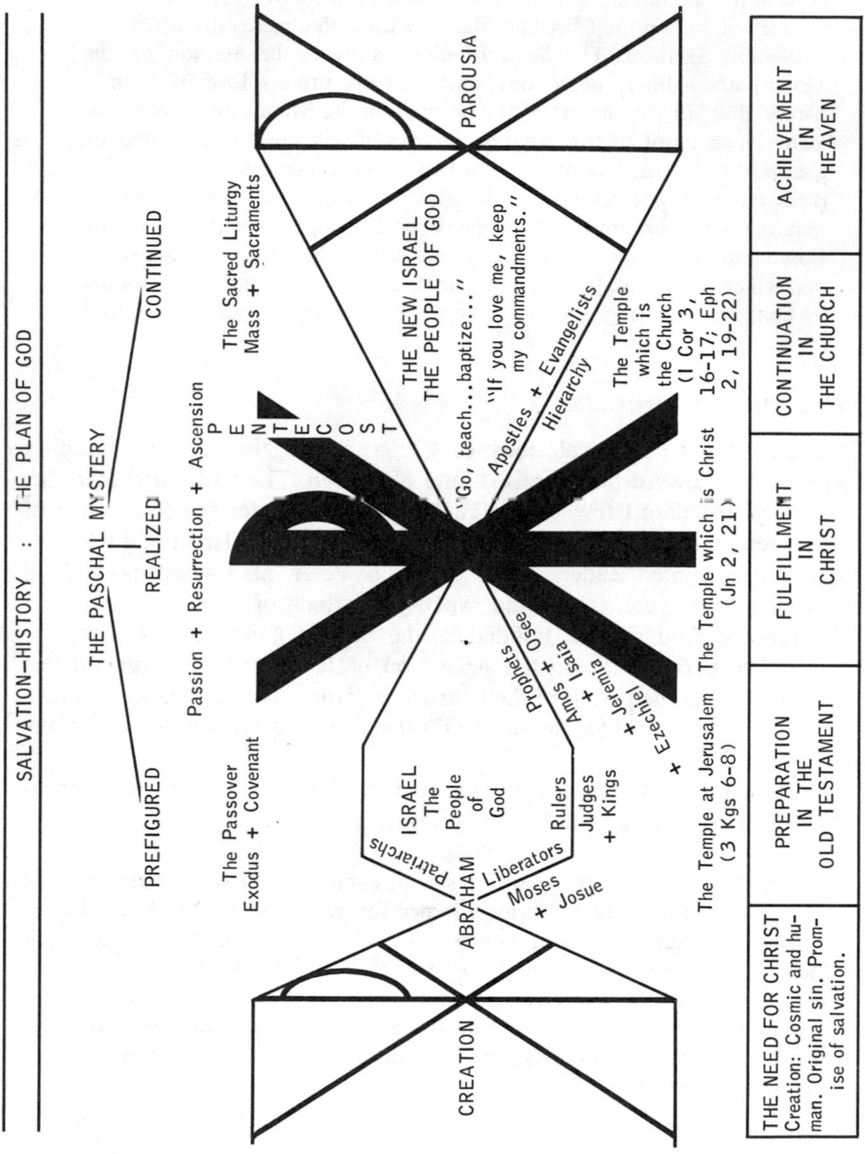

SALVATION–HISTORY : THE PLAN OF GOD

THE PASCHAL MYSTERY

PREFIGURED   REALIZED   CONTINUED

PAROUSIA

The Sacred Liturgy
Mass + Sacraments

Passion + Resurrection + Ascension

THE NEW ISRAEL
THE PEOPLE OF GOD

"Go, teach...baptize..."

"If you love me, keep
my commandments."

Apostles + Evangelists

Hierarchy

P
E
N
T
E
C
O
S
T

The Temple
which is
the Church
(1 Cor 3,
16-17; Eph
2, 19-22)

The Passover
Exodus + Covenant

Prophets

Amos + Osee

+ Isaia

+ Jeremia

+ Ezechiel

ISRAEL
The
People
of
God

Rulers
Judges
+ Kings

Patriarchs

Liberators

Moses

+ Josue

ABRAHAM

The Temple which is Christ
(Jn 2, 21)

The Temple at Jerusalem
(3 Kgs 6-8)

CREATION

THE NEED FOR CHRIST Creation: Cosmic and human. Original sin. Promise of salvation.	PREPARATION IN THE OLD TESTAMENT	FULFILLMENT IN CHRIST	CONTINUATION IN THE CHURCH	ACHIEVEMENT IN HEAVEN

Figure 1.

three

THE NATURE OF
BIBLICAL INSPIRATION

I. INTRODUCTION

IT IS PART of Christian Faith to believe that certain books are "sacred" because they are "inspired by God." Jesus often referred to the books of the Old Testament as the Word of God (Mt 22,31-32; Jn 10,34-35). The apostles and evangelists were convinced that those who composed the books were men of God who "spoke as they were moved by the Holy Spirit" (2 Pt 1,21). The primitive Church accepted the Scriptures of the Old Testament and soon added other books to the collection. St. Paul taught that "all Scripture is inspired by God. . . ." (2 Tim 3, 16). The Fathers of the Church received the collection of Sacred Books, and in their own writings they affirm that God is the true author. The official teaching of the Church has always been that the contents of the Bible are the inspired word of God. The official declarations of the Magisterium have often re-asserted this fundamental truth of the Christian Faith.

Words have meanings. This is a truism which is often neglected in many discussions. It is important that the meaning of the word "inspiration" be understood. Since it is a word that has acquired a variety of meanings in everyday speech, there is a danger that such meanings will be attached to it in the study of the Bible. The result will be misunderstanding and confusion concerning the nature of the Scriptures, and the Church's teaching that the Bible is "inspired by God." It is the word of God in human language.

> For as the substantial Word of God became like to men in all things, 'except sin,' so the words of God expressed in human language, are

27

made like to human speech in every respect, except error. In this consists that 'condescension' of the God of providence, which St. John Chrysostom extolled with the highest praise and repeatedly declared to be found in the Sacred Books.[1]

II. FALSE NOTIONS

A. The words "inspire" and "inspiration" are often used in reference to literary and artistic accomplishments. It is said that a poet or artist is moved by some interior intuition by which, almost inexplicably, he transforms the things of the world which others take for granted into a "new creation." This creative intuition in both art and poetry is involved in productions which are labeled "inspired" and "inspirational," for example: "This is an inspired masterpiece."

The ancient Greeks and Latins referred to this talent of certain men as a "gift from the gods." Nowadays, even those who do not believe in the supernatural order can be heard to say that someone or something is "truly divine."

These contemporary usages, even if legitimate when properly understood, must not be confused with Biblical Inspiration. Poets, artists, musicians, and other gifted persons are exercising a gift, which is God-given, but which is on the natural level; Biblical Inspiration is supernatural.

B. Sometimes the Fathers of the Church spoke of the human authors as writers to whom God "dictated" His message; therefore, many Catholics and Protestants followed the *Theory of Verbal Dictation* in explaining Inspiration. This view, which was common up to the eighteenth century, considered the human authors of the Biblical books as mere transcribers, men to whom God dictated His words. The human writers were looked upon as some sort of "phonograph" on which God placed his ready-made records containing revelation.

This development rested on a misunderstanding of the meaning of the word "dictation" as used by the Fathers. Studies have shown that the word did not imply the same amount of passivity for them as it does for us. It is true that God *could* use a human person in the capacity of an intelligent secretary. But this hardly befits a God whom we consider all-wise, all-gentle, good, and just. Moreover, the human character of the Biblical works is evident to all who take the time to read them intelligently. A careful reading of the Bible would be enough to convince anyone that Inspiration and dictation are not synonymous. The style and approaches in the book of Isaia, a member of the aristocracy, are different from those of Amos, a herdsman; the writings of St. Paul are certainly different from those of St. John. The author of the third Gospel, St. Luke, tells us that he spent a good deal of time collecting the sources that

[1] DAS, 37.

he used in the writing of the Gospel (Lk 1,1-4). The personalities of the human authors, their peculiar characteristics, their ability or lack of ability in the use of language, are apparent in the books which form the Canon of the Scriptures.

III. CORRECT NOTIONS

The Church teaches that the Bible is the Word of God, the Books have God for their Author. But the *infallible magisterium* of the Church has not given a technical definition of Inspiration. The encyclical of Pope Leo XIII contains a descriptive definition which is basic to a proper understanding of the Catholic position on the matter: "By supernatural power, He so moved and impelled them to write—He so assisted them when writing—that the things which He ordered, and those only, they, first, rightly understood, then willed faithfully to write down, and finally expressed in apt words and with infallible truth. Otherwise, it could not be said that He is the Author of the entire Scripture." [2]

This definition makes clear that God is the Author of the Bible because (1) the impulse to write comes from Him, and He assisted the authors throughout their work, (2) the work contains what He wills, (3) the influence of God touched both mind and will of the human author, and (4) the influence was involved in the choice made concerning the words used by the author. The whole Scripture is conceived, willed, and carried through under the impulse of God.

However, it is important to remember that the definition of Leo XIII was not a full account of the phenomenon of inspiration. The Church has not defined in minute detail the exact nature of Divine Inspiration. It would be up to theologians to study the fact and to present a closer analysis of its nature. The last 80 years have witnessed a variety of theological studies concerning Inspiration. These include, among others, the work of Cardinal Franzelin, S.J.; Marie-Joseph Lagrange, O.P.; Pierre Benoit, O.P.; and Karl Rahner, S.J. The solution proposed by Benoit has been received very favorably by many scholars who consider it most acceptable, at least in its general approach.[3]

[2] Pope Leo XIII, *Providentissimus Deus,* in *Rome and the Study of Scripture,* p. 24.

[3] See P. Benoit, O.P., "Inspiration," *Guide to the Bible,* I, 9-52; also by the same author, *"Scriptural Inspiration"* in Paul Synave, O.P., and Pierre Benoit, O.P., *Prophecy and Inspiration,* trans. Avery Dulles, S.J., and Thomas L. Sheridan, S.J. (New York: Desclee Company, 1961), pp. 84-168. An evaluation of the various approaches to Biblical Inspiration appears in the excellent article by David M. Stanley, S.J., "The Concept of Biblical Inspiration," *Proceedings of the Catholic Theological Society of America* (1958) pp. 65-89. The following article should be read in order to keep a proper balance between the role of the individual inspired author and the community of the People of God which is Israel (Old Testament) and the Church (New Testament): John L. McKenzie, S.J., "The Social Character of Inspiration," *The Catholic Biblical Quarterly,* XXIV (April, 1962), 115-24.

IV. NATURE OF INSTRUMENTAL CAUSALITY

Theologians make use of the principle of instrumental causality in their attempt to come to a better understanding of the nature of Biblical Inspiration. We have to remember that this is man's attempt to understand a Divine activity. Consequently, we are actually making use of an analogy when we apply the principle to the mystery of Inspiration. Every analogy limps. The explanation is not satisfactory in every detail. Nevertheless, it is very useful in coming to a better understanding of the way God acts when He chooses human persons in order to externalize His mind through human thought and modes of expression.

First, a few definitions and distinctions are necessary. Philosophers define a cause as a principle, by force of which something is produced; it is that which positively influences the being of another. Then they point out that there are four kinds of causes: (1) material, (2) formal, (3) final, and (4) efficient.[4]

We have said that a cause is a principle. A principle is that from which anything proceeds in any manner whatever. It implies only an order of origin; it does not include any notion of influence on those things which follow it. For example, dawn is the beginning of a day. But dawn does not make the day. In philosophical language, we would say that dawn is the principle of the day. A cause, on the other hand, positively influences something in such a way that that which proceeds from a cause depends upon it for its very existence. A man carves a statue out of a piece of wood. He is the cause of the statue; the statue depends on him for its very existence.

The four causes mentioned by philosophers may be defined as follows:

(1) A Material Cause is that out of which something is made. In the example already used, the statue is made of wood; the wood is the *material* cause.

(2) A Formal Cause is that which determines the material cause. It is that which makes the effect of such a kind that it distinguishes it from all other things. It is that into which something is made. For example, a statue is not *just* a statue but is a particular type or kind of statue. A man is not just a living being; he is a particular kind of living being, one who possesses a rational soul. That which distinguishes one kind of statue from another kind, and man from animals, is the form. It is this intrinsic cause that determines the matter in such a way that the result is "The Thinker" by Auguste Rodin or, in the case of a man, John Jones.

---

[4] This matter is covered in books of Scholastic philosophy that deal with the nature of causality. This presentation is based on R. P. Phillips, *Modern Thomistic Philosophy*, (2 vols., Westminster, Md.: The Newman Bookshop, 1935), II, 232-44.

(3) A Final Cause is that for the sake of which something is done. It is the reason, the purpose, goal, end, etc. A man works to support a family; the artisan carves a statue in order to win a prize, etc. There are proximate and final causes. Any series of acts necessary for the attainment of a distant goal contains a chain of final causes, some proximate, others remote; the last of the final causes is the Ultimate Final Cause; it is that which is intended for its own sake and not as a means to something further.

(4) An Efficient Cause is that by which something is made; it is the agent that produces something. The artist who paints, the man who builds, etc., are the efficient causes; they are the ones who produce the effects.

Efficient Causes are further divided into:

(a) *First Cause* and *Second Cause*. The First Cause does not receive its power from any other being; this is God. The Second Cause depends on another cause. This is everything else outside of God because there is nothing in the order of creation that does not depend upon another for its activity. Ultimately, all things depend upon God who is the Cause of causes.

(b) *Principal and Instrumental Causes*. A Principal Cause produces its effect by its own powers. A man who acts to produce some effect is an example of such a cause. The Instrumental Cause is one which produces an effect only when moved by an agent. It is something which is raised up by the power of the principal cause in order to produce an effect that is of an order higher than itself. For example, a lifeless piece of chalk is used by a teacher to produce words on a blackboard. It should be noticed that the two causes, principal and instrumental, are both responsible for the total effect produced.

The treatment above of the meaning and kinds of causes contains philosophical implications that are difficult to grasp immediately. Upon some reflection, however, it will be seen that these basic notions enter into every action performed by us as humans. In fact, they enter into all activity, including that known as Biblical Inspiration. The notion of Efficient Causality is particularly important in the theological study of Inspiration as presented by many modern-day scholars, particularly Pierre Benoit, O.P., whose work is considered a classic treatise on the subject.[5]

The Sacred Writer of the Biblical Books is the instrument of the Holy Spirit. "As a principal cause uses an instrumental cause by making the latter's peculiar efficiency subservient to its own higher efficiency, so that the resulting work is at the same time and fully the effect of both causes, of both together and of each according to its rank, so God by his sovereign activity influences the activity of the inspired writer so thoroughly that the resulting work will

---

[5] See P. Benoit, *op. cit.*, and Stanley, *op. cit.*, pp. 76-79.

be entirely His work and entirely the work of that man, and simultaneously, though in different degrees." [6]

However, the use of the principle of instrumental causality must not mislead us. Efficient Causality is involved when a teacher uses a piece of chalk to write on the board; the teacher is the principal cause; the chalk the instrumental cause. The chalk, which is inanimate and devoid of reason and will, must do what the teacher wants; the teacher on the other hand is limited by the quality of the chalk as far as the quality of the writing is concerned; white and smooth chalk will produce white and smooth letters, etc. In the case of Biblical Inspiration, the human author is not a dead instrument. He is an instrument that is "living and reasonable." He possesses human faculties of mind and will; he has a memory; he possesses a particular language and style. Consequently, God does not use him as if he were an inanimate piece of chalk, or a pen, or some tool. God respects the nature of the instrument He uses. God inspires a human being, not an automaton. It is because of this that one who reads the Bible must not neglect "any light derived from recent research, endeavor to determine the peculiar character and circumstances of the sacred writer, the age in which he lived, the sources written or oral to which he had recourse and the forms of expression he employed." [7]

God inspired human beings, not "talking dummies" or "secretarial automatons." The human author was not exempted from the processes that are part of the writing of any other kind of book. He gathered the necessary materials and organized them in a way that would express the thoughts he deemed necessary. In accomplishing all this, he made use of a series of judgments, illumined by the Spirit of God, concerning what should be used and what would be the suitable mode of expression. During the process, he was not necessarily aware of *inspiration* any more than we are aware of, or feel, Sanctifying Grace.

Sometimes a Biblical book has gone through a long and complicated history before it arrived at the state in which it is now in the Canon or list of inspired Books. Many of the books of the Old Testament are the result of a combination of various traditions, oral and written. They are the work of several individuals who lived in different ages. All those who contributed to produce the book benefited from the *charism* or grace of inspiration. Because of this, we may speak not only of an inspired author but also of any *inspired tradition.*

V. SPOKEN WORD TO WRITTEN WORD

Long before the Old Testament existed as a collection of written books, it existed as *oral teaching,* at least to a very large extent. It was handed down from one generation to another before writing came into general use. To

[6] Benoit, "Inspiration," *Guide to the Bible,* I, 19.
[7] DAS, 33.

understand and appreciate this we have to forget our approaches as members of a *paper civilization,* one where the emphasis is on the written word more than on the spoken word. We take books and written papers so much for granted that we can hardly imagine civilizations where these did not exist. Our dependence on the written word often stifles the operations of the faculty of memory; it impoverishes the approach to literary compositions, and poetical and artistic insight suffers. In antiquity, writing was used as an aid and guide; it was not a substitute for memory.

Such was the case in ancient Israel. Authors often had a well-trained memory and a great ability for art and aphorisms (short, pointed sentences expressing a truth or precept). Learning by heart was part of the process involved in the composition of a work and the *oral style* is often noticeable in the written version. We know that some teachings existed in oral form long before they were written; this was the case, for example, with the Psalms, the Canticle of Canticles, and the Prophetical Books.

There were three main periods in Israel's history during which the books of the Old Testament were written and edited.[8]

1. *The Period of the Ancient Monarchy.* This was the time of David and Solomon (1010-931 B.C.). A confederation with a political and religious center at Jerusalem replaced the federation of clans and tribes that existed from the time of the conquest under Josue (1200 B.C.). The widespread written and oral compositions were collected. The books consisted mainly of historical and religious traditions and popular accounts about the past.

2. *The Pre-Exilic Prophetic Period* (750-587 B.C.). The people went through a difficult crisis because of the rivalries between the two kingdoms caused by the schism after the death of Solomon. The Prophets were the outspoken champions and spokesmen of the Lord. In this period the literature is given to moralizing; social and religious abuses are condemned; lofty religious ideas and themes are developed. An increased spiritual outlook was introduced; emphasis was on moral uprightness and fidelity to the Covenant that God made with Israel. It was the time of Isaia, Amos, Osee, and Jeremia.

3. *The Post-Exilic Period* (after 538 B.C.). The community returned from Babylon and rose from new foundations. The work of Ezechiel and the anonymous author, Second Isaia, bore fruit in the renewed religious spirit of the people, particularly the *remnant.* This was the period of the greatest output of Biblical writings. Many works from previous periods were recast; new editions of the following books appeared: Josue, Judges, Samuel, Kings, Amos, Osee, Isaia, Jeremia, and Ezechiel. The Pentateuch, the first five books of the Bible, received its present form; many Psalms were

[8] This follows the division of Charlier, *The Christian Approach to the Bible,* pp. 101-104.

composed for use in the rebuilt Temple at Jerusalem. It was at this time that the following books were written: Second Isaia, Chronicles, Ezra-Nehemia, Ruth, Esther, Tobia, Ecclesiastes, Daniel, Sirach, and Wisdom.

B.C.	BIBLICAL HISTORY	BOOKS OF THE OLD TESTAMENT	SECULAR HISTORY
2000			
1850	Patriarchal Period		Hurrian Movements
	Abraham, Isaac, and Jacob		Amorite ("Western Semites") Invasions
1700	Hebrews in Egypt		Hammurabi (1728-1686)
			Hyksos Rule in Egypt
1300	Exodus under Moses		Pharaoh Rameses II (1290-1224)
1200	Conquest of Canaan under Josue		Merneptah (1224-1212)
	Period of the Judges		Fall of Troy (1184)
1100			
1050	Philistine victory over Hebrews		
	Saul (1030-1010)		
1000	David (1010-970)		
	Solomon (970-931)		
950			
	Schism: Roboam and Jeroboam I		
900	JUDA — ISRAEL		Pharaoh Shishak in Palestine (918)
850	Elia / Eliseus		Stele of Mesha
800			Homeric Poems
	Jeroboam II		
750	Achaz Isaia — Amos and Osee		Foundation of Rome (753)
			Tiglath-Pileser III (745-727)
700	Ezechia Michea — Fall of Samaria		Sargon II (722-705)
650	Josia / Jeremia	Sophonia / Nahum	
600	Fall of Jerusalem	Josue 1-2 Samuel Amos Isaia	Fall of Nineve (612)
	Exile in Babylon	Judges 3-4 Kings Osee	Nabuchodonosor (605-561)
550	Ezechiel	Jeremia Lamentations Habacuc	Buddha (563-483)
	Return from Exile	Aggai Ezechiel Michea	Confucius (557-479)
500		PENTATEUCH	Fall of Babylon (539)
			Cyrus the Persian
		Canticle Proverbs	Pythagoras
450	Ezra	Ruth Job	Battle of Marathon (490)
	Nehemia	Jona Malachia Abdia	Socrates
400			Thucydides
		Tobia Ezra Nehemia Joel	Plato
350		1-2 Chronicles	Aristotle
		Esther (Hebrew) Zacharia	Alexander the Great
300	Hellenization	PSALTER	Seleucids and Ptolemies
250		Ecclesiastes	Punic Wars (260-146)
200	Antiochus IV Pharisees	Daniel Sirach	
150	Revolt of Maccabees Sadducees	Esther (Greek) Baruch	Fall of Carthage (146)
	Qumran Community Essenes	Judith	Cicero (106-43)
100	Roman Domination	1-2 Maccabees	Caesar (102-44)
	Herod the Great	Wisdom	Horace (65-8)
50			
7-6	BIRTH OF JESUS CHRIST		

NOTE FOR TABLE I   This Table shows the general development of Biblical and Secular history. The central column shows the approximate periods in which the books of the Old Testament were edited in their present form. Many of them had a long and complicated oral and written history; the lines drawn to the books indicate this fact.

four

BIBLICAL LITERARY FORMS

I. INTRODUCTION

THE FACT THAT the Biblical books are the writings of diverse human authors who, inspired by God, wrote during many centuries and in different places is enough to prepare the reader for what will be found in the Bible— a variety of literary forms. A particular age and locale are often mirrored in a literary work. So it is with the Scriptures. The inspired authors wrote for people of their time. The thoughts they wanted to express were often in advance of their age, but they had to use the ideas and the language of their contemporaries in order to teach them. Only thus could the message of God be brought to them.

Each author had a distinctive personality which influenced the approach and style of his literary work. Although it was the message of God it was "colored" by the distinctive traits of the human instrument used. God, so to speak, accommodated Himself to the human beings. "For as the substantial Word of God became like to men in all things, 'except sin', so the words of God, expressed in human language, are made like to human speech in every respect, except error." [1]

Pope Pius XII wrote: "For the ancient peoples of the East, in order to express their ideas, did not always employ those forms or kinds of speech which we use today; but rather those used by the men of their times and countries. What those exactly were the commentator cannot determine as it were in advance, but only after a careful examination of the ancient literature of the East. The investigation, carried out, on this point, during the past forty or fifty years with greater care and diligence than ever before, has more clearly shown what forms of expression were used in those far-off times,

---

[1] DAS, 37.

whether in poetic description or in the formulation of laws and rules of life or in recording the facts and events of history. . . . For of the modes of expression which, among ancient peoples, and especially those of the East, human language used to express its thought, none is excluded from the Sacred Books, provided the way of speaking adopted in no wise contradicts the holiness and truth of God." [2]

II. MEANING OF LITERARY FORM

A literary form (genre) is the form of expression which an author chooses to present his thought; the very form of his work is an indication of how he wishes it to be understood. Each genre will be governed by laws proper to it, and in order to determine these forms accurately the literary genres of the Ancient Near East must be studied; they were the ones used by the inspired author.[3]

The literary form has to be understood before the truth which it teaches can be grasped. A knowledge of such forms is a primary requisite in our day, not merely because of the apologetical value which is gained from such knowledge, but because it is indispensable for an understanding of the Word of God by His people. "By this knowledge and exact appreciation of the modes of speaking and writing in use among the ancients can be solved many difficulties, which are raised against the veracity and historical value of the Divine Scriptures, and no less efficaciously does this study contribute to a fuller and more luminous understanding of the mind of the Sacred Writer." [4]

The Old Testament contains a variety of literary forms, some of them having an apparent similarity to modern ones. There are historical narratives, parables, lyrical and love songs, epic fragments, fables with a lesson, genealogies, and works of didactic fiction. This creates a danger because the similarities are liable to lead us to the conclusion that our modern understanding of the form in question is the same as the one of the inspired author. We have to keep in mind a fundamental principle in this matter of literary forms: *each form must be understood in the sense intended by the inspired author*. Every author has a purpose in mind when he writes. He has the right to expect that his readers will keep that in mind and read his work from his point of view. These remarks are as true of the Bible as they are of such works as Dante's *Divine Comedy,* the plays of Shakespeare, or more recent works such as William Faulkner's *The Sound and the Fury,* Virginia Woolf's *Orlando,* and William Golding's *Lord of the Flies.*

---

[2] *Ibid.,* 36-37.

[3] Charlier, *op. cit.,* pp. 142-46. See also Levie, *The Bible, Word of God in Words of Men,* pp. 222-24.

[4] DAS, 39.

III. KINDS OF LITERARY FORMS

We will consider three of the more common literary forms found in the Old Testament.

1) *The Poetic Genre.* The poet has always exercised rights which are proper to him. He has been permitted a great degree of liberty in the choice of words for the expression of his ideas. We expect to find metaphors, similes, and exaggerations in poetry; these are part of the privilege which we refer to as poetic license. Therefore, we do not find it too difficult to understand the poetry of the ancient Israelites if we also understand something about their beliefs, their environment, and their outlook on life, as well as their habit of using parallelism, presenting the same thought in two or more balanced and symmetrical phrases. We are not particularly surprised, therefore, when we read the following poetic presentation of God in the Psalms:

> Bless the Lord, O my soul! O Lord, my God, you are great indeed!
> You are clothed with majesty and glory, robed in light as with a cloak.
> You have spread out the heavens like a tent-cloth; you have constructed
> your palace upon the waters.
> You make the clouds your chariot; you travel on the wings of the wind.
> You make the winds your messengers, and flaming fire your ministers.
> *Ps 103,1-4*

Neither does it surprise us to hear the inspired poet of Israel use the following expression to tell about the joy of the people when they left Egypt at the time of the Exodus: "The mountains skipped like rams, the hills like the lambs of the flock" (Ps 113,4). But it does take a little more reflection to appreciate the meaning of the following description of a beautiful bride:

> Your eyes are doves behind your veil. Your hair is like a flock of
> goats streaming down the mountains of Galaad.
> Your teeth are like a flock of ewes to be shorn, which come up
> from the washing, all of them big with twins, none of them thin and barren.
> Your lips are like a scarlet strand; your mouth is lovely.
> Your cheek is like a half pomegranate behind your veil.
> Your neck is like David's tower girt with battlements;
> a thousand bucklers hang upon it, all the shields of valiant men.
> *Ct 4,1-4*

2) *The Apocalyptic Genre.* The Greek word *apocalupsis* means "revelation." This genre, which is foreign to our mentality, implies a revelation made by God to man concerning hidden things. The authors who use it "let their imaginations run wild." They employ all kinds of imagery and symbolism which appeal to the imagination of the ancients: visions, dreams, numbers,

colors, precious stones, fantastic beasts with many heads and horns, lions and leopards with wings. To the modern reader, this genre seems artificial and even pedantic. But if we enter into the spirit of the literature, if we "play along with the author," we will be surprised at how much meaning there is to be found. It is a type of literature that requires us to forget our own age and milieu and "go back wholly in spirit to those remote centuries of the East and with the aid of history, archaeology, ethnology, and other sciences, accurately determine what modes of writing, so to speak, the authors of that ancient period would be likely to use, and in fact did use." [5]

Very often, the genre is used in the Old Testament when the authors speak about some aspect of the future, for example, the coming of the Day of the Lord which signified the coming of the Lord in power and majesty to vanquish His opponents and establish His kingdom.

> The earth will burst asunder,
>   the earth will be shaken apart,
>   the earth will be convulsed.
> The earth will reel like a drunkard,
>   and it will sway like a hut;
> Its rebellion will weigh it down,
>   until it falls, never to rise again.
> On that day the Lord will punish
>   the host of the heavens in the heavens,
>   and the kings of the earth on the earth.
> They will be gathered together
>   like prisoners into a pit;
> They will be shut up in a dungeon,
>   and after many days they will be punished.
> Then the moon will blush
>   and the sun grow pale,
> For the Lord of hosts will reign
>   on Mount Sion and in Jerusalem,
>   glorious in the sight of his elders.
>   *Is 24,19-23*

Much of this apocalyptic genre has an eschatological perspective; it is concerned with the triumph of God at a future time or at the end of time. The compositions belonging to this literary form often originated during a period of suffering or calamity when the just believers looked forward to the intervention of the Lord on their behalf. The post-Exilic period saw the development of this genre in the books of Ezechiel, Joel, Zacharia, and Daniel. Many works written in this form are apocryphal, not part of the Old Testament Canon, for example, the Book of Henoch, the Apocalypse of Moses, the Fourth Book of Esdras, and the Apocalypse of Baruch; all these were written in the period extending from about 200 B.C. to 150 A.D.

[5] *Ibid.,* 35.

The apocalyptic style, with its interest in cosmic phenomena, provided some of the language that Jesus used in His teaching. If we compare the Old Testament use of this genre with the words of Jesus when He spoke about the destruction of Jerusalem and the *Parousia,* His glorious Second Coming, we will realize that His words referred to the significance of the events rather than to a literal prediction of cosmic catastrophe.

Jesus said:
But immediately after the tribulation of those days, the sun will be darkened, and the moon will not give her light, and the stars will fall from heaven, and the powers of heaven will be shaken.
Mt 24,29

Isaia said:
Lo, the day of the Lord comes cruel, with wrath and burning anger; to lay waste the land and destroy the sinners within it! The stars and constellations of the heavens send forth no light; the sun is dark when it rises, and the light of the moon does not shine.
Is 13,9-10

Joel said:
Sun and moon are darkened, and the stars withhold their brightness. The Lord roars from Sion, and from Jerusalem raises his voice; the heavens and the earth quake, but the Lord is a refuge to his people, a stronghold to the men of Israel.
Jl 4,15-16

An understanding of the apocalyptic genre as used in the Old Testament helps us to get the meaning of many texts in it and also in the New Testament, particularly the book of the Apocalypse which contains sections that are almost verbatim borrowings from the books of Ezechiel and Daniel.

3) *The Historical Genre.*   Unlike the two preceding genres, the historical genre, as used by the authors of the Old Testament books, presents serious difficulties. Most people are willing to admit that in the poetic and apocalyptic genres we should expect to find exaggerations, metaphors, similes, and other examples of license. But they find it difficult to understand that we must allow certain similar privileges to the historical genre as it is found in the Bible. Once the words "history" or "historical" are mentioned, a whole series of acquired intellectual characteristics appears and forces a meaning upon these words which is the result of a combination of Greek culture and the historico-critical approach. Much of modern historical writing has been influenced to a great extent by the philosophy and methodology of Leopold von Ranke (1795-1886) called the "father of modern scientific history," Theodor Mommsen (1817-1903) and Eduard Meyer (1885-1930). In the minds of many people, "history" means the presentation of strictly objective data; scientific objectivity is considered the basis of the science of history.

The Bible does contain history, but it is history written according to the laws of the Semitic mind. That mind often used a style characterized by popular, anecdotal, and epic qualities.

> The historical books of the Old Testament are neither photographic representations nor tape recordings of the deeds and words of the Israelites. They are not history in our modern sense; they are books conveying religious and cultic teaching. Their authors are historians in the profound sense of the word, that is to say, they are theologians who interpret and express the meaning of the naked facts. The ancient writers of the Old Testament were guided not only by the historian's eye but also by faith, because to them the Bible was the narration of God's action. It can be said in summary that the Biblical notion of history rests on the conviction that God has in the past revealed Himself in the framework of human events.[6]

The Hebrew authors of the historical books of the Old Testament were interested in what had happened. They were not indifferent to the objective realities of their people's history, but their outlook was theological, not historico critical. The archaeological labors of the nineteenth and early twentieth centuries have shown that the Biblical historical accounts are to be respected. The findings of the archaeologists have mitigated, if not completely destroyed, the charges directed against the Biblical narratives by the members of the rationalistic school of literary criticism. But we still have to remember that the general orientation of the Biblical accounts is theological, and based on that distinctive view of the Hebrew authors who saw the "hand of the Lord" in all that happened.

Biblical history, because it is concerned with revealing the Lord of history, presents a *heilsgeschichte,* a sacred history, which is the account of God's revelation of Himself through acts accomplished in our world. It was by means of this *heilsgeschichte* that the plan of God, "the mystery which has been hidden for ages," was revealed dimly and partially in the Old Testament and then brilliantly and fully in Jesus Christ and the Church (Col 1,26-27; Eph 3,8-13).

These remarks about the genre of Biblical history will help us to understand the meaning intended by the inspired authors of books such as Genesis, Exodus, Josue, Judges, Samuel, and Kings. We will see that the accusations of error which are directed against the Biblical recital of history are very often based on a lack of knowledge of the real purposes which the authors had in

[6] Philip J. King, *The Book of Judges* (New York: The Paulist Press, 1960), p. 13. See also Levie, *op. cit.,* pp. 225-30, John L. McKenzie, S.J., *The Two-Edged Sword* (Milwaukee: The Bruce Publishing Company, 1956), pp. 60-71, and Patrick W. Skehan, "Why Leave Out Judith?" *The Catholic Biblical Quarterly,* XXIV (April, 1962), 147-54.

mind when they wrote. The purposes, or final causes, of the Biblical works have to be understood, as well as the literary genres used by the authors. Only then will we be able to attain a proper, intelligent, and truly religious understanding of the inspired Books.

five

INTRODUCTION TO THE
PENTATEUCH

I. MEANING OF THE NAME

PENTATEUCH is the name given to the first five books of the Bible: Genesis, Exodus, Leviticus, Numbers, and Deuteronomy. The name originates in a Greek word which means "a work consisting of five books," *pentateuchos*. The Jews call this collection of books the Torah, the Law or the Teaching. Jesus often referred to it during His ministry, and the Gospels contain almost 30 references to it, for example, Mt 5,7; 22,36; Lk 16,16; Jn 1,17.

The Palestinian Jews divided Torah into five books and gave each one a name according to the Hebrew opening of each book:

Bereshith	—"In the beginning"
We'elleh Shemoth	—"And these are the names"
Wayyiqra'	—"And he called"
Wayyedabber	—"And he spoke"
'Elleh Haddebarim	—"These are the words"

The Greek-speaking Jews of Alexandria followed this division in the Septuagint, the translation made about two centuries before Christ, but they named the books according to content:

Genesis	:	the beginnings of the world and the Chosen Race.
Exodus	:	the story of the departure from Egypt under the leadership of Moses.

42

Leviticus	:	the laws concerning sacrifice, legal purity, ordinations, and other matters of special interest to the priests, who came from the tribe of Levi.
Numbers (Arithmoi)	:	the census of the Israelites in the desert and a special concern with numbers throughout.
Deuteronomy	:	repetition of many of the laws found in the previous books with additions or explanations; the name means "Second Law."

Christianity has followed the Septuagint names and refers to the whole work as the Pentateuch. Although it is divided into five books, it really is a single work that centers around the great event in the history of Israel, the Covenant of Sinai. Its legislation is basically the one given by Moses in view of the Covenant. The Hebrew people exist only because of the Covenant; first, the covenant made with Abraham, which included the promise of a people not yet in existence, then, the Covenant made at Sinai. Broadly speaking, the Pentateuch is a Biblical account of the world from the creation to the death of Moses.

II. PURPOSE AND LITERARY CATEGORY

The Pentateuch was written to teach the Jews who they were, how God had chosen them, and the things He had done for them. It is history written from a religious point of view.

The authors of the Bible, particularly those who produced the Pentateuch, have given us history, but it is history as the ancients conceived and composed it. Ancient history was the oral and later the written transmission of the collective memory of a family, clan, or nation. At times, imaginative reconstruction was employed. The collective memory of the past is sometimes referred to as "folklore" or "popular tradition," and it was the usual way that the past was preserved for posterity outside of the annals, which were the official records kept in the royal archives. We must keep this in mind; otherwise, we will look for documentary evidence of events which could not possibly produce such evidence, as for example, those which took place in the prehistoric period of the world and mankind. It is important that we remember this especially when we study the first 11 chapters of Genesis and, to a lesser extent, the chapters dealing with the Hebrew patriarchs.

Moreover, the authors made use of a variety of literary forms when they wrote history. Therefore, it will not surprise us to find examples of the following devices in their portrayal of the history of the People of God—hyperbole, satire, epic, poetic pieces, and legends.

III. THE TRADITIONS

The Pentateuch is the result of sources which were woven together after
the Babylonian Exile, toward the end of the sixth or the early part of the fifth
century B.C.[1] At least four distinct traditions, or cycles of traditions, have
been combined into the work as it now stands. These four traditions are the
(1) Yahwist, (2) Elohist, (3) Priestly or Sacerdotal, and (4) Deuteronomic.

(1) The Yahwist Tradition (Y.J), which uses the sacred name
Yahweh for the Lord, is concrete, vivid and colorful in style, anthropomorphic in language. It speaks of the Lord in human terms and portrays
Him with human qualities: the Lord works like a potter when He creates
man, He walks in the garden, He wrestles with Jacob.

The theme of the Yahwist is the wonderful promises which the Lord
made to the ancient patriarchs and the way in which they were fulfilled
in the various periods of history, reaching their culmination in the time
of David. The prime concern of this tradition is salvation-history, the
intervention of the Lord in history to save mankind, particularly through
the Covenant which He makes with Israel.

A careful study of this tradition, whose influence extends even beyond
the Pentateuch, reveals that its historical allusions are almost all from
a period earlier than the tenth century B.C. The Yahwist editor collected many old traditions which had circulated freely among the Hebrews. It is possible to say that the basic elements of this tradition were
set by the time of the establishment of the monarchy, particularly the
time of David and Solomon (1010-931 B.C.).

The artistry of the Yahwist is one of the great accomplishments in the
history of thought; theological profundity goes hand in hand with simplicity of form and clarity of expression. There is "more than meets the
eye" in this literary production.

(2) The Elohist Tradition (E) uses the name Elohim for God. This
tradition is less vivid and colorful than the Yahwist. It avoids the use
of anthropomorphic language and pictures God as being transcendent,
more remote and invisible. The basic interest of the Elohist Tradition
is the Covenant, and it insists on observing the demands which God had
made and the people had accepted.

It is difficult to ascertain the exact extent of the presence and influence
of this tradition in the Pentateuch. Much of it is in the nature of supple-
mentation to the Yahwist but usually it does not have the splendor and
perfection of that tradition. The date of this tradition is uncertain, but
scholars are of the opinion that it possessed its essential features by the
ninth or early eighth century B.C.

(3) The Deuteronomic Tradition (D) developed in the same circles

[1] See Neil J. McEleney, C.S.P., *The Law Given Through Moses* (New York: The Paulist
Press, 1960), pp. 17-30.

in which the Elohist developed and is greatly, but not exclusively, concerned with legislation. In 721 B.C., when Samaria fell into the hands of the Assyrian armies, the northern kingdom (Israel) came to an end. The priests sought to protect the sacred traditions of the nation by codifying them and giving them an historical framework. It is most probable that this tradition was preserved in the southern kingdom (Juda) and there, near the end of the seventh century, gave birth to the basic elements of the book of Deuteronomy. This tradition has a theology which sees the Jews as the chosen people of God, who owe Him complete, undivided, all-absorbing love and fidelity.

The Deuteronomist editor, a deeply religious person, saw that the preceding history of Israel was filled with the saving Acts of God—election, deliverance, covenant, and conquest. These Acts of the Lord demand the response of love on the part of the people. Faithfulness to God will bring reward and blessedness; infidelity will result in punishment and retribution. This theological perspective of Yahweh's love and man's response also influenced the composition of other books, Josue, Judges, Samuel, and Kings.

(4) The Priestly or Sacerdotal Tradition (P) shows a great concern with everything that pertains to worship. Its approach is greatly influenced by a desire to classify material and to systematize it. Its style is lucid and precise, but greatly lacking in the warmth and vividness that is characteristic of the Yahwist. This tradition is the work of priests who, during the years of the Babylonian Exile (587-38 B.C.), took the material which had already been codified in the southern kingdom (Juda) and added new material concerning sacrifices and legal purity. Therefore, the final redaction or edition of this tradition appeared after the Exile.

IV. THE BASIC UNITY OF THE PENTATEUCH

All four traditions go back ultimately to the period in which Israel was formed as a nation under the dominating personality of Moses. It was Moses who played the leading part in the formation of Israel and its age-old traditions. Hence, the *Mosaic authorship* of the Pentateuch. Albright gives the following summary of the way in which the Pentateuch arrived at its present state:

> Turning now to the question of the way in which the Old Testament assumed its present form, we enter into a field where literary criticism based on internal evidence held the field undisputed until recently. Now we see extrinsic evidence pouring in from archaeological discoveries in all the countries around Palestine, especially Egypt, Syria, Mesopotamia, and Asia Minor. Combining this evidence with other finds, including the indications of cultural relationships which have been recovered from Palestinian mounds . . . We are now able to paint a fairly satisfactory picture of the actual situation. The Hebrews brought

with them from their original Mesopotamian home the hallowed cos-
mogonic stories which they had learned there. To these ancient stories,
handed down for uncounted centuries by word of mouth, were added
the poetic narratives of the Patriarchs, which were subsequently adapted
to the form of prose saga in which they have survived in the Hebrew
Bible. Then came the soul-shaking events of the Exodus and the Wanderings, which were handed down in poetry and prose, together with the
teachings and institutions of Moses. Gathered together in various com-
pilations, the documents of the Mosaic Age were gradually formed into
a single collection, which was completed in approximately its present
form before the Restoration at the end of the sixth century B.C. The
contents of our Pentateuch are, in general, very much older than the
date at which they were finally edited; new discoveries continue to confirm the historical accuracy or the literary antiquity of detail after detail
in it. Even when it is necessary to assume later additions to the original
nucleus of Mosaic tradition, these additions reflect the normal growth
of ancient institutions and practices, or the effort made by later scribes
to save as much as possible of extant traditions about Moses. It is, accordingly, sheer hypercriticism to deny the substantially Mosaic character of the Pentateuchal tradition.[2]

V. THE THESIS OF THE PENTATEUCH

The purpose of literary criticism, or as it is usually called *form criticism,*
is not to analyze the contents of the sacred books to such a degree that we
are left only with a collection of unrelated units lacking any theological meaning, but to study and to understand the manner of composition used by the
inspired authors and the purpose which they had in gathering the great variety
of materials. Literary criticism proposes to study the literary structure in order
to discover the particular theological theme which the author intended to
teach the people.

Long before the Pentateuch was finally edited, the Hebrews recited credal
summations of all that the Lord had done for them.

> Then you shall declare before the Lord, your God, "My father was a
> wandering Aramean who went down to Egypt with a small household
> and lived there as an alien. But there he became a nation great, strong
> and numerous. When the Egyptians maltreated and oppressed us, im-
> posing hard labor upon us, we cried to the Lord, the God of our fathers,
> and he heard our cry and saw our affliction, our toil and our oppression.
> He brought us out of Egypt with his strong hand and outstretched arm,
> with terrifying power, with signs and wonders; and bringing us into
> this country, he gave us this land flowing with milk and honey."
>
> *Dt 26,5-9*

[2] William F. Albright, *The Archaeology of Palestine* (Baltimore: Penguin Books, Inc., 1960), pp. 224-25.

There are other examples of these Israelite creeds in Dt 6,20-24 and Jos 24,2-13. It is probable that these *credos* established the guiding lines along which the inspired editors of the Pentateuch fashioned the traditional material and presented their *heilsgeschichte,* their theologically interpreted view of history.[3]

The fundamental theme of the Pentateuch is: God created the world, called the fathers of Israel and promised to give them the land of Canaan. After the Israelites had spent several centuries of sojourning and also captivity in Egypt, God delivered them. He proved His love by many acts in their favor, and finally brought them into the land of promise.

The thesis of the Pentateuch is that it is a divine, immutable plan which progresses gradually toward an objective which is the formation of Israel as a theocracy, in the land of Palestine, under a charter which is the Law of Moses.

VI. OUTLINE OF THE BOOKS OF THE PENTATEUCH

GENESIS

1-11: This section is concerned with the primeval drama of creation, the progressively widening cleft caused by man's rebellion against God, and the Lord's continuing mercy. The book opens with the account of Creation. It sketches the relationship of God and man in the period before Abraham by using stories taken from the Semitic background of the Chosen People. The period of sacred history before Abraham is sometimes called that of the "Cosmic Covenant."

12-50: Then it goes swiftly to the call of Abraham, and from that point on, it unfolds the history of the Chosen People. This part artistically and powerfully unfolds the events and implications contained in the ancient *credo* of sacred history pronounced by the Hebrews (Dt 6,20-24; 26,5-9). It presents the wanderings of the patriarchs—Abraham, Isaac, Jacob. It tells of the sale of Joseph into Egypt, and thus sets the stage for the scenes of the Exodus and the Covenant of Sinai.

EXODUS

1-18: Moses leads the Hebrews from Egypt into the desert, as far as Sinai.

19-24: At Sinai the great Covenant (Alliance) is concluded and the laws are promulgated.

25-31: This section speaks of how the Lord is to dwell with His people.

---

[3] This is the thesis of Gerhard von Rad's *Genesis,* trans. John H. Marks (Philadelphia: The Westminster Press, 1961), pp. 1-42; see also G. Ernest Wright, *God Who Acts* (London: SCM Press Ltd., 1952), pp. 70-76. Admittedly, the probability that the "cultic credos" influenced the formation of the Pentateuch is only one of several solutions offered by scholars, but there is much in this view that recommends it.

It describes His dwelling place, ministers, and the worship that is to be given to Him.

32-34:   The sin of the people severs the Covenant; Moses obtains pardon and the Lord renews His alliance with them.

35-40:   This section contains a description of the construction of the dwelling place of the Lord and its furnishings.

LEVITICUS

1-27:   This book marks a break in the historical development. It speaks of the ritual of sacrifice, ordinations, and other elements of the new worship of the Lord.

NUMBERS

1-10:   The narrative is resumed with the people and their stay in the desert of Sinai.

10-22:   The move to the plains of Moab is described.

22-36:   This part deals with the new ordinances and the preparation to enter the Promised Land.

DEUTERONOMY

1-11 and 27-30:   The story of Moses is completed. Two sections of discourses are included.

12-26:   A development of the laws, religious and civil, is inserted between the discourses.

31-34:   The book ends with the death of Moses and· thus closes the Pentateuch.

six

THE BOOK OF GENESIS

I. THE PURPOSE OF GENESIS

THE BOOK OF Genesis was written to teach fundamental truths of theology. The first 11 chapters teach the existence of God, the creation of all things by Him, the original state of man as a creature who is made to the image and likeness of the Creator, the disobedience of the first pair of humans, their punishment and the spread of evil in the human race. These chapters are a sort of theological preface to the sacred history which the authors of Genesis wanted to present concerning the origin of the Jews from Abraham. Reading this book, the People of God learned how they were chosen to be the bearers of the message of God's intervention in this world. They were brought right back to the beginnings of things and thus were taught how God promised salvation and how that salvation gradually was made available to mankind through the children of Abraham.

II. GENESIS AND SCIENCE

Genesis was not written by scientific men, or for cultivated people. Its purpose was to give simple answers to people who were far less developed and scientifically educated than the countless numbers who would read its contents through the ages. The authors of Genesis knew much less than we do about the actual way in which the universe was formed. Scientists are still at work trying to answer the great question: How did the world begin? The inspired authors had no intention of presenting a scientific explanation of the origin of things.

The accounts of cosmic and human origins are written from the point of view of theology, not science. On June 30, 1909, the Biblical Commission asserted that Catholics were not "strictly and always bound, when interpreting these chapters to seek for scientific exactitude of expression" because "it was not the intention of the sacred author, when writing the first chapter of Genesis, to teach us in a scientific manner the innermost nature of visible things." The Commission agreed with the view that the sacred author wanted "to furnish his people with a popular account, such as the common parlance of that age allowed, one, namely, adapted to the senses and to man's intelligence." [1]

On January 16, 1948, the Biblical Commission reminded Catholics that they were to pay attention to the literary processes of the early Oriental peoples and the ways in which they expressed themselves. It said that the first chapters of Genesis "relate in simple and figurative language, adapted to the understanding of a less developed people the fundamental truths presupposed for the economy of salvation, as well as the popular description of the origin of the human race and of the Chosen People." [2]

The late Pope Pius XII, in an address to the Pontifical Academy of Sciences on November 22, 1951, said that although the figures of 5 and 10 billion years which scientists use when speaking of the origin of the universe may seem astounding, "even to the simplest of the faithful, they bring no new or different concept from the one they learned in the opening words of Genesis: 'In the beginning . . . ,' that is to say, at the beginning of things in time. The figures we have quoted clothe these words in a concrete and almost mathematical expression, while from them there springs forth a new source of consolation for those who share the esteem of the Apostle for that divinely revealed inspired Scripture, which is always useful, 'for teaching, for reproving, for correcting, for instruction' (2 Tim 3,16)." [3]

III. ANTHROPOMORPHISM

Anthropomorphism means attributing to God human qualities.

It cannot be emphasized too strongly that the anthropomorphic conception of Yahweh was absolutely necessary if the God of Israel was to

---

[1] The Biblical Commission, "On the Historical Character of the First Three Chapters of Genesis," No. 7, *Rome and the Study of Scripture*, p. 122.

[2] "Response of the Biblical Commission to Celestine Cardinal Suhard," *Rome and the Study of Scripture*, pp. 150-51. Pope Pius XII commented on this document in his encyclical *Humani Generis*: "Just as in the biological and anthropological sciences, so also in the historical sciences there are those who boldly transgress the limits and safeguards established by the Church. In a particular way must be deplored a certain too free interpretation of the historical books of the Old Testament. Those who favor this system, in order to defend their cause, wrongly refer to the Letter which was sent not long ago to the Archbishop of Paris by the Pontifical Commission on Biblical Studies. This Letter, in fact, clearly points out that the first eleven chapters of Genesis, although properly speaking not conforming to the historical method used by the best Greek and Latin writers or by competent authors of our time, do nevertheless pertain to history in a true sense, which however must be further studied and determined by exegetes; the same chapters, (the Letter points out), in simple and metaphorical language adapted to the mentality of a people but little cultured, both state the principal truths which are fundamental for our salvation, and also give a popular description of the origin of the human race and the chosen people. If, however, the ancient sacred writers have taken anything from popular narrations (and this may be conceded), it must never be forgotten that they did so with the help of divine inspiration, through which they were rendered immune from any error in selecting and evaluating those documents."

[3] *The Proofs for the Existence of God in the Light of Modern Natural Science* (Washington, D. C.: National Catholic Welfare Conference, n.d.), p. 14.

remain a God of the individual Israelite as well as of the people as a whole. For the limited few who are natural mystics or have learned to employ certain methods to attain ecstatic state, the theological concepts attached to deity matter relatively little. . . . For the average worshipper, however, it is very essential that his God be a divinity who can sympathize with his human feelings and emotions, a being whom he can love and fear alternately, and to whom he can transfer the holiest emotions connected with memories of father and mother and friend. In other words, it was precisely the anthropomorphism of Yahweh which was essential to the initial success of Israel's religion. . . . All the human characteristics of Israel's deity were exalted; they were projected against a cosmic screen and they served to interpret the cosmic process as the expression of God's creative word and eternally free will.[4]

Anthropomorphism is found in many places in the Old Testament. Besides the obvious examples in Gn 2-3, the following are interesting ones: God closes the door of the ark in the story of Noe (Gn 7,16), He smells the odor of Noe's sacrifice (Gn 8,21), He laughs at those who conspire against Him (Ps 2,4), He whistles (Is 7,18), He has ears (Is 22,14), and feet (Nah 9,4); and even drives a chariot (Hab 3,8).

IV. SEMITIC COSMOGONY

The ancient Semites had an understanding of the universe which was very different from ours. Modern man tends to forget that many of the facts which he takes for granted or for which he possesses an accurate or relatively accurate, scientific explanation, are the result of the work of scientists and scholars who lived during the last few centuries. It is hardly necessary to point out the innumerable scientific discoveries of the last few decades.

Nowadays, explanations of cosmic phenomena are based on many factors—high-precision scientific equipment, mathematical processes, etc.—which were unknown to the ancients. The Semites of the Biblical period antedated by thousands of years the discoveries, particularly the astronomical ones, of our age. In considering the make-up of the universe, they had to rely on judgments which were based simply on observation and appearances.

The ancients thought that light was a substance separate from the light-giving bodies in the heavens; the sun, moon, and stars were the bearers of this substance, light: "Tell me if you know all; which is the way to the dwelling place of light, and where is the abode of darkness, that you may take them to their boundaries and set them on their homeward paths?" (Job 38,19-20). The sky was thought to be a massive construction, somewhat like a high

[4] William F. Albright, *From the Stone Age to Christianity,* 2nd ed. (Baltimore: Johns Hopkins Press, 1957), p. 265. See the comments of Edmond Jacob, *Theology of the Old Testament,* trans. Arthur W. Heathcote and Philip J. Allcock (New York: Harper & Row Publishers, Inc., 1958), pp. 39-42.

inverted bowl, which was supported on columns, the mountains, located at the ends of the earth. This construction was known as the *firmament;* on it were fixed the sun, moon, and stars. Vast bodies of water were thought to be located both above and below the earth, and it was only because the firmament was solidly attached to the ends of the earth that these waters did not flood the land. The phenomenon of rain was explained as the result of the opening of the "windows" located in the firmament. These "windows" were known as the "floodgates of the heavens" or the "windows on high" and are mentioned in several texts of the Old Testament (Gn 7-11; 8,2; 4 Kgs 7,2; Is 24,18). Deep in the earth was a place known as *Sheol,* which was depicted as a shadowy and depressing locale where the dead continued to exist.[5]

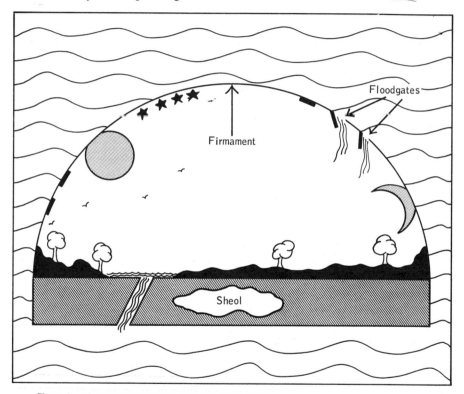

Figure 2. SEMITIC COSMOGONY: THE WORLD AS THE ANCIENT SEMITES UNDERSTOOD IT

[5] See Bruce Vawter, C.M., "A Note on 'The Waters Beneath the Earth'," *The Catholic Biblical Quarterly,* XXII (January, 1960), 71-73. A study of the Hebrew beliefs concerning Sheol is in Edmund F. Sutcliff, S.J., *The Old Testament and the Future Life,* 2nd ed. (Westminster, Md.: The Newman Press, 1947), pp. 44-69. Also Paul Heinisch, *Theology of the Old Testament,* trans. William Heidt (Collegeville, Minn.: The Liturgical Press, 1950), pp. 255-59; Jacques Guillet, *Themes of the Bible,* trans. Albert J. LaMothe, Jr. (Notre Dame: Fides Publishers Association, 1960), pp. 147-66.

An acquaintance with these ancient Semitic beliefs, which were based on appearances and naked-eye observation, rather than on the conclusions of advance natural sciences, will help in understanding the first chapter of Genesis. There we find theological truths about the existence of God and His creative action presented in a literary form which makes use of the ancient Semitic ideas of cosmogony.

V. THE CREATION OF THE UNIVERSE

A. MONOTHEISM VERSUS POLYTHEISM.

The account in Genesis breathes a pure monotheism. The text repudiates the idea of struggle between chaos and order, which was a common element in the pagan myths about creation found in Babylon and Egypt. The author depicts an orderly creation without any trace of a cosmic struggle. This is seen in the repetition of the phrase "God said, Let there be. . . ." Albright has given the following summary of the ancient Israelite understanding of God. He says that the Hebrews possessed the belief in the existence of God:

> who is the Creator of the world and the giver of all life; the belief that God is holy and just, without sexuality or mythology; the belief that God is invisible to man except under special conditions and that no graphic nor plastic representation of Him is permissable; the belief that God is not restricted to any part of His creation, but is equally at home in heaven, in the desert, or in Palestine; the belief that God is so far superior to all created beings, whether heavenly bodies, angelic messengers, demons, or false gods, that He remains absolutely unique; the belief that God has chosen Israel by formal compact to be His favored people, guided exclusively by laws imposed by Him.[6]

The accounts of the creation in Genesis show at least some relationship to the pagan Babylonian myth of creation, the *Enuma elish,* written shortly after the beginning of the second millenium B.C. This myth was written on seven clay tablets, and tells how in the beginning the universe was a formless chaos in which two deities begot offspring, the other deities of Mesopotamia. During a fierce quarrel, one of the gods, Marduk, fought with Tiamat, a fierce warrior and mother of all the gods. Tiamat was slain and her body was cut in two by Marduk who used one half of it to make the vault of the heavens and the other to make the earth. Marduk then proceeded to act as a creative deity who fashioned the heavenly bodies, plants, animals, and men. This is one version of the myth of creation with which the Hebrews probably came into contact

---

[6] William F. Albright, *Archaeology and the Religion of Israel* (Baltimore: Johns Hopkins Press, 1942), p. 116.

during their association with their neighbors in Canaan, a land full of Babylonian culture.[7]

Although there is a similarity in the basic cosmogony of the creation accounts in the Babylonian myth and Genesis, there is a complete dissimilarity in the basic concepts. In the *Enuma elish,* there is not only primeval chaos, but also a confusing plethora of gods who defy the deities of the chaos. In Genesis, there is one God, who existed before all things, and who is the cause of everything outside of Himself. The creative activity of this one God is exercised by a mere word. The visible universe is directed by the will of this God who possesses a supremacy which is both effortless and supreme. The sun, moon, and stars are not deities; they are created by one, all-powerful God. The rule and power of God are not the result of a victorious combat with other deities.

The general background of the present creation-composition in Genesis may be thus summarized:

> At some period in their history, perhaps at the time when they established themselves in Canaan, a land impregnated with Babylonian culture for some centuries, the Israelites became acquainted with the Babylonian traditions and shaped them according to their own genius and beliefs.

> This is the source of the history found in Gn 1-11, which, while having a great charm and attraction in itself, teaches us with such great authority the most fundamental truths of our Faith.[8]

B. THE TWO ACCOUNTS OF CREATION[9]

The first account (Gn 1-2,4) is from the Priestly Tradition and received its form shortly after the Exile (after 538 B.C.). Its characteristics are orderliness, repetition of certain formulas ("Then God said, let there be . . ."; "God saw that it was good."), absence of anthropomorphisms, and emphasis

---

[7] The text of the *Enuma elish* is in James B. Pritchard, (ed.), *Ancient Near Eastern Texts Relating to the Study of the Old Testament,* 2nd ed. (Princeton: Princeton University Press, 1955), pp. 60-72; see also D. Winton Thomas (ed.), *Documents from Old Testament Times,* Harper Torchbook (New York: Harper & Row, Publishers, Inc., 1961), pp. 3-16. A general study of the pagan religions is Etienne Drioton, *et al., Religions of the Ancient East,* trans. M. B. Loraine (New York: Hawthorn Books, Publishers, 1959). A good comparative study of the various pagan cosmogonies is in Nicolas Corte, *The Origins of Man,* trans. Eric E. Smith (New York: Hawthorn Books, Publishers, 1958).

[8] A. Robert, "The Literary Genres," *Guide to the Bible,* I, 483.

[9] The exact meaning of the verb used in Gn 1,1 is disputed. The Hebrew word *bara* does have the meaning "to create," but did the inspired author understand that to mean what philosophers call creation *ex nihilo,* the making of something from nothing? Is that what he intended to teach when he wrote the text? Some authors hold that creation *ex nihilo* is found in Gn 1,1. Among them is Paul Heinisch, *Theology of the Old Testament,* pp. 142-43; M. J. Gruenthaner, "The Scriptural Doctrine on First Creation," *The Catholic Biblical Quarterly,* IX (January, 1947), 48-58; see also the footnote to Gn 1,1 in the translation published by the Confraternity of Christian Doctrine. Other authors do not think that creation *ex nihilo* is the teaching of this text; see, for example, John L. McKenzie, S.J., *The Two-Edged Sword* (Milwaukee: The Bruce Publishing Company, 1956), pp. 82-89.

on the Sabbath rest. The second account (Gn 2,4b-25) is from the Yahwistic Tradition, which received its form around the time of the establishment of the Davidic-Solomonic monarchy (1010-931 B.C.). Its characteristics are woven around its concern for mankind, the origin of male and female, their relationship to God and each other, and the origin of evil. The temptation of the first pair of humans is described with remarkable insight. This account is marked by anthropomorphisms.

C. THE DAYS OF CREATION

The six days of 24 hours each are an artificial framework used by the author as a memory device which would foster the observance of the Sabbath —the seventh day—as a day of rest. This device is found in the first chapter of Genesis, which is attributed to the Priestly Tradition. Hence, the insistence on the Sabbath observance, something which would be of particular importance to the priests. The word "day" (Hebrew: *yom*) in the account means what it does for us. Admittedly, it can stand for a "long period of time," but if we remember the purpose of Genesis and the background of the author we will not try to force our knowledge of geological eras on him.

VI. THE ORIGIN OF MANKIND

A. The account in Genesis concerning the origin of mankind is concerned principally with theology, not biology or anthropology.

B. There is anthropomorphism in the account of the formation of man in Gn 2,7: God acts like a potter who molds his "creation." This literary form teaches the great truth: God created man. The man is not given any name in these chapters of Genesis except *ha-adam* which means "Man," rather than "the man." Nowhere else in the Old Testament is any individual called *ha-adam.*

C. The phrase "image and likeness" found in Gn 1,26 has given rise to a good deal of discussion. Some have interpreted it in a grossly materialistic sense, holding that the author implied some physical resemblance between God and man. The error of such a view is apparent to anyone who understands the nature of God. The Biblical account never reduces the Lord to the level of a physical being, even if it does delight in the use of anthropomorphisms. Others have seen in the phrase a Biblical description of the creation of the spiritual soul; this is the view expressed in the footnote to this verse in the Douay version of the Old Testament. This interpretation is inadequate. The ancient Hebrews did not possess our understanding of the soul as a spiritual, immortal principle of human life. They knew only man, a concrete individual who eats, drinks, thinks, generates, wars, loves, and after dying continues to exist in some form in Sheol. The Hebrews spoke of the "life principle" as the *ruah,* which we usually translate as "spirit," a word with profound connotations in Christian philosophy and theology. But the Hebrews did not recognize the body-soul relationship that is characteristic of our way of thinking. The individual living being was for them a *nephesh,* a word which we translate as "soul" but which would be more accurately rendered as "person." The philosophical study of man, with its refined analysis of the spiritual nature of the soul, is something that came much later than the writing of the passage of Genesis under consideration. Christian philosophy has come to a clearer understanding of the nature of man and the spirituality of the soul because of the positive contributions of the Greek philosophers, particularly Aristotle, the Fathers of the Church, and the Medieval Schoolmen, especially St. Thomas Aquinas. We have to resist the temptation to retroject our Christian understanding and beliefs upon the relatively primitive concepts of the ancient Hebrews.

It is the view of many that the "image and likeness" lay in the fact that man is endowed with the powers of intellect and will; in this he imitates God's perfection of understanding and willing. Others see the likeness in the fact that man shares in God's dominion over all creation. Man is to rule over the created universe which is below him in dignity—the animals, plants, and minerals. Man, a creature of God, is set at the head of creation; he receives the revelation of God and is able to rule as king.[10]

D. The account of the formation of Eve from the rib of Adam is part of the literary form used by the author. God who acted as a "potter" in making man, now acts as a "physician" in making woman. The text does not necessarily mean that woman was literally taken from man. Man is the exemplar of woman; thus it can be said that she came from him. The author wanted to teach what we, after centuries of Christian influence and teaching, take for granted: man and woman have the same nature. Contrary to the notion prevalent among many of the pagan peoples, woman is not inferior. She is not man's chattel. She is bone of man's bone and flesh of his flesh and, therefore, she has the same prerogatives. This Hebrew view of the nature of woman ran contrary to the belief of the surrounding pagan society which considered women a lower caste than men.

The Christian view was summed up by Pope Pius XII: "We have an absolute equality in personal and fundamental values, but different functions which are complementary and superbly equivalent and from them arise the various rights and duties of the one (man) and the other (woman)."[11]

E. The Garden into which man and woman are placed is also part of the

---

[10] See the following for a discussion of the meaning of "image and likeness": Jean DeFraine, S.J., *The Bible and the Origin of Man* (New York: Desclée Company, 1962), pp. 20-29; Claude Tresmontant, *A Study of Hebrew Thought,* trans. Michael F. Gibson (New York: Desclée Company, 1960), pp. 87-106; also G. Ernest Wright, *God Who Acts* (London: SCM Press Ltd., 1952), pp. 88-91, especially note 1, p. 88.

[11] Discourse delivered on October 14, 1956, "The Dignity of Woman," *The Pope Speaks,* III (Spring, 1957), 370.

literary form. It has a symbolic importance. Eden, which is not a Hebrew word, meant for the ancient Israelites what utopia means for us. It was a name that embodied all that one could hope to have on this earth. The author used the imagery of the garden to teach the elevated state of the human race in the beginning. Much later, Christian theology was to speak of the *Supernatural Gift* (Sanctifying Grace) and the *Preternatural Gifts* (Freedom from suffering, death, ignorance, and concupiscence) which were present when God created man and woman in the state of Original Justice.[12] The author of Genesis simply pictures man and woman living in a garden in a state of perfect intimacy and friendship with God. His interest is *theological, not geographical or botanical.*

F. The Biblical account of the origin of man and woman contains the following teachings:

1. *The dignity of mankind.* Man is the result of a deliberate act of God, and he is made to His "image and likeness." Man is completely apart from the rest of visible creation. Man's similarity to his Creator is seen, at least partially, in the fact that he has been created to have dominion over the created universe. Christian thought sees the "image and likeness" as referring to the fact that man possesses the powers of mind and will which make him like God and help him to share in the dominion over the universe.

2. *The dignity of marriage.* Monogamy was intended from the beginning and it is only when it is upheld that woman has protection for her dignity. It is only when a husband loves his wife as his own "flesh and bone" that there is a sure foundation for stable family-living and well-founded societies.

G. In the Babylonian myth of creation, the *Enuma elish,* the god, Marduk, fashions man from clay and the blood of a god; man comes at the end of a great deal of chaos and warfare among the gods. The Biblical account of the creation of man clearly stands in incomparable beauty upon the basis of a pure monotheism. "The spirituality of the ideas, the dignity of the style and the splendour of the imagery raise this first page of Genesis immeasurably above the Babylonian and all the other myths. . . . What a noble conception of God and man is revealed by the Bible narrative, compared with the degraded idea of both which emerges from the Babylonian myth."[13]

---

[12] For a discussion of the Church's teaching concerning Original Justice see John F. Clarkson, S.J., *et al.* (eds.), *The Church Teaches* (St. Louis: B. Herder Book Co., 1955), pp. 155-64; also B. V. Miller, "The Fall of Man and Original Sin," in George D. Smith (ed.), *The Teachings of the Catholic Church* (2 vols.; New York: The Macmillan Company, 1949), I, 320-59.

[13] Reprinted by permission of Hawthorn Books, Inc. from *The Origins of Man* by Nicolas Corte. Copyright © 1958 by Hawthorn Books, Inc., 70 Fifth Avenue, New York 11, New York.

VII. GENESIS AND EVOLUTION

A. The word evolution has various meanings. *Philosophically,* it is the position of those who repudiate all that is absolute, firm, and immutable; *scientifically,* it refers to every change which can be observed in the various categories of phenomena—physical, biological, human. It will be used here to refer to the development of the body of man from previously existing forms.

B. There are two types of evolution: (1) *Theistic,* which acknowledges the existence of God, His creative activity, and providential care; (2) *Materialistic,* which denies the existence of God and attributes the origin and continuance of matter and life to some other principle, which, fundamentally, was the chance clustering of atoms and molecules in suitable proportion.

C. Theistic evolution does not contradict the theological teaching of Genesis. However, we must not force an evolutionary outlook upon the Biblical text. The author of Genesis did not hold to an evolutionism of which he could not possibly have been cognizant, living as he did in a pre-scientific age. Theology, biology, and anthropology are greatly interested in man, but for different reasons. In philosophical language, the *material object,* the thing studied, of these sciences is the same, man, but the *formal object,* the aspect under which the material object is studied, is different—theology studies man as a creature of God, who fell from a state of Original Justice because of the Original Sin, a creature who has been redeemed by the Death and Resurrection of Jesus, destined for membership in the Church, and for happiness in heaven; biology and anthropology are interested in man's material nature and how he fits into the series of living things witnessed by the paleontological record.

D. The exact origin of the body of man is an anthropological, not an exegetical question. It is the task of scientists to study and determine the evidence of the biological evolution of man.[14]

E. The position of the Church on evolution was stated by Pope Pius XII:

> The Teaching Authority of the Church does not forbid that, in conformity with the present state of human sciences and sacred theology, research and discussions, on the part of men experienced in both fields, take place with regard to the doctrine of evolution, in as far as it inquires into the origin of the human body as coming from pre-existent and living matter—for the Catholic faith obliges us to hold that souls are immediately created by God. However this must be done in such a

[14] The following are recommended for the study of the important and complicated theory of biological evolution: René Biot, *What Is Life?,* trans. Eric E. Smith (New York: Hawthorn Books, Publishers, 1959); Remy Collin, *Evolution,* trans. J. Tester (New York: Hawthorn Books, Publishers, 1959); René Le Troquer, *What Is Man?* trans. Eric E. Smith (New York: Hawthorn Books, Publishers, 1961). A study of the findings of science and their relationship to the Biblical teachings is in Jean DeFraine, *op. cit.,* pp. 3-64. See also Vittorio Marcozzi, S.J., "The Origin of Man According to Science," *Theology Digest,* II (Winter, 1954), 43-47.

way that the reasons for both opinions, that is, those favorable and those unfavorable to evolution, be weighed and judged with the necessary seriousness, moderation and measure, and provided that all are prepared to submit to the judgment of the Church, to whom Christ has given the mission of interpreting authentically the Sacred Scriptures and of defending the dogmas of faith. Some however rashly transgress this liberty of discussion, when they act as if the origin of the human body from pre-existing and living matter were already completely certain and proved by the facts which have been discovered up to now and by reasoning on those facts, and as if there were nothing in the sources of divine revelation which demands the greatest moderation and caution in this question.

When, however, there is question of another conjectural opinion, namely polygenism, the children of the Church by no means enjoy such liberty. For the faithful cannot embrace that opinion which maintains either that after Adam there existed on this earth true men who did not take their origin through natural generation from him as from the first parent of all, or that Adam represents a certain number of first parents. Now it is in no way apparent how such an opinion can be reconciled with that which the sources of revealed truth and the documents of the Teaching Authority of the Church propose with regard to original sin, which proceeds from a sin actually committed by an individual Adam and which through generation is passed on to all and is in everyone as his own.[15]

VIII. THE FALL: ORIGINAL SIN

A. Symbolism and anthropomorphism are the media by which the author teaches the theology of the temptation and fall of Adam and Eve in Gn 3,1-13.

B. Some authors have held the view that the events in Gn 1-11 were revealed to the inspired author by means of visions. Concerning this view we have the remarks of a contemporary Biblical scholar:

> We cannot, of course, rule out the possibility of God revealing this whole story in a vision to the inspired author. Miracles can happen, but they are not to be unnecessarily multiplied when there is a quite natural explanation for some phenomena. If God saw fit to reveal all the details of this story to the hagiographer, it is hard to see why He

---

[15] *Humani Generis*, 36-7. The important questions raised by the scientific view concerning polygenism and its relation to the Biblical and Magisterial teachings concerning the origin of man and the doctrine of Original Sin are discussed in de Fraine, *op. cit.*, pp. 65-85. The following should also be consulted: Karl Rahner, S.J., "Theological Reflexions on Monogenism," in the collection of his articles entitled *Theological Investigations,* trans. Cornelius Ernst, O.P. (Baltimore: Helicon Press, 1961), pp. 229-96; J. DeFraine, S.J., *Adam et son lignage: Études sur la notion de "personalité corporative" dans la Bible* (Louvain: Desclée de Brouwer, 1959). Summaries of these studies are in *Theology Digest,* X (Spring, 1962), 99-105. See the comments of Bruce Vawter, C.M., *A Path Through Genesis* (New York: Sheed & Ward, 1956), pp. 62-63.

should have taken so many elements from the pagan mythologies, even though purged of their unbecoming aspects, or why He should have had the conversation in Paradise include so many plays on words which make sense only in Hebrew, a language which was certainly not spoken in Paradise.[16]

C. The "tree of knowledge of good and evil" and the "forbidden fruit" (Gn 2,17; 3,1-13) are part of the author's way of teaching that man's happiness was to be subordinate to his obedience of a divine command.

D. The "serpent" is used as a symbol of man's ancient foe. Hebrew writers will later call him Satan, "the adversary." Christian belief is that he is a fallen angel: "And he laid hold on the dragon, the ancient serpent, who is the devil and Satan . . ." (Apocalypse 20,2). The presentation shows him as a cunning being who exercises his rational powers with a considerable amount of craft. The use of the "serpent" was probably the author's attempt at attacking the many forms of worship current among the Canaanites in which the image of the serpent appeared as a fertility symbol.[17]

E. What was the sin of Adam and Eve? The inspired author did not know the precise nature of the sin, and neither do we. All we can say is that the sin involved pride and disobedience. The attempt to interpret the sin as some form of illicit sexual pleasure is not justified by the evidence, particularly when we view the account of the Fall in the light of Gn 2, in which we find a beautiful presentation of the normal role that sex plays in human life.

It should be noted that the text nowhere mentions an "apple." Popular views on this have been influenced by a mistranslation of Canticle of Canticles 8,5. It is interesting to note that in Jewish tradition the "fruit" was thought to have been grapes, olives, or wheat; the Greek Fathers of the Church spoke of a fig, the Latin Fathers of an apple, probably influenced by the fact that the Latin word for "evil" and "apple" is *malum*.

F. The loss of intimacy with God is presented under the literary form which speaks of Adam and Eve being expelled from the garden.

G. The doctrinal position of the Church on Original Sin should be studied

---

[16] Louis F. Hartmann, C.SS.R., "Sin in Paradise," *The Catholic Biblical Quarterly,* XX (January, 1958), 29.

[17] The serpent as a symbol of sex was fairly common in the ancient Near East. This is witnessed by the representations which archaeologists have discovered in that area. It also had other connotations; for example, it was used as a symbol of life and also of magic. "The author of Gn 2-3 probably had all, or at least most, of these various aspects of the serpent in mind when he made it the villain of his story": Hartmann, *op. cit.,* p. 40. See McKenzie, *op. cit.,* pp. 96-101, and by the same author, "Literary Characteristics of Genesis 2-3," *Theological Studies,* XV (December, 1954), 541-72; also Alexander Jones, *Unless Some Man Show Me* (New York: Sheed & Ward, 1951), pp. 99-107.

in the light of the teaching of the books of the New Testament : Rom 5,12-21; 1 Cor 15,21-22; also Jn 8,44 and 1 Tm 2,13-14.[18]

H. The Liturgy of the Easter Vigil refers to the Original Sin as the "happy fault which merited such a Redeemer" (Exultet).

I. The account of the Fall is an artistic presentation of the psychology of temptation. If we compare the various steps that were involved in that primeval drama with the moments involved in an individual's personal temptations, we can say with all honesty: "The author knew what he was talking about."

STEPS IN THE FALL	TEXTS: GENESIS 3,1-10
1. Temptation makes its appearance:	The serpent said to the woman: "Did God say, 'You shall not eat of any tree of the garden?' "
2. Delay occurs:	The woman answered the serpent, "Of the fruit of all the trees in the garden we may eat; but 'Of the fruit of the tree in the middle of the garden,' God said, 'You shall not eat, neither shall you touch it, lest you die.' "
3. The person is fooled:	But the serpent said to the woman, "No, you shall not die; for God knows that when you eat of it, your eyes will be opened and you will be like God, knowing good and evil."
4. Desire is aroused:	The woman saw that the tree was good for food, pleasing to the eyes, and desirable for the knowledge it would give.
5. Sin is committed:	She took of its fruit and ate it, and also gave some to her husband and he ate.
6. Effects are felt:	Then the eyes of both were opened, and they realized that they were naked; so they sewed fig-leaves together and made themselves coverings.

[18] See A. M. Dubarle, O.P., "Original Sin in Genesis," *Cross Currents*, VIII (Fall, 1958), 345-62; also by the same author, "Original Sin and God's Justice," *Theology Digest*, VI (Autumn, 1958), 139-42; Stanislaus Lyonnet, S.J., "Original Sin and Romans 5,12-14," *Theology Digest*, V (Winter, 1957), 54-57. See also Cyril Vollert, S.J., "Original Sin and Education," *Review for Religious*, V (July, 1946), 217-28.

7. Remorse is experienced: When they heard the sound of the LORD
                             GOD walking in the garden in the cool
                             of day, the man and his wife hid them-
                             selves from the LORD GOD among the
                             trees of the garden.

8. Tension results: The LORD GOD called the man and said
                             to him, "Where are you?" And he said,
                             "I heard you in the garden, and I was
                             afraid because I was naked; and I hid."

IX. THE PROMISE OF SALVATION

A. The text of Gn 3,15 is often called the *Proto-evangelium,* the first
glad-tidings: "I will put enmity between you and the woman, between your
seed and her seed; he shall crush your head, and you shall lie in wait for his
heel."

B. This text has been used often in the writings of the Fathers of the Church
and the pronouncements of the Popes. Many of them have applied it to Jesus
and our Blessed Mother. Its meaning, however, has not been formally defined.
Consequently, leaving the final judgment to the Church, it is possible to
study this text and see in it something other than a direct literal reference to
Jesus and Mary.[19]

1. The noun "seed" to which "he" refers is probably a collective noun
   in this verse, and it means the children of the woman Eve. In the
   literal sense the woman is Eve, and the seed is the human race.

2. Some Fathers of the Church have seen Christ and Mary predicted
   in this verse, and comparatively recent Papal documents have presented the same view, but they have not formally defined the meaning of the text of Gn 3,15.

3. Since the seed of the woman, according to the literal sense of the
   text, is the entire human race, every human being is contained in it.
   The victory which is predicted is that of the race over Satan. Not
   every member will be victorious, but that does not change the fact
   that the race as such will be triumphant eventually. Later revelation

[19] A well developed and documented article on this matter is Myles M. Bourke, "Papal
Teaching on Genesis 3,15," *Conference Bulletin of the Archdiocese of New York,* XXXII
(March, 1955), 15-28. See also McKenzie, *The Two-Edged Sword,* p. 104. For another view
of the matter see B. Rigaux, O.F.M., "The Woman and Her Seed in Genesis 3:14-15,"
Theology Digest, VI (Winter, 1958), 25-31.

brought a fuller understanding of this victory. It was won chiefly by
the Passion, Death and Resurrection of Christ, whose role is indispensable.

4. In the *sensus plenior,* a deeper understanding of the literal meaning
arrived at with the help of other Biblical themes and later revelations,
the seed of the woman is principally, and in the first place, Christ.
Later revelation brings out the fact that Mary, also a member of the
seed of Eve, is intimately linked with her Son in His victory. Therefore, in the *sensus plenior,* the seed of the woman is also Mary, in a
role which is secondary and subordinate to Christ.

5. In the *typical sense,* the sense whereby some event or person in the
Old Testament prefigures what was to be accomplished in the New
Testament, Mary is foreshadowed by Eve, the woman. However,
the typology is antithetical; Mary's obedience makes up for Eve's
disobedience.

X. THE ROLE OF CAIN AND ABEL

A. The stories in Gn 4 are a simple, yet deceptively profound, illustration
of what St. Paul would say much later: "Through one man sin entered into
the world" (Rom 5,12). The original sin of Adam and Eve unleashed moral
evil which then spread throughout time and among all peoples.

B. There are a few incongruities in the account of Cain and Abel. They
are pictured as the sons of Adam and Eve and, although the Bronze Age did
not occur in the Near East until about 3000 B.C. and the Iron Age not until
about 1200 B.C., they live in an environment where bronze and iron are in
use. Moreover, tent-dwelling and shepherding are presumed in an age which
certainly preceded by countless millennia the advent of such developments
(Gn 4,2,20-22).

C. The Yahwist editor did not want to present absolute genealogies or
objective descendency. His purpose was to bring home the lesson: Once man
rebels against God he becomes an enemy even to his fellow man. Therefore,
he used a traditional story in which God favored a good shepherd over his
wicked brother who was a farmer. This was a story that would be treasured
and appreciated by the Hebrews who had been a pastoral people before they
settled in Palestine.[20]

[20] The French theologian Jean Daniélou has written about the story of Cain and Abel and
the reasons why the latter is given a prominent place in the Liturgy: *Holy Pagans of the Old
Testament,* trans. Felix Faber (London: Longmans, Green and Co. Ltd. 1957), pp. 29-41.

D. It should be noted that nowhere does the account in Genesis tell us why, or how, the sacrificial offering of one brother was accepted and the other was rejected. It is mere conjecture to say that it was because the dispositions of one were better than those of the other. Cain's sin was not in his dispositions but in his jealousy of the favor granted to his brother. The fundamental mystery and theme is that of the *freedom of divine choice*. God does not choose someone because of any merits in that person. This story is the first to demonstrate that freedom of divine election which runs through all the history of salvation.

XI. THE GENEALOGIES

A. The genealogies in chapter 5 follow a symmetrical pattern with the repetition of certain phrases (When X was . . . years old, he became the father of Y. The whole life span of X was . . . , then he died). The source of this chapter is the Priestly Tradition (P) and this explains the similarity with the pattern of the seven-day division in the account of creation in Gn 1.

B. The use of 10 generations from Adam to Noe is evidence that the author followed a recognized literary form. Later, in chapter 11 we find 10 generations between the Flood and Abraham.

C. Babylonian parallels clarify why the genealogies of Genesis use the basic unit of 10 and fantastic ages. The famous tables that were discovered at Larsa, a city on the Euphrates river in Babylon, date from the twentieth century B.C. and contain the lists of kings that ruled there before and after the Flood. A look at the list, which is found in two recensions (editions), will show how moderate the Hebrew author really was when he chose his figures for the patriarchs. Evidently, the numbers did not always have the same meaning in the countries of the ancient Near East that they have in our modern civilization.

SOVEREIGN	LENGTH OF RULE	SOVEREIGN	LENGTH OF RULE
Alulim	67,200 yrs.	(There are only eight kings	
Alagar	72,000 "	in this recension).	
(. . .)-kidunnu-sha-kinkin	72,000 "	Alulim	28,800 yrs.
(. . .)-ukku	21,600 "	Alagar	36,000 "
(Dumuzi), the shepherd	28,800 "	En-menluanna	43,200 "
En-menluanna	28,800 "	En-mengalanna	28,800 "
En-sibzianna	36,000 "	Dumuzi, the shepherd	36,000 "
En-menduranna	28,800 "	En-sebzianna	28,800 "
Sukurlam	28,800 "	En-menduranna	21,000 "
Zi-ud-sud-du	36,000 "	Ubardudu	18,600 "
	420,000 yrs.		241,200 yrs.

A later version of the list, with the names and years changed, is found in the writings of Berosus who was a priest of the god Marduk at Babylon during the early part of the third century B.C.

SOVEREIGN	LENGTH OF RULE
Alorus	36,000 yrs.
Alaparos	10,800 "
Amelon	46,800 "
Ammenon	43,200 "
Megalaros	64,800 "
Daonos or Daos	36,000 "
Euedorachos	64,800 "
Amempsinos	36,000 "
Otiartes	28,800 "
Xisouthros	64,800 "
	432,000 yrs.

D. The inflated figures are not historical and were never intended to be taken as such. Anthropology has shown that the life span of primitive man was probably shorter, not longer than that of man today. The symbolic nature of the figures can be seen in the way in which they have been changed in the three ancient versions of the Old Testament: the Hebrew text, the Septuagint (LXX), and the Samaritan Pentateuch.

In the chart that follows, the numbers in the first column, in each case, represent the ages of the patriarchs when the next generation began; the second column shows the total life span. The addition of the numbers in the first column, plus the 100 years from the birth of Noe's sons and the Flood, gives the years between the Creation and the Flood.

	Hebrew		Samaritan Pentateuch		LXX	
Adam	130	930	130	930	230	930
Seth	105	912	105	912	205	912
Enos	90	905	90	905	190	905
Cainan	70	910	70	910	170	910
Malaleèl	65	895	65	895	165	895
Jared	162	962	62	847	162	962
Henoch	65	365	65	365	165	365
Mathusale	187	969	67	720	187	969
Lamech	182	777	53	653	188	753
Noe	500		500		500	
	100	950	100	950	100	950
	1656		1307		2262	

E. The purpose of the inflated figures was: (1) to bridge the vast time gap between Adam and the Flood, and (2) to teach the greatness and goodness of the ancient peoples who were mighty individuals, about whom the Hebrews learned from ancient traditions. The gradual shortening of life span also was a technique used to teach that evil spread after man's sin. This is understandable in the light of the ancient Hebrew belief that life on earth was the ideal, and man's longevity was determined by his relationship with God: the longer a man lived the more holy and blessed he was in the sight of God.

XII. THE FLOOD AND NOE

A. Traditions of a great flood are found in the writings of ancient peoples other than the Hebrews. Such a tradition was well known to the Sumerians who lived in lower Mesopotamia. Archaeologists have discovered several versions of a Babylonian account of a flood which contain striking parallels with Genesis. The *Epic of Gilgamesh,* a masterpiece of ancient writing which was known throughout the Near East in ancient times, contains what is perhaps the classic account. The Epic itself dates back to the time of Hammurabi (1728-1686 B.C.) and contains the exploits of the hero after whom it is named. Gilgamesh desires immortality and sets out on a journey to visit his ancestor, Utnapishtim, who was favored with that gift after the flood. Utnapishtim relates the account of the deluge.[21]

B. A comparison of the Babylonian and Genesis accounts does not prove that one copied from the other. It appears that both have a common, more remote source. There is evidence of a great aquatic catastrophe in the Near East sometime before 4000 B.C. This historical fact left behind deep impressions in the minds of the people who then transmitted them through the media of ethnic traditions and popular stories. It is probable that the Biblical account depends indirectly upon these traditions, which were brought from Babylonia by the ancestors of the Hebrews. Certainly the account in Genesis shows that the traditions have been passed through a "spiritual filter" and thus purged of polytheistic references.

C. The Biblical account of the Flood reveals a certain amount of repetitiveness as well as a number of inconsistencies. The following events are among those reported *twice* in the account:

God observes the wickedness of men	—	Gn 6,5; 6,12
God predicts the flood	—	Gn 6,13,17; 7,4
God orders Noe to enter the ark	—	Gn 6,18; 7,1
Noe obeys and enters the ark	—	Gn 6,22; 7,5-7; 7,13
The flood begins	—	Gn 7,10; 7,11
All living beings die	—	Gn 7,21; 7,22
The waters subside	—	Gn 8,1; 8,13

[21] A study as well as the complete text of the *Epic of Gilgamesh* are in Pritchard, *op. cit.,* pp. 72-99. The story of the flood is on the eleventh of the twelve tablets which make up the *Epic,* pp. 93-7. See the following for a presentation in parallel columns of the story of the Flood in both the *Epic* and the book of Genesis: Giuseppe Ricciotti, *The History of Israel,* trans. Clement Della Penta, O.P. and Richard T. A. Murphy, O.P. (2 vols.; Milwaukee: The Bruce Publishing Company, 1955), I, 158-61. See also John Bright, "Has Archaeology Found Evidence of the Flood?" *The Biblical Archaeologist,* V (December, 1942), 55-62.

There are also some conflicting details in the account. One example will suffice to illustrate this point. In Gn 6,19-22 and 7,15-16 Noe is concerned with taking one pair of every kind of living creature into the ark; in 7,2-3 a distinction is made between "clean" and "unclean" animals, a result of later Jewish dietary laws, and Noe takes seven pairs of the former and two of the latter into the ark.

All this shows that the author has taken two versions of the tradition about the Flood and, without removing the differences, has woven them together to form the account as it is in Genesis. The Yahwist version is the more colorful. It even says that the Lord closed the door of the ark after Noe entered (Gn 7,16).

D. The important question is: What purpose did the inspired author have in mind when he presented the account of the Flood? Remembering what was said about the purpose for which the book of Genesis was written, we know that we must not look to the Bible for answers to scientific questions.

The author wanted to teach the important lessons of theology in simple form—the lesson of the power of God, the terrible nature of sin, its spread, the wickedness of men, and the justice and mercy of God. The story of the Flood is a simple but meaningful parable of how God deals with men: justice causes Him to punish the wicked, mercy causes Him to spare the good and to give them another chance to fulfill His design. The story teaches the same lesson that another book of the Bible would put in the following way: "But thou, a forgiving God, gracious, and merciful, longsuffering, and full of compassion, didst not forsake them" (Neh 9,17).[22]

XIII. THE TOWER OF BABEL

A. The story of the building of a Tower is taken from a Mesopotamian background and probably was a primitive, naive attempt to explain the origin of the many languages of the world.

B. The most characteristic architectural form of temples in ancient Mesopotamia was the ziggurat; this was an artificial mountain, built of clay, bitumen, and unburnt bricks, and located in the flat plain. It was considered a high place for a god, whose shrine was located on the top of the structure. More than two dozen ziggurats have been discovered by archaeologists, the most famous one being the great one at Ur, which was built around 2000 B.C. in Babylon, in the time of Hammurabi. It was dedicated to the god, Marduk, and was known as the "House of the Foundation Platform of Heaven and Earth."

[22] St. Peter used the account of Noe to instruct the newly baptized Christians about the significance of Baptism. He saw in the water of the flood an instrument of salvation for the good, Noe and his family (1 Pt 3,20-22). The waters of the Baptism are the instrument of salvation for Christians, through the merits of the Risen Christ who acts in the Sacrament. See the excellent study of the theme of the Flood in the writings of the Fathers of the Church in Jean Daniélou, S.J., *From Shadows to Reality*, trans. Dom Wulstan Hibberd (Westminster, Md.: The Newman Press, 1960), pp. 69-112, and by the same author, *The Bible and the Liturgy* (Notre Dame: University of Notre Dame Press, 1956), pp. 70-85.

C. It is probable that the building of one of the ziggurats in Babylon, possibly the one at Ur, is behind the story of the Tower of Babel, which has been composed according to the special purpose that the author had in mind. It is quite likely that the city in the story is called Babel because the Hebrews thought that it was the oldest city in the world; moreover, the Hebrew word, *babal,* means "confuse," and it sounds enough like Babel to be used in folk etymology for the city in which the "confusion of tongues" first occurred.

D. It is important to note that, although originally the story was a fanciful explanation of the origin of languages based on folk history, yet there are definite evidences in the text which tell against its being used for that purpose by the inspired author. The Book of Genesis already mentions different languages and peoples in Gn 10,5,20,31 and 32. The author was trying to teach *theology not linguistics.*

E. The purpose of the story of the Tower of Babel was to teach the pathetic nature and foolishness of the type of pride that causes men to pit themselves against the Lord. The plans of those who direct their efforts against God seem to succeed for a time, but they are doomed to eventual failure. The lesson of this story is like the thought expressed in the Psalms: "Unless the Lord build the house, they labor in vain who build it" (Ps 126,1).

F. The story of the Tower of Babel provides a skillful and interesting background for the beginning of Sacred History proper. Mankind has sinned; it had rebelled against God and thus merited His condemnation. Left to itself, even with the aid of the power and human ingenuity of world empires which seek to establish unity among peoples, it could never re-create the primeval union with God. Under the sentence of God, and in no way deserving His further attention, mankind was still the object of His interest and love. The stage is set, now the Word of the Lord comes to Abraham and he, out of countless millions, is chosen to be the instrument through which all the nations of the earth will be truly blessed. It is at this point in Genesis that primeval history dovetails with Sacred History and we begin to see the implications of St. Paul's statement "where the offense has abounded, grace has abounded yet more" (Rm 5,20).

XIV. THE PATRIARCHAL PERIOD

It is only within recent times that there has been a retreat from the extreme skeptical position which denied the very existence of the ancient Hebrew patriarchs. Members of the rationalist critico-literary school of Biblical study often considered them as mere personifications of tribes that lived in a distant past, characterized by a lack of evidence. Even those who admitted the existence of the patriarchs refused to accept the Biblical narratives connected with them. They considered the stories nothing more than retrojections of ideas and customs which existed only in the period of the dual monarchy existing from the schism to the end of the northern kingdom (931-721 B.C.).

The labors of archaeologists and linguists during the last 25 years have forced a change in attitude. The ancient Near East is "coming alive" each time that an archaeologist uncovers a mound of dirt and produces artifacts, monuments, and literature from the past. Much of the culture and customs which are found in the narratives dealing with the Patriarchal Period in Genesis is now more fully understood. Many of the customs mentioned in the Biblical narratives have been substantiated and clarified by the study of the legend documents discovered in the Near East.

Many tablets discovered at Mari in Mesopotamia have been of great value in reconstructing the past. Scholars are at work translating and editing them and

> every new publication of theirs helps us better to understand the life and times of the Hebrew Patriarchs. Abraham, Isaac, and Jacob no longer seem isolated figures, much less reflections of later Israelite history; they now appear as true children of their age, bearing the same names, moving about over the same territory, visiting the same towns (especially Haran and Nabor), practicing the same customs as their contemporaries. In other words, the patriarchal narratives have a historical nucleus throughout, though it is likely that long oral transmission of the original poems and later prose sagas which underlie the present text of Genesis has considerably refracted the original events.[23]

XV. ABRAHAM, ISAAC, AND JACOB : GN 12-36

A. The Liturgy calls Abraham "our Father" (Canon of the Mass). This title emphasizes the fact that we are all spiritual Semites. We are men who believe in the one God who revealed Himself to Abraham, Isaac, and Jacob.

B. Why did God choose Abraham and the Hebrews to be His people? This question will come up again when we study the book of Deuteronomy. At this time, we will say that the only satisfactory answer that can be given is that the choice is another example of the freedom of divine election.

It is not the intrinsic merits of a person which cause God to act as He does. His choice is absolutely free. The call of Abraham and the covenant with him involves the first of the promises that God made to the fathers of the Hebrews. The theological synthesis of the Yahwist editor teaches that the choice of Abraham initiated the Divine plan for the salvation of nations.

---

[23] Albright, *The Archaeology of Palestine*, p. 236; see also by the same author, *From the Stone Age to Christianity*, pp. 200-243, and Kathleen M. Kenyon, *Archaeology in the Holy Land* (New York: Frederick A. Praeger, Publishers, 1960), pp. 162-194; H. H. Rowley, "Recent Discovery and the Patriarchal Age," *Bulletin of the John Rylands Library*, XXXII (September, 1949), 44-79. An authoritative study of the archaeological discoveries in the Negev, the region in which the Patriarchs did much of their wandering, is Nelson Glueck, *Rivers in the Desert. A History of the Negev* (New York: Farrar, Straus and Cudahy, Inc., 1959); see especially the article by the same author, "The Age of Abraham in the Negev," *The Biblical Archaeologist*, XVIII (February, 1955), 2-9.

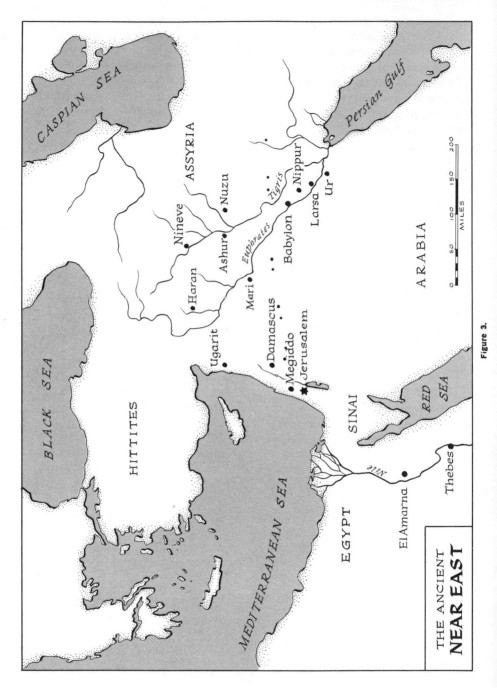

THE ANCIENT
NEAR EAST

Figure 3.

The purpose of the call was not limited to the Hebrews; eventually it was to embrace all mankind (Gn 12,1-3). Unlike Adam, Abraham obeyed God.

All who lived in the period of the Old Covenant believed in what was to come. We believe in what has come. But the object of our faith is one; we are the sons of Abraham who was the first to believe. In him the program of God's love and mercy begins to unfold. It is a program that will reach its climax in the Paschal Mystery of Jesus—His Passion, Death, Resurrection, and Ascension.

C. Abraham came from Ur of the Chaldees, in lower Mesopotamia, during the nineteenth century, probably around 1850 B.C. He traveled to the land of Canaan at a time when there were vast movements of peoples throughout the Near East.

The Accadians and Sumerians had ruled Mesopotamia for more than a hundred years; the Third Dynasty of Ur (2060-1950 B.C.) was one marked by great splendor. Soon, however, foreign tribes, like the Elamites, were attracted by the luxury of the well-cultivated land and moved into Mesopotamia. Then the Amorites sacked the capital city of Ur, established control over the land, and remained in power until about 1830, when the First Dynasty of Babylon was established.

This was also the time that foreigners known as *Habiru* came into the area. There are many ancient texts that mention these people; in fact, a variation of the name appears also in Egyptian texts where the "Apiru" are mentioned. Phonetically, the word "Hebrew" corresponds closely with *Habiru;* in Gn 14,13 Abraham is called a "Hebrew," and the Israelites are called the "Hebrews" in Gn 39,14 and other texts. Since the name means "foreigners" or "immigrants" we can see that it was a suitable title for Abraham and his people.

Abraham lived in Mesopotamia, and traveled to the land of Canaan at the time of the Amorite invasions and Hapiru movements. He was not a "typical nomad" accustomed to the wide open spaces; he came from an area that had an old civilization. There he witnessed a rich and relatively advanced culture. He brought some of this background with him when he left home to go to the land to which the Lord called him (Gn 12,1-3).

D. There is no need to be amazed at what took place in the Sara-Agar accounts found in the book of Genesis (Gn 16; 21). Monogamy was practiced by the Hebrews, but polygamy was also in vogue. This will be seen later in Israel's history when the custom of harem is adopted, and we will see people like Saul, David, and Solomon with several wives. The tablets discovered at Nuzu in Mesopotamia reveal that it was a custom for a childless wife to provide a handmaid for her husband so that children could be born to him. Abraham followed the custom of his time when he accepted Agar and had a child by her. The Nuzu tablets also explain why Abraham was disturbed when Sara decided to get rid of Agar; the child of a handmaid could not be driven out according to the accepted custom.[24]

E. Circumcision was a rite practiced among many of the ancient peoples. Therefore, the Israelites were not unique in the practice of this custom, but for them it had a religious significance. It was the sign of the covenant that the Lord made with Abraham (Gn 17,9-14, 23-27). The Patriarchs observed the custom (Gn 34,13-24) and we are told that it was practiced even when the Israelites were in Egypt before their liberation under Moses (Jos 5,4-5). It was continued after the conquest of the Promised Land, and even during the Babylonian Exile it was the distinctive mark of the one who belonged to Israel and thus to Yahweh. It is still observed by the Jews of today. It is usually performed by a skilled individual known as a *mohel;* after the rite of circumcision the father of the child says: "Praise be Thou, O Lord our God, ruling Spirit of the Universe, who in sanctifying us with His commandments has asked us to bring our son into the covenant of Abraham, our father."

The covenant that God made with Abraham has passed and so has the need for physical circumcision in the sense of a rite of religious significance. "In him (Christ), too, you have been circumcised, with a circumcision not wrought by hand, but through putting off the body of the flesh, a circumcision which is of Christ. For you were buried together with him in Baptism, and in him also rose again through faith in the working of God who raised him from the dead" (Col 2,11-12). The following texts also should be read: Acts 15,5-11; Gal 2,3; Rom 2,25-29; Gal 4,21-31; 5,6.

F. The events connected with the destruction of Sodom and Gomorra have been the subject of discussion for centuries (Gn 18,16-19,28). The Yahwist editor attributes the destruction of the two cities to Divine punishment for their wickedness and large-scale immorality, particularly the practice of unnatural vices. Sodom and Gomorra were remembered by the Israelites as the chief examples of a Divine judgment on a wicked people, who in their view were typical of the Canaanites among whom their forefathers lived (Is 1,9-11; Jer 49,18; Ps 10,6). The destruction of the cities was probably due to an earthquake that released the hydrogen sulphide gases and ignited the subterranean deposits of petroleum. The coastal areas of the Dead Sea along whose southeastern shore the two cities are believed to have existed are still rich in deposits of asphalt and sulphur. The Biblical author gives a theological reason for their destruction: sin was their ruin.[25]

G. Along the shore of the Dead Sea are rock formations of various bizarre

---

[24] Roger T. O'Callahan, S.J., "Historical Parallels to Patriarchal Social Customs," *The Catholic Biblical Quarterly,* VI (October, 1944), 391-405; also C. H. Gordon, "Biblical Customs and the Nuzi Tablets," *The Biblical Archaeologist,* III (February, 1940), 1-12.

[25] For a study of the location of Sodom and Gomorra and their destruction see the articles by J. Penrose Harland in *The Biblical Archaeologist Reader,* eds. G. Ernest Wright and David Noel Freedman (New York: Doubleday & Company, Inc., 1961), pp. 41-75.

shapes formed by severe erosion. The strange pillars of salt were explained by stories which delighted the imagination of the ancient Hebrews. Lot's wife turned to salt is a legendary element, a piece of incidental ornamentation based on a story about a woman who perished in the catastrophe. It was used by the inspired author to teach, among other lessons, the truth, "decide or perish". Man must not be a spectator to Divine events. He must respond to the Word of the Lord and do His bidding; if he delays, he will perish.

H. The account of Lot and the incestuous union devised by his daughters is coarse literature which carries the impression of the period in which it first was composed (Gn 19,30-38). The Ammonites and Moabites, although Semitic in origin and thus related to Israel, were the long-standing enemies of the Israelites. Throughout their history, the Hebrews had to suffer a great deal at their hands. The story in Genesis is a piece of popular wit; it is satire at the expense of Israel's enemies.

I. Abraham was asked to sacrifice his only son, the son of the promise (Gn 22,1-19). This was a tragic moment in the life of the Patriarch. It was not only that he was asked to give up his son; this would not appear too strange a request on the part of Yahweh, since Abraham had heard about, if not witnessed, human sacrifices offered to the gods in his original homeland, Mesopotamia. Now he was being asked to give his son to the true God, at least so he might have reasoned. The serious, basic problem was that *this child* was the "child of promise." Everything the Lord had promised depended on this child, his only son (Gn 17,15-19).

Faith for the heroes of the Bible was not just an intellectual assent; it involved the commitment of the whole person to a God who manifested His love and mercy in the acts which He performed in their favor.

Abraham proved his faith, his total commitment to the Lord, and in his act of sublime obedience we have the climax of his entire life. There is a lot implied in the short phrase found in the book of Sirach, "when tested he was found loyal" (Sir 44,20), and in the epistle to the Romans, "he did not waver through unbelief but was strengthened in faith, giving glory to God, being fully aware that whatever God has promised he is able also to perform" (Rom 4,20-21).

The account is basically Elohist with a few Yahwist elements, for example, Gn 22,15-18. Some scholars see in this account an implied condemnation of human sacrifices, particularly those involving infants as practiced by the Canaanites. The Lord does not want such offerings!

Moreover, there is an implicit liturgical significance which the Israelites would understand. The first-born belongs to the Lord and he is to serve his God by living a dedicated life. The death of the first-born is not desired by God. He wants a life of total dedication to His service.

J. The theme of the Just Sufferer is seen in the person of Isaac, the innocent victim who carries the wood for the sacrifice. Christian tradition has seen in him a type of Jesus, the innocent and Just Sufferer, who carried His cross to Calvary.

K. We do not know the year that Abraham died. His life will stand forever not only as a great example of the implications of true Faith, but also as a witness to the meaning of such basic virtues as fraternity (Gn 13,8-10), hospitality (Gn 18,3-5), justice, forgiveness, and intercession in the name of others (Gn 18,23-33).

L. The Israelites trace their descent from Jacob, whose name was also Israel, because, in the words of the Yahwist editor, he was the one who "contended with God and men, and triumphed" (Gn 32,29). Jacob was the twin brother of Esau, also called Edom, from whom the Edomites trace their descent.

M. Jacob's use of fraud to gain the birthright from his aged father is something which Christian morality does not condone. Here we have another example of how the Biblical authors present even their heroes as men of flesh and blood who sometimes do not hesitate to stoop in order to conquer. The same can also be said of Rebecca, the scheming mother, who did not hesitate to take advantage of her blind husband in order to get the "first place" for her "fair-haired boy." Much later in salvation-history we have the example of the mother of the sons of Zebedee who went right up to Jesus and asked for the "first seats" for her two sons, James and John (Mt 20,20-22). At least we can commend her forthright honesty. Rebecca was a different type of person. Yet the Roman Ritual does not hesitate to set her up as an example of what a bride should be like: "May you be as wise as Rebecca" (Nuptial Blessing). The means she used are not at all praiseworthy, but she does reveal an element of the magnanimous in her ambitious plan.

The outcome of the deceit again illustrates, in a unique way, the freedom of divine choice which acts independently of the merits of a person.

XVI. JOSEPH THE MAGNANIMOUS

A. Joseph is not as important as Abraham, Isaac, and Jacob, but his story is the longest one in the book of Genesis. Except for chapters 38 and 49 which are intrusions into the story, Joseph's history fills Gn 37-50. It is a presentation which shows the genius of the inspired author in its organically constructed and rich narrative. A few sections are from the Priestly tradition, but the major part of the work is an artistic composition made from Yahwist and Elohist traditions. Although much of the Egyptian background and many of the customs have been proven to be accurate and reliable, the work is not a piece of critico-historical writing. It is part of religious or sacred history, *heilsgeschichte.*

B. Scholars are of the opinion that the period into which the account of Joseph and his brothers fits best is the time of the Hyksos domination of

Egypt. The name *Hyksos* has received various interpretations: "shepherd kings," "kings of desert," "princes of the shepherds," "foreign chiefs," and "rulers of foreign lands."

The Hyksos were well established in Egypt about 1700 B.C. and their rule lasted until about 1570 B.C. They were probably of mixed racial stock but the main element was Semitic. The Roman-Jewish historian of the first century A.D., Josephus, went so far as to call them the ancestors of the Jews, but he was wrong. What he should have said was that the ancestors of the Jews were in Egypt at the time that the Hyksos were in power. But this he could have known only from reliable documentary evidence or archaeological research, and neither was available in his time. We are in a better position as far as sources are concerned, and, therefore, we can say with a high degree of probability that it was during the Hyksos domination that "Israel went into Egypt" (Gn 46).

Since the Hyksos were of Semitic stock we can understand why Joseph attained a choice position there, and also why the Israelites received preferential treatment to such a degree that they were permitted to settle in the best land in Egypt, the land of Gesen, sometimes called Goshen (Gn 47).

C. The account of the early days of Joseph in Egypt comes principally from the Yahwist tradition. We should notice the colorful and interesting way in which the character of Joseph is presented in the event involving the Egyptian's frustrated wife (Gn 39). The reasons why Joseph refuses to satisfy her lustful desires are a beautiful summary of why anyone who believes in God should thwart similar temptations; the sin would involve a betrayal of trust placed in him by the husband, an injustice, since she is the Egyptian's wife, and above all it would be a "sin against God" (Gn 39,8-9). In this simple but important episode the inspired author teaches his readers a vital truth: for believers, morality is not just naked ethics; it is something which flows from the fact of God's existence and man's allegiance to One who has revealed Himself in His acts.

The account in Gn 39 mentioned several times that the *"Lord was with Joseph* so that he was successful" (vv 2,3,5). At the moment of trial and temptation we are shown how Joseph refused to betray God; when the test came, Joseph was not found wanting, *he was with God.* Then, God who is never outdone in generosity, rewarded Joseph for his fidelity. "The Lord was with Joseph" in prison and he brought about his reinstatement in the Pharaoh's house (Gn 39,21-23; 41,37-46).

D. The account of the interpretation of the dreams is chiefly from the Elohist tradition (Gn 40-41). Joseph's interpretation of the dreams of the butler and baker prepares the reader for the great victory which is presented in Gn 41. There Joseph does what all the magicians and wise men of Egypt could not do; he interprets the Pharaoh's dreams correctly. There is irony in this fact; Egypt was the land that thrived on a reputation for wisdom. But it was Joseph, a Hebrew, who succeeded. The Israelites saw in this the special providence of God, not only over Joseph, their Patriarch, but also over them, His Chosen People.

Late in the period of the Old Covenant, the book of Wisdom, written in Egypt during the first century B.C., speaks of the success achieved by Joseph in the "land of wisdom" as the result of the action of Wisdom itself. "She (Wisdom) went down with him into the dungeon, and did not desert him in his bonds, until she brought him the scepter of royalty and authority over his oppressors, showed those who had defamed him false, and gave him eternal glory" (Wis 10,14).

E. The death and burial of Joseph are mentioned in Gn 50,22-26. His remains were embalmed according to the Egyptian custom, then buried. Later, when the Hebrews leave Egypt under Moses they will take the body with them (Ex 13,19), and when the land of Canaan is conquered under Josue "the bones of Joseph, which the Israelites had brought up from Egypt, were buried in Sichem" in the center of Palestine, on the border between the two tribes which descended from Joseph's sons, Ephraim and Manasses (Jos 24,32).

F. Near the end of Genesis there is a chapter which presents a collection of aphorisms often called the "blessings of Jacob" (Gn 49). Except for the words addressed to Joseph in vv 22-36 these statements hardly deserve such a title. The literary form of the contents leads to the conclusion that the present text was composed long after the death of Jacob. Most probably, the origin of the greater part of the contents should be dated to the period which followed shortly after the conquest of Canaan. However, it was not until the time of David (1010-970 B.C.) that the "blessing" of Juda was put into its present form; David was a descendant of that tribe from which the Israelites also expected the Messiah.

> The sceptre shall not depart from Juda,
>   nor the staff from between his feet,
> Until he comes to whom it belongs.
>   To him shall be the obedience of nations.
> *Gn 49,10*

seven

THE BOOK OF EXODUS

I. THE NAME

THE WORD EXODUS means "going out." It is a fitting title for the story of the deliverance of the Israelites from Egypt. The book, while it has some interesting parallels with our own history as a nation, is the inspired record of the intervention of God in human history. It is part of Sacred History which is God's plan for the salvation of the human race; it is part of that long record of God's intervention in our world, drawing men to Himself, communicating His life with them, and bringing about His universal reign.

II. IMPORTANCE OF THE EXODUS

The Exodus is the central point in the history and faith of Israel. It is the fact that gave rise to the unconquerable trust of the Israelites in the protection and fidelity of God. The prophets, the legislation, the religious history, and the liturgy of Israel are all permeated with the memory of this great event. The primary importance of the Exodus is that it was the time that Yahweh established the Covenant—the *berith*—at Sinai. The deliverance from Egypt was the fulfillment of the promises made to the Patriarchs; the Lord was faithful to His Word.

A. Each year the Hebrew peasant came to offer the first fruits of his field to God. During the ritual offertory, he recited a *credo* which expresses deep faith in the historical fact of the intervention of God in the life of His people at the time of the Exodus (Dt 26,5-10).

B. The books of the prophets have many references and allusions to the saving events of the Exodus. They contain predictions of a Second Exodus where God would duplicate and even surpass the marvels He performed at the time of Moses. As a matter of fact, the prophets before the Exile emphasize the Exodus and the wandering in the desert of Sinai; they do not

77

speak of Abraham and his wanderings. (Am 5,25; Os 2,14-17; 11,1; 13,4; Jer 2,2-7; Ez 20,5-26; and Is 40-55).

C. The Psalms, the prayers of the Hebrews, contain poetical descriptions of the Exodus (Pss 77; 104; 105; 113; 135).

D. Each year the events of the Exodus were, and still are, symbolically re-lived in the ceremonies of the Passover, the Seder. The ritual says: "In every generation it is the duty of a man to imagine that he himself has come forth out of Egypt."

III. EVIDENCE FOR THE EVENT

None of the early texts that have been found in Egypt contain any reference to the sojourn of the Hebrews in Egypt and their liberation under Moses. Likewise, none of the Biblical books mention the names of the Pharaohs under whom the Hebrews labored.

Many scholars hold the view that the settlement of Hebrews in Egypt occurred during the time that the land was invaded by mixed racial groups from Canaan called Hyksos. Their domination of Egypt began around 1700 B.C. and many of them settled in the rich Delta region. From there they dominated the entire country. Thus, if the Pharaoh was Semitic we can understand why Joseph, a Hebrew, would be promoted to the high office of the land. About 100 years after their conquest, the Hyksos were expelled by strong chieftains from the region of Thebes. The Delta region remained occupied largely by Semitic peoples. It was after the Hyksos defeat (*ca.* 1570 B.C.) that the great epoch began when Pharaohs like Amenophis I (1546-1525) to Thothmes III (1490-1435) expanded their possessions as far as the Euphrates. The kingdom collapsed under the rule of Amenophis IV (1370-1357) who was more of a religious reformer than a great worldly leader. It was he who spread the cult of the sun god, Aton, whom he declared to be the sole god and in whose honor he changed his name to Akhenaton which means "It is pleasing to Aton," or "the Splendor of Aton." After the death of his son-in-law Tutankhamon, the general Horemheb (1340-1310) seized the throne and began the final period of greatness for Egypt. After Horemheb the restoration was continued and reached its last peak of grandeur and strength under the Pharaoh Rameses II (1290-1224). It was then that the power of Egypt threatened to exterminate the people of Abraham.

IV. LITERARY FORM OF THE BOOK

There can be no doubt that the actual happenings during the period that the Hebrews were in Egypt and their liberation were far more complex than a casual reading of the Bible would suggest. It must be remembered that the accounts found in the book of Exodus are the last stages of an oral and literary evolution and that they show traces of their composite character. The Biblical accounts are substantially historical but they are presented in a form which represents the crystallization of the early spoken traditions of Israel concerning itself and its history. The events were handed down by word of mouth from one generation to another and were gradually molded into their present form by the context of the Israelite liturgy which formed the setting in which the marvelous deeds of Yahweh were recounted to the people. Like the other books of the Pentateuch, this book attained its final form after the Babylonian Exile, after 538 B.C.

The book of Exodus does not have for its purpose the recording of history as we conceive it. Its narratives, therefore, cannot and should not be judged by the standards of the modern historian. The book aims at bringing out the central and most important idea of the saving activity on the part of God for His people. It is a great religious epic built around a man, Moses, and an event, the Exodus from Egypt. It is in a style which is grand, heroic, and majestic. The influences of the liturgical service of the Passover can be felt particularly in chapters 1-15. The historical events have been "camouflaged" by details which emphasize the saving power of Yahweh.

V. BONDAGE IN EGYPT

There is no direct extra-Biblical evidence as yet which substantiates the account of Exodus concerning the bondage of the Hebrews in Egypt. However, a number of factors lend objective support. Egyptian names are prevalent in early Israel—Moses, Phinehas, Merari. There is evidence of the presence of *'Apiru* in Egypt throughout the empire period. The presence of this distinct social class may be inferred from references to state slaves. Some scholars connect this word with *'Ibri,* which means "Hebrew," and which is used in the stories of Joseph and the Exodus with a striking consistency. Whether or not the 'apiru were the 'ibri is a debatable point, but without question among the 'apiru were the components of the later Israel.

The situation in Egypt during the thirteenth century B.C. seems an ideal background for the Biblical data found in the book of Exodus. We are told in Ex 1,11 that the Hebrews were forced to labor at the building of Pithom and Rameses. The former was located in northeast Egypt; the latter was the ancient Hyksos capital known as Avaris which was rebuilt and again made the capital by Sethos I (1309-1290) and Rameses II (1290-1224) who called it the "House of Rameses". After the expulsion of the Hyksos rulers, the Semitic peoples who remained were disliked and mistrusted. Thus it is understandable that Rameses II should have forced them to act as laborers for his building projects.[1]

---

[1] For a study of Rameses II see Finegan, *op. cit.,* pp. 113-21, and L. H. Grollenberg, O.P., *Atlas of the Bible,* trans. Joyce M. H. Reid and H. H. Rowley (New York: Thomas Nelson and Sons, 1956), pp. 45-48, with illustrations.

VI. MOSES : EX 2-3

Moses means "son" in Egyptian; popular etymology, by a clever play on words, sees in the Hebrew name, *Mosheh,* the meaning "to draw out", *Mashah.* Hence, Moses is the one drawn from the water.

The story about his birth and his being saved in the basket seems to have been influenced by a similar story about Sargon of Akkad (*ca.* 2360 B.C.), in northern Mesopotamia. Sargon also rose to great power; he is often called the first empire builder of history. The story of Moses has many of the qualities of a glorified "rags to riches" biography.

He was brought up in the Egyptian court, attended the school of the royal children, and very likely had to experience the harsh methods then practiced in teaching. As a young man he no doubt enjoyed the many-sided and colorful life of the capital.

The religious practices of the time were steeped in magic; Moses had some idea of the religious practices of Canaan since he came into contact with the officials working in Palestine and also the Canaanites who lived in Rameses and sometimes even held offices of the court. The picture of the cult was not an attractive one; there were sexual excesses of all kinds, also a repulsive cult of serpents and even human sacrifices.[2]

Moses, one day in anger, slew one of the Egyptian overseers, and then took flight. He met some wandering Midianites and married the daughter of one of their priests, a man named Jethro, also known as Raguel. Moses now led quite a different life from the one he was used to at the Egyptian court. The lonely and impressive setting contributed to his formation and preparation for the revelation of Mount Sinai. He found his vocation, and had an experience which gave him a steadfast faith for the rest of his life: a strong faith in his mission, which was to lead the Hebrews out of Egypt and make them into a nation that would belong to Yahweh.

There are two descriptions of his vocation: the Yahwist-Elohist tradition in Ex 3,1-4,17 and the Priestly narrative in Ex 6,2-7,13. The vision in the Yahwist-Elohist tradition is similar to the visions had by the great prophets: Isaia (6), Jeremia (1), and Ezechiel (1-2). The account of the burning bush must be read with a "religious eye." Fire, which is often used in the Old Testament as a symbol of God, is used here to present the great mystical experience of Moses when he received his vocation from the Lord.

VII. MEANING OF THE NAME YAHWEH

Until the early centuries of the Christian era, the Hebrew language made use only of consonants. Therefore in Hebrew only the four consonants were used for the divine Name, YHWH. This is the *tetragrammaton.* During the

---

[2] Information about Egyptian religion is in Albright, *From the Stone Age to Christianity,* pp. 178-89, 209-28. A good survey is Etienne Drioton, "Egyptian Religion," *Religion of the Ancient East,* trans. M. B. Loraine (New York: Hawthorn Books, Publishers, 1959), pp. 16-59.

period after the Babylonian Exile, the name was not pronounced. Instead, the word *Adonai*, Lord, was used. It was during the Christian middle ages, in the thirteenth century, that the vowels of Adonai were combined with the YHWH; the result was the word usually written as Jehovah. It is certain that this is an erroneous spelling of the divine Name. Scholars have shown that the correct spelling is Yahweh.

The preferable meanings of the name are : "He causes to be" or "He who manifests His existence by mighty acts on behalf of His people." It may also signify nothing more than a refusal on the part of God to name Himself: I am who am.[3]

VIII. THE PLAGUES : EX 7-11

There is no exact historical certitude concerning the precise number of plagues. The way in which the various traditions have been combined by the editors of the Pentateuch makes it almost impossible to arrive at absolute certainty in this matter. No one of the traditions contains all ten plagues. An

Plagues	J	E	P
1. Water to blood	7:14, 16, 17a, 18, 24-25	7:15, 17b, 20b, 23	7:19, 20a, 21b, 22
2. Frogs	8: 1-4, 8-15a		8:5-7, 15b
3. Gnats			8:16-19
4. Flies	8:20-32		
5. Cattle plague	9:1-7		
6. Boils			9:8-12
7. Hail	9:13, 17-18 23b-24, 26-30, 33-34	9:22, 23a, 25, 35	
8. Locusts	10:1-20	(E elements in 10:12-13a, 20)	
9. Darkness	(J elements in 10:24-26, 28-29)	10:21-29	
10. Death of first-born	11:4-8 12:29-30	11:1-3 12:31-32	11:9-10

Table 2. **THE PLAGUES IN THE TRADITIONS**

[3] An excellent study is Myles M. Bourke, "Yahweh, the Divine Name," *The Bridge,* III (1958), 271-87. See also Albright, *From the Stone Age to Christianity,* pp. 15-16, 258-61.

analysis of the text on the basis of the style and vocabulary peculiar to each tradition is in Table 2.[4]

We should notice the marvelous artistry with which the traditions concerning the plagues have been combined to bring out the tension that existed between Moses and the Pharaoh and how the final victory was achieved by the spokesman of Yahweh.

There is nothing intrinsically miraculous about the plagues. The Egyptian magicians were able to perform similar wonders. Some authors point out that the first nine plagues have parallels in the natural phenomena proper to Egypt. They occur occasionally in the Delta region. For example, the first plague seems to be identical with the annual flooding of the Nile River, whose waters are reddened because of the stirring up of the soil and silt. The book of Exodus presents the plagues to point up the fact that there was a divine intervention at the time of the liberation from Egypt; God was directly involved in the Exodus of the Hebrews. The plagues were signs that God was present and active among His people. The main point was the faith of the Hebrews in a God who is the Lord of nature. Yahweh is indeed "wholly other." He is transcendent, but the works of nature reveal Him.

The death of the first-born of the Egyptians had a particular significance for the Israelites. Their worship of Yahweh included the sacrifice of the first-born of most animals and, since human sacrifices were forbidden, the redemption, "buying back," of the first-born sons who had to be offered to the Lord (Ex 22,28-29; 13,11-15; 34,19-20). This religious rite received a deeper theological meaning when it was seen against the background of the recital of the Exodus wonders, especially the tenth plague when "there was not a house without its dead" (Ex 12,30).[5]

IX. NUMBER WHO LEFT EGYPT

After the tenth plague struck, the death of the first-born of the Egyptians, the Hebrews left the land of Goshen. The exact number of people that left the land is a matter of dispute among scholars. It is almost certain that not all the original 12 tribes of Israel were involved in the Exodus. Many are of the opinion that the 600,000 mentioned in Exodus 12,37 (total population is set at about 2½-3 million when all the texts are studied) is an impossible number. Heinisch says: "If three million Israelites had been dwelling alongside the Egyptians in the delta, Pharaoh would never have dared to enslave them,

---

[4] Bernhard W. Anderson, *Understanding the Old Testament* (Englewood Cliffs, N. J.: Prentice-Hall, Inc., 1957), p. 42. Used with publisher's permission.

[5] See Roland E. Murphy, O.Carm., *The Book of Exodus* (2 parts; New York: The Paulist Press, 1960), I, 16-21; also Roland DeVaux, O.P., *Ancient Israel, Its Life and Institutions*, trans. John McHugh (New York: McGraw-Hill Book Company, Inc., 1961), pp. 443-44, 488-90. Material on the nature and meaning of miracles is in François Taymans, S.J., "Miracles, Signs of the Supernatural," *Theology Digest*, V (Winter, 1957), 18-23, and Robert W. Gleason, S.J., "Miracles and Contemporary Theology," *Thought*, XXXVII (Spring, 1962), 12-34.

and such a multitude would simply have crushed the soldiery pursuing them. How could these millions, together with their herds, have crossed the Reed-Sea in one night?"[6] Opinions vary from the 600 proposed by Premier Ben-Gurion to 36,000 given by Ricciotti.[7] Arbez, in his study of the book of Exodus says: "The actual total may have been *ca.* 6,000, perhaps a little more. The description of Israel in 13,18 moving out of Egypt 'in battle array', 'well-equipped' (so most translations) is questionable. More probably the text is to be read that they took with them their possession or went as free men."[8] This view is most reasonable but it is important to remember Roland Murphy's observation: "As in the case with so many figures in the Bible, we are unable to comprehend the meaning of such a large number (i.e., 3 million people). It has no mathematical value, but rather a symbolic one, indicating the large number of those to be saved."[9]

X. DATE OF THE EXODUS

The fact that there is no direct extra-Biblical evidence for the Exodus does not warrant the conclusion that it must not have taken place.

The Bible's own witness is itself so impressive as to leave little doubt that some such remarkable deliverance took place. Israel remembered the exodus for all time to come as the constitutive event that had called her into being as a people. It stood at the center of her confession of faith from the beginning, as is witnessed by certain ancient poems (Ex 15,1-18) and credos (Dt 6,20-26; 26,5-10; Jos 24,2-13) that go back to the earliest period of her history. A belief so ancient and so entrenched will admit of no explanation save that Israel actually escaped from Egypt to the accompaniment of events so stupendous that they were impressed forever on her memory.[10]

The information mentioned in No. V points to the existence of the Hebrews in Egypt during the thirteenth century B.C. The Stele of Merneptah, a piece of Basalt on which the Pharaoh Merneptah (1224-1212 B.C.) recorded his series of triumphs, contains the following inscription:

The kings yield and cry, "Peace."
All the vanquised are bowed down.
Libya is devastated and the land of the Hittites pacified;
Despoiled is Canaan and all her wickedness.

[6] Paul Heinisch, *History of the Old Testament,* trans. William Heidt, O.S.B. (Collegeville, Minn.: The Liturgical Press, 1952), p. 88.
[7] David Ben Gurion, quoted in *The New York Times,* May 18, 1960, p. 43; Giuseppe Ricciotti, *The History of Israel,* trans. Clement Della Penta, O.P. and Richard T. A. Murphy, O.P. (2 vols.; Milwaukee: The Bruce Publishing Company, 1955), I, 193.
[8] E. P. Arbez, "Book of Exodus," *Guide to the Bible,* I, 189.
[9] Murphy, *op. cit.,* I, 23.
[10] John Bright, *A History of Israel* (Philadelphia: The Westminster Press, 1959), pp. 111-12.

Ashkelon is fallen; Gezer is conquered; Yenoam is destroyed
ISRAEL IS RAVAGED AND HER SEED ANNIHILATED
Philistia stands widowed before Egypt.
All the lands are pacified.
All the nomads are in chains.[11]

There are scholars who see in these words the fact that at about 1220 B.C. a community of Israelites was living in the land of Canaan. Ricciotti, however, proceeds a little more cautiously. He points out that the inscription on the Stele does not prove conclusively that the Israel that is mentioned was definitely settled in Canaan. It is possible that it refers to the group of wandering and nomadic people who had gone out of Egypt but were still in the region of Sinai. On the other hand, if it does refer to an Israel already settled in Palestine, "this Israel would not necessarily be a people different from that of the descendants of Jacob, as the Bible itself allows for the possibility that even before the general exodus, some groups of the descendants of Jacob might have settled in Palestine, where they could have multiplied as did their fellow countrymen in Egypt." [12]

Another fact that points to the thirteenth century as the time of the Exodus is Israel's detour around Edom and Moab (Nu 20-21). These kingdoms were only established in that century. Therefore, the most probable conclusion is that Sethos I was the Pharaoh of the oppression mentioned in Ex 1,2, and Rameses II was the Pharaoh of the Exodus. Since available Egyptian records speak only of the victorious achievements of the Pharaohs we have a very likely reason for the absence of any mention in such records of the victory that the Hebrews achieved against the Egyptians at the time of the Exodus. The cumulative weight of the evidence permits us to date the Exodus not later than about 1250 B.C.; very probably about 1280 B.C.

XI. THE CROSSING OF THE SEA : EX 14,10-31

The shortest way out of Egypt would have been along the Mediterranean coast, which was called the "way of the Philistines" around 1200 B.C. The Jews, however, took a southern route which brought them to the lower part of the Sinai peninsula. The exact place where they crossed into the Sinai Peninsula cannot be determined with absolute accuracy. Some, like Ricciotti and Grollenberg, have maintained that at the time of the exodus the Red Sea extended much farther to the north and connected with the Bitter Lakes located in the region.[13] However, Bright, using evidence supplied by the

[11] Text as found in Grollenberg, *Atlas of the Bible,* p. 46. This Stele is the only ancient Egyptian source in which the name "Israel" appears.

[12] Ricciotti, *op. cit.,* p. 192. See Robert North, S.J., "Date and Unicity of the Exodus," *The American Ecclesiastical Review,* CXXXIV (March, 1956), 161-82.

[13] Ricciotti, *op. cit.,* I, 184; Grollenberg, *Atlas of the Bible,* p. 48.

archaeologist Albright, rejects that view.[14] The crossing probably occurred in the area of Lake Timsah and the Bitter Lakes that are located to the east of the Delta region. It should be noted that although we usually speak of the Red Sea, according to the Hebrew text we should speak of the Sea of Reeds or Rushes, *Yam Suph,* a marshy area found near the lakes. The Septuagint translated the Hebrew as Red Sea and so it has remained.

The literary presentation of the crossing has the same grand, majestic, epic qualities that are characteristic of the genre of the book of Exodus. Substantially it comes from the Yahwist tradition with Elohist additions. It is difficult to disengage the exact historical occurrence from the literary details which have been used by the inspired author to highlight the religious significance of the event.

It is interesting to read how the author of the book of Wisdom, written during the first century B.C., spoke of the event. He did not hesitate to add his own details:

> Out of the Red Sea an unimpeded road, and a grassy plain
> out of the mighty flood.
>
> *Wis 19,7*

XII. THE MANNA AND THE QUAILS : EX 16; NU 11,6-35

The discontent of the people and their desire to return to the land of Egypt were answered by the coming of manna and quails. What was this heaven-sent food? According to many modern-day scholars the food described as manna really was a sweet, sticky substance produced by the excretion of insects that suck the sap from the tamarisk bushes that are even today found in the central valleys of Sinai. The incident of the quails can be explained by the great flights of quails that migrate annually from Europe to the warmer climate of Africa. The flight over the Mediterranean Sea exhausts these birds and they often drop to earth and are easily captured. This is most likely what happened when the Israelites murmured against Moses. The quails arrived and the people greedily devoured the meat which was providentially presented to them.

These explanations offered by scholars should not cause us to forget the fact that it was the providence of God which was at work in the events which brought food to His people when they were in dire circumstances in the Sinai Peninsula. The Hebrews often recalled the events of the Exodus and how the "outstretched arm of the Lord" protected them. They did not forget that the Lord "commanded the skies above and the doors of heaven he opened; he rained manna upon them for food and gave them heavenly bread . . . he rained meat upon them like dust, and, like the sand of the sea, winged fowl, which fell in the midst of their camp round about their tents" (Ps 77,24-28).

[14] Bright, *op. cit.,* p. 112.

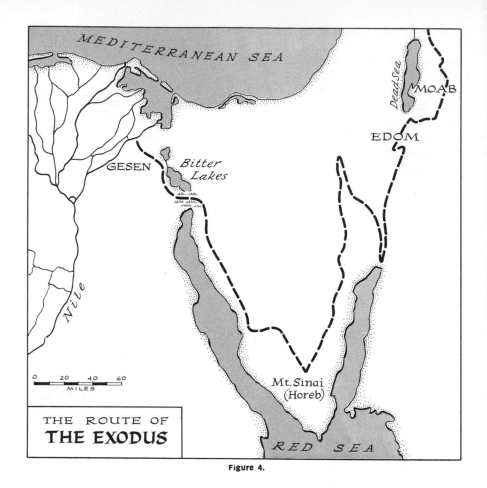

THE ROUTE OF
THE EXODUS

Figure 4.

The author of the book of Wisdom added picturesque details to his presentation of the events, the manna "blended to whatever flavor each one wished" (Wis 16,21).

XIII. MT. SINAI : EX 19-24

The exact route followed by the Hebrews is still the object of study by scholars. Even the location of Mt. Sinai is not absolutely certain. Yet there is sufficient evidence to support the view that after crossing the Reed Sea, the Hebrews traveled southwards. Making their way from oasis to oasis they penetrated deeply into the peninsula until they came to the granite range of mountains near the southern tip. They encamped near the highest peak, Jebel Musa, which rises about 7,500 feet above sea level. There God made the covenant with His people.

The accounts found in Exodus are not intended to be an exact historical report of all that took place at Mt. Sinai. Their purpose was to give a theological interpretation of the events. In the past, some authors attempted to explain the theophany at Sinai as a volcanic eruption which was given a religious interpretation by the Hebrews. There are absolutely no grounds for maintaining the existence of a volcano in all Sinai. Albright suggests that the present picture of the Sinai theophany makes use of folk memories of volcanic eruptions and thunder-storms with which the Hebrews were familiar from other regions, especially Arabia or Syria. The imagery used in Exodus is like that used in other books of the Bible to describe the greatness and holiness of God (3 Kgs 19,11; Is 2,21-22; Job 28,9-10; Ps 28,3-9; Neh 1,5).

XIV. THE COVENANT : EX 20-24

God intended His People to be a community, bound to Him by a covenant, an alliance which was not a legal burden but a Divine Act of *hesed,* love.[15]

> You have seen for yourselves how I treated the Egyptians and how I bore you up on eagle wings and brought you here to myself. Therefore, if you hearken to my voice and keep my covenant, you shall be my special possession, dearer to me than all other people, though all the earth is mine. You shall be to me a kingdom of priests, a holy nation.
>
> *Ex 19,4-6*

The Covenant-idea pervades the entire Old Testament; the Israelites were the People of the Covenant established at Sinai. They never forgot the fact of divine Election and the Covenant. Recent studies have thrown a good deal of light on the origin of the Covenant-idea and its implications. The study of ancient Hittite material from 1450-1200 B.C. has revealed that that people had two forms of pacts, *parity* treaties and *suzerainty* treaties. In the former, the parties involved are mutually bound to observe the same stipulations; in the latter, the ruler bound his vassals to faithfulness and obedience to himself. There is evidence of such covenant-pacts as early as the second millenium B.C., but the Hittites seem to have developed the idea more than the other ancient peoples, or at least there is more evidence from them than from others on this point.[16]

The suzerainty covenant was unilateral, only the vassal took the oath of obedience; in return, the king would protect his subjects from foreign attacks. The Hittite suzerainty covenant contained the following: (1) a Preamble

---

[15] Two well-written essays on this point are Mother Kathryn Sullivan, R.S.C.J., "The God of Israel, God of Love," *The Bridge,* IV (1961-62), 27-43, and J. Giblet, "God's Covenant with Men," *The God of Israel, the God of Christians,* trans. Kathryn Sullivan, R.S.C.J. (New York: Desclee Company, 1961), pp. 23-42.

[16] See George E. Mendenhall, "Ancient Oriental and Biblical Law," *The Biblical Archaeologist,* XVII (May, 1954), 26-46, and "Covenant Forms in Israelite Tradition," *ibid.,* (September, 1954), 50-76. A technical and detailed study of an example of a suzerainty treaty of the eighth century B.C. is in Joseph A. Fitzmyer, S.J., "The Aramaic Suzerainty Treaty From Sefire in the Museum of Beirut," *The Catholic Biblical Quarterly,* XV (October, 1958), 444-76. See also Neal M. Flanagan, O.S.M., "The Covenant and How It Grew," *The American Ecclesiastical Review,* CXLIII (September, 1960), 145-56, and P. VanImschoot, "Covenant in the Old Testament," *Theology Digest,* II (Spring, 1954), 86-89.

which identifies the author of the covenant, (2) a Historical Prologue which emphasizes the good actions which the Hittite sovereign had performed in the past for his vassal, (3) stipulations which include the obligations imposed on and accepted by the vassal, (4) a provision for the deposit of the treaty in the temple and a periodic public reading in order to bring it to the attention of all the people, (5) a list of the gods who acted as witnesses to the covenant, (6) a formula of blessings and curses which flow from obedience or violation of the terms of the covenant, (7) an oath taken by the vassal during a solemn ceremony, and the procedure to be followed against him should he violate the terms of the alliance.

A reading of Exodus texts regarding the covenant indicates that the form at the time of Moses followed the classical Hittite lines—the Israelites assume the obligations, Yahweh remains free, but He will protect and support His people. Yahweh is the author of the covenant; Moses is His messenger; the benevolence of the Lord is seen in the *Mirabilia Dei,* the mighty acts of God, which marked the deliverance from Egypt; obedience must be given to the terms of the Covenant; there is a solemn ceremony involving the sprinkling of blood upon the altar and people; a copy of the Covenant is deposited in the Ark of the Covenant (Ex 25,16; 40,20), and the Law is to be read to the people throughout history.

The Old Testament Covenant contains no curses or blessings except the Commandment against the worship of other gods and the punishment that will come to those who fall into idolatry.

Israel used the suzerainty treaty that was in existence at the time among its neighbors, particularly the Hittites, to express the relationship which it had with Yahweh. It is an interesting fact that the covenant-form, common during the second millenium B.C., survived among the Israelites.

The Covenant made at Sinai was not to last forever. It was a preparation for the new and everlasting covenant which God would make one day with mankind. Jeremia the prophet referred to it as the "new covenant" which would be written on the hearts of men (Jer 31,31-34). Jesus accomplished it when in the insignificant setting of an upper room, surrounded by His apostles, He ate the Supper and initiated the Covenant in His Blood:

> And while they were at supper, Jesus took bread, and blessed and broke, and gave it to his disciples, and said, 'Take and eat; this is my body.' And taking a cup, he gave thanks and gave it to them, saying, 'All of you drink of this; for this is my blood of the new covenant, which is being shed for many unto the forgiveness of sins.'
>
> *Mt 26,26-28*

XV. THE TEN COMMANDMENTS : EX 20,1-17; DT 5,6-21

They are called the Ten Words, hence the word *Decalogue* in Greek. There are two reports of the Commandments. A careful study of the form and content of the laws found in the Pentateuch leads to the conclusion that the

Biblical tradition which attributes the law to Moses is well founded. In their primitive form the Commandments are Mosaic, but the present form in Ex 20,1-17 comes from the Priestly Tradition, and the one in Dt 5,6-21 from the Deuteronomic Tradition. The original form of the commandments, without the later additions and commentary, was probably somewhat like the following:

> I, Yahweh, am your God, who brought you out of the land of Egypt, that place of slavery.
>> You shall not have other gods besides me.
>> You shall not carve idols for yourselves.
>> You shall not take the name of Yahweh, your God, in vain.
>> Remember to keep holy the Sabbath.
>> Honor your father and your mother.
>> You shall not kill.
>> You shall not commit adultery.
>> You shall not steal.
>> You shall not bear false witness against your neighbor.
>> You shall not covet your neighbor's property.

The Catholic and Lutheran division of the Commandments follows that of St. Augustine (354-430 A.D.); the Jews and Protestants follow the division of Philo (? 40 B.C.-40 A.D.) and Josephus (37-100 A.D. ?). Some of the Fathers of the Church also adopted the latter division.

COMMANDMENT	CATHOLIC AND LUTHERAN DIVISION	JEW AND PROTESTANT DIVISION
I	vv. 2-6	vv. 2-3
II	v. 7	vv. 4-6
III	vv. 8-11	v. 7
IV	v. 12	vv. 8-11
V	v. 13	v. 12
VI	v. 14	v. 13
VII	v. 15	v. 14
VIII	v. 16	v. 15
IX	v. 17 a	v. 16
X	v. 17 b	v. 17

Table 3. THE DIVISION OF THE COMMANDMENTS BASED ON EX 20,1-17

XVI. PROHIBITION OF IMAGES : EX 20,4

The prohibition of images was aimed against the making of images of Yahweh such as those used by the pagans in their worship. It probably also contained a deeper meaning: the Lord is not a god who can be limited to one place in an image. Although the Hebrews often spoke about the Lord in anthropomorphic ways they did not make an image to depict Him.

XVII. THE GOLDEN CALF : EX 32

There are three possible views regarding the meaning of the golden calf: (1) it was an idol in the strict sense; (2) it was a pedestal, like the ones found in Canaan, on which the divine image stood. The Hebrews, however, did not put any image on it—the Lord remained invisible. (3) It was a commonly accepted symbol of divinity among the people of the Orient; therefore, the Hebrews were using it as a symbol of the Lord and they were adoring Yahweh under this form. It is very probable that the Hebrews followed the second meaning. Yet the danger of falling into idolatry would always be present, even if that view or the third one were followed. Therefore, the reaction of Moses is understandable.[17]

XVIII. THE CHARACTER OF MOSES

The figure of Moses dominates the book of Exodus. We have pointed out that various traditions grew up in ancient Israel concerning this great liberator and mediator with the Lord. All the traditions testify to the important role that Moses played in the plan of God, particularly the influence he exercised as the groups of Jews who left Egypt were fashioned into the nation Israel. There is absolutely no evidence to support earlier critical theories that were skeptical about the very existence of Moses.

Even today, however, there are those who are skeptical about the early traditions of Israel. One important source of skepticism is the school of Albrecht Alt and Martin Noth, which is probably the most important non-Catholic school of history writing. It reduces the figure of Moses to the vanishing point. He is not the "great link" that ties the themes of the Pentateuch together. He had no original part in the Exodus from Egypt and the Covenant at Sinai. Alt and Noth hold that the ultimate basis for the Mosaic tradition is a grave where Moses was buried. All that can be said with certitude about Moses is that he died. The Alt-Noth school is very influential. Its position should be known, at least in summary fashion, and answers to its views should be part of the intelligent Christian's equipment.[18]

---

[17] Albright, *From the Stone Age to Christianity,* pp. 298-301.

[18] For a critique of the School of Alt and Noth see John Bright, *Early Israel in Recent History Writing* (London: SCM Press Ltd., 1956), pp. 34-55, 79-110. Noth's views may be seen in his work, *The History of Israel,* rev. trans. P. R. Ackroyd, 2d ed (New York: Harper & Row, Publishers, Inc., 1960), and *Exodus, A. Commentary,* trans. J. S. Bowden (Philadelphia: The Westminster Press, 1962).

Heinisch draws the following portrait of Moses:

> He never used his office for personal aggrandizement. The prospect of
> becoming the father of a great nation did not allure him, and when God
> revealed his impending death, his first thought centered upon those who
> had been confided to his care. That he was not permitted to enter the
> land of his fathers grieved him intensely, but it did not overwhelm him
> —he continued to fulfill his duty. True, he was on the verge of despair
> and wished to die when the people whom God had flooded with miracles
> failed to trust in divine providence during a passing need, but even then
> he did not cast off the burden which God had placed upon his shoulders.
> Only once did he fall, and that not through selfishness or lack of a spirit
> of sacrifice, but by believing God's patience, which had repeatedly for-
> given the people, had reached its limits. . . . The great tragedy was
> that he found himself almost constantly at odds with his people, a peo-
> ple whom he loved so intensely that he would willingly have sacrificed
> his life for them. They simply were unable to appreciate his religious
> stature. Consequently he lived isolated in greatness, even as he died in
> solitude. . . . Moses was the greatest of the Old Testament prophets. . . .
> He, the founder of the old covenant, was privileged to appear at the
> transfiguration of the One destined to inaugurate the new covenant. He
> had prefigured the Savior as prophet, as law-giver, as mediator, as in-
> tercessor, as miracle worker, as a good shepherd ready to lay down his
> life for those confided to his care. As a martyr to a lofty mission, he
> suffered innocently, receiving no thanks in return for his oblation.[19]

During the second century B.C. the inspired author of the book of Sirach
(Ecclesiasticus) wrote the following testimonial to Moses:

> From him (Jacob) was to spring the man
>   who won the favor of all:
> Dear to God and men,
>   MOSES, whose memory is held in benediction.
> God's honor devolved upon him,
>   and the Lord strengthened him with fearful powers;
> God wrought swift miracles at his words
>   and sustained him in the king's presence.
> He gave him the Commandments for his people,
>   and revealed to him his glory.
> For his trustworthiness and meekness
>   God selected him from all mankind;
> He permitted him to hear his voice,
>   and led him into the cloud,
> Where, face to face, he gave the Commandments,
>   the law of life and understanding,
> That he might teach his precepts to Jacob
>   his judgments and decrees to Israel.
>   *Sir 45,1-5*

[19] Heinisch, *History of the Old Testament*, pp. 107-108.

XIX. THE EXODUS AND THE CHRISTIAN

Christian tradition has always seen the events of the Exodus as types and shadows of the realities of the New Testament. Jesus himself taught this relationship when, for example, he compared Himself, "the Bread that has come down from Heaven," with the Manna that was eaten by the people during the sojourn in the desert (Jn 6). The inspired literature of the New Testament, the writings of Christian Patrology, and the Liturgy of the Church are all permeated with this awareness.[20]

Before presenting a few examples from these three areas, it is important that we understand correctly what is meant by typology. It is the name given to the relationships that exist between the Old and New Testaments. Few have synthesized the aspects of this question as well as Daniélou:

> That the realities of the Old Testament are figures of those of the New is one of the principles of biblical theology. This science of the similitudes between the two Testaments is called *typology*. And here we would do well to remind ourselves of its foundation, for this is to be found in the Old Testament itself. At the time of the Capitivity, the prophets announced to the people of Israel that in the future God would perform for their benefit deeds analogous to, and even greater than those He had performed in the past. So there would be a new Deluge, in which the sinful world would be annihilated, and a few men, a 'remnant,' would be preserved to inaugurate a new humanity; there would be a new Exodus in which, by His power, God would set mankind free from its bondage to idols; there would be a new Paradise into which God would introduce the people He had redeemed. These prophecies constitute a primary typology that might be called eschatological, for the prophets saw these future events as happening at the end of time.
>
> The New Testament, therefore, did not invent typology, but simply showed that it was fulfilled in the person of Jesus of Nazareth. With Jesus, in fact, these events of the end, of the fullness of time, are now accomplished. He is the New Adam with whom the time of the Paradise of the future has begun. In Him is already realized that destruction of the sinful world of which the Flood was the figure. In Him is accomplished the true Exodus which delivers the People of God from the tyranny of the demon. Typology was used in the preaching of the apostles as an argument to establish the truth of their message, by showing that Christ continues and goes beyond the Old Testament: 'Now all

[20] M. E. Boismard, "Exodus: The March to God," *The God of Israel, The God of Christians*, pp. 219-29; Jacques Guillet, "Themes of the Exodus—the March Through the Desert," *Themes of the Bible*, trans, Albert J. LaMothe, Jr. (Notre Dame: Fides Publishers Association, 1960), pp. 1-19; Barnabas M. Ahern, C.P., "The Exodus, Then and Now," *The Bridge*, I (1955), 53-74: Jean Daniélou S.J., *The Bible and the Liturgy*, pp. 86-98, and by the same author, *From Shadows to Reality*, pp. 153-201.

these things happened to them as a type and, they were written for our correction' (I Cor 10,11). This is what St. Paul calls the *consolatio Scripturarum* (Rom 15,4).

But these eschatological times are not only those of the life of Jesus, but of the Church as well. Consequently, the eschatological typology of the Old Testament is accomplished not only in the person of Christ, but also in the Church. Besides Christological typology, therefore, there exists a sacramental typology, and we find it in the New Testament. The Gospel of St. John shows us that the manna was a figure of the Eucharist; the first Epistle of St. Paul to the Corinthians that the crossing of the Red Sea was a figure of Baptism; the first Epistle of St. Peter that the Flood was also a figure of Baptism. This means, furthermore, that the sacraments carry on in our midst the *mirabilia,* the great works of God in the Old Testament and the New: for example, the Flood, the Passion and Baptism show us the same divine activity as carried out in three different eras of sacred history, and these three phases of God's action are all ordered to the Judgment at the end of time.[21]

The question of the typological sense of Scripture is one that is being discussed a great deal among Catholic and non-Catholic scholars. It has to be approached carefully lest we strain to find hidden resemblances between everything in the Old and New Testaments. Exaggerations are the unfortunate consequences of the use of a good thing by the incompetent. But the basic premise of typology is valid : there is in certain Old Testament persons and events a prefiguring of a person or event in the New Testament. Moreover, as the Old Covenant prepared for the New, so the New prepares for the final stage of the History of Salvation, which will be initiated at the Parousia. Among these stages in the Plan of God there is a unity which is revealed and understood gradually.

A. THE BOOKS OF THE NEW TESTAMENT

1. The Gospel of St. Matthew contains many allusions to *Jesus as the new Israel* or *new Moses* who leads His people through a new Exodus. For example, like Moses, Jesus went up the mountain and remained there for forty days and nights (Mt 4,2; Ex 24,18; 34,28). The temptations and victories of Jesus over the devil are presented with texts from the book of Deuteronomy which deal with the temptations of the Hebrews during the years of wandering after the Exodus from Egypt (Mt 4; Dt 8,3; 6,16; 5,9); Jesus the Legislator gives the Charter of the New People while on a mount, recalling the events of Mt. Sinai when Moses received the Old Law and gave it to the people (Mt 5; Ex 20).

---

[21] Jean Daniélou, S.J., *The Bible and the Liturgy,* pp. 4-5. See also Walter J. Burghardt, S.J., "On Early Christian Exegesis," *Theological Studies,* XI (March, 1950), 78-116.

2. The Gospel of St. John also presents the life of Jesus in the framework of the Exodus.

> From the beginning in the Prologue, the Word appears as the Shekinah, the abode of Yahweh's glory, which dwelt in the midst of the people in the desert (Ex 40:36). Then he reveals himself as the serpent lifted up in the desert and healing those who looked upon it (3:14) as the manna coming down from heaven and healing God's people (4:31-33), as the spring which gushed forth from the rock for the benefit of those dwelling in tents (7:37-38), as the pillar of fire which followed the people (8:12), and as the Paschal Lamb whose blood washed away the sins of the world (1:29; 19:36).[22]

Judaism for a long time looked upon the Manna as something which had an eschatological significance; just as God nourished the people during the Exodus so He would do the same when the new Exodus would happen. As a matter of fact, rabbinic literature contains evidence that at the time of Jesus men thought that the Messiah would repeat the wonder of the Manna. It is with this in mind that we ought to read the sixth chapter of the Gospel of St. John in which Jesus evidently connects the Manna of the Exodus with both the Message which He came to proclaim, "the Gospel of Salvation," and the Food which would be His flesh and blood. Two themes are presented in Jn 6, the sapiential (Wisdom; Message), and the sacramental (Holy Eucharist).

3. The other books of the New Testament also give evidence of such relationships. St. Paul, writing to the Corinthians, calls the crossing of the sea and the gushing of water from the rock things which were "examples to us" (I Cor 10,1-11). He also declared that "Christ, our passover, has been sacrificed" (I Cor 5,7). St. Peter spoke in terms of the Exodus when he instructed the Christians concerning their dignity and obligations (I Pt 1,13-20; 2,1-10).

B. CHRISTIAN PATROLOGY

The early Christian writers, particularly the Fathers of the Church, frequently taught that the Old Testament is fulfilled in the New. St. Augustine coined a phrase which has often been quoted in this regard: "In the Old Testament, the New is concealed, and in the New the Old is revealed."

The documents of Christian Patrology reveal frequent uses of the themes from the Exodus when they speak of Jesus, the Church, and the Sacraments in which the power of God continues to manifest itself among His people. Here are a few examples.

1. St. Justin Martyr (*ca.* 100-165), the most important of the Greek

---

[22] Jean Daniélou, S.J., *From Shadows to Reality,* trans. Dom Wulstan Hibbe d (Westminister, Md.: The Newman Press, 1960), p. 161.

apologists of the second century and one of the greatest personalities of ancient Christian literature said:

> Those who were saved in Egypt, were saved by the blood of the Pasch, with which they anointed doorposts and lintels. For the Pasch was Christ, who was later immolated. And as the blood of the Pasch saved those who were in Egypt, so the blood of Christ was to preserve from death those who have believed in Him.
>
> *Dialogue with Trypho*

2. Tertullian (*ca* 155-220), who, except for St. Augustine, is the most important and original ecclesiastical writer in Latin, wrote:

> When the people were set free from the violence of the Egyptian king by crossing through water, it was water that exterminated the king himself with his entire force. What figure is more manifestly fulfilled in the sacrament of Baptism? The nations are set free from the world by means of water; and they leave behind the devil, their old tyrant, overwhelmed in the water.
>
> *On Baptism*

3. St. Cyril of Jerusalem (315-386), when writing about Baptism, gave a summary of what happened when Moses led the people out of Egypt, and then said:

> There, we have Moses sent by God into Egypt; here, Christ, sent by His Father to the world; there, that Moses might lead an oppressed people out of Egypt; here, that Christ might free a world oppressed by the burden of sin; there, the blood of the lamb turned aside the destroying angel; here, the blood of the Lamb without blemish is the refuge from demons. The first tyrant kept pursuing the ancient people even to the sea, and now the reckless, shameless demon-prince of wickedness has followed you even to the running waters of salvation. The first tyrant was drowned in the sea, and this one disappears in the waters of salvation.
>
> *On the Mysteries*

4. *St. Ambrose* (333-397) relates the Manna to the Holy Eucharist:

> The manna that God sent down on the people was a great marvel. The heavens nourished them with daily food, as it is written. 'Man ate the bread of angels.' Nevertheless, those who ate this bread died in the desert. But this nourishment that you receive, the Bread descended from heaven, communicates to you the substance of eternal life. It is the Body of Christ. As the light is greater than the shadow, the truth than the figure, so the Body of the Creator is greater than the manna from heaven.
>
> *On the Mysteries*

5. *St. Augustine* (354-430) made the following observation:

> Even as the earth was cleansed by the flood from the iniquity of sinners
> who were then destroyed in the water, while the good escaped by means
> of the wood (of the Ark), so God's people as they went forth from
> Egypt found a way through the waters by which their enemies were
> completely destroyed. And here, too, the mystery of the wood was not
> lacking. For Moses struck the sea with a rod that this miracle might
> be wrought. Both are symbols of Baptism, whereby the faithful pass over
> into a new life but their sins like the enemies are totally blotted out. But
> even more openly was Christ's Passion figured in the case of that people
> when they were commanded to kill and eat a lamb, and to mark with
> its blood their doorposts, to celebrate this rite every year, and to call it
> the Lord's Passover. Most distinctly, indeed, does the prophecy say of
> our Lord Jesus Christ that 'He was led as a sheep to be sacrificed.' And
> with the sign of His Passion and Cross, you today are to be signed and
> sealed upon your forehead, as it were upon a doorpost; and so are all
> Christians signed and sealed.
>
> *First Catechetical Instruction*

6. Theodoret (393-466), one of the authors of the Eastern Church, said:

> When the Egyptians pursued the Hebrews, the latter by passing through
> the Red Sea escaped the savage cruelty of the pursuers. The sea is the
> type of the baptismal font, the cloud of the Holy Spirit, and Moses of
> Christ our Saviour, the staff is a type of the Cross; Pharaoh of the devil
> and the Egyptians of the fallen angels; manna of the divine food and the
> water from the rock of the Saviour's blood. Just as they enjoyed a won-
> derful refreshment coming from a miraculous source, after they had
> passed through the Red Sea, so we, after the saving waters of Baptism,
> share in the divine mysteries.
>
> *Commentary on the Exodus*

C. THE LITURGY

The Mass, the Christian Pasch, is the sacramental re-presentation of the
saving-events in the life of Jesus—His Passion-Death-Resurrection-Ascension
—which were typified in the saving-events of the Exodus when Yahweh
acted for His People.

The Liturgy often makes use of quotations or themes from Exodus. Its
prayers speak of the relationship that exists between Moses-Exodus-Jews and
Jesus-Salvation-Christians. The Liturgical texts for Holy Week are filled with
this relationship. For example, the Reproaches that are sung during the
Adoration of the Cross on Good Friday: "O my people . . . because I led
you out of the land of Egypt, you have prepared a cross for your saviour;

OLD TESTAMENT	NEW TESTAMENT
Moses, the Liberator	Jesus, The Liberator
The Hebrews	The Christians
Captivity in Egypt	Bondage of sin
Passover Meal	Holy Eucharist: Mass
Unblemished lamb	Jesus, the Lamb of God
Blood of lamb on doorposts	Blood of Jesus; Sign of Cross on forehead of the newly baptized.
Pharaoh and Egyptians	Devil and fallen angels
Crossing of Sea	Baptism
Cloud by day; fire by night	Holy Spirit
Water from the rock	Blood of Jesus
Manna	Holy Eucharist: Communion
Promised Land	Church; Heaven

Table 4. TYPOLOGY OF THE EXODUS IN PATRISTIC WRITINGS

because I led you through the desert for forty years, and fed you with manna, and brought you into a land exceedingly good, you have prepared a cross for your savior. . . ."

The lessons read during the Vigil also make use of the Exodus theme: Second Lesson (Ex 14,24-31; 15,1); Third Lesson (Is 4,2-6); and, Fourth Lesson (Dt 31,22-30).

The great Easter song, the *Exultet,* sung during the Paschal Vigil, reminds us of the following: "This is the paschal feast in which the true lamb is slain, whose blood hallows the doorposts of the faithful. This is the night on which you brought our forefathers, the children of Israel, in the flight from Egypt, through the Red Sea. This is the night in which the light of the pillar of fire destroyed the darkness of sin. . . ."

Notice how the text chosen for the Epistle of Easter Sunday teaches the Passover-Easter relationship: "Brethren: purge out the old leaven, that you may be a new dough, as you really are without leaven. For Christ, our Passover, has been sacrificed. Therefore, let us keep festival, not with the old leaven, nor with the leaven of malice and wickedness, but with the un-

THE LITURGY OF THE PASCHAL MYSTERY

THE JEWISH PASSOVER		"DO THIS IN REMEMBRANCE OF ME"	
The First Passover of the Jews	The Annual Commemoration (Seder)	The Passover of Jesus the Christ	Liturgical Commemorations Made by the Mystical Body —the Church
The Hebrews were in bondage in Egypt. They called upon God for help. Moses was sent to deliver them. He was to be their Liberator and Prophet. Ex 1-11	Recalls the original event.	The slavery of the Hebrews was nothing compared to the condition of mankind in sin. The Father sent His Son to be the Liberator of Mankind. "The Law was given through Moses; grace and truth came through Jesus Christ." Jn 1,17	The Sacrament of Baptism delivers us from the bondage of sin and admits us to membership in the Church—The People of God. The Risen Christ is our Liberator and Head.
Moses, obeying the commandment of the Lord, ordered each family to prepare a meal—roasted lamb, unleavened bread, and bitter herbs. Ex 12,1-28	Recalls the original event. Ex 12-13 Lv 23,4-14	Jesus observed the Passover with His disciples. His last Passover Supper was during the week after His triumphal entry into Jerusalem. I Cor 11,23-30; Mt 26; Mk 14; Lk 22	Each year the Liturgy of Holy Week and each day the Liturgy of the Mass are the representations of the Supper, Death, and Resurrection of the Lord. We do this in remembrance of Him "until He comes" at the Parousia.

Table 5. THE LITURGY OF THE PASCHAL MYSTERY

leavened bread of sincerity and truth" (I Cor 5,7-8). The liturgical texts during the Easter Season also contain many allusions and texts concerning the Exodus theme fulfilled in Jesus.

> It is truly right and necessary, it is our duty and our salvation, to praise thee, O Lord, at all times, but with greatest jubilation on this night (day) above all, when Christ our Passover was sacrificed. He is the true Lamb who took away the sins of the world. By dying, he destroyed our death; by rising, he restored life to us.
>
> *The Easter Preface*

THE LITURGY OF THE PASCHAL MYSTERY

THE JEWISH PASSOVER		"DO THIS IN REMEMBRANCE OF ME"	
The First Passover of the Jews	The Annual Commemoration (Seder)	The Passover of Jesus the Christ	Liturgical Commemorations Made by the Mystical Body —the Church
During the night the Lord "passed over" Egypt; the first-born of the Egyptians died; the People of God was saved because of the blood of the lamb. Ex 12,29-30	Recalls the original event.	On Calvary, the offering of the true Lamb of God, Unspotted and Undefiled (I Pt 1,18-19), brought salvation to mankind. "Christ, our passover has been sacrificed." I Cor 5,7 Mt 27 Mk 15;23;19 Lk 23; Jn 19	We make our Christian Passover united with the Risen Christ in the Sacraments of Baptism and Holy Eucharist.
The Hebrews left Egypt—Moses was their leader. The Lord guided them in the "column of cloud" and "column of fire." The Lord led them through the sea, fed them with manna, and brought them to the Promised Land. Ex 13-16; Dt 31-34	Recalls the original event.	The victorious Passover of Jesus from death to life: the Resurrection of the Lord. I Cor 15; Rom 4,25	Our liberation from the slavery of sin and our progress toward the Promised Land, Heaven, are made effective by the Risen Christ who acts in the Sacramental Liturgy of the Church.

Table 5. THE LITURGY OF THE PASCHAL MYSTERY

> To the Paschal Victim
>> let Christians offer a sacrifice of praise.
> The Lamb redeemed the sheep.
>> Christ, sinless reconciled sinners to the Father.
>>> *The Easter Sequence*

> At the Lamb's high feast we sing
>> Praise to our victorious King,
> Who has washed us in the tide

Flowing from his pierced side
Praise we him whose love divine
Gives the guests his Blood for wine,
Gives his Body for the feast,
Love the Victim, Love the Priest.
Where the Paschal blood is poured
Death's dark Angel sheathes his sword;
Israel's hosts triumphant go
Through the wave that drowns the foe.
Christ, the Lamb whose Blood was shed,
Paschal victim, Paschal bread;
With sincerity and love
Eat we Manna from above.

Vesper Hymn during Easter Season

The liturgy of Benediction affirms the relationship when it has the Priest say: "You have given them bread from heaven," and the people answer: "Containing within itself all sweetness."

eight

THE BOOK OF LEVITICUS

THIS BOOK is called in Hebrew "And He Called." It is also known among the Jews as The Law of Priests. The Septuagint called it Leviticon and from that word is derived the title given to it in our Bible, Leviticus. This Book is the ritual-book of the Old Testament and is the best example of the Priestly Tradition (P). It contains a great many laws governing the way in which sacrifice was offered to God. It manifests a great concern for liturgical, chronological, and genealogical matters. Many of the laws on biology and hygiene make us feel a little uncomfortable, but it must be remembered that this book embraces the whole of human life, and the Israelites considered these laws an integral part of man's relationship with Yahweh. Leviticus regulates the life of the people chosen by God to be a "priestly kingdom and a holy people" (Ex 19,6).

II. STYLE

The style of the book is tedious and often dull. The study of Leviticus, however, helps us to understand the contents of many of the other books of the Bible, and particularly some of the references in the New Testament. For example, compare Lk 2,21-39 with Lv 12,8 and Mk 1,40-45 with Lv 14.

III. HISTORICAL BACKGROUND

Leviticus can be understood only against the background of Biblical history whose roots are embedded deep in the period of Moses, the great legislator of the Hebrew religion. The religion had five great periods of development, all of which contributed to the final formulation of the laws and ritual found in the book.[1]

[1] See Carroll Stuhlmueller, C.P., *The Book of Leviticus* (New York: The Paulist Press, 1960), pp. 6-7.

A. PERIOD OF MOSES: ABOUT 1280-1220 B.C.

The Hebrews were nomads living in the desert. During this period blood sacrifices were of primary importance, agricultural offerings played a secondary role. In order to worship God and acknowledge their dependence on Him the people offered sacrifice of livestock. They gave to God what was their mainstay.

B. PERIOD OF SETTLEMENT IN CANAAN : FROM ABOUT 1220 B.C.

The settlement in Canaan introduced a social structure which made necessary laws covering the various aspects of life. During the period of settlement, the Mosaic spirit gave a religious orientation to the various elements that were introduced. Religion remained a strong force in the lives of the people. In this period unbloody sacrifices became more common; some of the Canaanite feasts were adopted and transformed into feasts in honor of Yahweh.

C. PERIOD OF THE REFORM : 622 B.C.

After years of religious and moral decline, much of it due to the political and religious schism that occurred after the death of Solomon (931 B.C.), a reform was attempted by King Josia. He zealously worked to destroy the pagan influences that had crept into the life of the people and he tried to centralize worship at Jerusalem. The reform was aimed at recalling the people to fidelity to the Covenant made with Yahweh. It pursued policies that would reinvigorate the Mosaic heritage.

D. PERIOD OF THE BABYLONIAN EXILE : 587-538 B.C.

The faith of the exiles was protected and deepened by the teaching of prophets, especially Ezechiel and Second Isaia, so called because he is the anonymous author of chapters 40-55 of the book of Isaia.

E. PERIOD AFTER THE EXILE : AFTER 538 B.C.

This period witnessed the final codification of Priestly legislation. Now life revolved more and more around the restored Temple in Jerusalem. During the last few centuries preceding the Christian era, the Temple became more and more the focal point of the life of the people. Minute laws were written to regulate the worship performed there.

Throughout the five periods of development, laws were gradually added which were authentic expressions of Mosaic traditions. The new laws that were inserted into the ancient code were said to be spoken by God to Moses and his brother Aaron. This was the literary device used by the authors to bring home a truth of great importance: the laws, although later than the time of Moses, are reflections of his spirit and developments based on the foundation he established.

IV. SACRIFICES IN ISRAEL : LV 1-5; 15

The four chief sacrifices offered to God are mentioned in this Book: (1) the Holocaust, the sacrifice in which the victim was completely burnt on the altar; (2) the Cereal Offering, a sacrifice which presupposes agricultural life; (3) the Peace Offering, in which the choice parts belong to the Lord and the rest are consumed by those who offer the sacrifice (this included a sacred meal and was sometimes called a "Communion Sacrifice"); and (4) the Sin and Guilt Offerings, which were offered to remove sin, a state of uncleanness due to a moral offense but in many instances due merely to inadvertence. The Israelites considered transgressions due to inadvertence as violations of that cleanliness which everyone ought to have before the Lord.[2]

The most conspicuous feature of the sacrificial system of the Israelites was union with God. They believed that by means of the external worship they could express their internal feelings toward the Lord. Through the various rites, a gift was given to God; He received it, took away the guilt of the people, and became united with them. The ancient Hebrews knew that all things belonged to God; they were not so naive as to think that they were giving Him something which He did not already possess. "All things are thine: and we have given thee what we received from thy hand" (I Chr 29,14). By depriving themselves of the gifts and giving them to God, the people believed that He in turn would bind Himself to them. It is axiomatic that love seeks union. The Israelite sacrifices were motivated by a love which expressed itself in a "giving" which, it was hoped, would be returned by God.

It is true that there were times when the sacrifices were nothing more than external acts of ritual. It was then that the prophets violently attacked the sacrifices of the people (Jer 6,20; Am 5,21-27; Os 6,6). Some have seized upon these texts in order to discredit the whole notion of external sacrifices in religion. That such a conclusion is unwarranted may be seen from the contexts in which the denunciations are found and the historical milieu which formed the broader context of the prophetic activity. Although there is evidence of a prophetic polemic against sacrifices, we have to keep in mind that there was a continued insistence on the role of the Temple in the life of the Israelites, and the Temple implied sacrifices. The prophets denounced *externalism* and *formalism* in worship; they taught that God desired love and

---

[2] A detailed study of the origin, history, and religious significance of sacrifice in ancient Israel is in De Vaux, *op. cit.*, pp. 415-56.

knowledge of Him rather than sacrifices and holocausts which were only empty ritual; obedience is better than sacrifies so offered (Os 6,6; I Sm 15,22).

> Since this people draws near with words only and honors me with their lips alone, though their hearts are far from me, and their reverence for me has become routine observance of the precepts of men, therefore I will again deal with this people in surprising and wondrous fashion.
>
> *Is 29,13-14*

V. FEASTS IN ISRAEL : LV 23

The four traditions in the Pentateuch contain a calendar of the great religious feasts celebrated by the Hebrews: Exodus 23,14-17 (Elohist), Exodus 34,18-23 (Yahwist), Deuteronomy 16,1-16 (Deuteronomic), and Leviticus 23 (Priestly). To these feasts the liturgical regulations found in Numbers 28-29 have to be connected. As mentioned earlier, the religious life of the people went through a long period of development. Evidences of this are found in the fact that the ritual becomes more precisely formulated from text to text. However, the three great feasts of the Hebrews remained those which were mentioned in Ex 23. These feasts were so important that all adult males were to gather at the Sanctuary for their celebration.[3]

1. *Feast of the Unleavened Bread and Passover.*   This was observed in the spring and it commemorated the liberation of the people at the time of the Exodus (Ex 13,8-9). The feast had a very complicated history; at first, it was not even looked upon as the main feast. It is possible that the Israelites adopted the feast of the Unleavened Bread from the Canaanites, among whom it was observed as an agricultural celebration. Since the Passover was celebrated during the same month that the feast of the Unleavened Bread was observed, the two feasts were combined, and made to commemorate that memorable springtime when the "outstretched arm of Yahweh" brought the Israelites out of Egypt. The Deuteronomic editor refers to the unleavened bread eaten during the feast as the "bread of affliction," a memorial of the period of suffering during the Exodus (Dt 16,3).

2. *Feast of the Harvest.*   This was the second great feast of the year; it was also called the "Feast of Weeks" (Ex 34,22) and the "Feast of the First Fruits" (Nu 28,26). The ritual observed for this feast is found in Lv 23,15-21; it was celebrated seven weeks after the first cereals had been cut. It was probably adopted from the Canaanites after the Israelites had settled in Canaan. Once there were settled farmers, there was need for a feast on which the people would offer thanks for the harvest. This was done on the fiftieth day reckoned from the day after the sabbath

---

[3] *Ibid.,* pp. 468-517, presents a complete study of the liturgical calendar and the feasts.

on which the first sheaf was presented to the Lord. The Greek name for the feast was Pentecost. In time, the feast was considered a commemoration of the promulgation of the Law at Sinai.

It was on the occasion of this feast that the Holy Spirit was bestowed upon the Church. The Christian feast of Pentecost celebrates that event and the fact that all nations are called into the Church (Acts 2).

3. *Feast of Tents.* This was the most popular of the three annual pilgrimages to the sanctuary. It was celebrated in the autumn after all the fruits of the earth had been harvested and grapes and olives had been pressed. It was a time of great rejoicing and merriment which was carried even to the courtyards of the Temple where the leading men in the community danced and sang while they carried lighted torches.

In Hebrew the feast is called *Sukkoth;* the word means "Huts" and it reminds the people of the ancient custom, followed in Palestine, of making huts out of tree branches in the vineyards and orchards during the harvesting of the produce. In time the feast was related to the Exodus-situation, when the Israelites were obliged to live in "huts." Actually, this is stretching the point a bit, because the Israelites lived in tents not huts during their wanderings in the desert; huts are used by settled people.

This feast is mentioned in the Gospels; for example, in Jn 7 where we are told that Jesus went to Jerusalem for the Feast of Tabernacles, another name for Tents. Knowledge about the feasts of the Old Testament will help us to understand the references to them found in the New Testament.

During the course of Israel's history other feasts were observed: *Rosh Hashanah,* the civil New Year's Day, celebrated during the month of Tishri (September-October); *Purim,* celebrated during the month of Adar (March) to commemorate the deliverance of the people from a massacre (Est 9,21-22); *Hannukka,* or Dedication, celebrated during Kisleu (December) in memory of the re-dedication of the Temple after the Babylonian Exile (I Mc 4,59).

VI. YOM KIPPUR, THE DAY OF ATONEMENT : LV 16

One of the great religious holydays was *Yom Kippur,* also called *Yom hakkippurim.* It had no commemorative significance; its main concern was atonement for sin. It was celebrated during the seventh month, Tishri, as a day of strict fast when the Israelites would examine their consciences and ask for forgiveness. On this day the High Priest, dressed only in a garment of common linen, entered behind the veil which separated the Holy of Holies from the rest of the Meeting Tent, and later the rest of the Temple. He sprinkled blood on the Mercy Seat located over the Ark of the Covenant and pronounced the sacred name *Yahweh;* at the sound of the trumpet blasts the people who were outside fell prostrate to the ground. The scapegoat ceremony, also referred to in Lv 16, symbolized the removal of sin from the community.

The Epistle to the Hebrews refers to the ceremony of Yom Kippur, applying it to the act of reparation of Christ the High Priest which made perfect atonement for mankind's sins (Heb 9,3-17).

VII. THE "LEX TALIONIS" : LV 24,20

Lex = law; *talio,* in juridical language, denotes a punishment similar and equal to the injury sustained, like for like, retaliation in kind. In the book of Leviticus the *lex talionis* appears in the following words: "Limb for limb, eye for eye, tooth for tooth." The Code of Hammurabi of the eighteenth century B.C. contains applications of this same law. For example: "If a man ruins the eye of a free man, they shall destroy his eye"; "If he breaks the bone of another, his own bone shall be broken"; "If a man knocks out the tooth of another man of his own rank, they shall knock out one of his teeth." [4]

The *lex talionis* was intended not merely to enforce rigorous justice, but also to prevent unjust penalties. Its spirit was not one of merciless revenge; it was intended to counteract the harsh infliction of penalties which were often motivated by the spirit of the old song of Lamech : "I kill a man for wounding me, a youth for bruising me. If Cain shall be avenged sevenfold, Lamech seventy times sevenfold" (Gn 4,23-24).

VIII. LEVITICUS AND CHRISTIANS

Much of the ritual in the Old Testament is foreign to our mentality and we are tempted to wonder about the real importance of many acts involved in it. The rubrics concerning the choice of animals, their slaughter, and the blood ritual are enough to make us feel grateful that we are living in the period of the New Covenant.

Christ's unique sacrifice has made valueless the ceremonial of the Old Law, but the demands for purity and holiness found in it, and particularly in Leviticus, are lessons that will always be valid. The spirit of Leviticus is one of unreserved consecration to the all-holy and almighty God. It was this spirit that motivated the approaches to sacrifice : "Be holy, for I, the Lord your God, am holy" (Lv 19,2). We must detach ourselves from everything that is unclean in order to be worthy to serve and worship God as new men who have been "created according to God in justice and holiness of truth" (Eph 4,24).

---

[4] The Code of Hammurabi and its similarities with the laws of Israel are treated in Jack Finegan, *Light From the Ancient Past* (Princeton: Princeton University Press, 1959), pp. 58-62. See also Pritchard, *op. cit.,* pp. 163-80.

nine

THE BOOK OF NUMBERS

I. THE NAME

THE FOURTH BOOK of the Bible contains a great emphasis on quantitative elements, numbers, censuses, and sizes. There is particular concern for exactitude, statistical regulations, genealogies, and chronological material. In the Hebrew Bible this book is called "In the Desert" or "In the Wilderness" because it contains the story of the wanderings of the Israelites in the wilderness during the traditional forty years between the time of the deliverance from Egypt and the entrance into the Promised Land. The Septuagint translators, intrigued by the emphasis on statistics, numbers, and all kinds of calculations, called it Arithmoi, plural of the Greek word for "number," *arithmos*. Hence the title of the book in our Bible.

II. ORIGIN AND PURPOSE

The book was not written all at once. It is the result of a compilation of several sources containing material from different periods of Israel's history. Scholars are of the opinion that the book shows the influence of the Priestly Tradition in its present form although it contains much ancient material from the Yahwist and Elohist traditions. It is concerned with the history of the People of God from the point in time at which the book of Exodus broke off to the conquest of Transjordan. It presents its teachings theologically; it is not merely the presentation of events according to the standards of modern historiography. It is *sacred history,* the account of the presence of Yahweh in the life and events, victories and setbacks, of the Chosen People. It is the record of the continuing love of God for His People.

III. THE SHEKINAH

This was the name given to the presence of Yahweh manifested by a luminous cloud. In Nu 9 it is mentioned as the cloud that covered the Dwelling, the Tent of the Commandments. This is the same mysterious Presence of the

Lord mentioned in Ex 13,21-22 and 40,36-38. The Cloud is used as a symbol of Yahweh's presence; He is guide and protector. The Lord is with His people by day and night. Throughout the Pentateuch, this Presence is signified by various manifestations. The Yahwist tradition prefers to speak of the "column of fire" (Ex 13,21-22); the Elohist prefers the "heavy cloud" (Ex 19,16); the Priestly tradition associates the "glory of the Lord" with the cloud (Ex 24,16-18).[1]

IV. THE SIN OF MOSES : NU 20,7-13

The context of this event does not give any indication of the precise nature of the sin of Moses and Aaron. The sin does not appear to be the fact that Moses struck the rock twice, as is sometimes affirmed. A careful reading of the text points to a situation where Moses and Aaron upbraided the people. Moses, angry at the people, struck the rock and the water came forth. God had intended the incident as an expression of His divine power and mastery over nature, and of His constant providence over His people. It turned, however, into an occasion for denunciation instead of one of joyful revelation of Yahweh's power. If we see the incident in this light, we are able to understand why God punished Moses and Aaron. They had frustrated the plan of God.

V. THE STORY OF THE TALKING DONKEY : NU 22,22-35

The Pentateuch is not a reference manual for those who seek answers to the problems found in the study of the natural sciences. Its purpose is theological. It is the collection of the traditions of the People of God, and provided the Israelites with a religious interpretation of the events which occurred in their history since the promises made to Abraham. Geology, anthropology, and biology are important sciences, but theology, the science about God, is far more important and necessary to man. At least, so thought the ancient Hebrews, who knew little if anything of what we would call the "natural sciences" but who had a deep conviction of the existence and providence of Yahweh. They sought the deeper religious aspect of facts, figures, persons, and events. All this has been emphasized in the preceding sections of this book but it is important to recall these fundamental points now that we are to consider one of the most amusing incidents in the Old Testament, the talking donkey of Balaam, the famous soothsayer of the Ancient Near East.[2]

According to the Biblical text, the Hebrews had advanced to the plains of

---

[1] The significance of the Shekinah is discussed in Louis Bouyer, *The Meaning of Sacred Scripture,* pp. 98-116.

[2] See Frederick Moriarty, S.J., *The Book of Numbers* (2 parts; New York: The Paulist Press, 1960), II, 7; also David Stanley, S.J., "Balaam's Ass, or a Problem in New Testament Hermeneutics," *The Catholic Biblical Quarterly,* XX (January, 1958), 54-55.

Moab, and Balac the king of the land became alarmed. He called Balaam, his seer, and asked him to curse the advancing Hebrews. After some hesitation, which the text attributes to the intervention of Yahweh, Balaam went on his mission. On the way his donkey behaved strangely. Perhaps, that's putting it mildly. The ass began to speak to its master! After a dialogue between the "intelligent" and the "dumb," the journey continued but the seer was to say only what the Lord permitted.

There have been various interpretations of this part of the book of Numbers. Some, following the lead of St. Augustine, have defended it as a miraculous occurrence. Others see in it an example of a colorful folktale intended to teach a simple but profound lesson in theology.

A careful study of the chapter in which the incident of the talking ass is found reveals that here, as in many other places in the Pentateuch, there is a combination of traditional sources. Scholars are of the opinion that the whole section dealing with Balaam (Nu 22-24) has resulted from the union of Yahwist and Elohist traditions. The first chapter of the Balaam cycle (Nu-22) is essentially Elohist; notice, for example, the use of the divine name Elohim, God, and the generally sophisticated literary tone. The inspired author, however, wove into this material an account taken from the Yahwist tradition. This is evidenced by the switch in the divine names, from Elohim to Yahweh as well as the colorful, anthropomorphic elements which appear (Nu 22,22-35). The author made good use of his literary skill and used another source which would help him bring a message to his readers. We have to be careful about attributing the ridiculous to individuals whom God chose to transmit His message of salvation. This is what we do if we think that the inspired author was a naive, credulous individual who believed in talking animals.

Of course, miracles can happen. A miracle is something done by God outside the order of all created nature. No one would deny that God can make intelligible sounds come out of dumb animals. But it is a longstanding point in Catholic theology that miracles are not to be multiplied. This means that we are not to label as miraculous things which, while beyond the understanding of some individuals, might have some explanation within the order of nature. It is for this reason, backed up by a sound literary criticism of the text in its proper context and understood from the theological viewpoint of the author, that there are Catholic scholars who see the talking donkey incident as something other than a miracle.

Old Testament theology is certain about the power of God who makes use of all creation, the heavens and earth, the animate and inanimate, to bring His message of salvation to mankind. The author of Numbers used a folktale about the enigmatic Balaam, seer of Balac the Moabite, and made him a medium for the communication of a theological truth. The pagans put their trust in soothsayers who imagined that they had power over nature. The

Israelites could only pity the folly of such men who were so deceived as to think that they were powerful against the Lord and His people. The talking-ass incident was a popular story in the literary heritage of the Near East. The inspired author used and adopted it to bring out his religious intentions : the Lord is all-powerful, His plans are stronger than the whims and wares of His enemies. He can even use an ass to bring His Word to those who think they know everything!

ten

THE BOOK OF DEUTERONOMY

I. THE NAME

THE FIFTH BOOK does not have a name in the Hebrew Bible. It is usually called "These are the Words." The Septuagint translators called it *Deuteronomion,* which means "This second Law," and from that word we get the present title. The book contains repetitions of the Law found in the preceding books, and it enlarges the legislation promulgated in them. It is sometimes referred to as "the basic document of Judaism."

II. ORIGIN AND SPIRIT

Deuteronomy was not written all at once. It is the product of a long oral and written transmission. It is very probable that the book, at least in parts, dates from the eighth-seventh century B.C. At that time pieces which had existed separately were gathered and compiled into a single work. The Reform of Josia in 622 B.C. was the occasion of the compilation; the period after the Exile witnessed the formation of the book as it is now. This book is the best example of the Deuteronomic Tradition, which is, basically, legislation presented in a theology of history centered on the love of Yahweh for His people and the obedience which He demands. It is this Deuteronomic "theology of history" that pervades the accounts found in later books like Josue, Judges, Samuel, Kings, and Chronicles. Put very simply, the Deuteronomic view is that every victory experienced by Israel is a reward for fidelity to Yahweh, every setback is a punishment for infidelity; obedience to Yahweh leads to peace and the welfare of the country, disobedience leads to defeat and hardship.

The recurrent theme of the book is God's protecting love for Israel.[1] It

[1] See R. A. F. MacKenzie, S.J., "Deuteronomy," *A Catholic Commentary On Holy Scripture,* pp. 261-63; also Kathryn Sullivan, R.S.C.J., "The Book of Deuteronomy," *God's Word and Work* (Collegeville; The Liturgical Press, 1958), pp. 41-50.

is also the theme developed in the prophetic literature where, for example, Osee uses the imagery of the husband-wife relationship to teach the people of his time the meaning of the love of God, which is gratuitous and long-suffering (Os 1-6).

A profound religious spirit is present in Deuteronomy which is presented as a sort of last will and testament of the great lawgiver, Moses. The book has a strong oratorical style, particularly displayed in the series of discourses in which Moses speaks to the people. Mindful of their weakness and varying moods, he reminds them to obey the commandments of God "loving him and walking in his ways" (Dt 30,16).

III. THE CHOICE OF ISRAEL

William Norman Ewer summarized the view of many people when he wrote the epigram:

> How odd
> Of God
> To choose
> The Jews.

This thought becomes even more provocative when the history of the Chosen People is studied. The book of Deuteronomy attempts an answer to the question: Why did God choose Israel? It is an answer that shows the conviction of the inspired author in the gratuity of Divine election. No one should imagine that he has been chosen because of some intrinsic worth which God found irresistible, so to speak. Divine choice is perfectly free. It is often exercised in favor of those who seemingly are the least worthy. Divine election manifests and proves one thing—the love of God.

> You are a people sacred to the Lord, your God; he has chosen you from all the nations on the face of the earth to be a people peculiarly his own. It was not because you are the largest of all nations that the Lord set his heart on you and chose you, for you are really the smallest of all nations. It was because the Lord loved you and because of his fidelity to the oath he had sworn to your fathers . . .
> *Dt 7,6-8; also 10,15*

But why choose Abraham? The answer to this question is the one we saw in Genesis. God has a plan by which salvation will be made available to all mankind. Eternal in existence, but temporal in execution, this plan had "to begin somewhere" and so it began with Abraham in whom all the nations of the earth shall be blessed (Gn 12,1-3; Eph 1,3-14).[2]

---

[2] Read the comments about the privilege of Divine election and the price that Israel had to pay for it in G. Ernest Wright, *The Old Testament Against Its Environment* (London: SCM Press Ltd., 1950), 46-54.

IV. THE SHEMA : DT 6,4-9

The love God has shown in the choice of the Hebrews and in His continued mercies toward them must be returned. Love requires love. It is this truism that the book of Deuteronomy tries to instill into the people. A synthesis of this important requirement is found in the prayer which believing Jews still recite three times each day. It is called the *Shema* because this is the Hebrew for its first word.

> Hear, O Israel! The Lord is our God, the Lord alone! Therefore, you shall love the Lord, your God, with all your heart, and with all your soul, and with all your strength.
>
> *Dt 6,4*

This prayer should be read in light of the teachings found in Dt 10,12-22; 11,13-21 and Nu 15,37-41. It is the "watchword of Israel" because it is based on the pillars of the Hebrew faith: the unicity of God, the special election of Israel, loyalty to His commandments, belief in Divine Justice, hope in deliverance from enemies. The foundation of true religion is a reverential love of God, and a total commitment to Him shown in absolute conformity to His will.

The instructions found in Dt 6,8-9 and Nu 15,37-41 are the basis for the wearing of the phylacteries and tassels, even mentioned in the Gospels (Mt 23,5). The phylactery is a small box which contains verses from the book of Deuteronomy, and sometimes Exodus. Twice each day it is to be fastened to the left arm and on the forehead, as a reminder of the implications of the Shema. Another custom is the use of the *Mezuzah,* which means "doorpost," but which is a small wooden, metal, or glass case attached to the right doorpost of Jewish homes. It contains a piece of parchment on which the Shema is written and also a few other verses from Deuteronomy. It reminds the Jews of the presence and love of God.

Jesus cited the Shema in response to the question, "Master, which is the greatest commandment in the Law?" (Mt 22,36). He completed his answer with the commandment to love our neighbor; the statement used by Our Lord is from Lv 19,18. Christ taught us the full implications of this twofold love.[3]

V. THE HEBREW CREDO : DT 6,20-25; DT 26,1-19

The passage found in Dt 6,20-25 is a typical example of how the Israelites professed their faith in God. Abstract or theoretical thoughts are absent. Profound commitment to God, based on love, was considered the essential

[3] The concept of love of enemies in the Old Testament is discussed in Heinisch, *Theology of the Old Testament,* pp. 178-80 .

element of faith, and this was necessary because of all that the Lord had done for His people. The *mirabilia Dei,* the wonderful things of the Lord, required a response of total commitment which carried with it a loving obedience to the demands of the law.

The *heart of the Pentateuch* is found in the liturgical ceremony found in Dt 26. Each year the Israelite was commanded to offer to Yahweh a basket of the first fruits of the harvest. On that occasion he would recite a *credo* which recalled the great acts by which Yahweh had delivered His people from Egypt and given them their land. The contents of that *credo* may go back to ancient professions of faith that were recited during the liturgical ceremonies at the Tent housing the Ark of the Covenant. Another example of such Hebrew creeds is in Jos 24,2-13 which shows the influence of the Deuteronomist viewpoint.

VI. COMMAND CONCERNING PAGAN PLACES OF WORSHIP : DT 12

There is an important command given in Dt 12 concerning the destruction of all pagan places. Notice the use of the following expressions: "every place on the high mountains"; "the high places"; "under every leafy tree"; "sacred pillars"; and, "sacred poles." This command was aimed against debased practices that the pagans followed in the worship of their gods and goddesses. In order to appreciate the struggle that Israel would have to engage in against the religion of the people of Canaan it is important that a summary be given of that religion.

The Old Testament usually refers to the religion of the Canaanites as the worship of the Baals and Astartes (Jgs 2,13; 10,6; I Sm 7,4; 12,10). The word *Baal* means "lord" or "owner," and it was used to designate the male deity who was looked upon as the owner of the land and the one who controlled its fertility. That god's female partner or consort was known as *Baalath,* which means "lady." In many cases she is called *Astarte.* The people believed that these deities of fertility were connected with particular localities. Hence one could refer to the many Baals and Astartes. They were as numerous as the cities of the land. It was also possible to look upon these local deities as manifestations of the chief "lord" and "lady" who lived in the heavens. In that case Baal and Astarte were addressed in the singular as cosmic deities.

Since these deities were connected with fertility, the cooperation with the powers of fertility involved the dramatization in the temples of the story of the loves and wars of Baal and Astarte. Besides the dramatizations, a prominent feature of the worship of the Canaanites was sacred prostitution (Dt 23,18) in which the man identified himself with Baal and the woman with Astarte. It was thought that such actions could bring the two deities together in a fertilizing union. The erotic character of Canaanite religion is evident. The worship itself was carried out on hilltops or mountaintops, commonly called the "high places." There were also "sacred groves" where the same rites were performed. The altars of the gods were often surrounded by poles which were called *masseboth*, "sacred pillars" in honor of the male deity, Baal, and *asherat*, "sacred poles" which were wooden posts, probably in the form of a tree, used to represent the goddess, Astarte.

It is in the light of this information that the prohibitions against the "high places" must be understood. The practices of the pagans would continue to be dangerous attractions for the Israelites as they settled in the land of Canaan. The victory over them was not won overnight, as can be seen in the fact that at the time of the Babylonian Exile Ezechiel condemned the "high places" (Ex 6,1-8).

VII. THE HEREM : DT 2,34-35; 3,4-7; 7,2; 20,10-18

What is to be said about those actions of the Hebrews which involved the destruction of the inhabitants of captured cities? Such practices must be judged in the light of the customs and moral standards of the times. It was a common procedure among the ancient Semites to put to death those who belonged to the vanquished enemy. The Israelites acted accordingly. The fact that they attributed their action to a command of God means merely that they, like the other nations, gave a religious meaning to what they did.

On the Stele of Mesha (ruler of Moab during the ninth century B.C.) discovered in 1868 and now kept in the Louvre at Paris, we read that Mesha fought against certain cities in Israel. We are told that he "warred against the city, and I took it, and slew all the people of the city; a spectacle for Chemosh and Moab. . . . And I went by night and fought against it from daybreak to midday. And I took it; I slew all in it, seven thousand (men and boys) and women and (young) girls and slaves; since I made *herem* of them to Astarte Chemosh. And I took from there the objects of Yahweh and carried them to the presence of Chemosh." Chemosh was the god of Moab.[4]

The Israelites were convinced that their destiny demanded the complete destruction of whatever threatened the purity of their monotheism. We must not condone their practice but it must be viewed in the light of prevailing customs. The *herem* or *ban,* as the total destruction of the inhabitants of a captured city was called, practiced by the Israelites underscores the imperfection of Old Testament morality. This is not to say that God is indifferent to the moral conduct of people, particularly His Chosen People. But God chose humans to achieve His purposes and they were not intellectual or moral supermen. Slowly and patiently He educated the ones He chose; gradually, He led them to the full light of the revelation of His Son and His Church from whom the teachings of Christian morality are extended to all men for all time.[5]

[4] The text of the Stele of Mesha, also known as the Moabite Stone, notes and an illustration are in D. Winton Thomas, *op. cit.,* pp. 196-98, also Grollenberg, *Atlas of the Bible,* p. 80.

[5] For a study of the problems connected with the morality of the Old Testament see L. Johnson, "Old Testament Morality," *The Catholic Biblical Quarterly,* XX (January, 1958), 19-25; also Heinisch, *Theology of the Old Testament,* pp. 197-206, and Levie, *The Bible, Word of God in Words of Men,* pp. 240-45.

eleven

FROM THE DESERT TO THE
PROMISED LAND (1250–1030 B.C.)

THE CLANS that left Egypt with Moses were not an ethnically homogeneous group descended from a common ancestor. They were a mixture composed of descendants of the original twelve tribes and foreign elements (Nu 11,4). It was in the desert that these various elements were formed into a single unit having a common destiny. The hard life of the desert with its forced isolation, and the authority of a single leader, slowly but effectively molded the mass of people into a homogeneous unit.

After the events on Mount Sinai, the people of God traveled up the eastern side of the peninsula. A summary of this journey is found in Nu 33 in which the trip is divided into 40 stages, probably an artificial schematic arrangement based on the symbolic number 40. The places mentioned in the final stages of the journey are not mentioned elsewhere in the Bible, and most Biblical scholars hold that it is not possible to identify them definitively. Scholarly research has located Cades, also known as Kardesh, a location in the Negeb about 30 miles southwest of the Dead Sea; now called 'Ain Qadeis. This was an oasis that the Israelites found very attractive after their difficult journey. From this place Moses attempted an invasion of the Promised Land, but the attack met with defeat at Arad, a well-fortified town about 25 miles north of Cades. After this defeat, the Israelites remained in the area of the springs for several years.

Moses then tried a new tactic. The Israelites were related to some of the clans living on the borders of Canaan. These clans were descendants of the original Hebrews who, instead of following Jacob into Egypt had settled outside of Canaan and reached a fairly high level of civilization. Edom and Moab, at the time of the Exodus, had developed a monarchical type of government. Efforts to form an alliance with these peoples failed, however, and the Israelites were forced to continue their wandering for many more years. The time came when the Hebrew tribes found themselves strong enough to try another march to the Promised Land. They made their way in the direction of the Gulf of Aqaba and then moved northwards along the broad valley of the Araba. When they reached the Dead Sea, they veered to the east, bypassing the land of Moab they entered the area north of the Arnon, and finally set up their camp in the plains of Moab. The local rulers of the region between the Arnon and the Jabbok rivers were defeated and some of the Israelites settled in their land.

After the death of Moses, Josue ("Yahweh is Salvation") was commissioned to finish the work begun by the great liberator of the people of God. In the Pentateuch there are almost twenty references to Josue among them, the following: Ex 17,8-9; Ex 24,13; Ex 33,11; Nu 11,28; Dt 31,23.

II. THE BOOK OF JOSUE

Josue finishes the story begun in the Torah; some scholars see it as the sixth volume of the unit known as the Hexateuch. As in the case of the first five books of the Bible, there have been many attempts at a documentary analysis of this book but these attempts have not resulted in unanimity among scholars. Some scholars are skeptical of the idea that the Pentateuchal traditions (J,E,D,P,) carry over into this work. No doubt the book shows a mixture of styles, but the various traditions in it differ quite a bit in form and content from those found in the Pentateuch. Consequently, the theory, first proposed by Julius Wellhausen, that Josue is part of the *Hexateuch* should not be adopted hurriedly. Leading non-Catholic scholars like Gerhard von Rad, John Bright, and G. Ernest Wright continue to speak of the Hexateuch, but they are well aware of the modifications that are necessary in the view as presented by Wellhausen.

Josue is the beginning of a history in the spirit of the Deuteronomic reform, a history extending through the books of Josue, Judges, Samuel, Kings. These books, usually referred to as the *Former Prophets,* have all been edited from the Deuteronomic perspective of the seventh century, which was the conviction that the long history of successes and failures in Israel is explained on the basis of fidelity or infidelity of the People of God to the Covenant made with Yahweh. This point of view is evident for example in Jos 8,30-35 and 22,12-16.

In its present form, the book of Josue dates from about the time of the Babylonian Exile but scholars agree that much of the material in it comes from a much earlier period. The account of the conquest of Canaan (Jos 2-11) as well as the renewal of the Covenant (Jos 23-24) most probably achieved written form around the turn of the millennium, about 1000 B.C. Even in its most recent parts, the book is therefore, about 2,500 years old!

The book of Josue is an example of "epic history" or "meditated history" wherein the hand of Yahweh is seen in all the trials of His people. The author includes many epic traits, hyperbole, great numerical exaggerations, suppression of human factors involved in the successes, and insistence on the unusual and the marvelous. The inspired author has used his sources skillfully and has made them serve a preconceived religious plan. The fact that the book presents a theologically interpreted history does not thereby lessen its historical worth. This has been shown by the work of archaeologists who have worked in areas mentioned in the book.

III. THE CROSSING OF THE JORDAN : JOS 3,1-5,12

According to an Arab historian, in 1267 A.D. the Jordan stopped flowing for more than ten years because of a landslide in the region of Adama; in 1927 an earthquake caused another landslide in the same region. The possibility of a miracle may not be entirely excluded from the event recorded in Josue. But it is possible that in the Providence of God a natural phenomenon occurred just when His people needed it most; a landslide blocked the flow of water and the Hebrews were able to cross to the other side of the Jordan.

IV. BATTLE OF JERICHO : JOS 5,13-6,27

Excavations at the site of Jericho have produced negative results as far as substantiation of the Biblical recital of its conquest is concerned. The work of Miss Kathleen Kenyon has not produced any trace of a Jericho dating from the 13th century B.C. or thereabouts. The lower layers of Jericho appear to contain settlements from as far back as the eighth millennium B.C. This means that Jericho is the oldest known city in the world. What was formerly thought to be the Jericho destroyed by Josue must now be dated to the third millennium.[1]

V. BATTLE OF HAI : JOS 7,2-8,29

The town of Hai, whose destruction is described in Josue, has been located about ten miles north of Jerusalem and a mile and a half southeast of Bethel. The Hebrew name means "heap of rubble" or "the ruin." Excavations carried out at the site have shown that it was already inhabited around

---

[1] Important information concerning the archaeological work carried on at the site of ancient Jericho is in the following: Albright, *The Archaeology of Palestine,* pp. 61-63, 87-92; Kathleen M. Kenyon, *Archaeology in the Holy Land* (New York: Frederick A. Praeger, Publishers, 1960), pp. 39-57, 104-09, 209-12; A. Douglas Tushingham, "Excavations at Old Testament Jericho," *The Biblical Archaeologist,* XVI (September, 1953), 46-67; *ibid.,* XVII (December, 1954), 98-104; a well illustrated article is Kathleen M. Kenyon and A. Douglas Tushingham, "Jericho Gives Up Its Secrets," *The National Geographic Magazine,* CIV (December, 1953), 853-70.

3300 B.C. and was completely destroyed around 2400 B.C.; in Josue's time Hai was what its name implies, a heap of ruins.

There are four possible solutions: (1) the story in Josue 8 is a legend which was invented to explain the presence of the immense heap of rubble; (2) it possesses a core of historical truth, for the inhabitants of nearby Bethel had entrenched themselves in Hai against the invading Israelites; (3) the story originally concerned the conquest of Bethel, but when this town later became a flourishing Israelite city, Hai was made the subject of the narrative; and (4) Hai must be assigned a different location.[2]

VI. THE SUN AT GABAON AND MOON AT AIALON : JOS 10,12-15

The text presents two views of the battle fought by Josue, a prose form (10,7-11), and a poetical one (vv 12-14).

The quotation from a lost book of Israelitic poetry, the *Book of Jashar,* refers to both the sun and the moon; the sun is asked to stand still at Gabaon and the moon at Aialon. But, it is the sun-miracle which has been the source of interest and difficulties for readers of many ages.

Fundamentalists see in the text a record of an actual occurrence, the sun "stood still" because the earth stopped rotating for almost an entire day. They argue that there is nothing incredible about the affair because "God can do anything." Comment about such a view is hardly necessary.

The following are the views of two contemporary Catholic scholars:

A. Though we cannot determine precisely what took place on this occasion, the narrative has substantially preserved the record of a providential intervention of God in favor of His people. Once again, the writer gives a clear, theological interpretation of the event, in keeping with the spirit of the entire work which is describing God's gracious assistance to His people.[3]

B. Attempts have been made even in modern times to explain the sun's 'standing still' on the basis of a prolonged daylight due to refraction of light, or as a meteor shower or some other such phenomenon. These pseudo-scientific 'explanations' collapse of their own tortured weight. Happily, they are being replaced by a sane exegesis which recognizes the passage for what it is—a highly poetic version of an emotionally charged cry of Josue, who hoped for time, for daylight, in which to crush the enemy utterly. The enemy was crushed,

---

[2] Consult L. H. Grollenberg, *Shorter Atlas of the Bible,* trans. Mary F. Hedlund, (New York: Thomas Nelson and Sons, 1959), p. 85; see also Frederick Moriarty, S.J., *Foreword to the Old Testament Books* (Weston: Weston College Press, 1954), pp. 28-29, and Kenyon, *Archaeology in the Holy Land,* pp. 115-17.

[3] Moriarty, *Foreword to the Old Testament Books,* p. 29.

so the time was granted, and this is expressed poetically in verse
13a, prosaically in verse 13b.[4]

Another possible explanation is that the cry of Josue was for the prolonga-
tion of darkness rather than light. The phrase "stand still" can have the meaning "do not shine." Josue's cry would have been for the night to last long
enough for the Hebrews to reach their enemies under cover of darkness. The
storm was the answer to prayer; this is how the author of Sirach interpreted
the event (Sir 46,5-6). The author of the book of Judges used a similar idea:
"From the heavens the stars, too fought; from their courses they fought against
Sisara" (Jgs 5,20).[5]

VII. CONQUEST OF CANAAN

The book of Josue presents the conquest of Canaan in a very simplified way.
Once over the Jordan, Josue concentrated all his forces together in one immense camp on the bank. From there he planned a series of raids into the
interior. Jericho was unprepared and fell at a single blow, and the gateway to
the hill country was open. Josue marched up the valley behind Jericho, and
assaulted the two citadels of Hai and Gabaon in the very center of the mountain
range. This daring maneuver cut in two the numerous small Canaanite
principalities of the hill country before they had a chance to unite against a
common enemy. Later they did rally, and the southern princes formed a coalition under the leadership of the powerful key city of Jerusalem. Josue attacked, and with some difficulty defeated them at Gabaon. He then wheeled
against the northern princes, who were already demoralized by the news of
the victory in the south. His chief tactic was, again, speed of movement. He
caught them unprepared near Lake Merom and cut them into pieces.

Although the accounts of the battles are vividly presented in the Bible, the
victories did not completely vanquish the enemies of Israel. They gave the
Hebrews a foothold in the country, but it was a long time before the whole
work of occupation and final victory were achieved. As late as the time of
David (1010-970) the Philistines, "People of the Sea" who occupied the
coastal region, were a source of trouble for the Israelites.

VIII. THE AFTERMATH

The period after the death of Josue was a crucial one for Israel. The tribes
that had invaded Canaan dispersed and became isolated colonies in the land.
Often their strength was dissipated. Since they had been accustomed to a

[4] Joseph DeVault, S.J., *The Book of Josue* (New York: The Paulist Press, 1960), p. 20.
[5] This is the suggestion made by H. H. Rowley, *The Growth of the Old Testament* (London:
Hutchinson University Library, 1950), p. 56. For an authoritative study of the archaeological
researches carried on at Gabaon see James B. Pritchard, *Gibeon: Where the Sun Stood Still*
(Princeton: Princeton University Press, 1962).

nomadic existence they did not have much knowledge about tilling the soil. They were inferior also in culture. The result was that the Israelites had to learn from the conquered people, and this meant that they came under the influence of both pagan culture and religion, which was often a mixture of sensual cults. The only thing that held the Hebrews together was their faith in Yahweh and the symbol of His presence, the Ark of the Covenant which they venerated at Shiloh.

During this period of Israel's history outstanding figures emerged, who, by a special grace of God, re-established His rights among the people. These individuals were known as *Judges.* This name, which in Hebrew is *Shophet,* does not give a proper idea of their function. They were not magistrates, nor did they have any permanent juridical status. The term "liberator-prophet" comes nearest to suggesting their role. They were military and political leaders as well as great champions of the faith.

IX. THE BOOK OF JUDGES

This book shows definite signs of being the result of a combination of sources. It is probable that much of the material first circulated orally as isolated units; this seems to have been the case with regard to the units which deal with the chief characters in the book.

The first attempt at collecting the units was made after the fall of Samaria in 721 B.C., perhaps around the time of the religious reform of Josia (622 B.C.); after the Babylonian Exile the final redaction of the work was completed. The book of Judges shows at least some influences of the Deuteronomistic tradition. This is understandable in the light of its literary history. Punishment and oppression at the hands of enemies are the consequences of infidelity, reward and victory are the result of the people's sincere return to the Lord; sin is a violation of the Covenant. This theological viewpoint is the book's unifying theme. It is exemplified in the lives and activities of the 12 Judges who are the heroes of the book. Their accounts form the "rhythmic pattern of rebellion and return." Each "Judge" is an answer to the prayer of a repentant people.[6]

The exploits of the Judges are presented in a collection of epic-like stories in which the lives of traditional heroes are written with a certain amount of folkloristic elements. These elements, however, do not negate the basic historical value of the account. The legendary elements that have grown up around the lives of some of the saints do not mean that these saints never lived. Careful and patient study of the accounts can disengage the "historical nucleus" from

---

[6] McKenzie, *The Two-Edged Sword,* pp. 135-36; Bright, *A History of Israel,* pp. 154-59; Philip J. King, *The Book of Judges* (New York: The Paulist Press, 1960), pp. 5-28; Moriarty, *Foreword to the Old Testament Books,* pp. 30-32. See also E. O'Doherty, "Literary Problem of Judges I, 1-3,6," *The Catholic Biblical Quarterly,* XVIII (January, 1956), 1-7, and Sr. M. Laurentia Digges, C.S.J., "Gideon's Trumpet Call," *Worship,* XXXV (November, 1961), 644-52.

the story. This is what has to be done with the stories in the book of Judges. Although the book presents a rather haphazard chronology and delights in the use of anecdotes, it nevertheless is a source of some authentic historical information. The era of the *shophetim* was one marked by wars and troubles of all sorts. There was no political unity; the Canaanites were still belligerently active, the Moabites and Ammonites were very much alive, and the Philistines, who were about to join a monopoly in the manufacture and use of iron, were active along the coast. The political and religious orders were menaced by the lack of internal unity and the presence of external politico-religious enemies. The narratives about the liberator-prophets, in the book of Judges, fit into that historical milieu.

The Judges differ in their character and in the activities which they performed but they have one common trait: they all possess the special grace of divine election. They are "charismatic" individuals, men who have received a special outpouring of divine grace and who in their actions show that Yahweh was with them. This fact, however, did not prevent them from using some deplorable tactics, such as the extermination of people by mass murder. We have to remember the nature of the period in question. It was one in which the law of "survival of the fittest" appears to have been in force. The *philosophy of life* was a sort of "beat the enemy otherwise he'll beat you." The Judges, like many of their Hebrew contemporaries, were men of their time. It would take time for their moral behavior to catch up to their theological beliefs. Moreover, the Bible is a book of life and, without necessarily approving the deeds of its characters, it presents them as flesh and blood individuals who, at times, were large "vessels of clay" (2 Cor 4,7). Samson is an example of this. Despite his vices, which included a great weakness concerning women, God used him in His plan of salvation (Jgs 13-16).

The period of the Judges lasted for nearly 200 years, from about 1200 to 1030 B.C.

twelve

THE UNITED MONARCHY IN
PALESTINE (1030–931 B.C.)

I. INTRODUCTION

AT THE TIME the Hebrews were settling in Canaan, the land of Egypt was pretty well exhausted by the wars with the People of the Sea (Philistines) and by the internal disorganization of the country itself; its role as a potent ruling power ended after the reign of Rameses III (1197-1165). Egypt had reached its nadir; the Hebrews had nothing to fear from that power.

Neither did the lands of the north present any great problem. Southern Mesopotamia was faced with the failure of its irrigation systems; thus, an essential element for material and political progress was missing. The Assyrians under Tiglath-Pilesar I (1112-1074) had conquered northern Syria and had made the Phoenician states tributaries for a while; Assyria emerged as the greatest power in the Middle East. But at this time that nation held only a restricted territory, and this situation continued for the next 200 years.

In the Middle East there was a "dead calm" during the twelfth and eleventh centuries B.C. This made it possible for the Hebrews to create a strong and well-organized kingdom in Canaan.

Another element entering into the picture was the fact that the Iron Age was in progress in Palestine (1200-900 B.C.); archaeologists have established that iron was in general use in the eleventh century. The Philistines managed to gain a monopoly in the use of this metal, which gave them a superiority in arms. Their presence on the fertile coastal plain and their attempts to conquer the mountain country were also a spur to Israelite organization.[1]

Until this time the Hebrews did not have a centralized form of government. Instead there was an amphictyony, a league composed of tribes and clans organized around a central religious sanctuary.

[1] An introductory study of the Philistines is in Kenyon, *Archaeology in the Holy Land*, pp. 221-39.

Faced with the situation at the end of the first millennium B.C. the Hebrews could easily realize the truth of the maxim, "In unity there is strength."

About 1050 B.C. the Hebrews were defeated by the Philistines at a place called Aphek, about 30 miles northwest of Jerusalem. The tribes went to Shiloh, took the Ark of the Covenant, and went again into battle against the Philistines. They were defeated; the Ark fell into the hands of the Philistines, who exploited their victory to the fullest by establishing strong garrisons in the mountain region. Israel was threatened with hopeless servitude; this situation lasted for many years. To prevent the manufacture of weapons by the Israelites, and also to protect their own monopoly on iron, the Philistines deprived the Hebrews of their metal industry and made them dependent on the Philistine smiths for all services (1 Sm 13,19-22). As a matter of fact, iron did not become plentiful in Israel until the time of David; the earliest evidence so far available is an iron plow-tip that was found at Gibeah, dating from the time of Saul. The Philistines later returned the Ark when they were tormented by a plague (1 Sm 5-7); but it had remained with them at Kirjath-jearim for a generation. Archaeological research has shown that Shiloh was totally destroyed in the period mentioned in the Bible.

During this time Samuel was Israel's guiding spirit. He was no mere village seer but a man in the succession of Judges, "the minor judges" (Jgs 10,1-5; 12,7-15), who probably dealt with Covenant law among the clans. In the first book of Samuel we find him moving in a regular circuit among some of the important shrines in the land (1 Sm 7,15-17). After the Philistine victory of 1050 B.C., Israel endured a generation of humiliating subjection at the hands of the conquerors. It was then that Samuel intervened and anointed the first king of Israel, Saul.

II. THE SOURCES: THE BOOKS OF SAMUEL, KINGS, AND CHRONICLES

A. THE BOOKS OF SAMUEL

This period in Israel's history is treated in the two books of Samuel, originally a single volume. The present books are *composite in character,* and although remarkably reliable, a careful reading of them shows that they contain some inconsistencies. These books have all the characteristics of a compilation: repetitions, abrupt changes, and differences of style and point of view.

The compilers of the first book included an early account of the Ark of the Covenant in the hands of the Philistines, followed by a cycle of stories about the prophet Samuel who consecrated kings in the name of God. Tales of the adventures of the young David, his friendship with Jonathan, his difficulties with Saul, and his wanderings are presented without any careful regard for logical sequence. The second book of Samuel, from the ninth chapter on, gives a well-arranged account of the rise of the rule of David in the face of many obstacles and family feuds. This section, written in beautiful classical Hebrew, is considered the oldest written document in the books of Samuel and is thought to be the work of an eye-witness who belonged to David's retinue. It is sometimes called the "Court History of David." The episodes which concern Samuel, Saul, the youth of David, and the fortunes of the Ark, were written later.

B. THE BOOKS OF KINGS

The first edition of these books appeared before the fall of Jerusalem in 587 B.C.; the second edition was written during the Exile.

The events surrounding the succession of Solomon are told in the second book of Samuel and in the opening chapters of the first book of Kings. The rest of Kings is devoted to Solomon and the history of the two kingdoms of Israel and Juda. The books of Kings, originally two parts of one work, would be pronounced fragmentary and biased compared to modern historical works. In writing these books, the authors used existing documents. Their aims were exclusively religious. Facts which are important for military and political reasons are not included and have to be learned from archaeological investigations. The battle and invasion led by the Pharaoh Shishak, about 918 B.C., are mentioned only because the Temple was pillaged (3 Kgs 14,25-28). The Temple of Jerusalem occupies the main interest of these books.

The Deuteronomic historian of the seventh century who edited these books judged each king of Israel and Juda according to the standard of fidelity or infidelity toward Yahweh. He plainly tells the reader throughout the Books of Samuel and Kings, that if he is interested in learning more about these kings, he may go to the royal library and consult the archives, where he will find the Book of Chronicles of the Kings of Juda or Israel, which were the royal annals. These perished long ago and survive only in the fragments quoted in the Deuteronomic history. They are not to be confused with the books of the same name found in the Bible today. The author's purpose was to present to his own day the great lessons of the past which support his theological viewpoint. Not one king of Israel escapes the historian's blacklist, and his judgment falls pretty heavily on the kings of Juda as well.

The books of Kings teach that fidelity to the Covenant must be maintained; they illustrate this by showing the consequences of transgressions against God's law. Solomon's successes are a reward for his piety; his failures and the division of the kingdom are a punishment for his disobedience to Yahweh. Insistence is placed on the assertions that the kings of Juda are the lawful heirs of David, and the Temple of Jerusalem is the only lawful place of worship. Not all the kings receive unstinted praise, because some of them allowed the "high places," the pagan centers of worship, to continue. Only two kings receive unqualified approval: Ezechia, because he abolished the "high places" throughout the land and ordered that sacrifices be restricted to the Temple of Jerusalem; and Josia, who conducted a great religious reform during which the laws of Deuteronomy were made the universal rule of conduct. This was the Deuteronomic Reform of 622.

C. THE BOOKS OF CHRONICLES

These books, like those of Samuel and Kings, were originally a single work. In Greek they are called *Paralipomenon,* "things which were passed over," because it was thought that they contained material not found in the books of Samuel and Kings. The Greek name is used in some Catholic editions of the Bible.

The book of Chronicles was composed after the Exile, around the end of the fourth or early third century B.C. Their contents reflect the situation of the period in which they were written. The work attempts a synthesis of all that happened from the time of Adam to the Edict of Cyrus which freed the Hebrews from captivity in Babylon in 538 B.C.

The author of Chronicles shows a great devotion to the Law, the Temple, and Worship. He idealizes the past history of his people and expresses great hopes for the future. This can be seen, for example, in his account of the kingdom of David in which he glosses over the failures and weaknesses of his heroes. David's sins of adultery and murder are not mentioned, but his concern for the Temple and worship is emphasized. The Chronicler, as the author of Chronicles is called, was more interested in describing the Davidic kingdom as the ideal theocracy than he was in presenting historical fact. The genre of Chronicles is known as *midrash,* a meditative history of the past, in which embellishments are introduced in order to achieve the author's purpose, which is to inculcate religious teaching and thus to inspire rather than merely to inform his audience.

III. SAUL: FIRST KING OF ISRAEL (1030-1010)

During the Philistine occupation of Palestine, Saul was chosen the first king of Israel. In view of the situation it is not surprising that the people should have desired a king. The books of Samuel present two traditions concerning the origins of kingship. One was pro-monarchical, the other anti-monarchical. The first view is found in 1 Sm 9,1-10,16; the latter view is seen in 1 Sm 8; 10,17-27; 12. Some scholars are of the opinion that the anti-monarchical tradition really originated in a later age when the nation became disillusioned with the monarchy and disgusted with the abuses witnessed in the conduct of those who held the office of king. It seems better to hold that both views were current at the time Saul was chosen to be king. One group wanted a theocracy, with Yahweh alone as king; the other group favored an earthly monarch such as other nations had. Samuel, the prophet who anointed

Saul, at first opposed the idea of an earthly king, but then went and sought out Saul when he realized that it was God's will that the nation have a monarch.

Saul made no changes in the internal structure of the country. The tribal organization remained as it was and no administrative machinery was developed. Saul had no harem, no officer except his cousin Abner, and no splendid court. At first he enjoyed a considerable amount of popularity throughout the land and brought the country life-giving respite and renewed courage. However, his reign ended in dismal failure. Saul was a tragic figure who, although fiercely courageous, was emotionally unstable. Soon his mind was like a pendulum swinging between periods of lucidity and periods of hopeless confusion which prevented intelligent action. He was a manic-depressive personality.

The excavations at Gibeah, where Saul had his home, have revealed little outward splendor. This inclines some scholars to see him as little more than a "rustic chieftain." [2]

During his reign he was quite friendly with David, who was a skilled musician and known for his brilliant exploits, among which was his killing of the Philistine giant, Goliath.[3]

Differences between Saul and David forced the latter to flee. During the campaign when the Philistines were at Shunem, the Israelites pitched camp on the slopes of Mt. Gilboa. There Saul reached his tragic climax. After seeing three of his sons, including Jonathan, killed before his eyes, he realized that the power of the Lord had been withdrawn from him, and in despair he killed himself by falling on his own sword (1 Sm 28,31). The Philistines found the body of Saul, cut off his head, and hung it with the bodies of his sons on the wall of Beth-shan. Later the men of Jabesh-Gilead came, took the remains, and buried them.

Meanwhile, David gathered a band of fearless men around himself in the mountains of Juda. It was with these men that he roamed during his flight from Saul. A Philistine king had given him the town of Ziglag and he succeeded in winning the confidence of his patron and the sympathy of those who lived in the villages of Juda by protecting them from nomad attacks (1 Sm 27-30). He skillfully got out of the necessity of having to march with the Philistines against Saul near Gilboa. When he heard of Saul's death he sin-

---

[2] This is Albright's conclusion after having studied the archaeological excavations in the area of Gibeah; *From the Stone Age to Christianity*, p. 290.

[3] The death of Goliath is recorded in 1 Sm 17,1-18. In 2 Sm 21,19 it is said that Goliath was killed by a man named Elhanam (the Douay translation calls him Adeodatus). In 1 Chr 20,5 we read that Elhanam killed a brother of Goliath; this seems to be an attempt on the part of a later author to harmonize two different accounts about the death of Goliath. It is possible that the deed of a lesser warrior was transferred to David; it is also possible that because David's fame rested on some spectacular event the two accounts in the books of Samuel are really about him, each using a different name. See Bright, *A History of Israel*, pp. 171-72.

cerely mourned him and in 2 Sm 1,17-27 the compiler of the book has inserted the lament that David composed at the time.

Saul's death, while lamented by David, probably did not surprise him. He had laid his plans years before. The success of the Philistines gave them control of the mountains and the north. They began to threaten the other side of the Jordan, called Transjordan. While Saul did much to put an end to the power of the Philistines, a better king was needed to achieve complete success. David had been secretly anointed as king even while Saul was alive, and now hearing of the death of the king he went to Hebron. There the people proclaimed him king in Juda. At the same time, the only surviving son of Saul, Ishbaal, was proclaimed king by Abner, one of the king's generals. Now there was a king in Juda and another one in Israel.

IV. DAVID (1010-970)

The early chapters of the second book of Samuel recount the events leading to David's being proclaimed king over all the tribes: fierce battles between the house of David at Hebron and that of Saul's son in the north; great quarrels between Abner and Ishbaal, a weakling; finally, the murder of Abner and Ishbaal. David convinced the people that he was not responsible for the death of the king and his general; he even took Michol, Saul's daughter, as a wife. Envoys from Israel went to David; he accepted the kingship, and assumed the task of creating unity among the tribes.

The Philistines realized that David's acclamation as king constituted a declaration of independence on the part of a reunited Israel. They decided to destroy David at once, and sent armies in search of him (2 Sm 5,17). With his faithful followers, David met them (2 Sm 5,21). Quite familiar with the military tactics of the Philistines, David was able to defeat them. In a later battle he defeated them again, and drove them back to their own territory (2 Chr 14,16). The people were to remember these victories, and to look upon them as a turning point in their history. David was now free to organize the state.

Around 1000 B.C., David captured Jerusalem, a Canaanite city of the tribe of Jebusites. Located on the central ridge which was the only convenient route north and south through the hill country, Jerusalem, unless captured, would have remained a threat to the unity of the kingdom. The city became the capital and the great period of Israelite history, the "Golden Age" began. David brought the Ark of the Covenant to the new capital from Kirjath-Jearim, and thus transferred to Jerusalem the importance of the sanctuary of Shiloh, where the Ark had been before the Philistines captured it. So it was that the ancient city became the center of the worship of Yahweh, in keeping with David's aim to make Jerusalem both the religious and political capital of the kingdom.

David's administration was skillful. In the Bible, which is essentially a religious document, we find references to only a few aspects of his government. The Sacred Book makes more of God's promises made to David and his successors (2 Sm 7,14). David consolidated and completed the geographical unity of the country although he never annexed Philistia. Thus, the Israelites controlled a large part of the territory from the Euphrates River to the borders of Egypt.

The Bible gives only a sketchy summary of David's external wars; the campaign against the Ammonites is given because of its bearing on his family life—it was at the time of that battle that he sinned with Bathsheba and from his union with her came his successor, Solomon.

David became the ruler of extensive domains, including a ring of vassal states around the land of the 12 tribes, and the territory of Moab and Edom which was taken at the price of brutal force and terrible atrocities. In the administration of the country, David followed the Egyptian system in many ways and even brought in officers from Egypt. His royal guard was composed of foreigners, according to the custom of the Pharaohs and other rulers of the time, who thus protected themselves from the intrigues of their own countrymen. His personal army included soldiers from lands outside his own. The army of Israel was made up of able-bodied Israelites. It was with a dramatic suddenness that David's conquests and internal organization transformed Israel into a foremost power. As a matter of fact the nation was, for the moment, probably as strong as any power in its contemporary world.

David did much in the religious sphere. He acquired land in order to establish a national sanctuary on the hilltop of Jerusalem. He initiated plans for the Temple which his son, Solomon, was to build. He was responsible for the organization of worship, and particularly for the music used to praise the Lord. More will be said about this in the study of the Psalms.

But David failed to weld together the northern and southern parts of the kingdom. The story of Absalom provides tragic proof of this; he opposed his father and "stole the hearts of the men of Israel" (2 Sm 15,6). Had David's successor been a man of his stature, the breach might surely have been healed, and real unity achieved. Even before David's death, there were signs of plots against Solomon, and in support of another son, Adonia (3 Kgs 1). But Solomon remained David's favorite, probably because of his mother Bathsheba, whom David loved more than his other wives, and Solomon was anointed king (3 Kgs 1,32-53).

> From the viewpoint of impact upon Israel's religion and history Moses far outranks David, but David rose higher in the affections and love of the people. Moses was constantly fighting his fellow men, the rebellions against David were, after all, only passing episodes. Posterity regarded David as the "Servant of Yahweh," the ideal king. Such already was the verdict of the author of the Book of Samuel, more so that of the chronicler, who quietly passes over disreputable acts, his adultery and murder, the family scandals, Absalom's rebellion, and emphasizes David's contributions to divine liturgy. In dark hours and in times of national

collapse the people remembered David not merely because he had made them great as a nation, but rather because the great king of the future would, as Nathan predicted, be his son.[4]

V. NOTE ON THE DYNASTIC ORACLE: 2 SM 7,1-16

At the time of David, kingship in Israel was considered a covenant between the Lord and the king.

David expressed a desire to build a house for the Lord because he did not think that it was fitting that he should dwell in a "house of cedars" while the "ark of God is lodged within skins" (2 Sm 7,2). He confided his plans to Nathan the prophet who told him that his son, Solomon, would build the Temple but that his piety would be rewarded by God. The reward would be in the form of an eternal dynasty:

> Your house and your kingdom shall be confirmed before me forever;
> your throne shall be established forever.
>
> *2 Sm 7,16*

God, as we have seen, promised Abraham that he would be the father of many people and that in him all the nations of the earth will be blessed (Gn 12,1-3). Now that promise breaks through centuries of silence and God promises an eternal kingdom to David; this is the *Dynastic Oracle,* which will be echoed throughout Israel's history as it awaits the coming of the Messiah and his kingdom.

Old Testament messianism was dynastic in its origins; it was rooted in the family of David, the ideal king. The Oracle spoken by Nathan was the *magna carta* of that messianism; the Messiah who would come and rule was to be a "son of David." The Prophets developed this theme; and the Psalms contain it in their record of inspired song (Os 3,5; Ez 34,23-24; Ps 87,35-38; 109,1-12).

The promise found in the *Dynastic Oracle* is contained in the words spoken at the moment of the Annunciation when Mary receives the message of the Incarnation: "He shall be great, and shall be called the Son of the Most High; and the Lord God will give him the throne of David his father, and he shall be king over the house of Jacob forever; and of his kingdom there shall be no end" (Lk 1,32-33). Jesus, the son of David, and the Church, His kingdom, are the fulfillment of the Oracle.

VI. SOLOMON (970-931)

Unlike his father, who had to endure great difficulties and persecutions before he ascended the throne, Solomon was born and reared like a prince in a palace. Once he became king he often asserted his authority through

---

[4] Heinisch, *History of the Old Testament,* pp. 190-91.

despotic methods; he assassinated his brother, dealt severely with his enemies (3 Kgs 2), imposed a heavy yoke on the Canaanites, and compelled the Israelites to do forced labor.

Solomon dazzled men with his impressive projects; like other rulers he loved large palaces, harems, luxury, ostentation. Visitors to his court were amazed at the grandeur they saw there (3 Kgs 10). To maintain his way of living, Solomon levied heavy taxes on the people and made sure that there was no evasion of the forced labor. At this time, even more than during the period of David, the people who had been used to a peasant way of life were subjected to organization; their harvests were assessed by tax collectors and every able-bodied man was obliged to work for the king. Soon, class distinctions developed in the new society.

David had planned to build a temple in honor of Yahweh at Jerusalem; Solomon accomplished the task. The original area of the Temple lies beneath modern Jerusalem at the site of the Moslem sanctuary of the Mosque of Omar, in the center of which is the Dome of the Rock. Hence, we must depend on archaeological discoveries made at other sites to understand the description of the Temple and its decorations found in the Bible (3 Kgs 3-6). The layout involved great terracing operations; it is possible that portions of the surviving wall found at the southern end of the present structure are the work of Solomon. The available evidence permits us to say that the Temple was almost entirely Phoenician in character. One entered the long rectangular building through a porch, passed through a hall illuminated by windows, then went up a flight of steps and into the darkened Holy of Holies.[5]

The building of the Temple required 7 years, but 13 years were necessary for the building of the palace, government buildings, and the house for Solomon's Egyptian queen. Outside Jerusalem, "chariot cities" were constructed. Military fortifications were built at Gezer, about twenty miles northwest of Jerusalem, Megiddo, about fifty miles north of Jerusalem, and other sites (3 Kgs 9). One of the chariot cities, Megiddo, has been uncovered by archaeologists; the evidence shows that it contained about 450 stalls for horses. This substantiates the information found in the Bible.[6]

At the time of David and Solomon, which is often called the period of the Ancient Monarchy, the ancient traditions which had been handed down for centuries in oral and written form were collected under the influence of the court scribes. The great desire to gather the traditions, which had been circulating in the separate clans up to this time, is readily understandable.

Solomon's reign left behind the memory of a period of greatness. His rule, however, ended in failure. The exact and methodical organization brought

[5] The history, ornaments, and theology of the Temple are studied in De Vaux, *op. cit.*, pp. 312-30.

[6] See Kenyon, *Archaeology in the Holy Land*, pp. 244-51; Albright, *From the Stone Age to Christianity*, pp. 291-94; Grollenberg, *Atlas of the Bible*, pp. 74-75; Moriarty, *Foreword to the Old Testament Books*, pp. 38-39.

inevitable consequences; the heavy taxes and forced labor grew worse as Solomon's building projects grew greater. He was a capable and skillful individual, but not deeply religious; he did not hesitate to build temples in honor of the gods whom his many pagan wives worshipped.

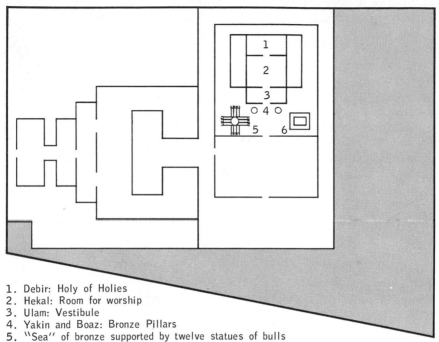

1. Debir: Holy of Holies
2. Hekal: Room for worship
3. Ulam: Vestibule
4. Yakin and Boaz: Bronze Pillars
5. "Sea" of bronze supported by twelve statues of bulls
6. Altar of Holocausts

Figure 5. THE TEMPLE AND PALACE OF SOLOMON

Solomon amazed the people by his splendor, but he won no hearts. Intoxicated by the spirit of enterprise and ambition, Solomon did not take into account the poor and undeveloped condition of his kingdom. He aimed to be on the level with the sovereigns of the mighty worldly kingdoms, but Canaan was so tiny. His projects involved too heavy a burden upon the resources of his subjects, his court expenses were too extravagant for the nation's economy, his policy of national development was too grandiose, and he disregarded the feelings of the people. . . . Through his conduct at public appearances, and especially through his attitude toward strange gods, he created a barrier between himself and pious Hebrews, and awakened opposition from the prophets. Even in the building of the temple he did not seek God's honor exclusively.[7]

[7] Heinisch, *History of the Old Testament*, pp. 201-202.

Figure 6.

thirteen

THE SCHISM: KINGDOMS OF
ISRAEL AND JUDA (931–587 B.C.)

I. INTRODUCTION

AFTER THE DEATH of Solomon, his son Roboam was chosen to succeed him. The people in the north wanted to make an alliance with Roboam which would be a sign of their full recognition of him as their king. But Roboam refused and replied with the remark: "My little finger is thicker than my father's loins" (3 Kgs 12,10). He continued his father's policies concerning taxation and forced labor, and surrounded himself with a circle of petty despots. The northern tribes cried out against the abuses (3 Kgs 12,16) and placed themselves under the leadership of Jeroboam, who had been in the service of Solomon, but had fled to Egypt after a clash with that king. The division of the kingdom was now an accomplished fact. The land of Israel in the north had a king in the old tradition, a king who, like Saul, had been designated by a prophet (Ahia) and proclaimed by the people. The schism was a terrible misfortune, and that could have been avoided if Roboam had exercised more tact and prudence.

Palestine was now divided into two kingdoms: Israel in the north with Samaria as its capital, and Juda in the south with Jerusalem as its capital. The kingdom of Israel lasted for two centuries; the Assyrians destroyed it in 724 B.C. (Samaria fell in 721 B.C.). The kingdom of Juda lasted for three and a half centuries until 587 B.C. when it was destroyed by the Babylonians.

The religious consequences of the schism were disastrous, more so in the north than in the south, which remained in possession of the Ark of the Covenant and the Temple, the only place in which Yahweh was to receive worship. For political reasons, the kings of Israel sought to prevent their subjects from going to Jerusalem. The situation gradually became worse and those who believed in the pure worship of Yahweh had to practice it secretly.

II. CHARACTERISTICS OF THE KINGDOMS

A. JUDA

Small in territory, the southern kingdom possessed a homogeneous population and relative geographical isolation. It was strongly loyal to the dynasty of David; the hereditary monarch lived in Jerusalem, the City of David. The fact that the Ark of the Covenant was located in the Temple gave a strong spiritual uplift to the people.

B. ISRAEL

The northern kingdom possessed extensive territory. It embraced ten of the original tribes and its land included not only a large part of Palestine but also Transjordan. The monarchy was less firmly rooted than that of Juda; the people could easily condemn the behavior of the ruler and persuade some other person to seize the throne. As a matter of fact, during the 200 years of its existence there were 19 kings, several of whom were assassinated during revolts or conspiracies.

The population was not thoroughly united; there were large numbers of Canaanites. Although Israel was politically and economically superior to Juda, the fact that it did not have an authentic center for the worship of Yahweh was a serious disadvantage.

III. BRIEF HISTORY OF THE KINGDOMS

A. KINGDOM OF ISRAEL (931-721)

1. *Jeroboam I (931-910)*

Jeroboam I, the originator of the schism, established his capital at Shechem. We know nothing about his administration other than that he dedicated two sanctuaries to Yahweh, one in the south at Bethel, the other in the north at Dan, to prevent the people from going to Jerusalem to worship Yahweh. In both sanctuaries he placed a statue of a golden calf. It is very likely that these statues were not intended as representations of Yahweh, but rather were "thrones" on which He was present invisibly. There are evidences from antiquity which show a god standing on the back of a young bull. However, even if Jeroboam's own monotheism can be defended, his actions paved the way for many of the false elements which crept into the worship of Yahweh. Since many of the inhabitants of the northern kingdom were former Canaanites, such a symbol was extremely dangerous, and made it easier to confuse Yahweh and Baal. The Bible refers to Jeroboam's action as his "sin" (3 Kgs 12,25-30).

2-5. *Nadab (910-909)-Zimri (885)*

Nadab, son of Jeroboam, continued his father's policies. He was murdered by Baasa (909-886), who also massacred the rest of the household and then took the throne. Ela (886-885) succeeded him; he in turn was assassinated by one of his officers, Zimri (885), who killed Baasa's house and made himself king. He ruled only seven days and then committed suicide when the armies of Omri, a general, moved on the city of Tirzah.

6. *Omri (885-874)*

Omri, an important king, was able to establish some stability after 50 years of disorder which had left Israel helpless against its hostile neighbors, especially Damascus, and Assyria, which at this time was rising as a new imperial power. His reign was brief, but thanks to his vigorous character he was able to establish a dynasty that held power to the third generation, and to initiate a policy that brought Israel a certain measure of strength and prosperity. He was a man of great ability, and even long after his dynasty had been overthrown, the Assyrians referred to Israel as "the House of Omri." His policies included friendly relations with Juda, close ties with the Phoenicians, and a strong hand east of the Jordan, especially against the Arameans. The Book of Kings confines its account to the fact that Omri founded Samaria and "acted wickedly above all that were before him" (3 Kgs 16,23-28).

The *Stele of Mesha* of the ninth century B.C., states that Omri ruled over the land of Moab: "Omri was king of Israel and oppressed Moab for many days, since Chemosh (the god of Moab) had been angry with his land. And his son succeeded him; and he also said: 'I will oppress Moab!' In my days he spoke (thus), I prevailed over him and his house and Israel has utterly perished forever!" [1]

7. *Achab (874-853)*

Achab surpassed even Omri in his wickedness. He was a man of some political and military standing. Under the influence of his wife, Jezebel, a daughter of one of the priests of the pagan goddess, Astarte, he set up in Samaria a sacred pillar to the goddess.

Jezebel was a strong-minded woman filled with a great zeal for her god and contempt for the cultural backwardness and austere religion of her adopted land. She sought to make the cult of Baal the official religion, particularly of the court. Although Achab remained a nominal believer in Yahweh, the court and the ruling class became paganized. The prophets of

---

[1] See complete text of the Stele in D. Winton Thomas, *op. cit.,* pp. 196-97.

Baal and Astarte enjoyed official status (3 Kgs 18). Loyal followers of Yahweh soon met with opposition and persecution. Jezebel, infuriated by the opposition created by the Yahwists, resorted to extremely harsh measures, including the execution of all who dared oppose her. She met a brutal death when she was thrown from a window and then devoured by wild dogs (4 Kgs 9,30-37). The daughter of Achab and Jezebel, Athalia, married Joram of Juda.

THE PROPHETS IN ISRAEL : ELIA AND ELISEUS

This period was a dangerous one for Yahwism. The "old time religion" of the people was beginning to weaken and gradually it was mixed with certain forms of pagan worship. The commemorative images in honor of Baal and Astarte became familiar objects: the *masseboth,* which was a phallic symbol used in the worship of the male deity, and the *asheroth,* a wooden pillar, often a tree, used in the worship of the god's consort. The influence of the pagan priests, supported by the royal family, increased and it did not take long for them to introduce a mixture of religious rites, Yahwistic and pagan. These were the ingredients of what is known as syncretism, a *pot pourri* of elements from several religions, which led to a practical indifferentism. Many of the people did not see the hidden purposes of those who conducted the worship of Yahweh and were unaware that it was tied up with the worship of the gods and goddesses of the storm, wine, seasons, and fertility. The campaign was so waged that the people were led to believe that they were worshipping Yahweh in other forms when they worshipped his various "manifestations" in the things of nature. This is not difficult to understand since many of the feasts of the Hebrews were related to the cycle of nature.

Religion and politics had never been separate things for the Hebrews, and "separation of church and state" would have had no meaning for them. The political schism at the time of Jeroboam and Roboam caused a religious schism which led to indifferentism and then to heresy and idolatry.

It was at this crucial moment that the Lord raised up individuals who were to be his spokesmen. The prophets were the die-hard defenders of the rights of Yahweh, fearless champions of His Word. There had been prophets as early as the time of Samuel, about 1040 B.C., but it was at this time that the Golden Age of Prophetism began; it was to continue until the fifth century B.C. A detailed treatment of the prophets and their role in the history of salvation will appear later in this book. Here it will suffice to say something about the important role of two individuals who waged a relentless war in the defense of Yahwism at a time when it would have been more "prudent" to do otherwise. These were Elia and Eliseus.

The story of Elia is in 3 Kings 17-19. It is a dramatic portrayal of a man who challenged the power of the king, the queen, and the entire entourage of Baal. The author of the Elia-cycle presents him in ways which are reminiscent of the great leader of the Hebrews in another period of dire need, Moses. It was while the Hebrews were in Egypt, land of sin and captivity, that Moses manifested the existence and power of Yahweh by means of signs and wonders that become traditional among the Hebrews. During the sojourn at Mt. Sinai (Horeb), Moses spoke with the Lord for 40 days and nights. He received the revelation in the midst of thunder and lightning, and experienced a tender intimacy with the Lord "in the hollow of the rock" (Ex 19; 24; 33). Elia demonstrated that the Lord, the true God, exists and He alone is to be worshipped when, at his request, fire consumed both victim and altar while the prayer of the priests of Baal effected nothing (3 Kgs 18). He too spent 40 days and nights in the desert of Sinai, and at the holy mountain he heard the voice of the Lord; not in the majestic notes of the theophany which had occurred while his forefathers were in the desert but in the "whistling of a gentle air," and at the entrance of a cave he was brought to a renewed awareness of his mission (3 Kgs 19).

God reveals Himself in various places and times. No one can predict the way that He will choose to make Himself and His message known. It was in a "gentle breeze" that Elia realized the intimacy of the Lord, an intimacy that was to be continued in the relations between Yahweh and the prophets that would come later. Filled with courage, born of faith and sustained by revelation, Elia was the living witness of the Lord before a people who often strayed from true worship. He was able, at least for a time, to bring the king, Achab, to his senses and to have him do penance (3 Kgs 21,17-29).

The death of Elia is presented in a manner faithful to the way in which he had acted throughout his life. He who had often called down fire to consume sacrifices and even captains and their company (4 Kgs 1), was taken away by a fiery chariot and fiery horses (4 Kgs 2,11). Fire was the classical accompaniment of divine manifestations in the ministry of Elia. This exodus from earth has all the charm of a story told by followers faithful to their master. Some are of the opinion that it may have been a mystical experience similar to the one which St. Paul underwent and which he described as being "caught up to the third heaven" (2 Cor 12,2). We cannot be sure of the exact manner of Elia's departure from earth, only that he was united with the Lord. He, whose name means "The Lord is my God," is with God. In time, the belief spread that Elia would return. The book of Malachia, written around the middle of the fifth century B.C. speaks of the return of Elia (Mal 3,23). This received a literal interpretation in Jewish tradition. Jesus declared that the promise was fulfilled in John the Baptist (Mt 17,10-13; Mk 9,8-12).

The importance of Elia in the history of salvation, and the relationship between him and Moses may be seen in the Transfiguration theophany where these two spokesmen and champions of the Lord appeared conversing with Jesus (Mt 17,1-8; Mk 9,1-7; Lk 9,28-36).

The account of Eliseus is found in a cycle of stories which developed around this important figure whose name means "God is my salvation" (4 Kgs 2-9; 13). These stories were composed quite early, probably in the first half of the eighth century B.C., in the northern kingdom. Eliseus the "man of God" was the sole intimate friend of Elia but, unlike him, he was associated with groups of prophets who lived together and who were known as "sons of the prophets." His portrait is filled with the miraculous. This is seen, for example, in the beautiful account of the resurrection of the son of the woman of Shunem and the cure of Naaman the leper (4 Kgs 4-5). The fact that Eliseus was believed to possess divine power is also seen in the anecdotes that were related about him. Examples of these are the stories about the vision of the blood-red water seen by the Moabites (4 Kgs 3,20-24), and the floating axe-head (4 Kgs 6,2-7). These accounts are the work of an author who utilized popular traditions about a religious hero to whom later generations of Israelites would owe a great debt of gratitude for his work in the preservation of Yahwism. They are told against the background of the political history of Israel, particularly the contest caused by the revolt of the Moabites during the reign of Joram (852-841). More than Elia, Eliseus was involved in the political situation of his time to such a degree that, as a result of his command, Jehu was anointed to succeed Joram. This led to a "blood purge" which marked the end of the dynasty of Omri and the elimination of the cult of Baal in Samaria (4 Kgs 9-10).

8. *Ochozia (853-852)*

Ochozia, son of Achab, continued to do "evil in the sight of the Lord, and walked in the way of his father and mother" (3 Kgs 22,53). His reign lasted less than two years. He suffered a fall from which he did not recover and was succeeded by Joram.

9. *Joram (852-841)*

This king attempted to return Moab to tributary status. He renewed Israel's alliance with Juda and fought Moab. He had initial victories against the Moabites, but the siege against Moab was discontinued after a "mighty wrath descended upon Israel,"—perhaps a plague. The Moabites retained their independence. Joram tried to remove the more objectionable objects of the pagan cult, but did not succeed very much since Jezebel was still alive. At the instigation of Eliseus, the king was replaced by Jehu whom one of the "sons of the prophets" anointed king over Israel, the people of the Lord (4 Kgs 9,1-10).

10. *Jehu (841-814)*

Jehu led a *coup d'etat* against the house of Omri and its entire policy. His move turned into a bloody bath which included the wanton slaughter of a delegation from Jerusalem.

Jehu was proclaimed king with a good deal of fanfare. Supported by the power of the mutinous army he purged Israel with thoroughness and brutality. He rode his chariot into the city of Jezreel, where he murdered the king, Joram, by sending an arrow through his heart. He also murdered Ochozia of Juda who had come to visit his sick uncle, Joram, and later massacred Ochozia's brothers who also had come to pay their respects to their uncle. Jezebel, the queen-mother, then met her end. In order to protect himself against any possible claimants to the throne, Jehu ordered the decapitation of Achab's 70 sons (4 Kgs 9-10).

After he had butchered the house of Achab, Jehu set out to exterminate the prophets of Baal. He announced that he was going to worship the pagan deity with a great sacrifice. It turned out that the "sacrifice" was the application of the *herem* to the followers of Baal assembled in the temple. The holocaust was completed by the burning of the "pillar," which probably was the asheroth, an image honoring the goddess of fertility, and the pagan temple was then converted into a latrine.

It should be noticed that the Deuteronomist historian who edited the Book of Kings was somewhat impressed by Jehu's zeal for Yahweh and hardly moved by his ruthless extermination of the house of Achab and the worshippers of the Baal. The historian denounced Jehu only when he failed to remove the idolatrous shrines which Jeroboam I had erected in Bethel and Dan (4 Kgs 10).

On the Black Obelisk of Shalmaneser III, king of Assyria (859-824), now in the British Museum, the Assyrian leader boasts of his victories. A carved relief depicts Jehu, king of Israel, bowing low at the feet of Shalmaneser, who is offering a libation. Jehu is called the "son of Omri," since the Assyrians continued to designate Israelite kings after the name of Omri.[2]

11. *Joachaz (814-798)*

During the rule of this king, conditions worsened considerably for Israel. He fostered the worship of the gods of the Canaanites (4 Kgs 13,6).

12. *Joas (798-783)*

The northern kingdom experienced further setbacks during the reign of Joas. The armies of Damascus inflicted a heavy defeat upon him and besieged Samaria. The famine that occurred during this period was so severe that mothers killed and ate their own babies. During the latter part of his reign, Israel was able to reduce the kingdom of Juda to a position of helplessness (4 Kgs 14,1-14; 2 Chr 25,5-24). After defeating the armies of

---

[2] For the text, commentary, and illustrations see Thomas, *op. cit.*, pp. 53-57; also Grollenberg, *Atlas of the Bible*, pp. 88-89.

Juda at the battle of Beth-shemesh, Joas moved on to Jerusalem. He looted the city, broke down a section of its walls, and then retired with hostages. Joas took the king of Juda, Amazia, as a hostage at the battle of Beth-shemesh, but he later released him and allowed him to return to his capital.

13. *Jeroboam II (783-743)*

This king was the most successful of the rulers of the northern kingdom and under him Israel reached its zenith. Jeroboam is one of the strong military figures in the history of Israel. Political conditions were such in the neighboring countries that he was able to extend the borders of his country almost to where they had been during the reign of Solomon. The increased trade poured wealth into the country so that it experienced a prosperity unknown since the time of that monarch. Archaeology has shown that industries of various kinds, like weaving and dyeing, flourished in some cities: for example, Debir, mid-way between Gaza and the Dead Sea. Indeed, the Israelites boasted of being the first among the nations of the world. The splendid buildings and rich ivory inlays of the eighth century, Phoenician or Damascene in origin, found by archaeologists at Samaria give us some idea of the luxury that the upper classes of Israel enjoyed at this time.[3]

However, this glowing picture must not obscure the fact that in spite of its prosperous appearance, the kingdom was in an advanced state of decay—socially, morally, and religiously. Although Yahwism remained the national religion many of the people gave only lip service to the Covenant. Covenant law often meant very little in practice.

> Though the great shrines of Israel were busy, thronged with worshippers, and lavishly supported (Amos 4:4f.; 5:21-24), it is evident that Yahwism in pure form was no longer maintained. Many of the local shrines were no doubt overtly pagan; the fertility cult with its debasing rites was practiced everywhere (Hos., 1-3; 4:6-14). . . . Although we have no way of measuring the degree of it, it appears that even the official state religion had absorbed rites of pagan origin (Amos 2:7f.; 5:26; Hos. 8:5f.) and, what was worse, accorded the cult the wholly pagan function of appeasing the Deity by ritual and sacrifice in order to secure the peace of the *status quo*. A Yahwism so diluted could scarcely be expected to have any keen feeling for covenant law or effectively to rebuke breaking it.[4]

It was at this time that two important figures appeared on the stage of Israel's history, the prophets Amos and Osee.

---

[3] Pictures of some of the ivory pieces are in Grollenberg, *Atlas*, p. 75, and Albright, *Archaeology of Palestine*, pp. 136-37.
[4] Bright, *A History of Israel*, p. 242.

AMOS: PROPHET OF THE GOD OF JUSTICE

Amos was a native of the southern kingdom, a shepherd from the village of Tekoa, situated a short distance south of Bethlehem. He was the first of the writing prophets and one of the great individuals in the succession of spiritual leaders whose vocation was to remind the people that they must be worthy of Yahweh's love and call.[5]

The bulk of Amos' oracles were pronounced late in the prosperous reign of Jeroboam II. The book that bears his name is composed of units which were spoken at various times by the prophet and then gathered by him or some of his close associates; it is a sort of "anthology of familiar quotations." Although born and raised in the south he exercised his ministry in Israel, principally in the vicinity of the schismatic sanctuary of Bethel. His oracles, however, were directed to the "whole family that I brought up from the land of Egypt" (Am 3,1).

Faithful to his name which means "Strong," Amos hurled his denunciations at the high and mighty ones in Israel and predicted their ruin: the rich women were like fat cows that would be slaughtered (Am 4,1-3), the wanton leaders of the people would be the first to go into exile (Am 6,1-7), the religious sanctuaries would be turned into desolate sites (Am 7,9). The oracles of Amos were too dire for the royal and priestly families of Israel to accept. Driven from the land, he warned that his predictions would come true when the "day of the Lord" would arrive and punish sinners (Am 5,18-27). That "day" would purge the dross from Israel but it would not be the end of the people. A "remnant" composed of the just ones would survive, the "fallen hut of David" would be the instrument which the Lord would use to bring about a national resurrection through a descendant of David.

> I will not destroy the house of Jacob completely, says the Lord. For see, I have given the command to sift the house of Israel among all the nations, as one sifts with a sieve, letting no pebble fall to the ground. By the sword shall all sinners among my people die, those who say, "Evil will not reach or overtake us." On that day I will raise up the fallen hut of David; I will wall up its breaches, raise up its ruins, and rebuild it as in the days of old, that they may conquer what is left of Edom and all the nations that shall bear my name, say I, the Lord, who will do this.
>
> *Am 9,9-12*

Amos' book proclaims a return to monotheism, and although directed to Israel, contains tones of universalism. His oracles extend the morality of the

---

[5] For a brief and informative study of Amos see Louis Bouyer, *The Meaning of Sacred Scripture,* pp. 52-60; also Marcian Strange, O.S.B., *The Books of Amos, Osee & Michea* (New York: The Paulist Press, 1961), pp. 5-13.

Law of Israel to other nations. He does not say how this is to be done, but it is evident that other nations are included in the plan of the Lord (Am 9,7). After the Babylonian Exile, this "speck" of universalism was to be enlarged into a great "beam" through the work of the post-exilic prophets and authors. Finally, Jesus would command the Word to be brought beyond the confines of the land of the Jews: "Go, therefore, and make disciples of all nations . . ." (Mt 28,18-20).

OSEE: PROPHET OF THE GOD OF LOVE

Osee was a native of the northern kingdom who exercised his prophetic function at the same time as Amos. He also preached during the reign of Jeroboam's successor, Menahem. He described the covenant which Yahweh had sealed with the people as a wedlock in which the Lord expects Israel to give Him the faithfulness a husband expects of his wife. Set against the background of the prophet's own unfortunate marital life with a woman who turned out to be a harlot, the oracles of Osee are a mixture of strong denunciations and tender calls to penance. The Lord loves His people but they turn to other gods; they will be punished but will turn back and seek the Lord (Os 3,1-5). He condemned the worship of the pagan gods as "adulteries" which would not go unpunished, but one day Yahweh would forgive Israel and restore the covenant bond.[6]

Osee is the great prophet of the *hesed* of the Lord, the love of Yahweh for His people, a love which demands the return gift of love and total commitment on the part of the beloved: "It is love that I desire, not sacrifice, and knowledge of God rather than holocausts" (Os 6,6). The eleventh chapter of Osee's book contains one of the most beautiful and tender expressions of Old Testament theology of *hesed;* the covenant between Yahweh and His people is pictured as the love of a father for his son.

> When Israel was a child I loved him, out of Egypt I called my son. The more I called them, the farther they went from me, sacrificing to the Baals and burning incense to idols. Yet it was I who taught Ephraim to walk, who took them in my arms; I drew them with human cords, with bands of love; I fostered them like one who raises an infant to his cheeks; yet, though I stooped to feed my child, they did not know that I was their healer.
>
> *Os 11,1-4*

Seven centuries before Jesus, the prophet Osee sketched the outlines of a picture which Our Lord was to complete and transform in the parable known to us as "The Prodigal Son" but which might be better entitled "The Parable of the Forgiving Father" (Lk 15,11-32).

---

[6] Bouyer, *The Meaning of Sacred Scripture,* pp. 61-67; Strange, *op. cit.,* pp. 34-42.

The death of Jeroboam II witnessed the beginning of Israel's downfall. The history of the northern state became a tale of unmitigated disaster. Israel's internal sickness erupted into the open, and the state found itself racked with anarchy just when it was called upon to face a resurgent Assyria—an Assyria which would present the gravest external threat ever encountered in Israel's history. Hardly 25 years would pass until Israel would be no more.

14-19. *Zacharia (743) to Osee (732-724)*

The ten years following Jeroboam's death saw five kings on the throne of Israel, three of whom seized the throne by violence, none with the slightest pretext of legitimacy. Jeroboam's son, Zacharia, was murdered after a reign of six months (743) by Shallum, who was in turn liquidated, within a month, by Menahem (743-738). The motives behind these actions are not known, but they plunged the nation into a civil war that was characterized by unspeakable atrocities (4 Kgs 15,16). When Tiglath-Pileser, the true founder of the Assyrian empire, advanced to the west, Menahem gave tribute to him —a heavy tribute which was raised by means of a head tax on every landholder of Israel, about 60,000 at that time. The Assyrian leader is called Pul (Phul) in the Bible. It is probable that Menahem had little choice in the matter but, on the other hand, it appears that he surrendered his country's independence willingly, hoping that Assyrian aid would support him on his shaky throne.

Menahem was succeeded by his son Pekahia (738-737) who was soon assassinated by one of his officers, Peka (737-732). Actually, the names of the king and the assassin are identical. Some scholars are of the opinion that Peka usurped both the throne and the throne name of his predecessor. The Douay translation of the books of Kings refers to Pekahia as Phaceia, and Peka as Phacea.

The social crimes that had been denounced by Amos the prophet had torn the fabric of Israel's society, setting class against class, section against section —there was no longer a unified kingdom. The removal of the strong hand of Jeroboam and the mounting Assyrian threat only laid bare the extent to which social disintegration had already advanced. At the same time, widespread paganism showed itself in the drunkenness, debauchery, and sexual license which were practiced under the aegis of religion, corroding the national character (Os 4,11-14,17-19; Is 28,1-4). Once the stern morality of Yahwism lost its place among the people, there was no integrity, no basic principle that could furnish the basis for the necessary public-spirited action that alone could save the nation Israel. Lacking internal cohesion and theological strength, the nation found itself incapable of intelligent and concerted action. Instead of manifesting wisdom, its leaders showed a complete inability to evaluate the realities of the situation, and they plunged Israel to its doom.

Peka represented the element in Israel which wanted to resist the advances of Assyria. In order to do this, he formed a coalition with Rezin, king of Damascus, and tried to get the king of Juda, who at this time was Joatham, to join. Joatham refused and Peka and Rezin decided to force him into line by invading Juda (4 Kgs 15,37). Joatham died before the invasion began and was succeeded by his son Achaz. To defend himself against the northern coalition, the king of Juda appealed to Tiglath-Pileser for aid, refusing the advice of the prophet Isaia, who warned that such a move would bring about dire consequences for Juda. Tiglath-Pileser fell upon the coalition and destroyed it completely. He overran all the Israelite lands of Galilee and Transjordan, destroyed many cities, and deported portions of the population. In the meantime, Peka was murdered by one called Osee (4 Kgs 15,30), who immediately surrendered to the Assyrians and gave tribute. After the fall of Israel, Tiglath-Pileser attached Damascus, ravaged it, deported many of the inhabitants, and executed Rezin.

Osee (732-724) ruled Israel as an Assyrian vassal. After the death of Tiglath-Pileser, thinking that he could liberate himself from the foreigners, he withheld the tribute from Shalmaneser V, (727-722) the new Assyrian leader. He also made overtures to Egypt for help. That was Israel's suicide.

In 724, Shalmaneser attacked, and Osee was taken prisoner. The Assyrians occupied the land, except for the city of Samaria, which held off the invaders for about two years. While the invasion was in progress, Shalmaneser died and was succeeded by Sargon II (722-705) who conquered Samaria in 721. According to Sargon's annals, 27,290 Israelites were deported into the region of Upper Mesopotamia and Media where they ultimately lost their identity. Israel was repopulated with colonists from Babylon, Elam, and Syria.[7]

B. THE KINGDOM OF JUDA (931-587)

1-2. *Roboam (931-913)—Abiam (913-911)*

Roboam and his son Abiam did little to force northern Israel back into the realm. The condition of religion continued to deteriorate as the syncretist type of worship introduced by the foreign concubines of Solomon made progress. The invasion by the pharoah of Egypt, Shishak, and his sack of the Temple and palace in Jerusalem, was considered part of the Divine punishment for the infidelities present in the land.

The invasion by Shishak happened about the year 918 B.C., while Roboam was king. The pharoah was a Libyan noble who hoped to re-assert Egyptian authority in the East. The Bible says that Roboam yielded to enormous tribute in order to induce Shishak to withdraw. This leaves the impression that Shishak's attack was directed against Jerusalem alone. Actually, there was more to the affair. The Shishak inscription which was discovered at

---

[7] Sargon's text and comments about it are in Thomas, *op. cit.*, pp. 58-63.

Karnak lists 150 places which the pharaoh claims to have taken. From this information we get the impression that the Egyptian armies devastated Palestine from end to end. The blows left both Israel and Juda in desperate condition. Fortunately, Shishak was unable to follow up his initial victories and re-establish the Egyptian empire in Asia. Egypt was faced with internal weakness and the armies were forced to abandon their gains. They withdrew from Palestine, leaving behind a few garrisons.

3. *Asa (911-870)*

This king was a true worshipper of Yahweh. He was hostile to any form of compromise with idolatry. But he was not successful in abolishing the "high places." During his reign, the armies of Israel invaded the frontier and captured Rama, five miles north of Jerusalem. In desperation Asa sent gifts to the king of Damascus, Ben-hadad I, begging him to break his treaty with Baasa of Israel. Ben-hadad, with characteristic duplicity, complied and sent an army to trouble northern Galilee, thus forcing Baasha to withdraw from Juda. This action on the part of Asa was looked upon as a lack of confidence in the Covenant which he had renewed with Yahweh.

4-5. *Josaphat (870-848)—Joram (848-841)*

Like his predecessor, Josaphat was a true worshipper of Yahweh. In order to spread the knowledge of the Torah, he sent priests and Levites throughout his country with the "book of the Law of the Lord" (2 Chr 17,9), and set up in Jerusalem a court of judges to interpret the Law in disputed cases. He won a bloodless victory over the Moabites and Edomites by means of fasting and prayer. He was not successful in a project for maritime trade, because he undertook it in partnership with Ochozia of Israel. This is how the sacred author states it. However, a storm or bad seamanship may have been the cause of the failure. The sacred authors, as we have said before, do not see the events on merely the natural plane, but see everything as directly connected with God's decrees.

The king's son Joram married Athalia, daughter of Jezebel, who exerted an evil influence in the kingdom. She persuaded her husband to kill all his brothers and to re-establish the worship of the pagan gods. Joram's reign ended in failure which was looked upon as a divine punishment.

6-7. *Ochozia (841)—Athalia (841-835)*

Ochozia was king only for a short time; he was murdered at the order of Jehu (4 Kgs 9,27). After his death, the kingdom was seized by Athalia; to make sure that she would enjoy it alone for some time, she put to death all the members of the royal family. She built a temple in honor of Baal.

One of Ochozia's sons, Joas, escaped the massacre, and was brought up in the Temple by the high priest Joiada. When the boy was seven years of age, Joiada showed him to the people who proclaimed him king; Athalia was put to death.

8. *Joas (835-796)*

Since he was raised in the Temple, this king was very devoted to the worship of Yahweh. He restored the Temple but was not successful in destroying all the pagan places of worship that had been erected during the reign of Athalia.

After the death of the high priest, Joiada, Joas fell into a syncretic form of worship. Upon being reprimanded by Zacharia, the high priest, he proceeded to have him put to death in the courtyard of the Temple. The martyr's dying prayer was that Yahweh should avenge the evil deed (2 Chr 24,21; Mt 23,35). Punishment came when the Assyrian armies invaded the land and the treasures of the Temple had to be delivered to the conquerors under Hazael to prevent them from besieging Jerusalem. The people were greatly embittered by the actions of Joas.

Before his reign was over, Joas had made himself bitterly disliked. This perhaps was due to his religious laxity, his military failures, or other reasons. Finally he was assassinated: certain high officials and priests who were incensed by the religious policies of the king and his crime against Zacharia formed a conspiracy, and put him to death.

9. *Amazia (796-781)*

Amazia decisively beat the Edomites, went to war against Israel, and was totally defeated. He was taken prisoner and later released by Joas of Israel. He returned to his throne; soon there was a plot to remove him. He got wind of it and fled to Lachish, a city southwest of Jerusalem, where he was caught and assassinated (4 Kgs 14).

10. *Azaria (781-740)*

Azaria was 16 years old when he came to the throne. He repaired the defenses of Jerusalem that had been destroyed by Joas of Israel, built up offensive operations, maintained control of Edom, and further consolidated his position along the trade routes by operations against northwestern Arabian tribes. He reopened the port and industries of Ezion-Geber on the Gulf of Aqaba, which led into the Red Sea. He was stricken with leoprosy toward the end of his reign (4 Kgs 14-15).

11. *Joatham (740-736)*

During his reign Peka, king of Israel, entered into a coalition with Rezin, king of Damascus, in order to stem the tide of Assyrian domination. The two kings wanted Joatham to join them, but he preferred to follow an independent policy and rejected the proposal. Unwilling to have a neutral and potentially hostile power in their way, Peka and Rezin formulated steps to subdue the kingdom of Juda. At that point Joatham died and was succeeded by his son, Achaz.

12. *Achaz (736-716)*

The forces of Peka and Rezin invaded Juda and drew close to Jerusalem (4 Kgs 16,5). To add to the problem, the Edomites, who had been subject to Juda throughout most of the eighth century, regained their independence and drove the troops of Achaz from Ethan (Ezion-Geber) which, as archaeological investigations have shown, they destroyed. It is almost certain that the Edomites also joined in the attack on Juda. Moreover, the Philistines who inhabited the coast of Palestine raided some of the border towns and occupied them. Juda was thus invaded from three sides. It was in the face of these events that Achaz, his throne endangered and he himself helpless, concluded that there was no alternative but to appeal to the Assyrian ruler for help.

Tiglath-Pileser III was the king of Assyria (745-727); he was a vigorous and very able leader whose avowed aim was to establish an empire that would encompass the entire Fertile Crescent. It was this ruler who inaugurated the deportation system by which the population of a conquered city, if it had not been exterminated during hostilities, was moved to another part of the empire and then replaced by colonists from other regions. In this way he hoped to destroy the nationalism of the vanquished and negate all patriotic feeling capable of fostering resistance.

Achaz was warned by the prophet Isaia not to enter into the alliance with Assyria but to trust in the promises of Yahweh (Is 7). Achaz refused the advice, sent an enormous gift to Tiglath-Pileser III, and asked for his help (4 Kgs 16,7-8). The Assyrian ruler acted swiftly. He moved down along the coast of Israel and cut off all possible Egyptian help. Then he struck at Israel with full force, destroying many of the cities and deporting portions of the population (4 Kgs 15,29). He also struck at Damascus, ravaging the city and executing the king, Rezin.

Since Achaz had not joined the anti-Assyrian coalition, Juda escaped the calamity that befell Israel. But its freedom was lost! As a result of the deal that Achaz made with Tiglath-Pileser III, Juda became a vassal state of the Assyrian empire.

Achaz left the reputation of having been a wicked ruler. His reign is remembered as the worst period of apostasy ever known in Juda. He introduced innovations in the Temple of Jerusalem, erecting in it an altar to the Assyrian gods. He was without faith or zeal for the religion of Yahweh, and did not, therefore, make any effort to keep the defenses against the introduction of pagan practices. The Biblical historian and the contemporary prophets speak of the pagan customs which flourished, together with all sorts of foreign cults and superstitions (4 Kgs 16,3-4; Is 2,6-8; Mi 5,12-14). Achaz went so far as to practice human sacrifice by offering his son to the god of the Canaanites, Moloch. Concerning this event, the Bible speaks of making "his son pass through fire," which almost certainly is a reference to human sacrifice and not merely to some form of ordeal (4 Kgs 16,3; 17,31).

The economic and social conditions of Juda were also in terrible condition during the time of Achaz. Much of the territory annexed by preceding kings was lost during the conflict between the Assyrians and the coalition formed by Peka and Rezin. This meant a great loss of revenue. Moreover, the tribute demanded by Assyria was so heavy that Achaz was forced to empty his treasury and even strip the Temple in order to raise enough money to pay it (4 Kgs 16,8,17).

Social and moral decay set in throughout the country. The poor were severely oppressed by the remaining great landowners, and the rich managed to continue to live in luxury without any concern for the plight of the less fortunate members of Juda (Is 3,16-26; 5,11-25). Although things were not so bad as they were in Israel, the difference was only of degree not of kind.

13. *Ezechia (716-687)*

The exact date of Ezechia's accession to the throne of Juda cannot be established with certainty because the Biblical evidence is conflicting. The year 716 is commonly accepted by scholars.

Ezechia understood the lesson in the destruction of the Northern Kingdom: he knew that the foreign influences and religious corruption had led to its ruin. Insisting that the nation's strength was to find its true basis in the purity of the faith which it has in Yahweh, he set out to achieve radical reform.

Before the fall of Israel, the prophet Isaia had foretold that Assyria would be Yahweh's rod of correction for the kingdom of Juda, and that only a "remnant" would remain (Is 5,26-30; 7,17-25; 8,6-8; 10,19-23). The prophet Michea also foretold the judgment that would occur against Juda (Mi 1,5; 2,1). The people saw how the threats of the prophets had been fulfilled upon the Northern Kingdom of Israel and so they were prepared for some reform.

Ezechia was a pious man; he and Josia are the only two kings who are praised without qualification in the book of Kings (4 Kgs 18,3-6,23,25). He ordered the Temple cleansed of all pagan objects and then dedicated anew. He renewed the Covenant with Yahweh, re-established the celebration of the festivals, and had the Scriptures that were in circulation committed to writing. The Canaanite high places were destroyed. To bring back the true worship of Yahweh he ordered that sacrifice be restricted to the Temple at Jerusalem. In this way he hoped to protect worship from the pagan excesses that had crept in at many of the local sanctuaries.

Tiglath-Pileser III died in 727 and was succeeded by Shalmaneser V (727-722), against whom, as we saw earlier, the last king of Israel (Osee) revolted by refusing to pay the tribute. The results of that move are already known—Shalmaneser acted quickly by attacking Samaria. He died during the battle and was succeeded by Sargon II (722-705) who captured Samaria after a three-year siege. The successor to Sargon was his son Sennacherib (705-681), a man of far less ability. It was probably this fact that caused Ezechia to think that he could throw off the Assyrian yoke, first by refusing to pay the tribute and then by claiming independence.

The prophet Isaia warned Ezechia against such a move. He told the king that Assyria would one day perish (Is 33); Ezechia did not heed the prophet's message and went ahead with his plans, even entering a coalition with other nations that also wanted to rid themselves of the Assyrian rule. He quickly busied himself with building up his defenses and ensuring his water supply in preparation for the revolt and expected siege (2 Chr 32,3-5). It was at this time that he dug the tunnel of Siloam which has become one of the great archaeological discoveries. The tunnel brought water from the spring under the hill of Jerusalem to a pool within the walls of the city.[8]

In 701 Sennacherib struck at those who had joined forces against Assyria. He first moved down along the coast and crushed the opposition. Then he turned on Juda and, according to his own records recently discovered, reduced 46 of its fortified cities, and made Ezechia a prisoner in his own palace "like a bird in a cage." He effected a slaughter at Lachish, which, when it was discovered by archaeologists, produced striking evidences of the destruction—a huge pit into which about 1,500 bodies had been buried, covered with a layer of animal bones, most of which were those of pigs, presumably the garbage of the Assyrian army.[9]

Sennacherib triumphed to the point of arriving at the gates of Jerusalem in 700 B.C. Ezechia was forced to pay tribute (4 Kgs 18,13-16) and had to remove the bronze from the Temple doors. The Assyrian ruler demanded the unconditional surrender of Jerusalem. Ezechia turned to Isaia for advice and the prophet told him that he should not fear because: "He (Sennacherib) shall not come into this city" (4 Kgs 19,32). Sennacherib did in fact fail in his attempt to capture the city; Assyrian records gloss over the setback with fine words. The Bible regards the retreat of the Assyrian armies as a miracle: "It came to pass that night, that an angel of the Lord came, and slew in the camp of the Assyrians a hundred and eighty-five thousand" (4 Kgs 19,35). It is very probable that a sudden outbreak of a plague or epidemic forced the retreat. However, Juda remained a tributary to Assyria. The brave attempt at independence, which cost Juda heavily, had failed.

---

[8] Illustrations in Grollenberg, *Atlas*, p. 84.

[9] A description of the battle of Lachish as found in records dating from the time of Sennacherib and also related illustrations are in G. Ernest Wright, *Biblical Archaeology* (Philadelphia: Westminster Press, 1957), pp. 164-69.

Ezechia is regarded as the king who remained faithful to Yahweh throughout his life: "The Lord also was with him, and in all things, to which he went forth, he behaved wisely" (4 Kgs 18,7). But, although the religious policy of Ezechia was successful as far as the rites and external observances were concerned, it did not greatly affect the interior disposition of the people. As a matter of fact, the reform he initiated did not survive him. His successor was one of the most godless kings of Juda, Manasses.

ISAIA: PROPHET OF THE HOLINESS OF GOD

Isaia, "The Lord is salvation," was born about the year 765 B.C.; at about the age of fifteen he received his prophetic vocation from Yahweh. It was while he was in the Temple of Jerusalem that he was called by God to announce the punishment of both Israel and Juda because of the infidelities of the people. As Isaia stood facing the Holy of Holies, he was filled with a sense of the tremendous, indescribable holiness of the Lord, and heard the voice of Him who is "Wholly Other." The transcendent Lord of heaven and earth revealed Himself to Isaia and showed that, as in the days of the Patriarchs and particularly Moses, He was a God who was with His people, Emmanuel. He was One who desired to cleanse His people and remove their sin.

> In the year King Ozia died, I saw the Lord seated on a high and lofty throne, with the train of his garment filling the temple.
> Seraphim were stationed above; each of them had six wings: with two they veiled their faces, with two they veiled their feet, and with two they hovered aloft.
> "Holy, holy, holy is the Lord of hosts!" they cried one to the other. "All the earth is filled with his glory!" At the sound of that cry, the frame of the door shook and the house was filled with smoke.
> Then I said, "Woe is me, I am doomed! For I am a man of unclean lips, living among a people of unclean lips; yet my eyes have seen the King, the Lord of hosts!" Then one of the seraphim flew to me, holding an ember which he had taken with tongs from the altar.
> He touched my mouth with it. "See," he said, "now that this has touched your lips, your wickedness is removed, your sin purged."
>
> *Is 6,1-7*

It was that vision that left an indelible mark on the personality of Isaia; it is the event which explains the tone of the Isaian message.

> The vision of the Lord enthroned in glory stamps an indelible character on Isaia's ministry and provides the key to the understanding of his message. The majesty, holiness and glory of the Lord took possession of his spirit and, conversely, he gained a new awareness of human pettiness and sinfulness. The enormous abyss between God's sovereign

holiness and man's sin overwhelmed the prophet. Only the purifying coal
of the seraphim could cleanse his lips and prepare him for acceptance of
the call: "Here I am, send me!" [10]

Isaia's career as a prophet lasted through the reigns of three kings: Joatham
(740-736), Achaz (736-716), and Ezechia (716-687); he witnessed the
fall of the kingdoms of Damascus (732), Samaria (721), and Ashdod (711).
He counseled kings and people against foreign alliances and warned Achaz
not to ally himself with Tiglath-Pileser III of Assyria. Faced with opposition
on all sides, particularly from those eager for pacts with nations that were
unfriendly to Assyria, Isaia faithfully and courageously strove to make the
king aware of the "wrong steers" that his advisers were giving him. Trust in
Yahweh was Juda's only salvation, the Lord of history will be true to His
promises. These must be the guiding principles for king and people. His voice
was drowned out by the opposition forces. He was forced to watch as Juda
made its covenant with death (Is 28,15). The king, his advisers, the masses,
preferred to honor God with their lips rather than with actions. They were
like those of today who do not see the implications of the words "In God we
trust." They say and read the words but put their trust in arms and alliances.

Isaia's faith remained strong in the hope that the all-Holy Lord would be
with His people and would restore the "remnant" and have it "lean upon the
Lord, the Holy One of Israel, in truth" (Is 10,17-22).

Nothing is known about the end of Isaia's life. There is little foundation
for the traditional Jewish story that he was martyred during the reign of
Manasses.

Although the book of Isaia is written in a style that is worthy of a great
poet, its general structure is hardly one that will satisfy the modern reader
who has a penchant for definite chronology and logical sequence. Like the
works of the prophets Amos and Osee, that of Isaia is really an anthology
of units composed by the prophet himself and some of his followers, members
of the Isaian school. Scholars generally attribute chapters 1-39 to Isaia
himself, and chapters 40-55 to someone other than the prophet of the eighth
century. The author of the second part is unknown; it is generally referred
to by the title *Deutero-Isaia,* Second Isaia. The period of composition is
thought to have been around the end of the Babylonian Exile.

The book of Isaia contains many profound theological ideas and themes.
God is the Holy One of Israel. He is the Strong One, the Powerful One. He
is King. Isaia is the great preacher of faith, total commitment to the Lord is
the only thing that matters. The Isaian slogan may be summed up in the
phrase, "Believe or perish!"

---

[10] "Introduction to the Book of Isaia," *The Holy Bible, The Prophetic Books* (Paterson,
New Jersey: St. Anthony Guild Press, 1961), p. 1. See the study of Isaia in Bouyer, *The
Meaning of Sacred Scripture,* pp. 68-81; also John E. Huesman, S.J., *The Book of Isaia*
(2 Parts; New York: The Paulist Press, 1961), I, 5-32; II, 5-21.

Absolute confidence in God is the mark of a true believer. This idea was developed by later prophets, for example, Sophonia, who taught in the late seventh century (Sop 3,12). It was ideally personified in the heroic individuals of post-exilic times, the *anawim,* the Poor of the Lord.

Isaia is a witness at an important stage in the history of salvation. He was the founder of a spiritual society which was distinct from the national group. The members of this prophetic circle were to make an alliance with the Lord and put their trust in Him until the time that He would accomplish His promises. This was the beginning of that remnant which the prophets had announced and which would make ready the way of the Lord. It would be tested and tried; it would be brought into exile and then would return to the land to which the promises were tied. The members of this remnant awaited the coming of the One who was to be the fulfillment of the promises. Finally, God, who exalts the lowly, regarded the lowliness of His handmaid, Mary, and Jesus the Lord, meek and humble, came into the world (Lk 1,46-55). He established the kingdom in which the *anawim* are heirs to the promises: "Blessed are the poor in spirit, for theirs is the kingdom of heaven" (Mt 5,3).

Some of the Messianic themes in the book of Isaia will be treated later in the special section on the prophets.[11]

14. *Manasses (687-642)*

Manasses came to the throne when he was 12 years of age. The country came more under the influence and domination of Assyria and this resulted in the renewed importation of the pagan gods and cults. The sanctuaries which Ezechia had destroyed were rebuilt and the people who had been inclined to pagan forms of worship again went to the "high places." The Assyrian worship of astral deities made its appearance (4 Kgs 21,5). The return to idolatry brought with it all types of superstition which now spread quickly —including sorcery and necromancy (claiming to foretell the future by alleged communication with the dead). Pagan cults connected with the fertility religion and the ritual of sacred prostitution were allowed to take place even within the Temple of Jerusalem (4 Kgs 21,7; 23,4-7). That such a change took place in the land shows that the spirit of Ezechia's reform had not affected the masses. There was some opposition from the loyal followers of Yahweh. To silence it Manasses ordered a persecution which the Biblical author can describe only by saying that he shed "very much innocent blood, till he filled Jerusalem up to the mouth" (4 Kgs 21,16).

In 681 Sennacherib was murdered; his death touched off a revolution in Mesopotamia. His successor was Esarhaddon (681-669) who was able to put down the revolt and to march into Egypt and take its king captive. The next king was Ashurbanapal (669-633). Although by this time Assyria was the greatest empire in history, there were signs that the sprawling kingdom

[11] See pp. 208-210.

was disintegrating. A revolt in Babylon shook it to its foundation even though it was put down by the king. The later years of Ashurbanapal are relatively unknown. Scholars are of the opinion that it was at this time that he found time for works of peace, among which was the collecting of a great library where copies of the myths and epics of ancient Babylon, including the stories of creation and the flood, were preserved. When he died, in 633, the end of the Assyrian empire was near; it was to last hardly 20 years more. In 626, Nabopolassar, a Chaldean prince, led a revolt for independence; he was the founder of the new Babylonian empire. The Assyrians were defeated outside Babylon and the prince established his throne there. Nineve fell to the Medes and Babylonians in 612. Continued battles brought the definitive collapse of Assyria in 609 B.C. when the Babylonians defeated its armies and their Egyptian allies at Haran.

15. *Amon (642-640)*

Amon continued the policies of his father, Manasses. He was assassinated after a short reign as a result of a conspiracy among high officials of the state. But the "people of the land" remained loyal to the house of David. They lynched the assassins and placed Amon's son, Josia, on the throne (4 Kgs 21,19-26).

16-17. *Josia (640-609)—Joachaz (609)*

Josia was the last great king of Juda. He returned to the principles of Yahweh. He cleansed the Temple and undertook to remove all traces of idolatry from the country. In the course of his reform (622 B.C.) the Book of the Law was discovered. This book was incorporated into the present book of Deuteronomy, which was probably written during the time that the scribes of Ezechiel were writing the traditions and narratives that had been transmitted orally. The Book of the Law was read to the people and the Covenant was renewed (4 Kgs 28). A religious reform was begun; the altars of the pagan deities were destroyed, and all traces of syncretism were removed. The reform extended not only to Jerusalem and Juda but also to such places as Bethel and the borders of Samaria which Josia had annexed to his kingdom.

While Josia was busy establishing control over northern Palestine, Assyria met its doom. Its capital, Ninive, fell to the Chaldeans and the Medes in 612. The Chaldean, Nabopolassar, who had wielded limited power in Babylon since about 626 B.C. gained control of the world empire. The Medes contented themselves with the mountainous regions of the north, although they were the ones who had destroyed the last vestiges of Assyrian power at Haran. Soon the Egyptian armies began their march to conquer the surrounding countries. The Pharaoh Necho marched to the north to support the crumbling power of Assyria (609 B.C.); Josia tried to block his path at Megiddo, a classic place to block an enemy coming from the south. The battle had hardly begun when Josia was wounded and died.

> There is deep tragedy in the life of the pious king, Josia. From early youth he had dedicated his life to the service of Yahweh, favorable political conditions enabled him to extend his sway over a great portion of the land once ruled by his father David, yet before attaining the age of forty he lost his life defending his country. He was animated by religious idealism. To him it did not seem part of Yahweh's plan that Juda should again be enslaved after attaining freedom through the fall of Assyria. . . . Nevertheless, it was foolhardy for him to advance against the Egyptians without weighing the relative strength of their forces, and to devise his own independent political policy while the mighty nations of the earth were contesting for world supremacy.[12]

At this time the Deuteronomic theology of history developed. This was the view which saw a correlation between obedience to Yahweh and earthly success (blessing) and disobedience and failure (curse). The historical documents were put into order according to the spirit of this Deuteronomic reform. This was also the time of the first *redaction* of the books of Josue, Judges, Samuel, and Kings. A *redaction* is an edition which includes adaptation and rearrangement of the original material.

After the death of Josia, the people, perhaps because they suspected the pro-Egyptian sympathies of his eldest son, placed his second son on the throne of Juda. However, when the Pharaoh Necho returned from the campaign around Haran, he replaced Joachaz (609) with Joakim.

18. *Joakim (609-598)*

Joakim was a tool of Egypt and permitted many of the worse forms of religious syncretism to come into his country. He was a despot with little concern for the people. Jeremia, the prophet, reproached him for his deeds—impoverishing the land through levies, compulsory labor, extortion, illegal death sentences, and deterioration of the religious worship of Yahweh. The warnings and threats of Jeremia fell on deaf ears, and he himself was bitterly persecuted (Jer 20,1-3; 26,1-19). The prophet was also severe on those who favored an alliance with Egypt, whose activities drew down on Palestine the scourge of Nabuchodonosor, the king of Babylon and victor over the Egyptians at Carchemish in 605 B.C. The pro-Egyptian group, more attached to human viewpoints than to the will of Yahweh, did not listen to Jeremia, but allowed themselves to be guided by men who can best be described as "time-serving prophets"—men who said what they were expected to say and who did not hesitate to "divine for money." This pro-Egyptian group instigated much of

---

[12] Heinisch, *History of the Old Testament,* pp. 262-63.

the bitter persecution of Jeremia, but it did not succeed in destroying his prestige. Joakim rebelled against Nabuchodonosor, who, because he could not return to Juda immediately, allowed the surrounding nations who had remained loyal to him to devastate Juda. In 598 B.C. he did come, and with an army he laid siege to Jerusalem. Joakim, however, had died a few months earlier and had been succeeded by his son, Joachin (4 Kgs 24).

19. *Joachin (598)*

The Deuteronomic historian who edited the books of Kings says that Joachin continued the policies of his father (4 Kgs 24,9). His reign lasted less than a year. In order to avoid total devastation he went into voluntary exile in Babylon with the royal household, some notables, and skilled craftsmen. He was freed about 37 years later, when Nabuchodonosor's successor came to the throne of Babylon. Archaeological discoveries have brought to light tablets which provide extra-biblical confirmation of the events mentioned in the Bible.

20. *Sedecia (598-597)*

This king, whose name was changed from Matthanias, was the son of Josia (4 Kgs 24,17). A puppet placed on the throne by the Babylonian king, he was poorly endowed intellectually, and lacked initiative and determination. He was a weakling wholly under the influence of the officials of the court. He consulted Jeremia in secret, but left him to the mercies of his persecutors. However, he did not follow the counsels that he received (Jer 37,2). True religion continued to decline and idolatry flourished in the Temple. Sedecia wavered between the counsels of Jeremia, who told him to take the present situation as the will of Yahweh, and the pressure from the group who urged him to conspire with Egypt and the neighboring peoples against Babylon. This faction prevailed and the king rebelled. In 588 B.C. the armies of Babylon reappeared in Palestine. Detailed information concerning the campaign is lacking, and the texts that we now possess from the time of Nabuchodonosor do not describe his military operations. It is certain that in 587 B.C., after a siege which he interrupted in order to rout reinforcements that had been sent from Egypt, Nabuchodonosor destroyed the city of Jerusalem and deported the flower of the people to Babylon.[13] Sedecia was captured and he suffered the punishment of a rebel—he was obliged to witness the murder of his sons, and then his eyes were put out. Sedecia then followed his people into exile with this dreadful picture in his memory. The prophecy of Jeremia had been fulfilled: "Thus says the Lord: I am handing this city over to the

---

[13] A longstanding dispute among scholars concerning the exact date of the destruction of Jerusalem has been settled by the study of the tablets of the *Babylonian Chronicle*. The date was July, 587. See David Noel Freedman, "The Babylonian Chronicle," *The Biblical Archaeologist*, XIX (September, 1956), 50-60.

king of Babylon; he will destroy it with fire. Neither shall you escape his hand; rather you will be captured and fall into his hands. You shall see the king of Babylon and speak to him face to face. Then you shall be taken to Babylon" (Jer 34,2-3).

JEREMIA: PROPHET OF THE NEW COVENANT

Jeremia lived through the hectic events that marked the last days of the kingdom of Juda. He was born around the middle of the seventh century B.C. in the town of Anathoth, a short distance from Jerusalem. He supported the religious reform conducted by king Josia in 622 B.C. As a result of his loyalty to Yahweh, he had to suffer a great deal at the hands of those who were more interested in succeeding in this world than in following the demands of the Covenant.[14]

Jeremia saw that Juda's sinfulness and refusal to do penance had determined its fate, destruction at the hands of the Babylonians. He advised the nation to capitulate to the armies of Babylon because he saw in them instruments of divine vengeance and purification. His oracles were considered too demoralizing for a people who looked upon military alliances and force of arms as the guarantees of national survival. He was imprisoned, brought to Babylon, and later to Egypt by his own people. There he suffered the further heartbreak of witnessing the worship of a pagan goddess by the Jews. An ancient tradition says that he was murdered by his fellow countrymen when he was about 70 years old (*ca.* 575 B.C.).

Although Jeremia's life appears to have ended in failure, this was not the case. He became one of the spiritual guides of the Jews. His works influenced those of Ezechiel, the prophet during the Exile, and Deutero-Isaia who wrote after the Exile. While in Babylon, the people meditated on his teachings and came to a deeper appreciation of the Covenant and the meaning of true piety.

There are many unsolved problems in the book of Jeremia. We know that the prophet dictated a large part of his message to his companion Baruch, but the manuscript was burned by Joakim (Jer 36,1-32). A second manuscript forms the main portion of the present book, chapters 1-25 and 46-51. The autobiographical parts are sometimes called the *Confessions of Jeremia* (Jer 11,18 to 12,6; 15,10-21; 17,14-18; 18,18-23; 20,7-18). The remaining chapters were added later; it is almost certain that several parts were inserted by Baruch. The last chapter of the book is a fitting *finis* to the work of Jeremia whose oracles were fulfilled in the destruction of the Holy City (Jer 52; Jer 39,1-10 and 4 Kgs 24,18-25,30).

The book is filled with oracles which Jeremia proclaimed at various times in his career. Like the books of the other prophets it does not present logical or chronological sequences of events. Neither is there any strict thematic unity

---

[14] Bouyer, *The Meaning of Sacred Scripture*, pp. 82-90; also Neal M. Flanagan, O.S.M., *The Book of Jeremia* (2 Parts; New York: The Paulist Press, 1961), I, 5-29; II, 5-31.

in the work. The reader has to get used to leaps from one subject to another, from one period in Jeremia's life to another, without much attention being paid to exact time sequence. The work is filled with symbolism that is rich in variety and profundity of thought. Some of the symbols are strange and foreign to most readers of today. It is fortunate that they are explained in the text itself: see, for example, the use made of the symbol of the boiling cauldron (Jer 1,13-19), the basket of figs (Jer 24,1-10), the cup of foaming wine (Jer 25,15-38), the smashing of the potter's flask (Jer 19,1-20,6), and the bands and yoke bars over the prophet's shoulders (Jer 27,1-28,17).

Many themes in the book of Jeremia could be emphasized, but for the purposes of this introductory study it will be sufficient to say something about the theme of the New Covenant.

God had established His Covenant with His people. The Hebrews were the People of the Covenant and at Sinai it was sealed with the blood of animals (Ex 24). Valued in theory but often disregarded in practice, the Covenant remained the witness of the love of the Lord for His elect. The prophets labored to keep alive the memory of this Covenant and to call their hearers back to a practical obedience to its requirements. The history of Israel and Juda is the sad history of the neglect of the commitment which had been made by the early Hebrews: "We will do everything that the Lord has told us" (Ex 24,3; Jer 11 contains a plea for fidelity to the Covenant).

Obedience must be based on sincerity and truth. Formalism, mere external participation, is the destruction of the very thing that the Covenant-observance is intended to demonstrate—*hesed*, love. The condemnations the prophets directed against the sacrifices offered without proper interior disposition are a warning to all those who perform the "letter" of the Law but are far from its "spirit."

Jeremia realized this when he heralded what has become known as "the Gospel before the Gospel."

> The days are coming, says the Lord, when I will make a new covenant with the house of Israel and the house of Juda. It will not be like the covenant I made with their fathers the day I took them by the hand to lead them forth from the land of Egypt; for they broke my covenant, and I had to show myself their master, says the Lord. But this is the covenant which I will make with the house of Israel after those days, says the Lord. I will place my law within them and write it upon their hearts; I will be their God, and they shall be my people. No longer will they have need to teach their friends and kinsmen how to know the Lord. All, from least to greatest, shall know me, says the Lord, for I will forgive their evildoing and remember their sins no more.
>
> *Jer 31,31-34*

Table 6. THE KINGDOMS OF JUDA AND ISRAEL 931-587 B.C.

JUDA		B.C.	ISRAEL	
KINGS	PROPHETS		PROPHETS	KINGS
ROBOAM (931-913)		931		JEROBOAM (931-910)
ABIAM (913-911) ASA (911-870)				NADAB (910-909)
		900		BAASA (909-886)
				ELA (886-885)
				ZIMRI (7 days)
				OMRI (885-874)
JOSAPHAT (870-848)			ELIA ELISEUS	ACHAB (874-853) OCHOZIA (853-852)
JORAM (848-841)		850		JORAM (852-841)
OCHOZIA (841) ATHALIA (841-835) JOAS (835-796)				JEHU (841-814)
AMAZIA (796-781) AZARIA (781-740) JOATHAM (740-736) ACHAZ (736-716)	ISAIA MICHEA	800 750	AMOS OSEE	JOACHAZ (814-798) JOAS (798-783) JEROBOAM II (783-743) ZACHARIA (743) SHALLUM (743) MENAHEM (743-738) PEKAHIA (738-737) PEKA (737-732) OSEE (732-724)
EZECHIA (716-687) MANASSES (687-642) AMON (642-640) JOSIA (640-609) JOACHAZ (609) JOAKIM (609-598) JOACHIN (598) SEDECIA (598-587)	JEREMIA EZECHIEL	700 650 600 587		

This text is the climax of the book. Jeremia announces the establishment of a New Covenant but the old one is not to be rejected. The Covenant relationship between Yahweh and His People is not repudiated, it is transformed into a greater intimacy of the Lord with His People. The New Covenant will not be written on tablets of stone, as the old one had been; God will act directly upon the heart of man (Jer 31,32-34). Religion, he insists, is something personal, the union of the individual with God. Yet this emphasis on the personal element is not something which neglects the social nature of salvation. The individual must respond to the *hesed* of the Lord with a personal commitment that involves an interior transformation. All this takes place in an individual who belongs to a People. Jeremia was interested in the salvation of the group as well as of the individual and his prophecy is a sensible balance of collectivism and individualism.

Jeremia's insistence on the essential interior qualities of the Covenant can be traced back to other prophets, particularly Osee. It is also in line with the spirit of the Deuteronomic reform which took place during the reign of Josia (640-609). It appears to be motivated by the teaching found in the Great Commandment of Love, the Shema:

> Hear, O Israel! The Lord is our God, the Lord alone! Therefore, you shall love the Lord, your God, with all your heart, and with all your soul, and with all your strength.
>
> *Dt 6,4-5*

The New Covenant would have three aspects: (1) God will forgive sins (Jer 31,34); (2) the individual will bear the burden of personal responsibility and retribution (Jer 31,29); and (3) religion will be true only if it is a thing of the heart, the Spirit will create a new heart in man (Jer 31,33; this is expressed in Ps 50,12). The New Covenant will be an eternal one.

The prophetic teaching of Jeremia was fulfilled at the Last Supper when Jesus established the New Covenant: "This cup is the new covenant in my blood, which shall be shed for you" (Lk 22,20; 1 Cor 11,25). The apostles announced the establishment of the Covenant through Jesus: "He also it is who has made us fit ministers of the new covenant, not of the letter but of the spirit; for the letter kills, but the spirit gives life" (2 Cor 3,6).

fourteen

THE BABYLONIAN EXILE
(587–538 B.C.)

I. INTRODUCTION

THE EVENTS of 587 B.C. cannot be minimized. Although it is true that there was no total deportation of the people into Babylon, the disaster was terrible, and it signaled the disruption of Jewish life in Palestine. Juda was left desolate, and archaeological studies have shown that many of the towns were razed to the ground and in most cases were not rebuilt for many years to come. Albright notes:

> The results (i.e., of excavations) are uniform and conclusive: many towns were destroyed at the beginning of the sixth century B.C. and never again occupied; others were destroyed at that time and partly re-occupied at some later date; still others were destroyed and reoccupied after a long period of abandonment, marked by a sharp change of stratum and by intervening indications of use for non-urban purposes. There is not a single known case where a town of Juda proper was continuously occupied through the exilic period.[1]

The population of the land was decimated. Many people were deported into Babylon and thousands died in battle, or from starvation and disease. The Babylonians did not replace the deportees with people brought from other lands, as the Assyrians had done in Samaria and Israel. The population of Juda was about 250,000 during the eighth century and half that number even after the first deportation of 597. After the first exiles returned from Babylon it was scarcely above 20,000. During the intervening years it was sparse indeed. We know nothing about what happened in Juda during the half-century that followed the disaster of 587. Some refugees probably drifted back

---

[1] *Archaeology of Palestine*, pp. 141-42.

and joined the population that was left in the land. Their lot was miserable. The Temple, although in blackened ruins, remained a center of pilgrimage for the pious of Juda as well as of Israel. The crisis of 587 left the northern part of Palestine untouched; however, conditions there, too, were nothing to be proud about. Religion was permeated with pagan features and Yahwism was of a syncretistic type. The reform efforts of Josia during the seventh century had not effected any lasting revival of true religion among the vast majority of the people. Consequently, national life in both parts of Palestine was at its lowest ebb. The People of God was in exile!

The Jews that were in Babylon were the cream of their country's political, intellectual, and religious leadership. It is impossible to fix their number. Certainly it was not large. In the book of Jeremia the total number of deportees is given as 4,600 (Jer 52,28-30). This is a reasonable figure. Probably, it includes only the adult males and, consequently, the grand total was about three or four times that figure. In 4 Kgs 24,14 and 16, the figures of 10,000 and 8,000 are given for the first deportation. These were probably rough estimates of the total, including women and children. Estimates given by some authors who mention 50,000 to 70,000 are far too high. Whatever their number, it was these exiles who would, in God's plan, be the ones to shape the future of the Chosen People and bring about a restoration of the religious ideals.

II. SOCIAL CONDITIONS

It is difficult to imagine the profound despair of the deportees. Torn from the land of their ancestors and their God, deprived of their liberty and of almost all their property, brutally transported into a distant country and into an idolatrous environment, they had to lead a poor, sorrowful, and humiliating life, particularly at first. We do not have any direct information about the condition of the exiled Jews. The historical books of the Bible have omitted this period more or less completely and the Babylonian annals do not mention the Israelites. Indirectly, we can get a fairly adequate idea of the Babylonian captivity from the allusions to it contained in the narratives of the contemporary prophets.

From the economic and social points of view, the living conditions of the exiles, after the painful phase of initial settlement, do not seem to have been too bad, at least in general. Ordinarily, they were not treated as slaves in the strict sense. They were settled chiefly at Babylon and near that city they formed compact colonies which occupied themselves with agriculture. Later, they engaged in trade and commerce. In their new home the Jews came to enjoy considerable freedom, especially after the death of Nabuchodonosor, and they used their opportunities in both agricultural and commercial pursuits. Excavations at Nippur in southern Babylonia have unearthed ledgers of a business house named Murashu. This firm did business with the Jews and with others like the Persians and even the Egyptians.[2] "All in all, there is no evidence that the exiles suffered any unusual hardship above that inherent in their lot. On the contrary, life in Babylon must have opened up for many of them opportunities that would never have been available in Palestine." [3]

At first, the exiles regarded their lot as a trial of short duration, but later they built houses and planted gardens (Jer 29,5). This proves that they could acquire property. They soon were in comfortable positions and many became "well-off," as is shown by the large sums of money given to those who returned to Jerusalem (Ezr 1,6; 8,24-30).

III. RELIGIOUS REVIVAL

As mentioned above, the social situation of the exiles gradually improved. Their religious life, too, enjoyed a real revival. There were dangers to Yahwism since they were in a land dotted with pagan sanctuaries, temples, and customs. How many of the Jews fell away from Yahweh entirely, we do not know. Possibly, the percentage was higher among merchants who for profit motives sought closer union with the Babylonians, and among those who had been reduced to slave status and as a result lost all connection with their own people. Many Jews capitulated to the pressures of foreign culture and religion. However, most of the exiles did not yield to their old inclination to idolatry, but attached themselves to Yahweh more closely than ever. They learned the superiority of internal, moral spirituality over *mere* external sacrifice. They recognized that their present misfortune was a just punishment for their sins, and they repudiated the past completely. Emphasis was placed on a strict observance of the Law. Such sincere repentence and good resolutions were strong enough to guarantee the survival of the religion of Israel and of the nation itself.

The mood of the exiled people is reflected in the moving words of Psalm 136 which embodies the spiritual anguish experienced by the devout in a foreign land and their longing for their ancestral home.

PSALM 136 (137)

By the streams of Babylon we sat and wept
    when we remembered Sion.
On the aspens of that land
    we hung up our harps,
Though there our captors asked of us
    the lyrics of our songs,
And our despoilers urged us to be joyous;
    "Sing for us the songs of Sion!"

---

[2] Scholars are divided concerning the identity of Murashu. Some say that he was a Jew: for example, Ricciotti, *op. cit.,* II, 63, and Anderson, *op. cit.,* p. 377; others say that he was not, D. Winton Thomas, *op. cit.,* p. 96.

[3] Bright, *A History of Israel,* p. 326.

> How could we sing a song of the Lord
>   in a foreign land?
> If I forget you, Jerusalem,
>   may my right hand be forgotten!
> May my tongue cleave to my palate
>   if I remember you not,
> If I place not Jerusalem
>   ahead of my joy.

The conversion that was effected was not merely the result of circumstances. It was aided by the work of several prophets, particularly *Ezechiel,* who by the severity of his reproaches and the strictness of his precepts, as well as by the number of his promises, became the revered savior of the people. The Jewish community had its rebirth in the 50 years between the first deportations to Babylon and the return from the Exile.

EZECHIEL : PROPHET OF THE EXILE

Ezechiel, the great spiritual leader of Judaism during the Exile, was a complex individual. He was a man upon whom the hand of the Lord rested and whom the spirit of God transformed (Ez 1,3; 2,2; 3,12-22). He combined such contradictory elements within himself that some have not hesitated to call him a psychopathic personality. At times he would fall on his face (Ez 3,1; 3,23), go off into seclusion (Ez 3,24-27), become distraught (Ez 3,15), perform strange actions (Ez 4,4-8; 5,1-4), or experience ecstasies and visions (Ez 1,4-28; 37,1-4). All these things are true, but the judgment of his critics is false. Ezechiel was a prophet of the Lord, and his book, often symbolic in language, is the testament of a man sent by God to be His spokesman.[4]

Ezechiel arrived in Babylon in 597 when King Joachin of Jerusalem went into voluntary exile rather than have the Holy City devastated by the armies of Nabuchodonosor. The people thought that Jerusalem would not be destroyed; and, therefore, even in exile their hope for a bright future was comparatively high. But in Jerusalem, the things that the prophets had condemned earlier in the people's history continued: Yahwism was on the decline, idolatry was practiced in the Temple itself where a statue of Astarte was worshipped, and the pagan god of vegetation Tammuz, as well as the Egyptian god received homage (Ez 8).

The prophetic call of Ezechiel took place in 593. It is described in a majestic vision full of oriental imagery, similar to the theophanies experienced by some of the other prophets (Ez 1-2). The vision of God "riding upon the cherubim" emphasizes His transcendence and omnipotence. The ancient Israelites did not have our understanding of angels as spiritual beings; they

---

[4] See the following for introductory studies of Ezechiel: Bouyer, *The Meaning of Sacred Scripture,* pp. 91-97; Edward F. Siegman, C.PP.S., *The Book of Ezechiel* (2 Parts; New York: The Paulist Press, 1961), I, 5-32; II, 5-29.

pictured the members of Yahweh's heavenly court as cherubims, the sphinx-like beings with human heads and wings, similar to the *karibu* of the Syro-Phoenician people. Perhaps these artistic forms appear strange ones for angels, but we might wonder if they were not better suited to express angelic dignity and power than many of the "softer" cupid-like forms invented by the Renaissance artists and still used in religious iconography.

God is the Master of the world, and so in the vision He sits on the throne over the firmament, the dome-like structure which the Semites imagined covered the earth. Stormwind and flashing fire, burnished bronze and glittering crystal, sounds of wings and noise of roaring waters, all these enter into a vision in which Ezechiel saw the "likeness of the glory of the Lord" (Ez 1). In a second vision he received and ate a scroll which bore the words, "Lamentation and wailing and woe" (Ez 2,10). As God's spokesman, he was to predict the punishments that were to come to the people because of their infidelities; the scroll written by Yahweh meant that the words of Ezechiel would transmit the message of the Lord. Throughout his life, Ezechiel was filled with the convictions born at the moment of his call—God is holy and present everywhere but he himself is only a "son of man," a mortal. Yet he is one chosen to be the Lord's prophet.

For the next five years Ezechiel warned the people about their personal responsibility; he told them, furthermore, that they shared in the guilt of those who were still in Juda. They were not to think that their woes were due to the "sins of their fathers" and thus place the blame on previous generations. The proverb that they liked to quote was false: "Fathers have eaten sour grapes, thus their children's teeth are on edge" (Ez 18,2-4). Guilt and responsibility were theirs and they were responsible individually for what was taking place. The warnings of Ezechiel concerning imminent punishments are sometimes presented by symbolic actions which appear strange to our mentality. But we should realize that he spoke to an *oriental mentality* and that his actions would mean more than many of our words (Ez 4,1-5,15; 12). Through the prophecies of Ezechiel runs the refrain, "thus you shall know that I am the Lord." The people would learn that Yahweh is not only the God of mercy but also of justice.

> Thus says the Lord God: Disaster upon disaster! See it coming! An end is coming, the end is coming upon you! See it coming! The climax has come for you who dwell in the land! The time has come, near is the day: a time of consternation, not of rejoicing. Soon now I will pour out my fury upon you and spend my anger upon you; I will judge you according to your conduct and lay upon you the consequences of all your abominations. I will not look upon you with pity nor have mercy; I will deal with you according to your conduct, and the consequences of your abominations shall be in your midst; then shall you know that it is I, the Lord, who strike.

> See, the day of the Lord! See, the end is coming! Lawlessness is in full
> bloom, insolence flourishes, violence has risen to support wickedness.
> It shall not be long in coming, nor shall it delay. The time has come,
> the day dawns.
>
> *Ez 7,5-12*

The hand of the Lord struck in the disaster of 587 and people were punished because of their sinfulness. Nabuchodonosor's army destroyed Jerusalem,
leveled the Temple to the ground, and forced many people into exile in
Babylon. Now everything seemed lost and the "glory of the Lord" departed
from the Temple; the Ark of the Covenant, the throne of His invisible
presence, was lost. The exiles were thrown into a state of despair; Babylon
had won and its god Marduk seemed to have vanquished Yahweh! Now it
was Ezechiel's task to comfort the people and to raise their hearts above the
present catastrophe to that time when the Lord would bring about the restoration of His people. He tells them about the "new covenant" that God will
make with the people.

> I will give them a new heart and put a new spirit within them; I will
> remove the stony heart from their bodies, and replace it with a natural
> heart, so that they will live according to my statutes, and observe and
> carry out my ordinances; thus they shall be my people and I will be
> their God.
>
> *Ez 11,19-20*

Jeremia had used almost the same words when he spoke of the Covenant
written "upon their heart" (Jer 31,31-34). The two prophets often use the
same expression: "I will be their God and they shall be my people" (Jer
24,7; 30,22; 31,33; Ez 11,20; 37,23,27).

Like Osee, Ezechiel uses an allegory about a faithless wife as an example
of the infidelities of Israel toward Yahweh.

> They shall burn your apartments with fire and inflict punishments
> on you while many women look on. Thus I will put an end to your
> harlotry and you shall never again give payment. When I have wreaked
> my fury upon you I will cease to be jealous of you, I will be quiet and
> no longer vexed. Because you did not remember what happened when
> you were a girl, but enraged me with all these things, therefore in return
> I am bringing down your conduct upon your head, says the Lord God.
> For did you not add lewdness to the rest of your abominable deeds?
>
> *Ez 16,41-43*

The allegory is developed at length, and at times it is a little tedious. But
it does reveal in a vivid and realistic way the solidarity of the people with
their God. Yahweh threatens vengeance in tones that sometimes hurt the
sensibilities of believers. However, in the Semitic idiom used by the prophet,

we cannot fail to be outraged by the horribleness of the sins committed by the people. Perhaps this can serve as an antidote for our generation, which so often acts as if it has lost the very sense of sin.

The prophet uses the parable of the Shepherds in order to teach the people that Yahweh, the Shepherd of Israel, will take care of His Chosen Flock (Ez 34). He had sent representatives, kings, priests, and prophets, but too many of them had used their position for their own selfish purposes. The result was that the people were like abandoned sheep going astray. Yet, all the blame must not be put on the *shepherds;* the sheep, too, had a personal responsibility, and they must share the consequences. Yahweh says that He will punish the guilty, shepherds or sheep, and He will assume personal charge over the flock and guide it to the Promised Land. This prophecy about the Shepherds should be seen as the background for the figure used by Jesus when He called Himself the "Good Shepherd" who would protect His sheep; and, unlike the hirelings who deserted the flock when danger threatened, He would die for them (Lk 15,1-7; Jn 10,1-18). The Church is the Flock of the Lord.

The vision of the field of dry bones is a prediction of the restoration of Israel, the people of the Covenant. The bones are symbolic of Israel in the deadly despair of the Exile. No earthly power could save it and restore it to life. Yahweh alone gives life; He alone can give the Spirit that will bring His people back to life.

> Then you shall know that I am the Lord, when I open your graves and have you rise from them, O my people! I will put my spirit in you that you may live, and I will settle you upon your land; thus you shall know that I am the Lord. I have promised, and I will do it, says the Lord.
> *Ez 37,13-14*

The last chapters of the book contain a lengthy vision in which Ezechiel speaks of the New Temple (Ez 40-43,12), the altar, and worship (43,13-46, 24). This part of the book, filled with idealistic and symbolic ideas, is called the *Torah of Ezechiel.*

Standing between the period of destruction and that of restoration, Ezechiel, the prophet of transition, draws the blueprint for the new Israel. It will be built in a close relationship with the Temple, which he pictures as an idealized version of the one built by Solomon. It is from the Temple that a stream of water flows which makes fertile all the land that it touches and even causes fish to live in the Dead Sea (Ez 47,1-42). Thus did Ezechiel try to show the people who would form the post-Exilic community that the Temple was to be the focal point of their attention, the source of their unity and life. In these chapters, Ezechiel truly shows himself to be a *priest* interested in the worship of the Lord.

It was Ezechiel's influence that caused later prophets like Aggai and Zacharia, partners in securing the reconstruction of the Temple, to continue the plea for lives that were Temple-centered (Ag 1-2; Zach 1-8). Even Ezra and Nehemia, who were to be instrumental in the rebuilding of the land, were disciples of Ezechiel, prophet and priest.

The priests who were in exile in Babylon were influenced by Ezechiel and they instructed the people. They preserved the liturgical laws and customs of the Solomonic Temple, and looked to the day when they could return and exercise their ministry. Since it was their task to recount the Sacred History of their people, they took the older accounts, systematized them and high-lighted the features they considered more important. Thus many of the groups of people who were to return from the Exile were formed in the Priestly tradition, loyal to liturgical laws and stressing the need for holiness in those who serve a God who is holy. This Priestly tradition influenced the final formation of the Pentateuch, which is the result of an editorial process in which the Yahwist, Elohist, and Deuteronomic materials were formed into one great work. The book of Leviticus is the particular example of the work of the Priestly School. In it Israel is viewed as a cultic community in which the whole of life is related to the Law of Moses. It was this tradition that fashioned the first chapter of the book of Genesis, which contains Priestly doctrine in concentrated form in which God majestically brings into existence a world that is good; the six days of Divine labor culminate in the restful observance of the seventh, the Sabbath, blessed by God.

Ezechiel has been called the *Father of Judaism* because of the influence which his teaching exerted on the Exilic and Post-Exilic communities. Em-phasis was placed on the Law and Worship. Israel was not merely a nation but a cultic group, a "church." His vision of grandeur for the Temple did not materalize; the re-built Temple was far from grandiose. But his person and his teachings were important elements in the History of Salvation which culmi-nated in Jesus, *the Shepherd of the Flock* and *the Temple*.

fifteen

THE RETURN FROM EXILE AND
PERSIAN PERIOD (538–333 B.C.)

I. INTRODUCTION

THE RETURN from the exile became possible when Cyrus became King of the Persians (555) and through a series of victories conquered the Medes and declared himself their lord (549). By the year 546 Cyrus was master of Asia Minor, and in 539 his armies entered Babylon, whose power had steadily declined since the death of Nabuchodonosor (561). Cyrus was looked upon as the agent destined by Yahweh to liberate Israel (Is 41,2-5; 25; 45,1-3).

Cyrus the Persian was a tolerant individual. His treatment of vanquished states and princes strengthened the hopes of the oppressed while it undermined the opposition of their oppressors in every place. In an inscription written on a clay cylinder dating from the time of Cyrus we read the promulgation of one of the basic principles of Cyrus' reign: to resettle in their native lands the peoples who had been violently deported by previous kings, and to re-establish the cult of the gods.[1] It was, therefore, in complete harmony with his policy to grant the Jews permission to return to Palestine and to rebuild the temple of Yahweh. The decree was issued in 538, the first year of his rule. It is preserved in two forms in the book of Ezra (1,2-4 and 6,3-5). [Ezra 6,3-5 was copied from the original which was kept in the royal archives. The section that is given refers to the building of the Temple, not to the return of the Jews. The first reference contains the instructions concerning both the return and the building of the Temple.] There were scholars who used to look upon the decrees of Cyrus found in the Bible as spurious. However, the discovery of inscriptions of Cyrus in temples of Mesopotamia have shown that such an opinion cannot be sustained. The now-famous Cyrus Cylinder contains an account of his Babylonian triumph and his policy of allowing captives to

[1] The text of the Cyrus Cylinder is in Thomas op. cit., pp. 92-94.

return to their homelands and rebuild their temples. It took several months for the Jews to leave after the decree was issued. It should be noted that not all the Jews left the country. Many had established themselves very well and were not eager to give up all that they had acquired in order to return to the ruins of their homeland.

II. EZRA AND NEHEMIA

The Bible does not shed much light about the period that immediately followed the return of the people to Palestine. There is some little information in the books of Ezra and Nehemia. These originally formed one literary work together with the books of Chronicles (Paralipomenon)—a work which was compiled toward the end of the fourth century B.C. in an attempt to present the whole course of history from the Creation down to the time of the compiler. By reading these books as a unit we are able to get some idea of what happened at the time: the Jews returned in separate groups to Palestine; the building of the Temple, hindered by the activities of the hostile Samaritans, was completed in 515 B.C., 23 years after the return of the first group of exiles. This achievement aroused the jealousy of the people who had been imported to populate the plains of Palestine and they opposed the reconstruction of the walls of Jerusalem. Finally, however, the walls were rebuilt in spite of the Samaritan opposition (Ezr 3-6; Neh 1-6).

Ezra and Nehemia date their activities by the years of the reign of king Artaxerxes (Ezr 7,1; Neh 2,1). It would seem, therefore, that it is an easy matter to fix their dates accurately. However, the available sources do not permit anything like an absolute chronology. To begin with, there were three kings of Persia who were called Artaxerxes—Artaxerxes I (465-424), Artaxerxes II (404-358), Artaxerxes III (358-338). Scholars are not in agreement concerning the chronology of the period and about the lives of the two individuals under consideration. It is pretty much accepted by all scholars that Ezra and Nehemia exercised their duties during the reign of Artaxerxes I. But the problem remains: Who came first from Babylon to the city of Jerusalem, Ezra or Nehemia?

Some authors hold that Ezra went to Jerusalem in 458 B.C. at the command of the Persian king.[2] It was his task to re-organize the life of the Jewish people in accordance with the Mosaic Law. Nehemia made his first visit in 445 B.C., which was the twentieth year of the rule of Artaxerxes I (Neh 2,1). At that time he supplemented the religious re-organization with material programs, including the building of the walls of the city. The second visit of Nehemia to Jerusalem was made in 433 B.C. when he eliminated abuses that were present. Bright concludes his discussion of the problem by saying:

> We take the view, then, that Nehemia was governor from 445 until
> 433 when he returned to the Persian court for an unspecified length of

---

[2] Grollenberg, *Atlas*, p. 100; Moriarty, *Foreword*, pp. 44-45.

time. Circa 428, Ezra arrived, by which time Nehemia was almost certainly back in Jerusalem colliding, as he probably already had done
before, with apostates and back-sliders. Ezra's work was thus done during Nehemia's second term of office. . . . The reforms of the two men
ran, in part, concurrently and converged at the same point. Nehemia
tells his own side of it and claims the credit; the Chronicler, as one
would expect, gives the credit to Ezra.[3]

Particular attention should be given to Nehemia 9 wherein the author gives
an account of the renewal of the covenant with Yahweh. In that chapter we
find a profession of Israel's faith which contains a recital of the whole history
of Israel—the history of Yahweh's dealings with His people.

After the time of Ezra and Nehemia we know almost nothing about the
Jews until the revolt of the Maccabees in 166 B.C. There is, therefore, a
period of about two and a half centuries during which we have no information
from the Bible. Concerning that time it is impossible to lay a finger on a
single event and to say with absolute certainty that it happened. It seems that
during these centuries nothing happened which could be interpreted as an
intervention of Yahweh in the life of His people. We saw a similar situation
for the period between the time that the Hebrews went to Egypt during the
time of the patriarch Jacob in the seventeenth century and their liberation by
Moses in the thirteenth century—a period of about 400 years, of which the
Bible records nothing.

III. THE PERSIAN PERIOD

A. THE SITUATION

Early during the period which lasted from 550 to 330 B.C. Persian culture
reached a high level of development, as witnessed by the impressive remains
found at Persepolis, the main capital of the Persian empire.[4] Juda was incorporated into the huge empire, and the Persian kings recognized the territory, with Jerusalem as its center, as a sacral place administered by priests
in accordance with the Law of Moses. Jerusalem held a unique place in
the hearts of the Jews, who at this time were beginning to settle in many parts
of the empire.

The Diaspora, or Dispersion, dates from this time. Beginning in 587 B.C.
many Jews had gone to Egypt in order to escape the catastrophe of the
Babylonian Exile and had established themselves there, as well as in Babylon
where they achieved a certain amount of status, as was pointed out earlier.
Of the Jews in these foreign lands we have no information at all except for
the data supplied by the *Elephantine Texts,* which come from a Jewish community in Upper Egypt during the fifth century. The last text dates from the

---

[3] Bright, *A History of Israel,* p. 386; see pp. 375-86 for a study of the complicated Ezra-
Nehemia chronology.
[4] Illustrations in Grollenberg, *Atlas,* p. 99.

year 399 B.C. These sources tell us about the social and religious life of the Jews in that section of the Diaspora. Unfortunately, they were not too faithful to the demands of Yahwism and we are informed that they developed a questionable kind of religion under the surrounding pagan influence. Religion was highly syncretistic in nature, a mixture of Yahwistic and pagan beliefs and practices, and there was a temple dedicated to the god Yahu.[5]

Albright, in commenting on the Persian Period, says: "The Persian authorities allowed the people of Palestine a good deal of autonomy. For example, the high priests of Juda, like the contemporary high priests of Atargatis at Hierapolis in northern Syria, received permission to strike their own coinage and levy their own temple taxes. Silver coins, struck in imitation of Attic drachmas, but with the Hebrew or Aramaic inscription *Yehud*, 'Judah', are being found in increasing numbers."[6] Archaeological investigations, however, have not unearthed any significant works of construction dating from this period. There was a complete lack of large buildings and objects of art. The simple household utensils that have been discovered show how miserably poor was the life of the people at that time.

B. THE LANGUAGE

It was at this time that Hebrew was gradually replaced by Aramaic as the language of daily living. Aramaic was the language of the immediate neighbors as well as the official tongue of the Persian empire. Although Aramaic became popular at this time, it is at least as old as Hebrew. Both languages belong to a common family of Semitic languages, and the differences between them are somewhat like those between such Romance languages as Spanish and Italian. Aramaic was originally the language of the Arameans, who were sedentary or nomadic tribes. They never achieved the unity of a great empire, but their language spread over the whole Near and Middle East from the Mediterranean coast to modern Iran, and from the sources of the Tigris and Euphrates rivers to the Persian Gulf. In these regions the native languages gave way to Aramaic entirely, or at least as the language of business and diplomacy. In Palestine, at the end of the eighth century only the ruling class knew Aramaic. After the Babylonian Exile Aramaic began to spread widely. Soon Hebrew and Aramaic existed side by side. Hebrew was the ancestral language as well as the language of the Law and Liturgy; Aramaic was the "universal" language. Gradually, Hebrew came to be looked upon as a literary or classical language. In Palestine and throughout the Diaspora the spoken language was Aramaic.[7]

---

[5] See Emil G. Kraeling, "New Light on the Elephantine Colony," *The Biblical Archaeologist,* XX (September, 1952), 50-67.
[6] Albright, *Archaeology of Palestine,* pp. 142-43.
[7] H. Cazelles and E. Osty, "Languages," *Guide to the Bible,* I, 131-39.

C. THE BIBLE

During this time, a period upon which the Bible shed so little light, the Old Testament was given its present form. The Pentateuch and the books known as the Former Prophets (Josue, Judges, 1-2 Samuel, 3-4 Kings) received their final revision, and the works of the Latter Prophets (Isaia, Jeremia, Ezechiel, and the Twelve Minor Prophets) were worked over. Much that is contained in the division called *Writings* dates from this period: some Psalms, Proverbs, Job, Canticle of Canticles, Lamentations, Ecclesiastes, Tobia, Esther, Ruth, Daniel, Ezra–Nehemia, and Chronicles.

sixteen

THE HELLENISTIC PERIOD AND MACCABEAN RULE (333–63 B.C.)

I. INTRODUCTION

THE FOURTH century witnessed the gradual shifting of political power from the East to the West. Preludes of this development were the two battles that were fought in the previous century at Marathon and Salamis. In the former (490 B.C.), the Greek forces defeated the Persian armies of Darius I (522-486). The latter place, Salamis, was the scene of the defeat of the Persian fleet in 480 B.C. while Xerxes was king (486-465). Revolts broke out throughout the empire and the situation was complicated by the Peloponnesian War, which raged between Athens and Sparta (431-404) and culminated in the victory of Sparta. At the time the Persian king, Artaxerxes I (465-424) was able to recoup some of the losses that his kingdom had suffered, while the Greeks were destroying themselves. This period was the Golden Age of Athens, when Pericles, Socrates, Sophocles, Aeschylus, and Phidias walked the streets of the city and brought to their contemporaries the fruits of their genius. By the end of the fifth century, while Darius II was king (423-404), Persia's position was again secure but not for long. Within a very short time, rebellions broke out again in many parts of the empire. Soon almost the whole empire west of the Euphrates River was in revolt, and victories and defeats followed in short order. A brief period of renewed strength during the reign of Artaxerxes III (358-338) did not conceal the fact that the Persian empire was on its last legs. Murders and intrigues in the royal family finally wrote *finis* to the Persian colossus that had enjoyed vast power for two centuries.

II. ALEXANDER THE GREAT—(336-323)

During the reign of Artaxerxes III in Persia, Philip II of Macedon (359-336) was consolidating forces in the Greek states. Many of the Greeks feared his rise to power, but in 338 B.C. at the battle of Chaeronea all of Greece was brought under his rule. When Philip was murdered, his son Alexander became king (336-323). Tutored by the great philosopher Aristotle, and an enthusiastic admirer of Homer, particularly of his great work *The Iliad,* Alexander was destined to become the ruler of a mighty empire. Moved by a pan-Hellenic ideal, Alexander quickly set in motion a crusade aimed at the liberation of the Greeks of Asia from the Persian yoke. In 333 B.C. he routed the forces of Darius III (336-330) at Issus, in southeastern Asia Minor, and turned southward along the Mediterranean coast. He pressed through Palestine and entered Egypt where he was welcomed as a liberator and acclaimed as Pharaoh in 332. His other military exploits need not detain us since they are outside the scope of our survey. Enough to say that as a result of his genius Greek civilization was extended to distant lands, including Egypt and roughly that part of Asia that lay between the Mediterranean Sea and northern India. Alexander the Great heralded the beginning of the Hellenistic Age. His career came to an early end, in 323 B.C., when at the age of 33, he fell sick and died in Babylon.

On the tip of the Nile Delta Alexander founded the city of Alexandria, destined to become the cultural and commercial metropolis of the new age. It attracted the best minds of the Greek and oriental worlds. When he founded the city, Alexander issued orders which were to be very important in later years. He guaranteed the Jews, who had settled in the region in large numbers since the time of the Exile, the same rights as were accorded to his own countrymen. The city rapidly became a Jewish metropolis, and soon the Jews acquired Hellenic culture to such a degree that during the second or third century B.C. the Bible was translated into Greek in order to meet the needs of the Jews in Alexandria. This was the translation known as the Septuagint (LXX).[1] After the death of Alexander the Great his generals began to quarrel among themselves. The activities of only two of these generals need concern us because they have a relationship to the subsequent history of Palestine and of the People of God. These generals were Ptolemy and Seleucus.

III. THE PTOLEMAIC AND SELEUCID DYNASTIES

Ptolemy seized control of Egypt and made Alexandria his capital. He was the founder of the Ptolemaic Dynasty, the last representative of which was Cleopatra, who is remembered for having so successfully turned the heads of her contemporaries Julius Caesar and Mark Anthony. Seleucus made himself master of Babylon by the year 312 and extended his control westward into Syria and eastward across Iran; the capitals of his empire were Seleucia on the Tigris River and Antioch in Syria. Both generals desired Palestine and Phoenicia, but it was Ptolemy who, after various maneuvers, was able to gain complete possession of those lands by the year 301 B.C.

---

[1] See pp. 257-59.

The Ptolemies ruled Palestine for about a century. We know very little about Jewish life during this time. It is probable that few changes were made in the administrative system that was inherited from the Persians. It seems almost certain that the Ptolemies, following the example of Alexander the Great, treated the Jews with kindness. Although they favored Greek customs and ideas, they did not interfere with the religious organization of the country. The Jewish high priest continued to be the spiritual head of the community as well as the secular prince. It was during this time that a priestly aristocracy developed in the country. Provided that the levies were paid to the Ptolemaic state, the people were able to follow their normal course of life.

It must be remembered, however, that as soon as a Jew left Palestine—and many Jews continued to do so—he immediately passed into Hellenistic centers where Greek was the language, and where Greek statues, buildings, theatres, sacred groves, temples, and customs were to be seen everywhere. Thus the Jew could not help being affected by the Greek literature and philosophy which spread far and wide. Alexandria, as we mentioned earlier, became the center of world Jewry, and there, as in other places, the Jew lost his language, and, at times, his religion.

The year 198 saw a great change when, at the battle of Paneas (Panium), Egypt was defeated. Palestine soon passed under the domination of the Seleucids. Prior to this time the Seleucids had made various attempts to extend their holdings but it was only when Antiochus III (223-187) became king that Seleucid power was able to spread.

At the time that the Seleucids replaced the Ptolemies in Palestine the people received Antiochus III with great joy. They were happy to see the end of a war which had caused a great deal of suffering in their land. The Seleucid king in turn showed the Jews a great deal of consideration. He ordered the return of Jewish refugees and the release of captives. He reduced the levies and permitted the people the same freedom that they had enjoyed under the Ptolemies. They were even given money to complete the repairs of the Temple. Everything looked as if the Jews were in for a wonderful period of peace and freedom.

Soon the plan of the Seleucids became apparent. They wanted to absorb Palestine into the Hellenistic culture of their kingdom and therefore bring about the religious and social unity that would produce the united world Alexander the Great had dreamed about.

IV. THE PROCESS OF HELLENIZATION

At first, the Seleucids were tolerant in matters of religion, but their approach soon changed. Antiochus IV (Epiphanes) (175-163), who considered himself an incarnation of Zeus, did his best to destroy the religion of the Jews. He was tyrannical and crafty, and so eccentric that many believed that he was mentally deranged. He adopted a policy that soon drove the Jews to rebellion.

Shortly after Antiochus IV came to power, he was offered a large sum of money by Jason (in Hebrew, Josue) in return for the position of high priest. Jason also asked Antiochus for permission to build a gymnasium, after Greek models, in Jerusalem, in order to have a place where Jewish youths could be brought up in Hellenistic ways. The requests were granted, and soon there was a flow of Greek ideas and customs to the Jews, and of money to Antiochus. Jason's plan soon became so popular that many of the Jews neglected their religious duties in order to attend the games. The apostasy of Jason was so great that he did not hesitate to send money to Tyre for sacrifices to be offered in honor of the god Hercules. In 172 B.C. Jason was succeeded by Menelaus who offered a larger bribe to Antiochus. He soon showed that he was even less scrupulous than his predecessor. Unable to raise all the money needed for the bribe he had promised the king, he began to steal the vessels of the Temple and to sell them (2 Mc 4,27-32). He went so far as to have the legitimate high priest, who at this time was in Antioch, assassinated (2 Mc 4,33-38).

In 169 Antiochus entered Jerusalem, plundered the Temple, and killed many of the citizens of the city. He took away the seven-branched candlestick and the altar of incense, and ordered that the Temple be converted into a shrine of Zeus and that a Greek altar be placed over the Jewish altar of holocausts—this was the "abomination of desolation." Antiochus forbade the practice of the Jewish religion; the observance of the Sabbath, the possession of copies of the Torah, and the practice of circumcision were to be punishable by death. The Jews were forced to worship the pagan gods. Many of the Jews became apostates, but there were also many who were martyred because they refused to bow before the decrees of Antiochus. The faithful ones allowed themselves to be killed rather than defend themselves when they were attacked on the Sabbath (1 Mc 2,29-38; 2 Mc 6,11). Women who had circumcised their sons were put to death with their families (1 Mc 1,60-67; 2 Mc 6,10). Yahwistic religion was now in a great period of crisis. The attack on the God of Israel marked the beginning of a new period in the history of the Jewish people.

V. THE BOOK OF DANIEL

The persecutions of Antiochus Epiphanes are the milieu in which the book of Daniel was written. The Jews had been in similar disastrous situations during their history; God had humbled their conquerors—Babylonians, Medes, and Persians—and saved them. Now, faced with the persecutions of the Greeks, they were reminded of God's past mercies and acts of protection. He will again intervene in their behalf. He will humble Antiochus, who claims to be a divine manifestation (*Epiphanes*) and show that he is nothing but a madman (*epimanes*). It is with this in mind that we should read the book of Daniel.

The genre of the book is *apocalyptic* and, therefore, we should expect to find all the qualities that are peculiar to that literary form, particularly symbolism, visions, and an eschatological perspective.[2] Many of the stories in the book are popular tales about a hero who is supposed to have lived during the time of the Babylonian Exile. Scholars are divided on the question of Daniel's actual existence, but they agree that the book which bears his name was not intended as scientific history. There are indications which point to it being less than critico-historical; many dates and even the historical personages in the book lack scientific accuracy.[3]

The author has combined several stories about Daniel in such a way that the whole book is an inspiration to his persecuted co-religionists. The majestic vision of the Son of Man, who will receive dominion, glory, and kingship and whom nations and peoples will serve, was given to the Jews to strengthen their hope in that future when the ideal Israel will receive dominion over the earth (Dn 7,13-14).

The book was another important step in the History of Salvation. It was among the last books written during the period of the Old Covenant. Its importance is due to several reasons, among which is the fact that it provided some of the terms and ideas which Jesus used during His public life, for example, the "Son of Man" (Dn 7; Mt 12,32; Lk 11,30; Jn 8,28; Mk 14,41,62).

Its teachings concerning angels is another important doctrinal contribution. The earlier books of the Old Testament usually spoke of angels as beings who were members of God's heavenly court; they were the host of heaven. But the doctrine of angelology became clearer in post-Exilic books like Job in the fifth century, Tobia in the fourth century, and Daniel. It is in these books that the notion of angelic intercession for men began to appear, first dimly (Jb 5,1; 33,23-24), and then more clearly as in Tobia where the angel Raphael says he presented the petitions to God (Tb 12,12). The book of Daniel speaks of angels several times (Dn 3,49; 4,10; 6,23). It is in this book that we hear of Gabriel for the first time in the Bible; he explains a vision to Daniel (Dn 8,16; 9,21). We also meet Michael, the protector of God's people (Dn 10,13,21; 12,1). The meaning of the names of these two angels is interesting: Gabriel, "Strong man of God" and Michael, "Who is like God?" We meet them again in a few texts of the New Testament. Gabriel appears at the moment of the Annunciation to Mary (Lk 1,26-38), Michael in the book of Jude, in which he disputes with the devil over the body of Moses (Jude 1,9), and in the Apocalypse, where he is involved in a battle with the dragon, Satan (Ap 12,7).

The book of Daniel contains a magnificent hymn of praise which is part

<hr />

[2] For a study of the meaning of the apocalyptic genre see Bruce Vawter, C.M., "Apocalyptic: Its Relation to Prophecy," *The Catholic Biblical Quarterly*, XXII (January 1960), 33-46.

[3] See the following: Raymond E. Brown, S.S., *The Book of Daniel* (New York: The Paulist Press, 1962), pp. 5-12; Achille Brunet, S.J., "The Book of Daniel," *Theology Digest*, V (Winter, 1957), 58-63; Levie, *op. cit.*, p. 231; A. Gelin, "The Book of Daniel," *Guide to the Bible*, I, 334-38.

of the Divine Office recited by clergy and religious, and recommended for all members of the Church as a prayer of thanksgiving after Mass. All of creation is called upon to bless the Lord (Dn 3,52-90).

VI. THE BOOKS OF MACCABEES

The two books of Maccabees found at the end of the Old Testament are parallel accounts of the events that took place during the revolt of the Jews against the process of Hellenization. They were written at different times, 1 Mc written about 100 B.C. and 2 Mc a little after 124 B.C. Their style, contents, and manner of treatment also differ. That the two books are placed one after the other can be justified on grounds that they both treat of the same hero, Judas Maccabeus, and both are concerned with the liberation of the Jews from the Seleucids.[4]

The first book covers the period from the arrival of Antiochus IV in 175 to the death of Simon in 134 B.C. It was written in Hebrew but we have only its Greek translation. It is a valuable source of information about the history of the period, but we have to keep in mind its literary genre. The author is a good historian, but his purpose was to present religious history; this is seen in his contention that the trials which the Jews experience are punishments for their sins and their victories are due to Divine Help which comes as a reward for fidelity. We notice in this outlook the spirit of the Deuteronomic Tradition of earlier times. His report of the facts is simple and clear. At times, however, he betrays some deficiencies in knowledge and his judgments are prejudicial concerning foreigners.

The second book was originally written in Greek and was an abridgement of a five-volume work of Jason the Cyrene. It is history presented in an oratorical manner and intended to edify the readers. The author of 2 Maccabees used various sources and has produced a work which, like the books of Samuel, Kings, and Chronicles gives a theological interpretation of historical situations and events. Some place the book in the genre of "pathetic historiography," which presents facts in a way that will convey a lesson and move the readers to action.

The book was written for the Jews of Alexandria and tried to make them feel a sense of solidarity with their people in Palestine. The Temple plays an important role in this book.

Several important theological contributions are found in this work. It contains the doctrine of the resurrection of the dead (2 Mc 7,9-14). The martyrs will rise because of the power of the Creator (2 Mc 7,23).

The emphasis is on the resurrection of the just and not necessarily of all men. But, at least we do have here an explicit reference to a resurrection, which will receive further enlightenment in the teaching of Jesus (Jn 5,29).

[4] See Moriarty, *Foreword to the Old Testament Books,* pp. 54-58; A. Robert, "The Books of Maccabees," *Guide to the Bible,* I, 309-14.

These texts of 2 Mc about the resurrection should be read with Dn 12,2-3, written in the same century, where we find a clear teaching about the glorious resurrection of the bodies of the just. Prayers for the dead are mentioned in 2 Mc 12,41-46 where Judas has prayers and sacrifice offered for the dead. We also find mention made of the intercession of the saints in 2 Mc 15,12-16 where we are told that Jeremia, the prophet of God, is praying for the people.

VII. THE MACCABEAN REVOLT—(166-63 B.C.)

Resistance to the policies of Antiochus IV was formed by a group known as the *Hasidim* or "holy ones," "the pious," "the loyal ones." These were Jews who had fled from Hellenism and for a time put up a passive resistance. The continuing anti-Yahwist measures adopted by Antiochus soon made it clear that resistance would have to become active through the formation of some Yahwist organization. Mattathias, a priest in the village of Modin, refused to obey the command to offer sacrifice to the pagan god (1 Mc 2-22). When another Jew decided to comply with the royal request, Mattathias cut him down beside the altar together with the officer who brought the directive to the village. Summoning all those who were heroic enough to defend the Law and the Covenant, he fled to the hills. There he was joined by other Jews and by the Hasidim, who had decided that the time had come for open resistance. Guerrilla warfare ensued against the Seleucids and everything Hellenistic. Although these heroic Jews were very zealous for the Law, they did not hesitate to suspend the law of the Sabbath and to fight on that day (1 Mc 2,41).

After the death of Mattathias, the leadership of the forces passed to the third of his five sons, Judas Maccabeus. The name "Maccabeus" is commonly traced to the Hebrew word *maqqabhah,* which means "hammer." Hence it is said that Judas was the "hammer" that crushed the persecutors of Israel. The derivation is not free from all doubts and, therefore, we can say only that such an explanation is a possible or, at most, a probable one. Judas was a courageous and very competent individual. Under his direction, which lasted from 166 to 160 B.C., Jewish resistance fanned out into a full-scale active struggle for independence. The whole revolt is commonly referred to as the Maccabean War. Antiochus, who at this time was troubled by rising problems throughout his domain, thought that his troops in Palestine were sufficient to put down the uprising, which at first seemed to be no more than a localized skirmish. He was soon disillusioned. His forces, led by Appolonius and Seron, were thoroughly routed (1 Mc 3). Antiochus then ordered more troops into the Palestinian struggle. At Emmaus, about 20 miles northwest of Jerusalem, Judas attacked the enemy's camp and won a smashing victory (1 Mc 3,42-4, 25). In 164 B.C. at a place called Beth-zur (Bethoron), about 15 miles from Jerusalem, Judas inflicted a crushing defeat on the armies commanded by the deputy of the king, Lysias. Immediately Judas and his men marched triumphantly into Jerusalem and, after getting rid of the Seleucid garrison, cleansed the desecrated Temple (1 Mc 4,36-59). All the pagan objects were removed and a new altar was erected. In December, 164 B.C., three years after Antiochus had profaned it with the establishment of the cult of Zeus, the Temple was rededicated with a great deal of feasting. It is this event that the Jews commemorate each year with the feast of *Hannukkah;* the word means "dedication."

Spurred on by his success, Judas tried to consolidate the results of the religious revolution by gaining complete political independence from the Seleucids. In 160 B.C. he was killed before accomplishing his program. Antiochus IV died in 164 or 163 B.C. and was succeeded by his son Antiochus V, who ruled only a year and then was murdered by Demetrius I (162-150).

The successors of Judas were his brothers Jonathan (160-143) and Simon (143-134). During their reigns the territory of the Jews was recognized as independent when Syria granted political freedom in 142 B.C. while Demetrius II (145-138) was king. Simon assumed the hereditary title of Prince and High Priest and became the founder of the Hasmonean Dynasty, so called after Asamonaios (Hashmon), the great-grandfather of Mattathias who led the revolt against Hellenization. Simon was succeeded by his son John Hyrcanus who took the title of King (134-104). During his reign Antiochus VII (138-129) led an army against Jerusalem and was able to impose a tribute on Juda. John was captured and led away as a captive by Antiochus but he managed to escape and was even able to regain his country's independence.

At the death of John his son Aristobulus I came to the throne. Although he ruled for only a year (104-103) he was remembered as a harsh person who did anything to achieve his aims, even if it meant the murder of some of his own blood relations. His successor was his brother Alexander Janneus (103-76) who conquered more land, including Transjordan. He was the most aggressive of the Maccabean kings and was constantly engaged in political intrigues because of his mania for power. Alexander continued the practice of imposing the Jewish religion on the people by force, more for his own egotistical motives than for religious ones. He was bitterly hostile toward the Pharisees, whom he considered the internal enemies of his dynasty. This hostility was the result of the dissatisfaction of the Pharisees with their bellicose priest-king. They looked upon Alexander as one who usurped the rights of the descendants of David. "He was, for them, a common soldier who spent the whole year making war and mingling with uncircumcised foreigners; an Israelite whose hands were always wet with human blood and whose conscience was further burdened by thousands of Jews whose deaths were traceable to his craze for conquest; a politician who, because he was always on the move, fighting his battles, necessarily neglected the offices of high priest; a man who had espoused a widow in violation of the ancient Yahwistic law which forbade a priest to do so." [5]

Now the original situation was reversed—the descendant of the Maccabees

---

[5] Ricciotti, *History of Israel,* II, 289-90.

was attacked by the descendants of the Hasidim, the Pharisees. In an attempt to get rid of Alexander, the Pharisees appealed to Demetrius III of Syria, the descendant of the detestable Antiochus IV. Demetrius defeated Alexander but the Jews then rallied to the support of their king, and the Syrian was forced to withdraw. Alexander then took vengeance on his enemies at home. It is reported that some 50,000 Jews lost their lives in the ensuing years. During one of his bestial moods, Alexander ordered the crucifixion of 800 of his opponents and before the eyes of those agonized sufferers he had the throats of their wives and children cut.

Alexander was succeeded by his wife Alexandra (76-67) who restored the Pharisees to a position of great influence in the government and even granted them seats in the Sanhedrin, the Jewish "Senate" or "Supreme Court." This position of prominence was kept throughout the rest of Jewish history. Alexandra appointed her eldest son Hyrcanus II, a feeble man, as high priest. After her death Hyrcanus came into conflict with his younger brother Aristobolus II who was supported by the army commanders and the Sadduccees. The Pharisees supported Hyrcanus; in 67 B.C. he was forced to relinquish the throne to Aristobolus. During this rivalry between the two brothers, Antipater, a shrewd Idumean, called upon Aretas the king of the Nabateans, a race southeast of Palestine, to come to the aid of Hyrcanus. As a result, the Nabateans began to exercise considerable power in Palestine.[6] It was then that news came that the Roman commander Pompey had arrived in Syria to annex the remains of the Seleucid empire for Rome.

[6] A short and informative study about this race is in Jean Starcky, "Nabataeans: A Historical Sketch," *The Biblical Archaeologist*, XVIII (December, 1955), 84-106.

seventeen

THE ROMAN PERIOD (63–   )

I. INTRODUCTION

POMPEY, hearing that Jerusalem was in a state of siege because Nabatean troops were attacking, sent one of his legates to act as "peacemaker." Hyrcanus and Aristobolus both bargained with the Roman Legate, but the latter made a more favorable offer and won. The Nabateans were ordered to stop the siege and return to their country. When Pompey arrived, there was still a fierce rivalry between the two brothers, with Antipater on the side of Hyrcanus. Since the Nabateans had not yet been subjected to Roman power, Pompey decided to take care of them before deciding the Palestinian issue. Finally, he returned and was welcomed by Hyrcanus and his followers who joined the Romans in a siege of the Temple wherein Aristobolus and his followers had retreated. The attack was made and during the battle some 12,000 Jews lost their lives. Pompey marched into the sanctuary and even into the Holy of Holies. Hyrcanus was installed as high priest, though not as king, and ruled from 63 to 40 B.C.; Aristobolus was led away a chained captive.

Shortly after, when civil war broke out between Pompey and Caesar, Antipater assumed the role of a quisling. He sided with Caesar and had himself appointed as procurator of the Jewish state. He installed one of his sons, Phasael, as commander in Jerusalem, and another son, Herod, as commander of Galilee. In 40 B.C. a descendant of the Hasmoneans, Antigonus, was able to size the throne but was deposed after three years. Herod, who had to flee when Antigonus claimed the throne, made his way to Rome where the Senate proclaimed him king of Juda. He returned to Palestine and, with the help of Roman troops, occupied the land and captured Jerusalem after a bloody massacre. He established himself as king in 37 B.C. and retained the throne until his death in 4 B.C.

II. HEROD THE GREAT:
HIS RULE AND ITS CONSEQUENCES

Herod was a Jew by religion, but Idumean (Edomite) by race. He had to use every type of diplomacy in order to remain on friendly terms with Anthony during the crisis that marked the last years of the Roman Republic. This was especially necessary since Anthony's mistress, Cleopatra, was trying to obtain Syria and Palestine just as the Pharaoh's and the Ptolemies had done in the past. Immediately after the defeat of Anthony at the battle of Actium in 31 B.C., Herod, who was as cunning as his father Antipater, went over to the side of the victor, Octavian.

Herod is commonly given the appelation "The Great," but that title is one which belongs to him primarily on account of his political ability and his building.[1] He used his native ability for his own personal gain and showed himself incredibly jealous, vain, tyrannical, and cruel. In order to gain the good will of the Jews he married a member of the Hasmonean family, and also began the construction of a new Temple that would rival the one built after the Babylonian Exile. He systematically put to death all who could possibly claim the throne, and tried to further strengthen his position through visits to Rome. He put to death two of his sons, two of his brothers-in-law, his wife Mariamne (he had nine other wives), his wife's grandfather (Hyrcanus II), a great number of the aristocracy, and the members of the Sanhedrin. He maintained his authority with the help of Roman mercenaries, made up of uncircumcised rabble from all parts of the world. Herod also took control of the office of High Priest and appointed to it unworthy candidates whom he deposed and murdered whenever such moves suited his ruthless ambitions and policy. After essaying the building operations of Herod, Albright concludes: "One wonders, in less objective mood, whether it was Herod's conscience which drove him to seek refuge in ever more inaccessible strongholds from the ghosts of those he had so brutally murdered as well as from the living avengers of the dead."[2]

Herod fell gravely ill around 6 B.C. and rumors of his death spread among the people. This signalled an attempt on the part of the Pharisees to remove the golden eagle of Rome from the Temple; those who made the attempt were captured and burnt alive. Herod retired to the northern coast of the Dead Sea where he hoped to attain relief in the warm springs, and later to Jericho where he died in 4 B.C.

It was during the reign of Herod that Jesus was born in Bethlehem. Ironically enough, the thousands of pilgrims who throng the tiny village each year to venerate the birthplace of the Saviour hardly take notice of the solitary ruins nearby where the tyrant Herod the Great was buried.

---

[1] See Albright, *Archaeology of Palestine*, pp. 154-58; Grollenberg, *Atlas*, pp. 113-18; also Stewart Perown, *The Life and Times of Herod the Great* (New York: Abingdon, 1959).
[2] Albright, *Archaeology*, pp. 157-58.

After Herod's death there were terrible upheavals throughout the country. To restore order, the Roman emperor partitioned the country, assigning a part to each of Herod's three sons: Judea, Samaria, and Idumea to Archelaus, Galilee and Perea to Herod Antipas, and the northern territories to Philip.

During the reign of Achelaus (4 B.C.-6 A.D.) a delegation of Judeans and Samaritans went to the Roman emperor to complain of the mishandling of affairs in his territory. Archelaus was removed from office and sent into exile, and was replaced by a procurator. The Procurator was to live in the city of Caesarea, and to go to Jerusalem only to maintain order during the celebration of the Jewish feasts. During those periods he would reside in the magnificent palace that had been built by Herod, called the Praetorium. The Jews retained the right to administer the law, but could not pass the sentence of death. They could practice their religion freely, and their religious feelings were respected as much as possible by the Roman representative. Roman soldiers were forbidden to carry standards bearing the image of the emperor into Jerusalem; coins that were made in Judea did not bear the image of the emperor; the Jews were not required to worship the emperor as a god.

There were six procurators who governed Judea from 6-41 A.D. and among them was Pontius Pilate, Governor from 26-36 A.D. In character, Pilate combined arrogance and weakness. On one occasion he ordered that the Roman standards be carried into Jerusalem but when a storm of protest came from the Jews he withdrew his order. His role in the trial of Jesus is well known. There he showed his wish to do what was right, as well as the essential weakness of character which made him yield to the people's demand that Jesus be put to death. When he commanded his soldiers to attack a crowd of unarmed Samaritans gathered at Mt. Gerizim to hear a pseudo-prophet who promised to produce the sacred utensils of the time of Moses, Pilate was removed from office. The Samaritans complained of the massacre to the governor of Syria, who had the authority to intervene. Pilate was sent to Rome: we know nothing about the rest of his life.

Revolts led by groups of Zealots continued to break out during the Roman occupation of Palestine, and in 66 A.D. a war broke out during which the Romans were defeated and driven out. However, in 69 A.D. the rebels were crushed by Titus, who then destroyed Jerusalem, the Temple, and many Jews. The Roman victory was accompanied by unparalleled atrocities in 70 A.D. and in the following year Rome celebrated the triumph of the emperor Vespasian and his sons Titus and Domitian.

This was the end of the Jewish state.[3] There were those who saw in the

---

[3] Very few details are known about life in Palestine after the Roman victory of 70 A.D. until the final Jewish rebellion in 135. Led by Bar Kokhba, the Jewish insurrectionists captured Jerusalem, but soon the superior Roman forces crushed the revolt. The population which had survived the earlier revolts was further decimated, and the Holy City, Jerusalem, was populated by heathens. It was around this time that the country's name was changed to *Palestine*, a word derived from the older description of the coastal area as "the land of the Philistines." In this way, the Romans hoped to destroy the idea that the country was "the land of the Jews."

destruction of the Temple an event of profound significance. It was the confirmation of their belief that the world had reached a crucial turning-point in history, and that the last age had begun. These were the Christians, followers of Jesus the Christ, God born man, and man born king.

eighteen

PARTIES AND SECTS

I. INTRODUCTION

THE FOLLOWING is a brief treatment of some of the parties and sects in the Jewish world: (1) the Scribes, (2) the Sanhedrin, (3) the Pharisees, (4) the Sadducees, and (5) the Essenes. Their importance is not limited to the Old Testament. They were also in existence during the early decades of New Testament times and all of them, with the exception of the Essenes, are often mentioned in the inspired books of the New Testament.[1]

II. THE SCRIBES

The study and interpretation of the Law was in the hands of men who were called Scribes. Originally, it was the priests who interpreted the Law, but once the Law was accepted as the basis of Jewish life it was necessary to have a separate group whose main function was to determine its meaning and apply it to various situations as they arose. Actually, the Scribes had no official position, their opinions having only the weight of their own personal influence. But the very fact that they were legislators, teachers, and judges was enough to make their opinions binding, inasmuch as the devout Jew considered the study of the Law, *Torah,* the highest occupation of man. A Scribe was addressed as *Rabbi,* Master.

The interpretations of the Scribes grew into a second legal system, the oral law, which was looked upon as having the same authority as the Law of Moses. The oral law was the object of tradition. A famous Scribe usually gathered around himself a group of followers who would preserve his teaching and amplify it in their own generation. Memory was all-important, since there was

---

[1] Information about the history and beliefs of the parties and sects is in J. L. McKenzie, S.J., "The Jewish World in New Testament Times," *A Catholic Commentary on Holy Scripture,* pp. 732-33; A. Tricot, "The Jewish World at the Time of Our Lord," *Guide to the Bible,* II, 287-96; Heinisch, *History of the Old Testament,* pp. 387-90; Albright, *From the Stone Age to Christianity,* pp. 353-57; Bright, *A History of Israel,* pp. 448-52.

no written basis for the teaching of the Scribes until after the beginning of the Christian era. At times the various schools of Scribes were at odds. There was a great deal of casuistry in their opinions. The Gospels contain many allusions to the Scribes' over-emphasis on external observances, as well as to the devices by which they evaded the obligations of the Law (Mt 15,1-9; Mk 7,1-13). It was their function to "build a fence around the law," which meant that they were to see to the perfect observance of the Torah by surrounding it with additional regulations. The Scribes did this by studying the Law and deducing from it regulations which they considered necessary. Two types of interpretation were followed: (1) the *Halakhah,* which interpreted, applied, or extended the precepts of the Law and formed a rule of conduct, and (2) *Haggadah,* which amplified particular portions of the Law, especially the narrative sections, by adding a good deal of speculation and even legend.

Although it is true that the Scribes treated with contempt those who did not know the Law or did not observe it, it is likewise true that among them there were many who were close to true appreciation of the Kingdom of God. The first Jewish Christians almost certainly included many of these Scribes who had devoted their lives to the sincere and earnest study of the Torah of Moses and the Word of God.

III. THE SANHEDRIN

The word *Sanhedrin* means "assembly" or "council." It is not certain when this institution arose in Palestine. Throughout the early history of the Jews local government was conducted by a council of men whose age, rank, and wealth gave authority to their decisions. It was probably during the Hellenistic Period, after 333 B.C., that the Sanhedrin or Council of Jerusalem began to exercise legislative and judicial authority over all Palestinian Jews as well as those of the Diaspora.

The president of the Sanhedrin was the High Priest, the supreme magistrate under the imperial government of Rome. Originally, the 71 members of the council belonged to the aristocracy, the high-priestly families, and the high-ranking members of the laity. The field of competency of the Sanhedrin was originally very broad. It included all religious questions, as well as civil and criminal cases not reserved to the imperial government. During the period of Roman domination, after 63 B.C., the jurisdiction of the Sanhedrin was restricted considerably, capital crimes were declared beyond its sphere of competence.

IV. THE PHARISEES

The word *Pharisee* is derived from the Hebrew which means "to separate." It was used to designate those who, because of their exact observance of all the prescriptions of the Law, separated themselves not only from the Gentiles, but also from those Jews who did not observe all the legal prescriptions.

The Pharisees continued the tradition of the *Hasidim* of the Maccabean period who refused to compromise with Hellenism. They emerged as a party during the course of the second century B.C. and were very exact in their observance of the Law. They were hostile toward Alexander Janneus, and were involved in the Roman interference that occurred during the quarrels between John Hyrcanus II and his brother Aristobolus II. During the reign of Alexandra, the Pharisees became the leaders of the masses and obtained seats in the Sanhedrin. They were able to maintain their position of influence throughout the period of Roman domination. When Herod the Great was king they refused to give the oath of loyalty, kept themselves aloof from political affairs, and exercised their activity in the sphere of the religion.

The Pharisees taught that the kingdom of God would be established by some divine intervention, not by human efforts. They believed that government by foreign powers was a divine punishment for the sins of the nation, and as such should be accepted with submission. However, the presence of foreigners in the land was a profanation both of the land and of the Chosen People, and should be overthrown by rebellion. Since they were not organized as a political party, the Pharisees joined forces with others during the rebellions from the period of the Maccabees to the last great insurrection led by Bar Kochba in 135 A.D. Most of the Scribes were Pharisees.

The religious beliefs of the Pharisees may be summarized as follows: they believed in (a) personal immortality, (b) judgment after death, (c) resurrection of the body, and (d) the existence of angels. They allowed wide scope for man's freedom and also for the action of divine Providence. They awaited the coming of the kingdom of God upon earth, and professed a strong faith in the coming of the Messiah. The Pharisees kept alive Jewish piety during some of the most critical periods of the history of the people of God, although at times they reveled in excessive legalism. At times the religion of the Pharisees degenerated into mere external formalism, in which the observance of the most minute ceremony was their chief concern. At times they practiced their religion so that everyone could see them, as, for example, in the giving of alms. In the Gospels they are often censured for seeking to *appear* virtuous: Christ tells them that they resemble sepulchres which are white on the outside and filled with dead men's bones within (Mt 6.5; 6,16; 23,5-7; 23,27; Lk 18,9-14). Nevertheless, the Pharisees did represent what had been at one time a high and pure form of Judaism.

V. THE SADDUCEES

The origin and exact meaning of the name are not certain. They were a Jewish party whose members belonged chiefly to the priestly and aristocratic class. They claimed to be descendants of Zadok, one of the priests appointed by David when he transferred the Ark of the Covenant to Jerusalem (1 Chr 15,11).

The Sadducees accorded authority only to the Law (Torah) and rejected the body of oral law developed by the Scribes. They had, however, their own traditions and even included some Scribes in their party. The difference between them and the Pharisees, who accepted the oral laws, was not so much in the theory of interpretation, as in the binding force of tradition. Their great concern was that the cult of the Temple should be prosecuted and that the Law, especially where it concerned ritual and sacrifices, should be carried out under the supervision of the constituted priesthood. Of all the parties and classes in Judaism, the Sadducees were the most open and favorable to Hellenistic culture.

The Sadducees were practical men of the world whose ambition was to maintain the *status quo*. They readily cooperated with the secular rulers, whether these were the worldly-minded priest-kings of the Hasmonean family or the Roman procurators. Their great fear was anything that might disturb the present situation and cause an upset in the balance. Hence their animosity toward Jesus and His teachings. They did not have very much influence on the common people and no lasting influence on Judaism.

The religious beliefs of the Sadducees were: (a) they denied the possibility of retribution in the afterlife, (b) they rejected belief in bodily resurrection after death, (c) they held to a primitive concept about Sheol, the place where the dead continue to exist in a place below the earth, where conditions are shadowy and depressing, (d) they rejected belief in angels, (e) they stressed freedom of the will and refused to accept any intervention on the part of God in the course of events, and (f) they denied divine Providence.

VI. THE ESSENES

The Essenes constituted an important element among the Jewish people, particularly at the time of Jesus. The discovery of the documents in the caves along the shore of the Dead Sea has led to a renewed interest in this Jewish group. It is almost certain that the sect at Qumran was an Essene group.[2]

The Essenes originated during the period of the Maccabees. They were men who withdrew from ordinary life in order to live in communal groups. Among them were members of the Zadokite priesthood who were the successors of the priest at the time of David, Zadok (2 Sm 15,24-29); also others who looked upon the Hasmonean priesthood as illegitimate and apostate. Around the middle of the second century B.C. a group of Essenes withdrew from Jerusalem in the face of opposition and took refuge in the wilderness of Juda. Led by a person known as the Teacher of Righteousness, they put their trust in God's help and awaited their final victory when the armies of the "Sons of Light" would defeat those of the "Sons of Darkness." They did not repudiate the worship carried on in the Temple but disassociated themselves from it

[2] See pp. 242-55.

because in their eyes it was performed by impure priests who lacked the requisite holiness. The persecutions of Alexander Janneus and the unstable conditions during the latter part of Hasmonean rule were conditions favorable to the growth of the group at Qumran.

The Essene movement comprised other groups besides the one at Qumran. There were Essenes living in isolated villages in southern Syria. Scattered groups of Essenes who lived in other places are sometimes referred to as Essene "tertiaries," and the ones who established themselves in Egypt were known as *Therapeutae*.

The Essenes considered themselves the people of the New Covenant. They had their own interpretation of the Law, their own religious calendar, and a discipline that was rigorously enforced.[3] Their picture of the physical and spiritual world contained elements of determinism: human life is regulated by the movements of the heavenly bodies and they in turn are ruled by the angels; man is a plaything of the forces of good and evil. They awaited the imminent end of the world, and believed that there will be rewards and punishments after death.[4]

The Essenes were victims of the Roman persecution and after the destruction of Jerusalem in 70 A.D. they disappeared rapidly.

[3] For centuries the chronology of the last week in the public life of Jesus has been a much-discussed problem. The solutions proposed for the apparent contradiction in the Gospel's concerning the date of the Last Supper have been interesting in their diversity. The discovery of the *Jubilees Calendar* at Qumran has led some scholars to see in it the answer to the problem of chronology. See the following for a discussion of this question: Annie Jaubert, *La Date de la Cene: calendrier biblique et liturgie chretienne* (Paris: J. Galbada, 1957); Patrick W. Skehan, "The Date of the Last Supper," *The Catholic Biblical Quarterly*, XX (April, 1958), 192-99; J. F. Milik, *Ten Years of Discovery in the Desert of Judaea*, trans. J. Strugnell (London: SCM Press. Distributed in USA by Allenson's, Naperville, Illinois, 1959), pp. 107-113; also "The Date of the Last Supper," *Theology Digest*, VI (Spring, 1958), 120-22.

[4] One of the best studies of the history, organization, and teachings of the Essenes is Milik, *op. cit.*, pp. 44-128.

nineteen

THE PROPHETS AND MESSIANISM

I. INTRODUCTION

THE HEBREW PROPHET was one who spoke in the name of Yahweh. His task was to explain the role of Israel in relation to world events and to define the requirements of the Covenant with the Lord in the light of constantly changing circumstances. Already at the time of Samuel, about 1040 B.C., there were men who had ecstatic experiences when possessed by the spirit of God. They performed wild dances, often accompanied by music and sometimes they went so far as to wound themselves and tear their clothing. Groups known as "sons of the prophets" were associated with religious places of worship (1 Sm 10,5; 1 Sm 19,18-24; 4 Kgs 2,3; 4 Kgs 4,38). The prophets often took part in the struggle against the pagan policies of the kings and the syncretic forms of worship that made their appearance in the land. Elia and Eliseus, as we have seen, spent their lives in that sort of work, and a high price was demanded of them because they were the heralds of God. In general, we can say that the prophets were witnesses to the presence of God among His people, and also to the fact that such presence demanded faithfulness in the observance of the Covenant.

II. MEANING OF "PROPHET"

The Hebrew word *nabi* is used to refer to the men known as "prophets." There are several opinions concerning the exact meaning of this word.

A. Some are of the opinion that *nabi* comes from a word which means "to bubble up" or "to put forth." These authors point to places in the Old Testament where the word is used for men who acted in an ecstatic way while experiencing some religious emotion. This view is inadequate; it does not explain why men who did not act in such a way were called *nabis*.

B. Others are of the opinion that the *nabi* was one who foretold the future. This is the view that many people have when they hear the word "prophet."

Although the predictive element is present in the work of the prophets, it is not their essential value. Consequently, this understanding of the prophets is inadequate. Its application to the prophetical books causes the loss of the true meaning of the prophets and their mission in the history of salvation. It reduces the prophets to the level of men whose only purpose was to hide "needles in the haystack," texts which have to be searched for and when put together form a perfectly clear picture of the future. It is because many approach the prophetical books with this notion in mind that they fail to grasp their real importance.

C. Finally, there is the opinion that the word *nabi* is derived from the Hebrew which means "to speak" or "to call" or "to announce." The *nabi* was an individual who was called or who announced a message. He was a messenger and an interpreter of the Divine Word; he was the spokesman of the Lord. This view does justice to the evidence found in the Old Testament books regarding the prophet and his role in the plan of God.[1]

III. KINDS OF PROPHETS

We have said that the prophet was a man who spoke in the name of the Lord. But the word *nabi* is used in the Bible for men who do not seem to have had any special calling or right to speak in His name. Before we procede, therefore, it is necessary to say something about the two classes or prophets who exercised a ministry during the period of the Old Testament: the *professional* and the *vocational* prophets.

The *professional* prophets made their appearance about the time of Samuel, during the last decades of the second millenium. They were usually bands of enthusiasts who lived a sort of community life. At times, they performed strange and bizarre actions and engaged in dances accompanied by cymbals and lutes. In moments of excitement some of them even lacerated themselves. From among these men came those who are called "false prophets," persons who would flatter those in authority by making predictions which they knew were false but which would bring them some form of prestige or reward. They would even demand money for their services (3 Kgs 22,5-28; 4 Kgs 5,20-27).

Our judgment of the professional prophets tends to be severe because it is colored by present religious attitudes. To be sure, many of their activities, particularly those of the false prophets were reprehensible. Our worship of God does not include the free-play of the emotions witnessed in the mannerisms of these prophets; we do not use flutes, cymbals, and bells in our displays of religious fervor. But things were different in the times of the prophets, and even in our own time there are Christian groups in which prayer and religious song are performed in ways that are foreign to our twentieth century western

---

[1] See Joseph Dheilly, *The Prophets*, trans. Rachel Attwater (New York: Hawthorn Books, Publishers, 1960), pp. 15-16. Albright interprets the word *nabi* as "the one who is called, who has a vocation"; *From the Stone Age to Christianity*, pp. 17, 303.

mentality. True, the professional prophets were not specially called by God, but they did meet the challenge of their time and many of them were faithful to the native impulse which made them dedicate their lives to the service of Yahweh. In condemning the abuses of some of them, we should not forget the positive contributions which they made to the survival of Yahwism in times when devotion to Baal and the other pagan deities appeared to be more profitable and rewarding.

Although the Bible uses the word *nabi* to designate the professional prophets, the word is most accurately used when it refers to men who had an authentic experience of God and were entrusted with the vocation of "speaking in the name of the Lord."

The *vocational* prophets received a revelation of the holiness of God and His will; they pronounced a judgment on the state of affairs in their own times and viewed the future in the light of God's revelation. Sent by God, they reminded the people of the Divine plan and urged them to respond with obedience and love. Although some authors have attempted to explain Israelite prophetism by parallels observed among other ancient peoples, nowhere has the experience of the vocational type of prophet been duplicated.

We possess the teachings of prophets who are known as "Writing Prophets." They are the ones who have been memorialized by having books bearing their names in the Canon of the Old Testament. Many of their speeches circulated orally before they were written down. Often poetical in language, and presented in forms meaningful to their hearers, they brought the Word of the Lord to the people. When these prophets said, "Thus says the Lord . . ." their contemporaries stood up and took notice of what was said because their faith convinced them that it was Yahweh who communicated His message through the mouths of His spokesmen. In time, the speeches, which are usually called *oracles,* were collected and committed to writing. Very often this was done by close disciples of the prophets. Once the materials had been gathered, some biographical details were added and the whole work was presented in the form found in our Bibles.

IV. REQUIREMENTS FOR A PROPHET

Two requirements were necessary for the authentic vocational prophet: (A) a commission from God, and (B) Divine revelation.[2]

A. COMMISSION FROM GOD

1. The office of the prophet was not a privilege that belonged to a certain Israelite clan or particular family. It depended on a direct call from God (Am 7,15; Is 6,8; Jer 1,7; Ez 2,2).

2. It carried within itself proof of authenticity; at times miracles were per-

---

[2] See Dheilly, *op. cit.,* pp. 35-52; also McKenzie, *The Two-Edged Sword,* pp. 22-44.

formed by the prophet (Is 38,7-8), at other times a prediction was quickly verified (Jer 22, 18-19). But the inspired writings contain a warning against too quickly accepting the message of a person who makes predictions which come true:

> If there arises among you a prophet or a dreamer who promises you a sign or wonder, urging you to follow other gods, whom you have not known, and to serve them: even though the sign or wonder he has foretold you comes to pass, pay no attention to the words of that prophet or that dreamer; for the Lord, your God, is testing you to learn whether you really love him with all your heart and with all your soul. The Lord, your God, shall you follow, and him shall you fear; his commandment shall you observe, and his voice shall you heed, serving him and holding fast to him alone.
>
> *Dt 13,2-5*

This warning is valid for our own times. False prophets are not limited to any one period of history, and signs and wonders are not necessarily proofs of holiness or orthodoxy. Just as the inspired authors of the Old Testament warned their people to be careful about hasty judgments based on "signs and wonders" so Jesus has cautioned His people. Even the "elect" must be careful lest they be led astray (Mt 24,24; 2 Thess 2,9).

3. The main test of the true prophet was whether or not his teaching was in conformity with the doctrine of Yahweh. Conformity to the religious tradition of Yahwism was the essential guarantee of authenticity. Prophecy had its roots in the soil of the religion of Israel. Just as the true Israelite was the one who was faithful to the "religion of the fathers" so the true prophet, the true spokesman of the Lord, was the man whose teaching was faithful to the religious heritage of Israel. Although the unique vocation of the Old Testament prophets is not shared by preachers and teachers in the Church today, we realize that the test of the authenticity of their message is not whether they make successful predictions or perform signs and wonders; the essential criterion is whether or not their words are faithful to the tradition of the Church. Departure from that tradition or contradiction of its message is certain proof of the erroneous nature of the message transmitted by a speaker or author.

B. DIVINE REVELATION

1. God inspired the prophets to speak in His name. They were men "whom God sanctified, carried away, as they spoke, by the Holy Spirit" (2 Pt 1,21).

2. The communication of God with the prophets was supernatural; its manner was diverse. The prophets at times received the communications from God by means of visions, either internal or external to themselves, by dreams, and also by ecstacies. Very often, however, there was no extraordinary in-

ternal psychic manifestation or external phenomenon. God affected the intellect directly. The prophet, convinced that he had experienced the Divine, then communicated the message to his contemporaries by means of words or symbolic actions adapted to their mentality. The usual and most common form of communication was the use of words introduced by the phrase, "Thus says the Lord. . . ." This was the *oracle* of the prophet.

V. THE WORK OF THE PROPHETS

The prophets were teachers given to the Israelites by God to keep them faithful to their mission. They were also sent to prepare the way for the establishment of the Messianic kingdom. They were the heralds of God to the world and the outspoken champions of His rights. The vocational *nabis* worked in three areas of life : (1) *Political*—they dissuaded rulers from entering foreign alliances. They pointed out with great insistence that the enemies of Israel were enemies of Yahweh (Is 7). (2) *Religious*—they insisted on the relation of God with His people and on the obligations which flowed from the relation. Punishment would come if the obligations were neglected. The Prophets were the bitter enemies of polytheism. They insisted on a more spiritual form of religion and not just mere external rituals (Am 5,14; Os 6,6; Is 1,11-17; Jer 6,20). They were also the heralds of the Messianic age. (3) *Moral*—the prophets condemned the oppression of the poor, and of widows and orphans (Am 2,6; 5,12; Is 1,17-23; 5,23; 10,2; Jer 7,5; 22,3). They bitterly rebuked the avarice and injustice of king and priest (Is 1,23; Jer 2,8; 5,31; 6,13). In no uncertain terms they denounced the pride and luxury of the people at large (Is 3,16; Am 4;6).

VI. THE TEACHING OF THE PROPHETS

In the religious development of Israel, the prophets played a most important role. Not only did they recall Israel and its people to a true understanding of God, but they were the ones used by God to add to the progress of Revelation. Each of the prophets contributed his "stone" to the total edifice of doctrine. Their contributions can be grouped into three key concepts: *monotheism, morality,* and *messianism.*[3]

A. MONOTHEISM

The emphatic manner in which the prophets teach that there is only one God is not something new for the religion of Israel. We have seen how, throughout the history of the Chosen People, there was the dogma that the

---

[3] These are the three concepts developed in *La Sainte Bible* (Paris: Les Editions du Cerf, 1955), pp. 971-76.

Lord God is one, and that the gods of the pagans do not exist. Reading the prophet Amos we note his insistence on the fact that Yahweh is the only God, and that He is the ruler of the forces of nature and master of all mankind. Amos, however, is not saying anything new, he is merely putting emphasis on a truth which at times was neglected by the people. Yahweh is involved not only in the history of the Chosen People but also in the destiny of the other nations (Am 9,7); He judges both the small and the great (Am 1-2), and at times He makes use of the pagan nations as instruments by which He punishes the offenses of the people (Am 6,11; Is 7,18-19; Jer 5,15-17). The prophets proclaimed that Israel is in a special way the land of Yahweh, and that the Temple is His dwelling (Is 6; Jer 7,10-11). They also proclaimed that the Sanctuary of Yahweh, the Temple, would be destroyed (Mi 3,12; Jer 7,12-14; 26) and that the Glory of Yahweh would forsake Jerusalem (Ez 10,18-22).

The prophets were the champions of Yahweh and they labored constantly to destroy the influence of the pagan cults among the Jews. They were the opponents of any form of syncretism (Is 44,6-23). The prophets insist that God is The Holy One who fills the earth with His glory (Is 6). Although there is a great insistence on the transcendence of God, the prophets do not fail to teach, as Deuteronomy did, that "no other nation is so great; no other nation has gods that draw near to it, as our God draws near to us whenever we pray to him" (Dt 4,7). The prophets made use of several figures of speech to stress the union that exists between God and His people; Osee, the prophet of love, used the symbolism of marriage (Os 2), so did Jeremia (2,2-7) and Ezechiel (16 and 23; see also 2 Cor 11,2 and Eph 5,25-33 for New Testament usage of this symbolism).

B. MORALITY

The holiness of God is the source of the moral demands that He makes. The morality found in the prophets is not something altogether new; it appears already in the Decalogue, The Ten Commandments, and it was a strong sense of moral goodness that prompted the action of Nathan toward David, after the king had committed his sins of adultery and murder (2 Sm 12). The prophets insist that it is sin that separates man from God (Is 59,2). Sin is an attack on the God of justice (Amos), the God of love (Osee), the God of holiness (Isaia). The prophets pointed out that it is both individuals and the nation as a whole that have sinned, and, therefore, punishment will follow when the great "Day of Yahweh" will occur (Is 2,6-22; 5,18-20; Os 5,9-14; Jl 2,1-2).

The prophets deepened the idea of the true nature of a religious person. They insisted that religion must "come from the heart"; they opposed mere external formalities (Is 1,11-17; Jer 6,20; Os 6,6; Mi 6,6-8). The prophets stressed that God must be found in the heart, and they brought the people

a little closer to that mystery which would be finally revealed in the revelation
of Jesus and which is faithfully echoed in the epistle to the Romans: "You
have received a spirit of adoption as sons, by virtue of which we cry, 'Abba!
Father!'" (Rom 8,15).

C. MESSIANISM

We must bear in mind that God's plan for mankind was unveiled gradually
in ways that long remained inadequate. The Messianic prophecies were
wrapped in a "material form" which contained their spiritual reality, as an
envelope contains a letter. The Jews of the time of Jesus made them even more
materialistic, and thus the most valuable elements in the expectation remained
hidden. In this matter, we must make a distinction between what is called
"real Messianism" and "personal Messianism." In the former, attention is directed to the good things that are to characterize the new order God will bring
about. In the latter, emphasis is on the Person who is to preside over the new
era, bringing it into being and embodying within himself all its values.[4]

The word "Messiah" is from the Hebrew "Mashiah," which means
"anointed." The Greek translation of the word is "Christos." During the
period of the Old Testament this term was applied to those who received
their power of office by means of an anointing with oil. Hence the kings (1 Sm
12,3; 25,7; 26,9; 2 Sm 1,14); the patriarchs considered as kings (Ps 105,15);
and the priests (Lv 4,3-5; 6,15; Nu 3,3) were called the *anointed* of the Lord.
The author of Deutero-Isaia does not hesitate to call Cyrus the Persian by this
title (Is 45,1). The term "Messiah" as a *technical term,* used to refer to the
ideal individual who was to come, does not appear in the Old Testament.
Scholars dispute whether or not the following are exceptions to this statement:
"The kings of the earth rise up, and the princes conspire together against the
Lord and against *his anointed*" (Ps 2,2); and "Know and understand this:
From the utterance of the word that Jerusalem was to be rebuilt until one
who is *anointed* and a leader, there shall be seven weeks" (Dn 9,25). Toward
the beginning of the Christian era the term "messiah" was applied technically
to the ideal individual referred to in the books of the Old Testament. The
word "messianic" is most often used in the strict sense to refer to the prophecies that relate to the person of the ideal individual, usually the king; in the
broad sense it is used to qualify those prophecies of the kingdom of God
which is to come and also everything which the New Testament fulfillment
brings under that kingdom: Jesus, the new Israel fulfilled the destiny of Israel.[5]

[4] Albert Gelin, *The Key Concepts of the Old Testament,* trans. George Lamb (New York:
Sheed & Ward, 1955), pp. 48-63.
[5] The views of a Jewish scholar on the subject of the Messiah and Messianism are in
Joseph Klausner, *The Messianic Idea In Israel,* trans. W. F. Stinespring (New York: The
Macmillan Company, 1955); see the review of the book by J. Edgar Bruns, *The Bridge,*
II (1956-57), 315-21. A short and informative article is A. I. Polack, "The Messianic Idea
in Contemporary Jewish Thought," *The Life of the Spirit,* XV (December, 1960), 250-57.

The king was looked upon as sacred, as someone set apart from the rest of the people. David was considered the ideal king. He was chosen by Yahweh who made a covenant with the House of David, a covenant that would last forever. "Your house and your kingdom shall be confirmed before me forever; Your throne shall be established forever" (2 Sm 7,14). The promise, the *magna carta* of royal messianism, is made even more solemn in some of the Psalms.

> The Lord said to my Lord: "Sit at my right hand
> till I make your enemies your footstool."
> The scepter of your power the Lord will stretch forth from Sion:
> "Rule in the midst of your enemies.
> Yours is princely power in the day of your birth, in holy splendor;
> before the daystar, like the dew, I have begotten you."
>
> *Ps 109,1-3*

> "I will not violate my covenant;
> the promise of my lips I will not alter.
> Once, by my holiness, have I sworn;
> I will not be false to David.
> His posterity shall continue forever,
> and his throne shall be like the sun before me;
> Like the moon, which remains forever
> a faithful witness in the sky."
>
> *Ps 88,35-38*

The Prophets, when they turn their eyes towards the future and see the perfect kingdom that God was to bring about, speak in terms that refer to a David *redivivus*. They look to the "new David" as one who, like the first David, but more satisfactorily, will bring to fulfillment the goal of peace, justice, mercy, and piety, and will fulfill the dreams of victory and greatness.

> Then the people of Israel shall turn back and seek the Lord, their God, and David, their king; they shall come trembling to the Lord and to his bounty, in the last days.
>
> *Os 3,5*

> On that day, says the Lord of hosts, "I will break his yoke from off your necks and snap your bonds." Strangers shall no longer enslave them; instead, they shall serve the Lord, their God, and David, their King, whom I will raise up for them.
>
> *Jer 30,8-9*

> I will appoint one shepherd over them to pasture them, my servant David; he shall pasture them and be their shepherd. I, the Lord, will be their God, and my servant David shall be prince among them.
>
> *Ez 34,23-24*

The prophets described the restoration of Israel in terms of the establishment of a golden period of peace and justice inaugurated by a new David
who would be a prince of peace. He would be endowed with the spirit of
wisdom, understanding, counsel, fortitude, knowledge, and fear of the Lord
(Is 9,1-6; 11,1-9; Jer 23,1-6; Ez 17,22-25; 34,23-24).

The exact time of the appearance of this great personage was not known
by the authors of the Old Testament books. At certain turning-points in
history, hopes were raised and vision was focused more keenly on this problem. During the Assyrian crisis, Isaia reassured the people that their hopes
were not in vain, and from his inspired pronouncements generations of believers were to draw their idea of the Messiah (Is 7,14; 9,5-6; 11,2-5,10).
After the Babylonian Exile the desire of Israel regarding the Messianic Age
was projected into the dim future and it thought of the one who, like David,
would establish the kingdom (Ps 2). It is with this in mind that we should
read about the entrance of Jesus into Jerusalem. Popular expectation was at
a high point, and the crowds saluted him as the one who came in the name
of the Lord; they saluted the coming reign of David (Mk 11,10).

Another current of thought in ancient Israel held that God would establish
the kingdom without the help of any human being, since the kings of the past
had been sad failures. The new kingdom was looked upon as the one that
would result from the "coming of God." The prophet Zacharia spoke of the
nations of the earth going up each year to the Holy City to worship "their
king, the Lord of hosts" (Za 14,16).

God's plan was unveiled gradually. The promises concerning the Messiah
and his kingdom were contained in a "material envelope" which preserved
their spiritual reality.

VII. SUMMARY OF BIBLICAL MESSIANISM

The following points summarize the manner in which the prophets spoke
of the Messianic future.

1. The prophets knew that the Messianic future would be quite different
    from the times in which they lived.
2. They did not possess a clear understanding of what the difference
    would be and, therefore, they described the future in terms of things
    existing in their own times. But they spoke of these things in such a
    way that they suggested that there would be a profound change in
    the future. The aim of the prophets was not merely to preserve what
    had been received from previous ages. They insisted that there was
    need for a profound renewal of the Covenant with the Lord. An
    inner renewal was necessary and urgent. The attempt made by Josia
    in 622 B.C. to bring about a renewal was short-lived. Therefore,
    the prophets told the people that God would grant a new Covenant

which would be more than external; it would be an inner reality by which all men were to live. The words of Jeremia on this point are the "high-water mark" of the Old Testament. They are closely linked to the New Testament revelation regarding Sanctifying Grace (Jer 31,31-34).

3. The prophets were men of their era. Consequently, at times, their religious horizons have a tone of nationalistic narrowness. They used the institutions of the Old Testament—for example, the Temple, the forms of worship, the Law, the political kingdom—to describe the New Testament. The institutions of the Old Covenant were symbols of the Messianic Age and preparations for it. The Old is fulfilled in the New. But, it must be remembered, no Old Testament author *adequately* foresaw the New Testament fulfillment.

4. The Prophets often spoke without temporal perspective. They spoke of things that would happen only after the passage of much time as of they were to happen immediately. It may be said that they saw the *whole,* happening at once. They contemplated the Messiah not in the perspective of the centuries that were to pass before he would come, but in an immediate manner, disregarding any connection with time. Therefore, they often associated Him and His kingdom with the circumstances of the present and they announced His coming as if it were imminent.

5. The prophets spoke in a fragmentary manner. None of them gave a complete picture of the Messiah or the salvation that would be brought about. Some were concerned with certain aspects of the New Age, others were concerned with pointing out one or another of the roles of the king who was to come. At times He is referred to as a great king who comes in triumph and majesty; at other times, as in the *Servant Songs* of the book of Isaia, he is depicted as the Suffering Servant of Yahweh (Is 42,1-4; 49,1,6; 50,4-9; 53,13; 53,12).

Here is my servant whom I uphold, my chosen one with whom I am pleased, upon whom I have put my spirit; he shall bring forth justice to the nations, not crying out, not shouting, not making his voice heard in the street.

A bruised reed he shall not break, and a smoldering wick he shall not quench, until he establishes justice on the earth; the coastlands will wait for his teaching.

Is 42,1-4

Therefore I will give him his portion among the great, and he shall divide the spoils with the mighty, because he surrendered himself to death, and was counted among the wicked; and he shall take away the sins of many, and win pardon for their offenses.

Is 53,12

None of the prophets saw that all these roles would be united in a unique manner in the person of Jesus Christ. The reason for the fragmentary manner in which the prophets spoke is that God accommodated Himself to the circumstances, the needs of His people and the individuality of the prophet. Because of the differing means used to portray the Messiah and His kingdom it is not difficult to see why the Jews did not have a clear picture of the nature of the One who was to come and bring about the kingdom of God. At the time of Jesus, there were different Messianic ideas because of the variety of descriptions present in the writings of the prophets. Thus, we can understand why even those who had an absolute certitude concerning the fact of messianic salvation were still uncertain with regard to the way in which that salvation would be accomplished by God. The faith and hope of the Old Testament were rewarded by the coming of Christ who did not merely fulfill the promises but vastly transcended them. "In uniting in Himself and refining the fragmentary utterances of Old Testament prophecy—and, be it noted, in discarding some of them—our Lord did a unique thing, a thing as unique as His own person. His was a work of fulfillment—never before or after has fulfillment been so complete or so satisfying—and it was a fulfillment that the prophets would not have disavowed, though they could not possibly have foreseen it without being Christians before their time."[6]

Jesus is the Prophet *par excellence* who has delivered to the world the definitive message and directions whereby it is to attain its goal.

> And all the prophets who have spoken, from Samuel onwards, have also announced these days. You are the children of the prophets and of the covenant that God made with your fathers, saying to Abraham, "And in thy offspring shall all the families of the earth be blessed." To you first God, raising up his Son, has sent him to bless you, that everyone may turn from his wickedness.
>
> *Ac 3,24-26*

> God, who at sundry times and in divers manners spoke in times past to the fathers by the prophets, last of all in these days has spoken to us by his Son, whom he appointed heir of all things, by whom also he made the world.
>
> *Hb 1,1-2*

VIII. THE PROPHET AND THE CHRISTIAN

1. The preceding treatment of the prophets has attempted to show that their role and message are not as incomprehensible as some Christians think. We owe it to every speaker or author to try to reconstruct the times in which

---

[6] Bruce Vawter, C.M., "In Many Fragmentary and Varying Utterances: The Use of Messianic Prophecy in Apologetics," *Proceedings of the Catholic Theological Society of America* (1959), p. 116. See A. Gelin, "The Expectation of God in the Old Testament," in *Son and Saviour,* trans. Anthony Wheaton (Baltimore: Helicon Press, 1960), pp. 13-26.

he lived and the purposes for which he composed his message. Certainly, we owe this to the prophets, who were men through whom God spoke "at sundry times and in divers manners." Their message is real and meaningful in proportion to the understanding that we have of their nature, role, and purpose in the history of salvation. They were not Christians before Christ, but what they did and said were important elements in the preparatory stage of the Old Covenant.

2. Jesus often referred to the prophets and their message. The prophetical books were the sources from which he drew a good deal of his message. However, he transformed it and fulfilled them beyond all expectation.

> And he came to Nazareth, where he had been brought up; and according to his custom, he entered the synagogue on the Sabbath and stood up to read. And the volume of Isaias, the prophet was handed to him. And after he opened the volume, he found the place where it was written, "The Spirit of the Lord is upon me because he has anointed me; to bring good news to the poor he has sent me, to proclaim to the captives release, and sight to the blind; to set at liberty the oppressed, to proclaim the acceptable year of the Lord, and the day of recompense."
>
> And closing the volume, he gave it back to the attendant and sat down. And the eyes of all in the synagogue were gazing on him. But he began to say to them, "Today this Scripture has been fulfilled in your hearing." And all bore him witness, and marvelled at the words of grace that came from his mouth.

Often he adopted the strong tone of the prophets when he castigated the unworthy and hypocritical members of the sects of the Pharisees, Scribes, and Sadducees (Mt 23).

Many of the themes which Jesus developed in his preaching were not altogether unfamiliar to the people. They had heard them read from the books of the prophets, for example: (1) The theme of the Good Shepherd (Ez 34 and Jn 10), and (2) The theme of the Vine and Branches (Is 3,14; Os 10,1; Ez 19,10-11 and Jn 15).

3. The Liturgy of the Church uses texts and themes from the prophetical books. Only if the Christian is familiar with these in their proper contexts can he appreciate and understand how and why the Mystical Body uses them in its public prayer. The Liturgy is the worship of the whole Christ, Head and Members.

The prophetical texts are most meaningful on the lips of those who worship in spirit and in truth in the New Israel. The *qahal Yahweh,* the assembly of the Lord of the Old Covenant is fulfilled in the *ekklesia Kyriou,* the assembly of the Lord which is the Church. The prophets are at home in the Christian Liturgy. Their message is important and necessary today: "Thus says the Lord. . . ."

4. The Christian, like the prophet, is one who is called by the Lord. There

are differences in the nature of the two vocations. Yet both involve a call on the part of God, a response on the part of the individual, and a mission to the world.

The Christian is called in Baptism and receives the faith which demands the response of *total commitment* to the Lord. The Church relies on each member to exercise his vocation as a "prophet," calling the attention of the world to the message that really matters, the message of salvation. The true Christian is a person who is sensitive to the role of the Holy Spirit in his life. A man of his time, like the prophet of the Old Testament, he is yet one whose horizons extend beyond time and space. The Christian is the "pilgrim of the Absolute," one who follows with living faith the all Holy God who spoke through Amos, Osee, Isaia, Jeremia, Ezechiel, and the other prophets, and who now speaks through the Church which continues the prophetic role of Jesus the Prophet. The Christian is to bring the message of God into his daily life and thus be a witness and if necessary a "suffering servant," who incarnates in his daily existence the transcendent truths of the Lord.

> Blessed be the God and Father of our Lord Jesus Christ, who has blessed us with every spiritual blessing on high in Christ. Even as he chose us in him before the foundation of the world, that we should be holy and without blemish in his sight in love. He predestined us to be adopted through Jesus Christ as his sons, according to the purpose of his will, unto the praise of the glory of his grace, with which he has favored us in his beloved Son.
>
> In him we have redemption through his blood, the remission of sins, according to the riches of his grace. This grace has abounded beyond measure in us in all wisdom and prudence, so that he may make known to us the mystery of his will according to his good pleasure. And this his good pleasure he purposed in him to be dispensed in the fullness of the times: to re-establish all things in Christ, both those in the heavens and those on the earth.
>
> In him, I say, in whom, we also have been called by a special choice, having been predestined in the purpose of him who works all things according to the counsel of his will, to contribute to the praise of his glory—we who before hoped in Christ. And in him you too, when you had heard the word of truth, the good news of your salvation, and be- 'lieved in it, were sealed with the Holy spirit of the promise, who is the pledge of our inheritance, for a redemption of possession, for the praise of his glory.
>
> *Eph 1,3-14*

twenty

MESSIANISM AND APOLOGETICS

I. INTRODUCTION

OUR STUDY OF the prophets and messianism will conclude with some comments about Old Testament texts which are often listed by those books presenting arguments in favor of Jesus being the One predicted by the prophets. Often the Old Testament is presented as if it served no other purpose than to predict the New Testament. The impression is given that all one has to do is to go to the Old Testament and collect a sufficient number of texts (contexts are not emphasized) and the result will be a mosaic of references which taken together cannot fail to identify Jesus as the One sent by God. The words of McKenzie on this point are worth quoting at length:

> The Old Testament was regarded not only as a prediction of the New Testament in whole, but also in detail. It predicted not only the future, but also the steps, the phases in which this future was to be realized. Consequently, by collecting a sufficient number of texts, it was possible to find a great many details in the life of Jesus foretold, enough to identify Him when He appeared. We know now that such exegesis is fantastic. It is impossible to imagine that God secretly revealed the future course of events in detail to the men of old, and that they distilled in cipher such details for the public as would sharpen its curiosity. If the sacred books were composed as a jigsaw puzzle to be assembled by the ingenuity of Christians who know the finished picture, then this manner of interpretation might stand; but we have to suppose that God spoke sense to the Hebrews also, and there is no sense in a fragment of a jigsaw puzzle.[1]

Textbooks have often followed the approach mentioned above, and have led their readers to imagine that they can find a complete Christology in the

---

[1] McKenzie, *The Two-Edged Sword*, p. 206.

205

Old Testament with even the most minute and trivial details of the life of Jesus foretold by the inspired authors. This approach is a very old one; Justin the Apologist used it in the third century.

Usually the reader is shown on one side of the page a list of "outstanding prophecies" in the Old Testament, and, on the other side, how these were fulfilled in the life of Jesus. This approach is known as the parallel-text argument. But if such an approach were valid, the prophecies would be rendered useless: that is, if they were so clear from the beginning, they could be artificially "fulfilled" by anyone who came later. As noted earlier, the language of the prophets contained obscurity, vagueness, and lack of temporal perspective, all of which usually did not point to a literal fulfillment. Although the prophet did at times foresee the future, he foresaw it within the limitations placed upon him because of his personal, historical, and cultural background and environment. It is a synthetic approach, one which tries to form a synthesis of all that the prophets said and did, which alone will give a proper understanding of the role of the prophets and the meaning of Old Testament messianism.

There are about seventy-five texts of the Old Testament which authors who follow the "parallel-text argument" use in their books.[2] The following are some of the texts which are used most often.

PROPHECY	FULFILLMENT
1. Lo, I am sending my messenger to prepare the way before me; and suddenly there will come to the temple the Lord whom you seek, and the messenger of the covenant whom you desire. Yes, he is coming, says the Lord of hosts. *Mal 3,1*	1. John the Baptist prepared the way for the coming of Jesus.
2. Therefore the Lord himself will give you this sign: the virgin shall be with child, and bear a son, and shall name him Emmanuel. *Is 7,14*	2. Christ was born of the Virgin Mary.
3. But you, Bethlehem-Ephratha, too small to be among the clans of Juda, from you shall come forth for me one who is to be ruler in Israel; whose origin is from of old, from ancient times. *Mi 5,1*	3. Christ was born in Bethlehem.

[2] An example of this approach is in William J. Keifer, S.M., *Biblical Subject Index* (Westminster, Md.: The Newman Press, 1958), pp. 19-20.

4. Then will the eyes of the blind be opened, the ears of the deaf be cleared; then will the lame leap like a stag, then the tongue of the dumb will sing.

Is 35,5-6

4. Christ performed many miracles.

5. Rejoice heartily, O daughter Sion, shout for joy, O daughter Jerusalem! See your king shall come to you; a just savior is he, meek, and riding on an ass, on a colt, the foal of an ass.

Za 9,9

5. Jesus entered Jerusalem seated upon an ass on Palm Sunday.

6. Therefore I will give him his portion among the great, and he shall divide the spoils with the mighty, because he surrendered himself to death and was counted among the wicked; and he shall take away the sins of many, and will pardon their offenses.

Is 53,12

6. Our Lord was crucified with thieves and prayed for those who killed Him.

7. Indeed many dogs surround me, a pack of evildoers closes in upon me; they have pierced my hands and my feet; I can count all my bones. They look on and gloat over me; they divide my garments among them, and for my vesture they cast lots.

Ps 21,17-19

7. Christ's hands and feet were pierced with nails, and the soldiers gambled for his garments.

8. Rather they put gall in my food, and in my thirst they gave me vinegar to drink.

Ps 68,22

8. During His suffering, Jesus was given common wine (vinegar) to drink.

9. I will put enmity between you and the woman, between your seed and her seed; he shall crush your head, and you shall lie in wait for his heel.

Gn 3,15

9. By her offspring Jesus, Mary overcomes the devil.

10. I saw one like a son of man coming, on the clouds of heaven; when he reached the Ancient One and was presented before him, he received dominion, glory, and kingship; nations and peoples of every language serve him.

Dn 7,13-14

10. Christ the Son of Man descended into heaven and ". . . sitteth at the right hand of God the Father . . . and of his kingdom there shall be no end."

II. COMMENTS ABOUT THE PRECEDING
OLD TESTAMENT TEXTS[3]

1. MALACHIA 3,1

The precursor announced in this text is Yahweh's, not his Messiah's. In the context v. 23, which is an addition made by another author so that the book would not end with the word "doom," the precursor is called Elia. The use of this text in the Gospel when speaking of the beginning of the Messianic Age and the preaching of John the Baptist is the result of Jewish speculation at the time of Christ concerning the character of the individual called Elia. Jesus said that Elia had come in the person of the Baptist (Mt 11,10).[4]

2. ISAIA 7,14

Many are familiar with this text because of its use in Mt 1,23, and therefore, they consider it in the context of the birth of Jesus rather than the context found in Isaia. The Hebrew text does not have the word "virgin": it speaks of *ha almâ,* which is similar to the English "girl," and neither supposes nor excludes virginity. An *'almu* was a young girl of marriageable age. The Greek translators of the Septuagint, which was made about two centuries before Christ, used the word *parthenos,* which does indeed mean "virgin." It is possible, although this is still a disputed point, that the Septuagint marks a forward step in the revelation made by God. Hence, the translation of Is 7,14 could be a further inspired clarification of the meaning of the original Hebrew text. However, it must be noted that the Septuagint also uses the word *parthenos* in a sense that does not necessarily carry the precise idea of virginity (Gn 34,3). Since many translators worked to produce the Septuagint it cannot be said with absolute certainty that the one who translated Isaia uses *parthenos* in the same sense as the translator of Genesis. Nevertheless, there is possibility that it meant the same thing for both.

It is most unlikely that Isaia foresaw the virgin birth of the Messiah. Isaia presents a contemporary sign for the king, Achaz, who is faced with the Syro-Ephraimite war which threatens his dynasty. The most obvious significance of the prophet's words is that he is referring to the king's son, Ezechia, who is the fulfillment of the prophecy in the *literal sense.* The name "Em-

---

[3] The material presented here is treated in more detailed fashion in the works of several contemporary scholars, particularly Roland E. Murphy, O. Carm., "Notes on Old Testament Messianism and Apologetics," *The Catholic Biblical Quarterly,* XIX (January, 1957), 5-15; Bruce Vawter, C.M., *The Conscience of Israel* (New York: Sheed & Ward, 1961), pp. 289-95, *et passim;* also by the same author, the article referred to ea lier, "In Many Fragmentary and Varying Utterances: The Use of Messianic Prophecy in Apologetics."

[4] See Carroll Stuhlmueller, C.P., *The Books of Aggai, Zacharia, Malachia, Jona, Joel, Abdia* (New York: The Paulist Press, 1961), p. 38.

manuel" does not carry any necessary implication of divinity for the one who bears it. It is in the *typical sense* that this prophecy is referred to the Virgin Birth.[5]

There are some unsolved problems concerning this text but the fact that many Catholic scholars hold the view just presented should make us pause before we assert *apodictically and without qualification* that Is 7,14 foretells the Virgin Birth of Jesus.

The Gospel of St. Matthew, without saying how the prophecy is being used (that is in the literal or typical sense) applies it to the event of the virginal conception that occurred through the power of the Spirit of God. Here the author was following a standard rabbinic way of using the Scriptures, which was to marshal as many texts as possible to prove a point or bolster a particular teaching, without necessarily implying that the texts in their original literal sense were meant to convey the point or prove the teaching under discussion. This is a device still used in Christian preaching.

Furthermore, the fact that the Matthean Gospel speaks of "Emmanuel" does not mean that originally Isaia understood the name to mean that the individual bearing it was divine by nature. For him, it meant only that there would be some extraordinary divine assistance. However, when the author of the Gospel used the name he knew what had occurred in the moment of the Incarnation, since he was writing about 80 years after the event with the fullness of the Christian faith. Consequently he wanted to convey the truth that the son of Mary is, in the strictest sense, "God with us."

3. MICHEA 5,2

This is a messianic prophecy. In the context, Ephratha is contrasted with the clans of Juda because it is where the Davidic dynasty had its origin. This text, with its reference to Bethlehem, signifies simply that the king of the future is to come from the royal line of David—not that he will necessarily be born in the town of David. Nothing obliges us to say that the prophet saw anything beyond the historical dynasty of David. The use of this text in Mt 2,5-6 gives us evidence of how it was interpreted at the time of our Lord, particularly at the time of the writing of the canonical Gospel sometime around 80 A.D. The author of the Matthean Gospel does not necessarily say that Mi 5,2 was a prediction of the birthplace of the Messiah.

4. ISAIA 35,5-6

Scholars are of the opinion that this text was written after the Babylonian Exile, hence not by Isaia, who exercised his ministry during the eighth century. The passage describes the happy state of Israel after the return from

---

[5] Read the comments of Huesman, *The Book of Isaia,* pp. 10-11.

Exile. The wonderful deeds mentioned are those of Yahweh. This text is not personally messianic.

5. ZACHARIA 9,9

The text, which is messianic, emphasizes meekness. It contrasts the kingly ideal which would be fulfilled in the Messiah with the sad experiences witnessed in Israel's history. Even if Christ had never used the animal to ride into Jerusalem on Palm Sunday, this text would be fulfilled in the sense that He was meek and humble of heart. It is possible that this detail was chosen by Jesus as a means of laying claim to the messianic role, although such literal enactment went beyond what the prophet had in mind when he wrote.

6. ISAIA 53,12

This text, together with Isaia 42,1-7; 49,1-9; 50,4-9; 52,13-53,12, is part of what are commonly called the "Songs of the Servant of Yahweh." These texts picture a perfect follower of Yahweh, who proclaims the true faith, suffers in order to expiate the sins of his people, and is glorified by God. There have been, and continue to be, many views and disputes concerning the texts and their interpretation.

Is the Servant the nation Israel, at least an ideal group in Israel, which represents the entire nation? Those who follow a collective interpretation answer in the affirmative. Is he an individual contemporary with the author? Is he an individual person who will come in the future and fulfill the destiny of Israel? Is the Servant to be looked upon in the collective *and* in the individual interpretation? In what sense are the title "Servant of God" and the general contents of the Servant Songs applied to Jesus in the New Testament? There are differences of opinion among both Catholics and non-Catholics. Those who hold that the Servant is the Messiah *as such* are in the minority. Pre-Christian Judaism did not understand the Servant as the Messiah either.

The teaching of the Songs of the Servant can be understood better if the concept of the "remnant of Israel" is remembered. Israel's hope was tied to the house of David. The oracle of Nathan (2 Sm 7,4-17) had made this clear.[6] The nation was often tempted to pride, and its history, as we have seen, was hardly one of continued fidelity to Yahweh. A purging of the dross was necessary. And out of the fire that would purify the nation would come the *remnant,* a new Israel that would inherit the promises of the Lord. The destruction of Jerusalem and the Exile in Babylon were the instruments used by Yahweh to bring judgment upon the nation and preserve the *remnant* (Is 10,20-22). This *remnant* would be the final destiny of Israel as a people, called to be a victim, to expiate the sins of the other Jews as well as those of other peoples.

[6] See p. 130.

The first three Songs (Is 42,1-7; 49,1-9; 52,13-53; 12) can be applied to the *remnant* which is the Servant of Yahweh. Primitive Christianity applied these texts to Jesus because He most fittingly fulfilled the promises; He is the most important member of the *remnant,* He is the Servant who expiates the sins of all mankind through His sufferings, death, and resurrection.

7 & 8. PSALM 21,17-19 AND PSALM 68,22

The sufferings described in these Psalms are similar to those endured by Jesus during His passion. The fact that the opening words of Psalm 21 were used by our Lord on the Cross naturally led to the interpretation which holds that the Psalm was a prophecy of the sacrifice of the Cross. Hardly any scholar of our times holds the ancient view that the Psalm is a messianic one in the literal sense.

These Psalms describe the sufferings of a just man who has been unjustly punished. They contain remarks which could be paralleled in the sufferings of other individuals, for example, Job. Moreover, there are elements in them which in no way can be applied to Jesus, for example, "O God, you know my folly, and my faults are not hid from you" (Ps 68,6).

Admitting that there is a reference to a messianic future in Psalm 21,28-32, there is no evidence to force the conclusion that the psalmist was *literally* speaking of Jesus. The individual in the psalm is a type of Jesus; the psalm is messianic in the *typical* sense. The verse "they have pierced my hands and feet" (Ps 21,17) which leads many Christians to apply the psalm literally to the crucifixion of Jesus is not certain. The translation relies on the Vulgate of St. Jerome, which is based on the uncertain text of the Septuagint. The Hebrew text for this verse also is difficult to ascertain. Some authors suggest that the phrase connotes the digging action of fetters rather than the piercing of the hands. It is an interesting fact that the authors of the Gospels, who used several other phrases in the psalm, did not refer to this verse.

> It is clear . . . that the New Testament writers interpreted the psalm as referring to the Messiah. This has also been the constant tradition of the Fathers and of other Christian writers (with the solitary exception of Theodore of Mopsuestia).
> The only question on which there is not agreement is as to whether it refers to the Messiah in the literal sense or only in the typical sense. Catholic scholars generally favour the former view. They maintain a) that certain passages of the poem obtain their full meaning only if they are taken to refer to Christ; and b) the conversion of the nations is the consequence of the death of Christ.
> Yet it is doubtful if these arguments are quite conclusive. For making due allowance for poetic hyperbole, there is nothing in the description of the psalmist's sufferings which cannot be paralleled in other psalms and in the Book of Job. It is also to be noted that the conversion of the

nations is not set down as the consequence of the sufferings of the
psalmist, but rather of the manifestation of God's justice in the deliverance of the sufferer and his restoration to happiness.[7]

9. GENESIS 3,15

This text was treated earlier in the section dealing with the book of
Genesis.[8]

10. DANIEL 7,13-14

The phrase "Son of Man" is used almost 70 times in the Gospels, for example Mt 12,32, Mk 14,41, Lk 11,30, Jn 8,28. During the trial before the
Sanhedrin Jesus declared, "You shall see the Son of Man sitting at the right
hand of the Power, and coming with the clouds of heaven" (Mk 14,62).
This statement has an obvious connection with the one in the book of Daniel.
The close association of Jesus with the title "Son of Man" causes many to
conclude that the text in Daniel is a literal prophecy about Jesus.

It is important to know that the book of Daniel was written about the time
that the Jews were being persecuted by Antiochus IV Epiphanes (175-163
B.C.). All human hope seemed futile. This fact helps in the understanding
of this prophetic book which contains a message of hope couched in symbolic
language.

The seventh chapter in Daniel is one where the author presents a great
vision, a summary of the many trials and visions found in the preceding parts
of the book. It is concerned with the triumph of the kingdom of God. Four
monsters are mentioned, each of which represents one of the empires which
persecuted the Jews: the lion with the wings of an eagle is the Babylonian
Empire, the bear is the empire of the Medes, the winged leopard is the Persian
Empire, and the beast that was different from all the rest is the empire founded
by Philip of Macedon which harassed the Jews during the Seleucid and
Ptolemaic periods in Palestine. It is only after these visions are presented that
the author speaks of the vision of "one like a son of man coming on the clouds
of heaven" who receives a kingdom.

The Aramaic expression "son of man" means an individual human being.
In the vision it is used as a personification of the People of God; it is a collective figure which stands for the "holy ones of the Most High" who will receive
the kingship (Dn 7,18). This is an example of the Old Testament concept of
corporate personality in which a group is summed up in an individual. One
name or term stands for the group, and the group is summed up in a personification.[9]

[7] Edward Kissane, *The Book of Psalms* (2 vols.; Westminster, Md.; The Newman Press,
1953), I, 95.
[8] See pp. 62-63.
[9] See Brown, *The Book of Daniel,* pp. 23-25.

Jesus, the perfect representative of the People of God, is the One in whom the kingdom was established on earth. He summed up within Himself the role and destiny of the "holy ones of the Most High." He brought to fulfillment the theme of the "Son of Man" which was only imperfectly realized in the Old Covenant. He is the One in whom and through whom the salvation of God's people was achieved. In Jesus the kingdom received its transcendent King.

twenty-one

INTRODUCTION TO THE
WISDOM LITERATURE

I. INTRODUCTION

THE SEARCH for knowledge is as old as man. Aristotle, the pagan philosopher, said that "all men by nature desire to know" and the records of ancient culture and civilization bear out the truth of his observation. Human wisdom, or philosophy in the general sense, was born as soon as primitive man arrived at the moment of self-consciousness, and the record of history shows that both the love and search of wisdom have never been the absolute possessions of any one race or culture. It is true that humanity had to await the advent of the Greek Sages for the initiation of the great developments in the field of philosophy. The great thinkers of ancient Hellas composed works which are a mine of information and wisdom. Yet, long before Thales of Miletus, the Sage of the seventh or sixth century B.C., there were "wise men" in other lands who exercised their natural intuition and sought the answers to the manifold problems of life. Long before man's natural and instinctive intellectual urge was combined with human genius in the persons of individuals like Aristotle, Plato, and Socrates, there were men who philosophized about the problems of life. However, they searched for solutions on the practical rather than the speculative level.

The "wise men" of ancient Egypt were the authors of some of the most ancient pieces of literature so far discovered. Their works include, for example, *The Song of the Harper, The Dialogue of a Misanthrope with His Soul, The Admonitions of an Egyptian Sage,* and *The Maxims of Ptah-hotep* all from before the second millenium B.C. About the beginning of the first millenium B.C. the Egyptian sages produced a work known as *The Teaching of Amen-em-ope,* which has some interesting parallels in the Biblical book of Proverbs.

From the Old Kingdom to the Greco-Roman period, these compositions represent an unbroken traditional teaching which formed the souls of

214

pupils in the schools for scribes and of an incalculable number of other readers. We hear in them a sage speaking from the distant past; he addresses his son and gives him a series of practical counsels, from which religion is not absent. They are the fruit of experience, and tradition confers on them an authority that puts them above all discussion. Their purpose is primarily to train functionaries, but also men, so that they may become masters of themselves, gracious, cultivated, upright, and worthy.[1]

Babylon also has sages who composed wisdom-literature, for example the work entitled *Let Me Praise the Lord of Wisdom,* written shortly before the first millenium and sometimes called "the Babylonian Job" because of literary similarities with the Book of Job in the Old Testament. There are superficial resemblances but profound differences. In general, the wisdom-literature of Babylon is bound up with magic and divination and is in the form of a fable or story which often deals with the problem of suffering. The lands of Canaan, Arabia, Tyre, and Edom were also places where literature of this type was produced by sages, some of whom are mentioned in the Bible (cf. 3 Kgs 4,30-31; Prv 30,1-14; Ez 28,2-7; Jer 49,7).

II. SAGES OF ISRAEL

Palestine, the land of divine-election, was so situated that contacts with its neighbors were not only unavoidable but even absolutely necessary. These relations were not only political but also literary. It is very probable that the early Hebrew settlers brought to their new home the literary compositions which were prevalent in the lands where they had lived. The long line of settlers which started in the days of the Patriarchs carried more than physical belongings from the land of Mesopotamia. The caravans, as well as the peaceful and warring Hebrew invaders at the time of the conquest and settlement during and after the time of Josue, brought with them more than the physical "spoils from Egypt." Gradually, the imported cultural and literary materials were passed through a "monotheistic filter" and transformed by a distinctive theological viewpoint, that of Yahwistic faith.

Israel, like its neighbors, had a special class of "wise men," individuals who were instructors in the practical art of living. They were neither priests nor prophets, but were moral advisers interested in the conduct of individual, personal life more than in the Law, Covenant, and Worship. They were interested in the individual as a human being. They pondered his destiny and commented on the terribly vexing problem of retribution. Why do the good suffer? When will those who do evil get their share? Their emphasis is more on Man and the "good life." Their approach is generally existential and humanistic; it is psychological and sociological rather than theological. Yet, one cannot escape the "theological perspective" in evidence in the literature,

---

[1] A. Robert, "Didactic and Lyric Poetry," *Guide to the Bible,* I, 499.

particularly the later books, such as Sirach and Baruch. Admittedly, this perspective is not always as evident as it is in other books of the Bible, but it is not difficult to sense the fact that in the wisdom literature human life and its actions are viewed and interpreted by those who possess the viewpoint of Yahweh. This point has to be emphasized because there are still some who see the sapiential literature of the Bible as nothing more than a collection of interesting parallels to the literature of Israel's pagan neighbors already mentioned.

In the days of the ancient monarchy, particularly the time of Solomon (970-931 B.C.), the sage was an accepted part of the life of Israel. Solomon himself was looked upon as one whose wisdom surpassed the "wisdom of all the Orientals and of the Egyptians, and he was wiser than all men" (3 Kgs 4,30-31). Many who know little about the role of Solomon in the history of salvation remember the folkloristic tale about this wise king who, during a dispute between two harlots who claimed the same child, restored the baby to his true mother by using the clever tactic of ordering the child to be cut in two, knowing that the mother would never be satisfied with "half a child." This beautiful tale circulated throughout the land, and all Israel "feared the king, seeing that the wisdom of God was in him to do judgment" (3 Kgs 3,16-28). There is another lesson in the story. It brought out the fact that in Israel, wisdom was looked upon as something more than human ingenuity. It was a gift from the Lord. Yahweh was the source of the wisdom and understanding found in the sage. Solomon left behind the memory of having been the Wise Man *par excellence,* the great Sage of Israel. That memory explains the literary fiction used by later authors who did not hesitate to attribute their works to him. It also explains the position of those who still think that Solomon was the author of the books of Proverbs, Canticle of Canticles, Ecclesiastes, and Wisdom, all works which are much later than the period of the united monarchy in Israel. (Proverbs, in its final form, dates from the fifth century B.C.; Canticle of Canticles also from the fifth century; Ecclesiastes from the third century; Wisdom from the early part of the first century).

The time of Solomon witnessed a great impetus for the wisdom tradition and also the confirmation of the conviction that wisdom is the gift of the Lord. In time, the sages conducted schools in which they taught the lesson of divine reward for those who do their work in due season (Sir 51,23-30). It was in such groups that the scribes were trained and, schooled in wisdom, they became the select attendants at the court of the king.

III. THE WISDOM BOOKS

The Wisdom or Sapiential Literature of the Old Testament (in Hebrew, *hokmah*), includes the books of Job, Proverbs, Ecclesiastes, Sirach, and Wisdom. Since not all scholars agree on the number of books that should be included in this category, sometimes the following books are also included: Canticle of Canticles, Tobia, Baruch, and some of the Psalms.[2]

Almost all of this canonical literature is post-exilic. Although the early period of Israel's history saw the beginning of this genre, at least in its oral form, and the Solomonic era witnessed the great sapiential impetus, it is the period after the Babylonian Exile (587-538 B.C.) that fathered the greater part. It was a product of that spiritual maturity which was formed in the crucible of exile and suffering. The Exile taught the lesson: "The fear of the Lord is the beginning of wisdom" (Prv 1,7). Thus did the Sage echo the teaching of the prophets which Jeremia summed up when he said:

> Let not the wise man glory in his wisdom, nor the strong man glory in his strength, nor the rich man glory in his riches; but rather, let him who glories, glory in this, that in his prudence he knows me, knows that I, the Lord, bring about kindness, justice and uprightness on the earth; for with such am I pleased, says the Lord.
>
> *Jer 9,22-23*

After the Exile, the sages of Israel became more interested in those things which were the particular concern of the priests and prophets. This is seen, for example, in the book of Sirach, written during the second century B.C. by a sage filled with love for the temple, priesthood, worship, and the holy books. Its author speaks of love of wisdom and of the Law of Moses and identifies Wisdom and the Law (Sir 23,23-4). This is also the case in the beautiful sapiential hymn found in the book of Baruch, written during the second century B.C. (Bar 3,9-4,4). The hymn praises Wisdom and speaks of the Law of Moses as a gift from God that endures forever. "All who cling to her (the Law) will live, but those will die who forsake her" (Bar 4,1). The reading of Sirach will also show how tenuous is the position of those who maintain that the sages of Israel were disinterested in the things that belonged to the worship of Yahweh:

> Appear not before the Lord empty-handed, for all that you offer is in fulfillment of the precepts. The just man's offering enriches the altar and rises as a sweet odor before the Most High. The just man's sacrifice is most pleasing, nor will it ever be forgotten. In generous spirit pay homage to the Lord, be not sparing of freewill gifts. With each contribution show a cheerful countenance, and pay your tithes in a spirit of joy. Give to the Most High as he has given to you, generously, according to your means.
>
> *Sir 35,4-9*

---

[2] The best book in English on the nature and contents of the Wisdom books is Roland E. Murphy, O. Carm., *Seven Books of Wisdom* (Milwaukee: The Bruce Publishing Company, 1960).

The wisdom literature of the Bible is the result of the efforts of sages who utilized not merely the best compositions of their neighbors but also their own personal observations and experiences. They studied life in the light of Yahweh's revelation and proven providence, and gave to the Chosen People a theological view of life which, although limited by the particular stage in the history of revelation, is vastly superior to the wisdom-literature of the pagan nations. The Sapiential Books were written under the inspiration of God by believers for believers, and the object of belief was Yahweh, the God who had chosen Israel as His People and who had acted continually in its behalf.

Wisdom, the wise-men of Israel said, is justice and piety. These lead to happiness. Folly, which is impiety, results in ruin. God is the one who will reward the good and punish the wicked: "The curse of the Lord is on the house of the wicked, but the dwelling of the just he blesses; when he is dealing with the arrogant, he is stern, but to the humble he shows kindness. Honor is the portion of wise men, but fools inherit shame" (Prv 3,33-35). The world and the lives of men are governed by a God who is both wise and just: "It is easy with the Lord on the day of death to repay man according to his deeds" (Sir 11,26). Wisdom is the gift of God and the man who possesses it is truly happy.

> Happy the man who finds wisdom,
>   the man who gains understanding!
> For her profit is better than profit in silver,
>   and better than gold is her revenue;
> She is more precious than corals
>   and none of your choice possessions can compare with her.
>   *Prv 3,13-15*

The Sages of Israel, with the Prophets, were the guides who led the People of God along the torturous paths that led finally to Incarnate Wisdom, Jesus, who brought the Good News of Salvation.

IV. THE LITERARY FORM : MASHAL

The Hebrew word *mashal* is used to designate the genre of the Wisdom Literature. It has the meaning of "likeness" but it is usually translated as "proverb." In the early stages of the development of this type of literature the word referred to maxims and aphorisms which caught the attention of the hearers. The book of Proverbs contains many examples of these.

> In the fear of the Lord is a strong defense;
>   even for one's children he will be a refuge.
>   *Prv 14,26*

> Pride goes before disaster
>   and a haughty spirit before a fall.
>   *Prv 16,18*

> Even a fool, if he keeps silent, is considered wise;
>   if he closes his lips, intelligent,
>
> *Prv 19,28*

In time, the word was used in an extended sense to mean parables, allegories, riddles, even derisory remarks and satire. It was applied to authoritative statements which used poetic and figurative forms. The *mashal* often uses parallelisms and picturesque imagery.

It often has a pedagogical purpose: to arouse the curiosity of the young, make them reflect, and thus impress on their minds a particular lesson which would influence the conduct of their lives. The books of Wisdom contain examples of all types of *mashal*.

V. THE BOOK OF JOB

Long before this book was written ancient Egypt and Babylon had witnessed similar literary attempts at solving the riddle of the sufferings of a just man. However, careful comparisons of the various "Jobs" show that the similarities between the pagan literature and the biblical Job are only superficial. The pagan writings never reached the spiritual height of the biblical Job.

Job who appears in this book was not a historical character. The book, written about the fifth or fourth century B.C., is a didactic piece of literature in which the main character is highly stylized. The author used a dramatic story filled with dialogue in the form of sublime poetry in order to present a concrete case of an innocent sufferer who trusts in God and hopes in Divine Justice.[3]

This book grapples with a problem that was taken for granted by most Israelites, temporal retribution. Throughout most of the Old Testament the people held the view that rewards and punishments were given out in this life. After death there was only a shadowy and gloomy existence in Sheol (Pss 6,6; 38,14; Jb 10,20-22). It was not until the second century B.C. that a clearer understanding developed about life after death and even that fell far short of the revelation made by Jesus concerning such a life.

The prologue of the book contains a folkloristic presentation in which God permits Satan, one of the heavenly company, to so act toward Job that all his possessions will be taken away (Jb 1,1-12). Job ponders what is happening and is unable to figure it out, because the punishments that he is experiencing are supposed to come only to those who are wicked and sinful, and *he* is a just man. In series of poetical speeches, Job's three friends, Eliphaz, Baldah, and Sophar try to convince Job that he is being punished for personal wrongdoing (Jb 4-5; 8; 11; 15; 18; 20; 22; 25). Job answers the remarks of his friends with what amounts to a flat refusal to accept their interpretation. At

---

[3] A scholarly study of this book is Myles M. Bourke, *The Book of Job* (2 Parts; New York: The Paulist Press, 1962).

times, Job's remarks are anything but praiseworthy; they are often aggressive and defiant, sometimes they are almost blasphemous (Jb 9,22-24). Yet he does make an act of faith in God.

> But as for me, I know that my Vindicator lives,
>   and that he will at last stand forth upon the dust
> Whom I myself shall see, and not another—
>   and from my flesh I shall see God;
>   my inmost being is consumed with longing.
>
> *Jb 19,25-27*

These verses are difficult to understand because the Hebrew text has been poorly preserved. The Vulgate of St. Jerome so presents these verses that Job appears to be convinced that whatever his end may be God will vindicate him and he will rise from the dead. The Douay translation, which is based on the Vulgate, has the same meaning, and those who composed the footnotes in that edition did not hesitate to say that the text shows Job's explicit belief in his Redeemer and in the resurrection of the body.

> For I know that my Redeemer liveth, and in the
> last day I shall rise out of the earth.
>   And I shall be clothed again with my skin: and
> in my flesh I shall see my God.
>   Whom I myself shall see, and my eyes shall behold;
> and not another. This my hope is laid up in my bosom.
>
> *Jb 19,25-27*

Although such a meaning is very consoling, it is not substantiated by either the Hebrew or the other ancient versions. All we can say about this text is that Job believes that God will be his vindicator and will defend his cause. Moreover, it cannot be said that the author stated a belief in a type of life after death which was different from the one normally held, that is, existence in Sheol.

The speeches of the individual named Eliu which were probably added to the book by someone other than the original author, continue the theme of suffering and punishment, but Eliu adds little to what Job's friends have said already (Jb 32-37).

Finally, Yahweh enters the scene and recalls the marvels of creation which man finds difficult to understand: why then should man try to understand suffering? He reproaches Job for his complaints (Jb 38-41). Job then recites his act of contrition, "I disown what I have said, and repent in dust and ashes." (Jb 42-6). Then the Lord restores him to his former blessed condition of life.

The problem of the suffering of the just and the apparent happiness of the sinful is a timeless one. But believers know that there is an answer, even though they cannot fully comprehend the mystery. If the finite mind of man does not understand all the marvels of nature, how is it going to comprehend the infinite wisdom of God. The Christian knows that suffering is not necessarily punishment for sin, and that earthly prosperity is not necessarily a reward for virtue. He believes that there is an after-life which will bring to those who love God and who are faithful to Him those things that eye has not seen nor ear heard (1 Cor 2,9). He does not have a complete answer to the problem of suffering, but in the Cross of Christ he has an answer that softens his pain and on the Resurrection he bases his hope. The book of Job teaches the Christian that he must be strong in his faith even when he is not blessed with earthly consolations.

St. Paul summed up the true Christian outlook when he said, "I reckon that the sufferings of the present time are not worthy to be compared with the glory to come that will be revealed in us" (Rom 8,18).

VI. PROVERBS

Collections of *mashals,* proverbs, were not the unique distinction of Israel. The sages of Egypt, Babylon, and other countries of the ancient Near East had produced similar collections. The Old Testament book received its present form about the fifth century B.C. but it incorporates parts which are much older, perhaps as old as the time of Solomon, to whom the book is attributed in popular tradition. There is even some affinity of the 30 proverbs in Prv 22,17-24,22 to the maxims of Amen–em–ope, the Egyptian sage.[4] The book, a composite work, is really an anthology of didactic poetry. Essentially a "collection of collections" introduced by a long prologue (Prv 1-9). The purpose of the work is to help men appreciate wisdom and discipline . . . "understand words of intelligence . . . receive training in wise conduct, in what is right, just and honest" (Prv 1,2-3). The book closes with an epilogue in which the domestic virtues of the ideal wife are eulogized (Prv 31,10-31).

The fact that the contents of the book date from various periods, explains why there are apparent differences in its doctrinal depth. It is plain human wisdom that received most attention in the older parts (Prv 10-22 and 25-29). Religious proverbs appear, but they are fewer in number than the humanistic ones. Usually they are characterized by a sort of *practical theological* outlook in which God is said to reward the good and punish the wicked in this life (Prv 10,3; 10,27; 15,25; 16,5; 22,4). There have been those who have seen sanctions beyond the grave in some of the texts.

> When the tempest passes, the wicked man is no more;
> but the just man is established forever.
> *Prv 10,25*

> In the path of justice there is life,
> but the abominable way leads to death.
> *Prv 12,28*

[4] Examples are given in Murphy, *Seven Books of Wisdom,* pp. 21-23.

> For you will surely have a future,
>   and your hope will not be cut off.
>
>   *Prv 23,18*

More detailed study has shown that the same theology of temporal retribution seen in Job is also found in the book of Proverbs. If the sages of Israel had attained the concept of a blessed life after death, they would have used it as a strong motive for right living on this earth.

The contents of Proverbs are very limited when viewed in the light of the revelation brought by Jesus, the Wisdom of God. But the axiom often used in Christian theology is true: the supernatural builds on the natural. With this in mind, the Christian reader will find that the book is not obsolete. He may sometimes smile at what seems naïve or slightly absurd in this book (Prv 17,21; 17,28; 26,14), but more often he will find matter for serious thought (Prv 10,21; 12,1-2; 16, 18-19; 22,1).

VII. ECCLESIASTES

Ecclesiastes is the transliteration of the Greek name given to the book which in Hebrew is called *Qohelet*. This name probably means "one who speaks to an assembly." Perhaps the book was composed by a person who was a leader of an assembly of sages. It is attributed to the "son of David," but that is merely an example of the literary fiction often used in ancient Israel, where books were assigned to famous individuals in order to give them greater dignity and authority. Ecclesiastes was written during the third century before Christ.

The book is in the form of a monologue which contains definite signs of its composite nature. The speaker discusses the problems of his day and of life in general, and he moves back and forth over his material with little attention to logical sequence. One scholar has made the suggestion that this genre of the book is best compared with the *Pensées* of Blaise Pascal.[5] Sometimes the speaker clarifies statements made earlier and at other times he introduces statements which clash with others in the book. He praises the value of wisdom (Eccl 7,11; 10,2-3) and also says that it is a vanity and it increases sorrow (Eccl 1,17-18; 2,15). The basic theme of Qohelet is the vanity of all that is in life. At times his tone is so pessimistic that he seems to be the sort of person that would have been at home with those Existentialists of our times who see life as something that lacks meaning and purpose, and in the final analysis is merely a hell (Eccl 2,17; 4,2). Everything, he says, is useless: knowledge, riches, love, even life itself (Eccl 1,14,18-23). As pessimistic as Qohelet appears to be, he is beyond doubt a firm believer in Yahweh and His Providence.

---

[5] Roland E. Murphy, O. Carm., "The Pensées of Qoheleth," *The Catholic Biblical Quarterly,* XVII (April, 1955), 184-94.

When I applied my heart to know wisdom and to observe what is done on earth, I recognized that man is unable to discover all God's work that is done under the sun, even though neither by day nor by night do his eyes find rest in sleep.

Eccl 8,16-17

He realizes that life comes from God and whoever is blessed with riches and property has received a gift from Him (Eccl 5,17-19). "For every man, moreover, to eat and drink and enjoy the fruit of all his labor is a gift of God" (Eccl 3,13). Like the authors of Job and Proverbs, he does not know of the existence of eternal retribution. Yet he has no doubt that God will judge both the just and the wicked "since there is a time for every affair and on every work a judgment" (Eccl 3,17). It is only if we pay attention to his statements of faith and see the basic perspective, which is that of a believer in Yahweh, that we will be able to balance the pessimism that appears in many texts.

Some would like to picture Qohelet as a model for pessimism or hedonism; partial and superficial reading of the book gives some backing to such a view. But no one who reads carefully and religiously can fail to see that Qohelet was a believer and a realist. He realized that some of his statements were only tentative; he did not intend them as absolutes upon which to base one's life.

We have to realize that the book was part of an earlier stage in the History of Salvation. Seen in this light it contained much to provoke thought among Qohelet's contemporaries. It was composed at a time when Hellenic influence was permeating Palestine and many Jews began to find Greek culture more attractive than the Faith of their Fathers. To the Christian, Qohelet seems quite limited. Yet even the Christian will draw from the book a sense of the vanity of so many of the things the world prizes. The book raises many questions in our minds; perhaps it even suggests the question posed by Wisdom Incarnate, "What does it profit a man, if he gain the whole world, but suffer the loss of his own soul?" (Mt 16,26).

VIII. THE THEME OF WISDOM PERSONIFIED

The theme of the personification of Wisdom in the Old Testament is one which has provoked a great deal of discussion. Some see it as an example of poetical personification similar to the text in which both Wisdom and Folly are personified: "Wisdom builds her house, but Folly tears hers down with her own hands" (Prv 14,1). Others see it as a revelation of the eternal existence of a distinct Divine Person in God. Therefore it would be an explicit revelation of the doctrine of the Blessed Trinity. We will consider this theme in the three books in which it appears principally, Proverbs (fifth century B.C.), Sirach (second century B.C.), and Wisdom (first century B.C.).

The Lord begot me, the firstborn of his ways,
the forerunner of his prodigies of long ago;

From of old I was poured forth,
    at the first, before the earth,
When there were no depths I was brought forth,
    when there were no fountains or springs of water;
Before the mountains were settled into place,
    before the hills, I was brought forth;
While as yet the earth and the fields were not made,
    nor the first clods of the world.

When he established the heavens I was there,
    when he marked out the vault over the face of the deep;
When he made firm the skies above,
    when he fixed fast the foundations of the earth;
When he set for the sea its limit,
    so that the waters should not transgress his command;
Then was I beside him as his craftsman,
    and I was his delight day by day,
Playing before him all the while,
    playing on the surface of his earth
    and I found delight in the sons of men.

Prv 8,22-31

We see that the author presents Wisdom as something more than a Divine attribute. It has the characteristics of a person who dwells with God "from of old." Earlier in Proverbs, the author had said that Wisdom has a universal mission to accomplish (Prv 8,1-5), and that it possesses the things which man works hard to obtain—knowledge, counsel, understanding, and strength (Prv 8,12-14). Wisdom loves those who love her, and those who seek will find her (Prv 8,17-21). In the book of Sirach she says:

From the mouth of the Most High I came forth,
    and mistlike covered the earth.
In the highest heavens did I dwell
    my throne on a pillar of cloud
The vault of heaven I compassed alone,
    through the deep abyss I wandered.
Over waves of the sea, over all the land,
    over every people and nation I held sway.
Among all these I sought a resting place;
    in whose inheritance should I abide?

Then the Creator of all gave me his command,
    and he who formed me chose the spot for my tent,
Saying, "In Jacob make your dwelling,
    In Israel your inheritance."
Before all ages, in the beginning, he created me,
    and through all ages I shall not cease to be
In the holy Tent I ministered before him,
    and in Sion I fixed my abode.

> Thus in the chosen city he has given me rest,
>   in Jerusalem is my domain.
> I have struck root among the glorious people,
>   in the portion of the Lord, his heritage.
>
> *Sir 24,3-12*

Of her, the author of the book of Wisdom says:

> Wisdom, the artificer of all, taught me.
> For in her is a spirit
>   intelligent, holy, unique,
> Manifold, subtle, agile,
>   clear, unstained, certain,
> Not baneful, loving the good, keen,
>   unhampered, beneficient, kindly,
> Firm, secure, tranquil,
>   all-powerful, all-seeing
> And pervading all spirits,
>   though they be intelligent, pure and very subtle.
> For Wisdom is mobile beyond all motion,
>   and she penetrates and pervades all things by reason of her purity.
> For she is an aura of the might of God
>   and a pure effusion of the glory of the Almighty;
>   therefore nought that is sullied enters into her.
> For she is the refulgence of eternal light,
>   the spotless mirror of the power of God,
>   the image of his goodness.
> And she, who is one, can do all things,
>   and renews everything while herself perduring;
> And passing into holy souls from age to age,
>   she produces friends of God and prophets.
> For there is nought God loves, be it not one who dwells with Wisdom.
> For she is fairer than the sun
>   and surpasses every constellation of the stars.
> Compared to light, she takes precedence;
>   for that, indeed, night supplants,
>   but wickedness prevails not over Wisdom.
> Indeed, she reaches from end to end mightily
>   and governs all things well.
>
> *Wis 7,22-8,1*

A studied reading of the passages above reveals that there is a progressive development which finally results in the text of the book of Wisdom, written in the century before Christ. Wisdom is "an aura of the might of God and a pure effusion of the glory of the almighty . . . the image of his goodness" (Wis 7,25-26). It is too much to say that we have in these texts the revelation of a Person who participates in the Divine Nature. Perhaps it is also claiming too much to say that the texts are examples of what scholars call the *sensus plenior,* that deeper, fuller meaning intended by God when He inspired the human authors, but seen in a Biblical text only in the light of further revelation of the mystery of the Blessed Trinity in the New Testament.

The Old and New Testaments are related: one prepares, the other fulfills, one is shadow, the other is light. Thus the Gospels and Epistles contain the revelation. But we can say that these texts prepared the ground for the later revelation of the Mystery of the three Divine Persons, and in the New Testament texts we notice a distinct relationship with the Wisdom of the Old Testament. Jesus is called the "Wisdom of God" (1 Cor 1,24); He is involved in the creation and conservation of the world: "All things have been created through and unto him, and he is before all creatures, and in him all things hold together" (Col 1,17). Jesus is the "image of the invisible God" (Col 1,15) and the "brightness of his glory" (Heb 1,3; Wis 7,25).

The Prologue of the Gospel of St. John attributes to Jesus, the Word, the qualities of creative Wisdom:

> In the beginning was the Word,
> and the Word was with God;
> and the Word was God.
> He was in the beginning with God.
> All things were made through him,
> and without him was made nothing that
> has been made.
>
> He was in the world, and the world
> was made through him, and the world
> knew him not.
> He came unto his own, and his own
> received him not.
>
> *Jn 1,1-3,10-12*

The Gospel of John presents Jesus as the Wisdom of God. An example of this is found in the sapiential theme which Jesus Himself develops in the discourse found in John 6,35-50; the heavenly bread of divine teaching brings eternal life to those who receive it.

The Sages of Israel saw the great distance between God and mankind; they declared that it could be bridged only by God who sends Wisdom to dwell in the world. They were unaware of the fact that the distance would be bridged in a unique way by the Person of the Word, the Wisdom of God, who was made flesh and dwelt among us (Jn 1,14). They did not know this; we do.

twenty-two

AN INTRODUCTION TO
THE PSALTER

I. NAME AND CONTENTS

THE PSALTER, from the Greek word *Psalterion*—a stringed instrument used to accompany singing, is the collection of Psalms traditionally numbering 150. In Hebrew the Psalter is called the *Tehillim,* "Hymns" or "Songs." The treasury of the religious songs of Israel is found in the Psalter, Israel's lyrical prayer. In its present form the Psalter is the collection used in the liturgy of the second Temple of Jerusalem, which was built after the Babylonian Exile and lasted until the Roman armies destroyed it in 70 A.D.

The enumeration found in the Hebrew Bible differs from that of the Septuagint (LXX) and, consequently, from that in the Catholic Bible, since it follows the LXX as far as the numbering is concerned. The difference can be summed up as follows: from Psalm 10 to 147 the Hebrew numbering is one ahead of the Septuagint; at Psalm 148 they again coincide. The following arrangement shows the exact situation:

Hebrew	Septuagint
1-8	1-8
9-10	9
11-113	10-112
114-115	113
116	114-115
117-146	116-145
147	146-147
148-150	148-150

Probably influenced by the five-book division of the Torah, the Psalter is divided into five books, each of which ends with a doxology.

Book		Psalms	
I		1-40
II		41-71
III		72-88
IV		89-105
V		106-150

It is interesting to note the conclusion of Psalm 71: "The prayers of David the son of Jesse are ended." It is possible that Psalm 150 is a doxology intended to conclude the whole Psalter.

A careful study reveals the presence of several doublets: Ps 13 and Ps 52 are the same; Ps 69 reproduces Ps 39,14-18; and Ps 107 contains Ps 56,8-12 and 49,8-14. Moreover, the use of the Divine Names varies. For example, the first book (Pss 1-40) is Yahwist, and the name "Yahweh" is used 272 times, compared with Elohim, which appears only 15 times. The second book (Pss 41-71) is Elohist, and "Elohim" appears 164 times, while Yahweh is used in only 30 cases; the third book (Pss 72-88) contains no notable preference (Yahweh is used 44 times and Elohim 43); the fourth (Ps 89-105) and the fifth book (Pss 106-150) are definitely Yahwist (Yahweh is used 103 and 236 times while Elohim does not appear at all in the former and only 7 times in the latter). Whatever the reason for the varying usage as regards the Divine Name, such differences, and the presence of doublets, indicate that the Psalter is the result of previously existing units or collections which were formed in different places and at different times.

II. AUTHORSHIP AND DATES OF THE PSALMS

Nearly all the psalms found in the first three books, and some of those found in the fourth and fifth, have titles or inscriptions which designate one of the following; (1) the character of the psalm, (2) matters connected with its musical setting, (3) liturgical use, (4) the historical situation for which it was written or which it illustrates, (5) its author.

A Psalm may have several such titles or, on the other hand, may have none, as is the case in the Hebrew text with 35 of the psalms called the "orphan psalms." The only titles that will be of concern here are those that refer to authorship. These are regularly introduced by the Hebrew word *Lamed,* a preposition which denotes some relationship to the noun it governs. That relationship may express authorship, norm, causality, finality, or advantage. The English translation of *Lamed* may be "of," "belonging to," "by," or "for." The following schema shows to whom the psalms are attributed in the Hebrew version:

David	Book I—all psalms except 1, 2, 32.
	Book II—Psalms 50-64; 67-69.
	Book III—Psalm 85.
	Book IV—Psalms 100, 102.
	Book V—Psalms 107-109, 121, 123, 130, 132, 137-144.
Sons of Core (Korah)—Psalms 41, 43-48, 83, 85-87.	
Asaph	Psalm 49, 72-82.
Solomon	Psalm 72, 126.
Moses	Psalm 89.
Heman the Ezraite	Psalm 87 (also attributed to the Sons of Core).
Ethan the Ezraite	Psalm 88.
Idithum	Psalm 38.

As we have already mentioned, the preposition used to introduce the proper name *may* denote authorship. Generally speaking, it is best to take it as meaning authorship, but such authorship need not be understood in the strict sense. There are scholars who maintain that the titles were not intended, from the very beginning, to designate the authors of the Psalms. For example, in the case of Asaph, authorship cannot be taken in the strict sense, because he lived in David's time (1 Chr 15,17; 16,5-7; 25,1) whereas the psalms attributed to him can be seen to have been composed in different times; some of them refer to the destruction of Jerusalem and the Exile. Likewise, in the case of the sons of Core, it can hardly be imagined that an entire group of singers would sit down to compose a psalm, and that each member would contribute something to it. In the case of those psalms assigned to Asaph and to the sons of Core, it is probably best to take the titles as meaning that the psalm formed part of the collection belonging to that group of singers. It is possible that the psalms were written by some member of the group.

The ancient testimony of the titles must not be overlooked. Long-standing tradition has assigned the authorship of the psalms to David, but a close study of the Psalter reveals that he cannot be looked upon as the sole author. Considering what is said in the historical books of the Bible with regard to David's talents as a musician (1 Sm 16,16-18; Am 6,5); his poetical bent (2 Sam 1,19-27 and 2 Sm 3, 33-34); his great interest in the worship of God (2 Sm 6,5,15-16), it is evident that he could be the author of some of the contents of the Psalter. In fact, Ps 17 is what appears in 2 Sm 22 as a poem attributed to David.

It is certain that not all the Psalms attributed to David are his. The Davidic tradition could not have started without some authentic support; the Hebrew version assigns 73 psalms to David; the Septuagint attributes 84 to him. The problem is to ascertain what that support was. Briefly, we may say the titles in the Hebrew version are not to be taken as absolutely certain, yet David must have played a role in the composition of the Psalter. The impulse provided by David continued for a long time after his death. The Psalter as it is today is the result of several centuries of poetical activity. The period after the Exile was a fruitful one as far as psalm-compositions are concerned—it was the time when worship was re-instated in the restored Temple; singers gained importance and were likened to the Levites; wise men used the genre of psalmody to teach lessons.

In 1910 the Biblical Commission issued a decree concerning the authorship of the psalms. It said that it must be held that David was the principal author of the Psalms and that those psalms that are assigned to him in either the Old Testament or the New Testament must be considered Davidic, for example, Pss 2, 15, 17, 31, 68, and 109.

The decrees of the Biblical Commission took into account the long-standing tradition concerning the Davidic authorship of the psalms, and because such a tradition was inexplicable unless David had a major role in the composition of the Psalter, it concluded that his role should not be discarded. Since the decrees of the Commission are subject to change, it left the possibility that at a future date such a tradition might have to be understood in a wider sense than that of strict authorship. Today a broader interpretation is given to the meaning of the titles of the psalms. There are Catholic scholars who hold that the titles found in the Hebrew version are not to be taken as absolutely certain. Furthermore, these scholars believe that when the authors of the New Testament cited the psalms, and assigned David as their author, they were merely conforming themselves to the opinions current at their time.

Concerning the authorship of the Psalms, it is helpful to remember that the ancient Hebrews did not always use the term "author" as we do today. The ancient Israelites gathered large pieces of the sacred writings under the names of such well known individuals as Moses, David, and Solomon, without necessarily affirming that every line in these literary pieces was written by the individual whose name was used. The Hebrews preferred not to leave any work anonymous. Consequently, the sacred writings were placed under the names of famous historical figures who were remembered for having been connected with such types of literature. Thus, very often, the individuals to whom the sacred books are attributed are to be looked upon as "patrons," rather than as literary authors in the modern sense.[1]

The contents of the Psalter were written gradually during Israel's history, from about the time of David (1010-970 B.C.) to the period after the Exile (after 538 B.C.); about half the Psalms are considered to be post-exilic. It seems almost certain that none of the Psalms were written after the fourth century B.C. One last point ought to be mentioned in this matter of dating the psalms: are there any psalms that come from the time of the Maccabees, the second century B.C.? Do Pss 43,73,78, and 82 date from that period? It is not necessary to go into great detail about the disputes concerning such psalms and their dating. It suffices to say that the arguments advanced by those who would like to give a late dating to the psalms are insufficient and, therefore, do not prove that there are psalms from the Maccabean period.

III. LITERARY GENRES (FORMS)

A good classification of the Psalms may be obtained from a study of the literary genres (forms). From this stylistic viewpoint, it is possible to distinguish three main types or genres: the Hymns, the Supplications (Lamentations), and the Thanksgiving. It is well to mention, however, that this division is far from being an exhaustive one. There are other secondary genres to which the names "Variant Genres" or "Combinations" may be given. There is also the category of Royal and Messianic Psalms.

[1] See R. A. F. MacKenzie, "Some Problems in the Field of Inspiration," *The Catholic Biblical Quarterly*, XX (January, 1958), pp. 1-8.

Much has been said about the importance of studying the literary forms found in the Bible. The emphasis placed on this point by Pope Pius XII in the Encyclical *Divino Afflante Spiritu* should be recalled:

> No one, who has a correct idea of biblical inspiration, will be surprised to find, even in the Sacred Writers, as in other ancient authors, certain fixed ways of expounding and narrating, certain definite idioms, especially of a kind peculiar to the Semitic tongues, so-called approximations, and certain hyperbolical modes of expression, nay, at times, even paradoxical, which help to impress the ideas more deeply on the mind. . . . Hence the Catholic commentator, in order to comply with the present needs of biblical studies, in explaining the Sacred Scripture and in demonstrating and proving its immunity from all error, should also make a prudent use of this means, determine, that is, to what extent the manner of expression or the literary mode adopted by the sacred writer may lead to a correct and genuine interpretation; and let him be convinced that this part of his office can not be neglected without serious detriment to Catholic exegesis.[2]

It is important to remember the role that the genre or literary form plays, particularly when a study of the Psalms is pursued. Just as in everyday life, a knowledge concerning the family to which some person belongs gives us an important insight into the person himself, so also, if we understand the literary family, *the genre,* of a Psalm, we will be helped greatly in understanding the message that the inspired author wanted to teach or express. The language that is found in the Psalms, the particular verbal expressions and formulas, must all be viewed from the point of view of the *"family"* to which the Psalm belongs. Even the words themselves take on a different meaning according to the genre of the Psalm. For example, the "cry" for help in times of distress or necessity is altogether different from the "cry" of joy in the hymns.

As a book of poetry, the Psalter demands that close attention be given to this question of genres. The forms that are found in this collection, Hymns, Supplications, etc., are characterized by a vocabulary that was, and often still is, traditional among poets.

A knowledge of the language of the Bible, particularly as seen in the Psalms, which are a sort of lyrical resumé of all the other inspired books, will facilitate the reading and understanding of Scripture. A study of the genres and verbal expressions found in the Psalter will aid in the understanding of the other parts of the inspired Word of God in both Old and New Testaments, and will make possible a better appreciation of the Sacred Liturgy, which is permeated with the Psalms.

[2] DAS, 37-38.

We return now to a consideration of the various genres that are found in the Psalter.

A. HYMNS

The word "Hymn" is used according to the meaning generally given to it in the Old Testament, i.e. a song of praise. The Psalms which are included in this division bring out the direct manner of speaking characteristic of Hebrew poetry. The following Psalms are among those usually included in this genre: Pss 8, 18, 28 (which some call the "Gloria in excelsis" of the Old Testament), 32, 45-47, 64, 67, 75, 83, 86, 92, 95-99, 102-105, 112, 113, 116, 121, 134, 135, 144-150.

The hymns contain a worship of Yahweh which is disinterested; the one praying does not do so because he wants the Lord to do something for him. His prayer is one of enthusiastic praise. Generally speaking, the characteristic quality of these Psalms is *altruism*—love and praise of God because of His kindness and fidelity towards His people. Sometimes the whole Psalm is centered on praising Yahweh because of His constant watch over Israel throughout its history. This is seen in Ps 104 in which, after an introduction, the individual praying recalls the promise of the Lord to the patriarchs, their wanderings in the land of Canaan, the story of Joseph, the period in Egypt, the plagues sent by the Lord on the Egyptians, the journey through the desert, and the victories in the promised land.

The literary composition of these Psalms is constant. Each begins with an exhortation to give praise to God. The body of the hymn gives the motif or reason for this praise, for example, the wonders accomplished by God in nature, especially in His creative work, and in history, the salvation that He have given to His people. The conclusion repeats the introductory idea or expression, or it expresses a prayer.

In this *genre* it is possible to distinguish, according to their subjects, two groups of psalms: (1) *Psalms of Sion* (Hymns of Sion) and (2) *Psalms of the Kingdom of God*.

1. *Psalms of Sion* are 45, 47, 75, 86. These praise the Holy City, the dwelling place of the most High and place of pilgrimages. Eschatological allusions are found in these psalms. Read, for example, Pss 83 and 121, which were part of the hymns that the Jews sang while on pilgrimage to the Temple for the annual feasts.

2. *Psalms of the Kingdom of God* are, for example, Pss 45,92,95-97. These celebrate the universal reign of Yahweh. Their style is reminiscent of that of the Prophets. The wording and images contained in these hymns refer to the accession of kings to their throne. Consequently, some exegets have seen in them a relationship with a feast dealing with the enthronement of Yahweh which was cele-

brated each year in Israel. They try to prove that there was such a feast as an Israelitic counterpart of the Babylonian feast celebrated annually in honor of the pagan deity, Marduk. The evidence does not warrant such a claim and so the hypothesis can be disregarded.[3]

B. SUPPLICATIONS (PSALMS OF LAMENTATION)

Unlike the Hymns, these Psalms do not recount the glories of God, but are addressed to Him. Usually, they begin with in invocation, and then an appeal for help, a prayer or expression of confidence. In the body of the psalm, there is an attempt made to move God by presenting the sad condition or situation of those who are supplicating. The Psalmist employs metaphors which in reality are clichés, and they are of such a nature as to rarely permit an exact determination of the historical circumstances of the prayer, or the concrete conditions that were the *sitz im leben* (life situation). The images or metaphors used include "lion's prey," "apple of your eye," "bulls that menace," "heart quakes within me," "the nether world" (Sheol), and "their teeth are spears and arrows, their tongue is a sharp sword."

God is reminded of His past good deeds; He is reproached for being unmindful of present needs. "Why, O Lord, do you stand aloof? Why hide in times of distress?" (Ps 9; See also Pss 21 and 43).

Examples of supreme confidence in God are expressed by these supplications: Pss 3, 5, 41, 42, 54-56, 62, and 129. Some of these Psalms of supplication are often merely long appeals based on deep confidence in God (Pss 4, 10, 15, 22, 61, 120, 124, and 130).

The supplication or lamentation is brought to an end, often very abruptly, with an expression of certitude that the prayer has been heard by God. This is seen in Pss 6, 21, 68, and 139, among others.

These supplication Psalms are either individual or communal (collective).

1. *Individual Supplications*

Pss 3, 5-7, 12, 16, 21, 24, 25, 27, 30, 34, 37, 41-42, 50, 53-56, 58, 62, 63, 68-70, 76, 85, 101, 119, 129, 139-142. These prayers are particularly numerous and their content is varied. They include references to the perils of death, persecutions, exile, old age, etc. Sickness, personal calamity, and sin are the evils from which the Psalmist usually prays for deliverance. The enemies against whom the individual prays are mentioned in such generalities as "those who do evil." It is likely that the references to enemies were part of the emotional language adopted by the author. The problem afflicting him leads him to imagine himself surrounded by enemies.

These psalms are not to be considered as the expressions of a "collective I," nor are they words of the king speaking for his people. These prayers are too

---

[3] For a discussion of this hypothesis and the reasons for not accepting it see DeVaux, *Ancient Israel. Its Life and Institutions*, pp. 504-506.

individualistic in tone and too devoid of allusions to the person of the king or royal conditions, to warrant the "royal interpretation." Some of these psalms were adopted and used as national lamentations as, for example, Pss 21, 27, 58, 68, 70, and 101. Moreover, there are some royal psalms included among them. Also, it is true that many became expressions of a common need, hence their inclusion in the Psalter. But they were composed for an individual, or by an individual, in a particular need. They are the cry of a soul and the expression of a personal faith.

2. *Communal (Collective) Supplications*

In studying Pss 11, 43, 59, 73, 78, 79, 82, 105, 122, 128, and 136 we find that each of these psalms was composed on the occasion of some national disaster, some destruction, some common or national need. The request is for salvation and the restoration of the people.

As one author has put it:

> In these the whole nation is threatened by some great danger, usually political; but the danger may also come from the forces of nature; drought, pest, plagues. One observes, in such petitions, that the poet recalls some past exhibitions of the Lord's power and good will as a motive why He should act in the present danger, and that the psalm often concludes with a note of thanksgiving as if the danger had already passed while the prayer was said.[4]

Pss 73 and 136 reflect, like the Lamentations attributed to Jeremia, on the ruin of Jerusalem in 587. Ps 84 expresses the sentiments of those who had returned to their home land; Ps 105 is a general confession of the sins of the nation.

C. THANKSGIVING

Pss 17, 20, 29, 32, 33, 39, 64-67, 91, 115, 117, 123, 128, 137, and 143. Like the Supplication Psalms, these are also either Communal (National) Thanksgivings, or individual acts of thanks. The people render thanks for deliverance from some peril, or for an abundant harvest, etc. The individual thanksgivings, after recounting the evils endured, thank God for His goodness, and exhort the faithful to praise God with the one who is rendering the thanks.

The literary structure of these psalms is like that of the Hymns.

D. VARIANT GENRES AND COMBINATIONS

The boundaries between the various genres or forms discussed above are not absolute and, consequently, we find that some of the genres appear in combinations. At times there is a sort of fusion of types or genres. For ex-

---

[4] McKenzie, *The Two-Edged Sword,* p. 268.

ample, in Pss 26 and 30, lamentations follow upon a prayer of confidence, and in Pss 27 and 56, lamentations are succeeded by thanksgivings.

Ps 88 begins as a hymn, with phrases reminiscent of older hymns; then the divine promises made to David (2 Sm 7,8-16) are recounted at considerable length; finally, the present sad state of affairs is spoken about wherein God seems to have forgotten His promises. Such a psalm seems to give evidence that it is the result of a combination of older sources: (1) Hymn, (2) Account of Past Promises, and (3) a Lamentation.

Ps 118, the longest (176 verses) and the least poetic composition in the entire Psalter, is a praise of the Law, a hymn of the Law. This psalm is an alphabetical one, that is, each of the eight verses of the first strophe begins with the first letter of the Hebrew alphabet, each verse of the second strophe with the second letter, and so on for all the 22 letters.

E. ROYAL PSALMS AND MESSIANIC PSALMS

We have already mentioned the eschatological character of some of the psalms, particularly the Psalms of Sion and the Psalms of the Kingdom of God (Yahweh). The universal restoration announced in these psalms is the one that will happen in the Messianic age.

The Psalter contains a number of "royal" hymns that do not belong to any one genre in particular. They are found in several of the genres. Pss 2 and 109 are oracles in favor of the king; prayers for the king are seen in Pss 19, 60, 71, and 83; thanksgiving for the king is found in Ps 20; prayers of the king in Pss 17, 27, 62, and 100; a royal processional song in Ps 131; a royal hymn in Ps 143. Ps 44 is an *epithalamium,* a nuptial song for a princely marriage. All of these are ancient poems dating from the monarchy, and reflecting the language and ceremonial of the court. As originally composed, these psalms spoke of the king as living at the time, and they directly visualized a king seated upon the throne of David, even as in Ps 44, a king of the northern kingdom.

The king of the chosen people is referred to as having received an anointing. He is the anointed one, in Hebrew, *Messiah.* He is the adopted son of Yahweh and the blessed one of God. The fact of such a benediction is the cause of the prosperity and success of his people. The promises of God to the dynasty of David contain within them a glimpse of a privileged descendant in whom God would be especially pleased. He would be the one that God would elect to bring about the plan of salvation.

The prophecy of Nathan in 2 Sm 7, is the first link in the chain of prophecies concerning the Messiah as the Son of David. "Your house and your kingdom shall be confirmed before me forever; your throne shall be established forever." Essentially, this prophecy was a promise of stability for the house of David, a guarantee for the Davidic line.[5] It emphasizes the immediate

5 See p. 130.

successor of David, his son Solomon. It is in that sense that it is taken up
again in Ps 88,29-38, and in Ps 131,11-12.

> Forever I will maintain my kindness toward him,
>   and my covenant with him stands firm.
> I will make his prosperity endure forever
>   and his throne as the days of heaven.
> "If his sons forsake my law
>   and walk not according to my ordinances,
> If they violate my statutes
>   and keep not my commands,
> I will punish their crime with a rod
>   and their guilt with stripes.
> Yet my kindness I will not take from him,
>   nor will I belie my faithfulness.
> I will not violate my covenant;
>   the promise of my lips I will not alter.
> Once, by my holiness, have I sworn;
>   I will not be false to David.
> His posterity shall continue forever,
>   and his throne shall be like the sun before me;
> Like the moon, which remains forever—
>   a faithful witness in the sky,"
>
> *Psalm 88,29-38*

> The Lord swore to David
>   a firm promise from which he will not withdraw:
> "Your own offspring
>   I will set upon your throne;
> If your sons keep my covenant
>   and the decrees which I shall teach them,
> Their sons, too, forever
>   shall sit upon your throne."
>
> *Psalm 131,11-12*

But this prophecy has been interpreted in an individual sense, as having
reference to a particular person. This is the case in the Acts of the Apostles,
2,29-36; therefore, while the prophecy points with emphasis to David's immediate successor, Solomon, it includes all the kings of Juda who will follow
him. The prophecy finds its final fulfillment in Jesus Christ, who established
an eternal kingdom (Lk 1,32 and Acts 2,29-36). Christ was descended from
David (Mt 1,1-17 and Lk 3,23-31).

After the fall of the monarchy, some of these ancient royal psalms were
incorporated into the Psalter, and with some retouching and additions they
became messianic psalms in the literal sense. The messianic nature of some
psalms is seen in Pss 2, 71, and 109. The last-mentioned psalm (109) is the
one that is most frequently used in the New Testament. The nuptial song in
Ps 44 was looked upon as an expression of the union between the Messiah
and the New Israel. The Epistle to the Hebrews applies this psalm to Christ
(Heb 1,8).

The New Testament and Christian tradition apply to Jesus some other psalms which although they were not royal psalms, express sentiments that are eminently applicable to Him who is the Just One *par excellence*. This is the case with Pss 15 and 21; also certain passages in Pss 8, 34, 39, 40, 67, 68, 96, 117, and 118. Likewise, the psalms of the kingdom of Yahweh have been applied to the kingdom of Christ. Although such applications exceed the literal sense of the psalms, they are legitimate because all the hopes that animate the Psalter are fully realized only in the coming to earth of the Son of God.

IV. PSALMS IN THE WORSHIP OF ISRAEL

The Psalter is the collection of religious songs of Israel. Songs had an important place in the ideas of those who had charge of the Temple, and, although, they are not explicitly mentioned until after the time of the Exile in Babylon, it is certain that they were in existence from the beginning of Israelite worship.

The feasts of Yahweh were celebrated with dancing and songs as witnessed by Jgs 29,19-21 and 2 Sm 6,5 and 16. According to the Prophet Amos, in the sanctuary at Bethel sacrifices were accompanied by songs (Am 5,23). During the time of David, the royal palace had its singers (2 Sm 19,36). The tradition which makes David the author of many of the psalms also gives him the honor of being the one who organized the worship and the singers. This tradition cites the fact that David played on musical instruments and danced before Yahweh when the Ark of the Covenant was brought to Jerusalem (2 Sm 6,5 and 16).

After the building of the Temple, a choir was formed for the liturgical services. Pre-exilic texts do not mention Temple singers but doubtless the Temple had its choir as did all the great oriental sanctuaries of the time. The present Psalter contains psalms which were sung by the professional singers who formed the choir.

Many of the psalms contain musical and liturgical references. Sometimes there is a reference to the rite that was performed while the psalm was sung. For example, in Pss 19, 25, 26, 65, 80, 106, 115, 133, and 134 we find reference to holocausts, the altar, and the solemn feast, probably the Feast of Tabernacles. These psalms, together with others like Pss 47, 64, 94, 95, and 117, evidently were recited within the precincts of the Temple. It is also known that the *Psalms of Ascents* or *Pilgrim Psalms* (Pss 119-133) were sung during the pilgrimages to the sanctuary of Jerusalem for the great feasts.

These examples are sufficient to show that numerous psalms were composed for the service of the Temple. Likewise, there were other psalms which, although not composed primarily for the Temple worship, were later adopted for use therein as, for example, Pss 124, 127, and 129.

The connection between the Psalms and worship, and the liturgical character of the Psalter taken as a whole, are undeniable facts. However, generally speaking, there is little information available which would help to determine the precise ceremony or feast during which a particular psalm was used. The Hebrew title of Ps 91 makes reference to "A song for the Sabbath day," and the Greek titles for Pss 9, 23, 47, 92, and 93 refer to other days of the week. Furthermore, according to the Hebrew, Ps 29 was used for the dedication of the Temple, and Ps 28, according to the Greek, was used during the Feast of Booths. These indications are not ancient ones, that is, they do not date from the time that the Psalm was composed. But they do testify to the fact that the Psalter was the book of songs used in the Temple, and later in the Synagogues, before it became the great book of religious songs for the Christian Church.

V. A NOTE CONCERNING THE HALLEL

The Triple Hallel

The Ordinary Hallel .... Psalms 113-117
    Passover, Pentecost, Feast of Booths
The Great Hallel ....,,,,,,,,,,,,,,,,,,,,,,,,,,,,,,, Psalm 135
    Seventh day of the Passover
The Final Hallel .... Psalms 145-150
    Morning Prayers

The word *hallel* means "praise"; *alleluia,* a combination of *hallel* and *Yahweh,* means "Praise the Lord."

The Ordinary Hallel is of particular interest to Christians. As mentioned above, it was sung during the three major feasts celebrated by the Jews. It is also called the Egyptian Hallel because it begins with Ps 113: "When Israel came forth from Egypt." It was sung in the Temple while the lambs were being slaughtered in preparation for the Passover supper.

During the Passover Supper Pss 113 and 114,1-8 were sung while the second cup of wine was being drunk; Pss 114, 9-26 to 117 were sung while the fourth cup was taken. If the Last Supper of Jesus was a passover meal, as seems most likely, those Psalms were sung by Jesus and the Apostles. The latter ones are those that the Gospels refer to when they say that Jesus and his followers left the room for Mount Olivet "after reciting a hymn" (Mt 26,20; Mk 14,26).

There is appropriateness in having Ps 115 among the prayers that the Church recommends in preparation for the offering of Mass, and also Ps 113 in the Vespers for Sundays. Vespers is the canonical hour which recalls the Eucharistic Sacrifice. When sung at the proper time, in the late afternoon, it falls about the time of day at which Jesus ate the Paschal Supper, and when the Eucharistic Liturgy was celebrated in the early Church.

It is interesting to note that our Lord's last liturgical prayer before His passion was Ps 117. Rejected by His people, He, the cornerstone of the Church, was offering Himself for the salvation of mankind, and He sang:

> The stone which the builders rejected
> has become the cornerstone.
> By the Lord has this been done;
> it is wonderful in our eyes,
> This is the day the Lord has made;
> let us be glad and rejoice in it.
> O Lord, grant salvation!
> O Lord grant prosperity!
> Give thanks to the Lord, for he is good;
> and his kindness endures forever.
> *Ps 117,22-25,29*

VI. TEACHINGS IN THE PSALMS

The Psalter, as has been seen already, is not a homogeneous unit. It developed throughout a long period of Israel's history. Consequently, any attempt to present a synthesis of the religious teachings of the Psalms, or of their theology, is difficult. There is a danger that certain religious developments which occurred late in Israel's history might be projected into an earlier period. However, while acknowledging the general way in which the Psalter originated, it is possible to point out some of the principal doctrinal themes that are contained in it.

The *hymns,* the most characteristic literary form of the Psalter, have as their principal object God and His greatness. Everything is directed to or related to Him. Although a certain amount of anthropomorphic language is present, it is evident that it is deliberately being used by an author whose monotheism is unquestionable.

There is only one God and He is the Creator of all that exists (Pss 8, 32, 89, 90, 102); He is all-just (Pss 8, 110); all-good (Ps 35); all-merciful (Pss 102, 129); and present everywhere (Ps 138). The world, which is His work, demonstrates His existence, power, and grandeur (Pss 8, 18, 28, 88). Only a fool can fail to admit the existence of God (Ps 13).

The authors of the Psalms devote their thoughts continually to God, communing with Him, praising Him, thanking Him, and calling upon Him for help. God was not a philosophical abstraction for them. He was a living being who participated in all the events of their lives. The Psalms contain a deep gratitude for all that God has done (Pss 17, 29, 39, 65, 115), and this leads the psalmists to affirm a deep trust in Him (Pss 3, 4, 5, 10, 15, 16, 19, 27, 30, 45, 55, 61, 62). The service of God results in true joy and happiness (Pss 1, 4, 5, 15, 62, 83).

In times of need, God is called upon for help and the prayer of the psalmist is urgent and unrestrained (Pss 6, 12, 21, 43). The yearning for God is a thirst (Ps 41) and the great desire is to abide in the Temple forever (Ps 26).

The Psalter, in general, adheres to the theology of temporal retribution, that God rewards the good and punishes the bad in this life. The psalmists loved God and they knew that they were loved by Him. Death was powerless to separate them from Him (Ps 15,10).

The Psalms teach that God wills justice and that He loves the poor and the humble. He comes to their aid (Pss 10, 68, 69, 93). The worship which pleases Him is prayer and moral living (Ps 49). Man must acknowledge his guilt before God and he moved to sincere repentance (Pss 30, 31, 37, 40, 50, 129).

The sentiments of praise, adoration, trust, love, and faith which are found in the Psalms make the Psalter a book of permanent religious value. Hebrew prayer had a very important place for the praise of the Lord. It can be said that in this the Hebrew approach attained a height not reached by the prayer of many Christians who regard prayer as petition only. On the other hand it must be noted that charity toward enemies is absent from the Psalms, and, at times, their maledictions are rather surprising (Pss 58, 68, 108). But the strong language is aimed at the impious and the persecutors of those who believe in the Lord and follow His ways; the angry words are directed to those who have resisted efforts at converting them to the Lord. The words are part of the literary heritage of the times, and the sentiments belong to a particular stage in the development of religion as regards man's relationships with his friends and enemies. Christ had not yet come, and love of enemies was not looked upon as a cherished virtue of the true follower of the Lord.

VII. RELIGIOUS VALUE OF THE PSALMS

The religious value of the Psalms is evident to all who study them. They were the prayers of the Old Testament, wherein God Himself inspired the sentiments that His children should have with regard to Him. The Psalms were recited by Jesus, by the Blessed Virgin, by the Apostles. The Church, without changing them, made the Psalms its official prayer. By their adoption in the Church, the Psalms have received a great deal of added richness as far as their meaning is concerned. In the New Testament (Covenant), the faithful praise and thank God, who has revealed to them the mysteries of His own intimate life and who has redeemed them with the blood of His Son. They praise Him who has granted them His Spirit. The supplications of antiquity become even more ardent after the Supper, Cross, and Resurrection of Jesus showed men the infinite love of God, the universality and gravity of sin, and the glory promised to the just. The hopes and aspirations embodied in the songs of the Psalter have been realized; the Messiah has come, He reigns, and all nations are called to praise Him.

The Sacred Liturgy makes great use of the Psalter. It furnishes the substance of the Divine Office which is recited by priests and others who are granted the privilege by the Church. A glance at the prayers of the Mass found in the Missal shows how many of the Introits, Graduals, Tracts, Alleluia Verses, Offertories, and Communion Verses are taken from the book of Psalms. The Church, as the heir of Israel and the true Jerusalem, has taken the greatest part of its public prayer from the Bible, and very often from the Psalter. This should give us a clue as to where we can find a nourishing diet for our prayer-life. As Pope Pius XII pointed out in his important encyclical on the Sacred Liturgy:

> The Psalms recall to mind the truths revealed by God to the Chosen people, which were at one time frightening and at another filled with wonderful tenderness; they keep repeating and fostering the hope of the promised Liberator which in ancient times was kept alive with song, either around the hearth or in the stately temple; they show forth in splendid light the prophesied glory of Jesus Christ: first, His supreme and eternal power, then His lowly coming to this terrestrial exile, His kingly dignity and priestly power and, finally, His beneficent labors, and the shedding of His blood for our redemption. In a similar way they express the joy, the bitterness, the hope and fear of our hearts and our desire of loving God and hoping in Him alone, and our mystic ascent to divine tabernacles.[6]

The use of the Psalms should find a special place in our private prayers. They will give to our prayers that simplicity and strength that are essential requisites for sincere praying.

The following is a list of suggested Psalms for particular occasions:

1. To express adoration or to praise the glory of God in His works: Pss 32, 33, 67, 91, 99, 103, 144, 145, 146, 148, 150.
2. To thank God for His blessings: Pss 9, 29, 64, 102, 117, 146.
3. To express sorrow for one's sins: Pss 6, 31, 37, 50, 101, 129, 142.
4. To appeal for help, while at the same time expressing trust in God: Pss 3, 4, 5, 7, 27, 41, 53, 69.
5. To meditate on the peace that comes to the one who lives a life of obedience to God: Pss 15, 19, 24, 61, 111, 124.
6. To express confidence: Pss 39, 119-133.

[6] *Mediator Dei,* 148 (New York: The America Press, 1954), pp. 62-63.

twenty-three

THE DEAD SEA SCROLLS

I. DIARY RELATED TO THE FINDINGS

SPRING, 1947:

A SHEPHERD, Mohammad ed-Di'b (Mohammed the Wolf), while looking for a stray goat, threw a stone into a hole in the side of a hill located about eight miles south of Jericho and about a mile from the Dead Sea. The stone hit against some pottery. Frightened by the noise the boy fled. The next day he returned, and with the help of a friend, he climbed through the hole and found a narrow cavern. The floor was strewn with broken pottery, and at the back there was a row of eight unbroken jars covered with lids. All the jars were empty except one; it contained three scrolls which the two boys took away with them. A few weeks later the scrolls were taken to an antiquities dealer in Bethlehem.

SUMMER, 1947:

The Monophysite Syrian Patriarch residing at St. Mark's Convent in Jerusalem, Mar Athanasius Yeshue Samuel, purchased four scrolls from some Bedouins who had found them in the area of the Dead Sea. The price is reported to have been $150.

WINTER, 1947:

Hebrew University in Jerusalem acquired three manuscripts. Professor E. L. Sukenik, who was the first to recognize the great age of the scrolls, thought that they might be of Essene origin.

SPRING, 1948:

Mar Athanasius left Palestine and arrived in the United States with his scrolls. He found it difficult to sell them and it was not until 1955 that they were finally bought by the State of Israel for the sum of $250,000. The sale was the result of an advertisement in the *Wall Street Journal,* June 1-3, 1954:

242

"The Four Dead Sea Scrolls. Biblical Manuscripts dating back to at least 200 B.C. are for sale. This would be an ideal gift to an educational or religious institution by an individual or group."

Among the scrolls found in the first cave at Qumran were the following:

1. *The Isaia Scroll* (1QIs^a), which is practically a complete copy of the book of the prophet of the eighth century B.C. It is a roll of parchment twenty-four feet long and about ten inches wide. Its state of preservation is exceptionally good. The text is substantially the same as the standard Massoretic Text. It dates from at least the first century before Christ, perhaps earlier, and is considered the oldest of the manuscripts found in the caves, with the exception of some of the small fragments. There is another *Isaia Scroll* (1QIs^b), which is badly disintegrated. It contains portions of several chapters and almost all of the text from chapter 38 to the end of the book.

2. *The Habacuc Commentary* (1QpHab) contains two chapters from the book of Habacuc and a commentary on the text. The roll has suffered a good deal of disintegration, and as a result the text is incomplete. It is a little more than four feet long and slightly less than six inches wide. It is the richest scroll as far as historical allusions are concerned. It mentions persons, and events, but unfortunately there is so much vagueness that the contents are open to several possible explanations.

3. *The Manual of Discipline,* also known as *The Rule of the Community* (1QS), contains both disciplinary and liturgical instructions to be followed by the community at Qumran. It is a parchment roll about six feet long and nine inches wide.

4. *The Genesis Apocryphon* (1QApoc) is an Aramaic version of several chapters of the book of Genesis with stories and legends not found in the canonical Genesis. It is about nine feet long and twelve inches wide.

5. *The War of the Sons of Light and the Sons of Darkness (1QM)* contains accounts of the conflict which is expected to break out between the "sons of light" and the "sons of darkness." The community belongs to the former, the latter are also referred to as the Kittim. Details about war equipment, tactics, prayers before battle, and a hymn of thanksgiving are included. The roll is well preserved and measures over nine feet in length and six inches in width.

6. *The Thanksgiving Psalms,* also called *The Hodayot* (1QH), is a collection of hymns, similar in style to the Psalms, in which thanks are offered to God for His deeds of kindness. It is in a fragmentary condition, but originally it formed a roll about six feet long and thirteen inches wide.

SPRING, 1949:

A Belgian United Nations observer, Philippe Lippens, and some members of the Arab Legion went to search for the original cave (1Q). It was found that clandestine diggers had already been there and removed practically all the contents. However, a thorough search uncovered hundreds of manuscript fragments. Potsherds of jars and lamps, as well as linen pieces in which the scrolls had been wrapped, were also found. These were to prove very valuable for dating the scrolls.

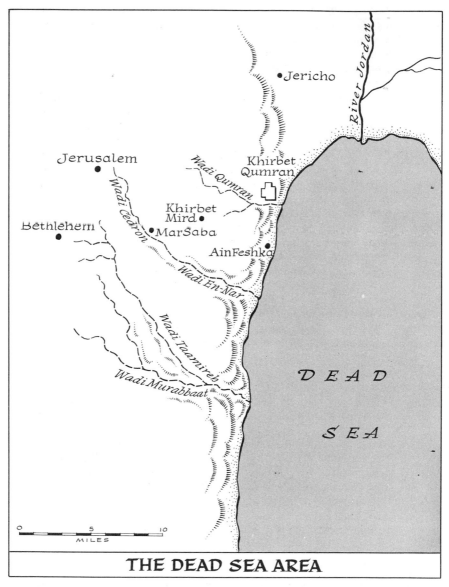

THE DEAD SEA AREA

Figure 7.

FALL, 1951:

During this period a team of archaeologists excavated the ruins at Khirbet Qumran. The main building was uncovered and it measured about 118 feet by 94 feet. During the work bronze coins were found in almost all the rooms. The dates of these coins ranged from the beginning of the Christian era to the time of the first Jewish Revolt (66-70 A.D.). A large amount of pottery was also found which included an intact jar of the same type as the ones which contained the manuscripts in the first cave that was discovered (1Q).

A study of the building refuted the view, which had been held for some time, that the site had been only a Roman Fort. The plan of the building as well as the type of its construction showed that it was a meeting place for a community of individuals who had lived in caves or tents nearby. The excavations and studies conducted at this time led to the conclusion that there was a connection between the materials found in Cave I and the ruins being studied. The charred reeds and timbers indicated that the building had been destroyed in a violent catastrophe. A cemetery was discovered near the ruins.

WINTER, 1952:

Work began at Wadi Murabbaat in January. Evidence was found of occupation in Chalcolithic times (4000-3000 B.C.), Middle Bronze II (2000-1600 B.C.), Iron (eighth-seventh century B.C.), and Graeco-Roman periods. Among the texts that were found there is a non-biblical one written in Hebrew on a papyrus palimpsest which dates from the eighth century B.C. There are also biblical fragments which date from the first and second centuries A.D., including some of Genesis, Exodus, Deuteronomy, and Isaia. Two letters were discovered which were signed by Simon bar Kokhba (Ben Koseba), famed leader in the Second Jewish Revolt of 135 A.D. They were written to a certain Joshua bar Galgola. There is no connection between the material found in these caves and the Qumran community.

A few handfuls of fragments were found in a cave (2Q) a little south of the one discovered in 1947.

SPRING, 1952:

Archaeologists examined a five-mile radius around Khirbet Qumran. They found about 40 caves, in some of which were discovered remains of Roman pottery similar to material found in Cave I. Fragments of the Hebrew Old Testament were also found. In Cave III (3Q) were discovered the famous copper scrolls presenting information about large deposits of treasure hidden throughout the Palestinian countryside, mainly in the region of Jerusalem. The total weight of the treasure is said to be about 200 tons. Scholars generally are of the opinion that the scrolls are folklore and not intended as fact.[1]

[1] See J. T. Milik, "The Copper Document From Cave III, Qumran," *The Biblical Archaeologist*, XIX (September, 1956), 60-64.

Archaeologists worked in Cave IV (4Q), which had already been found and dug by the Bedouin who removed thousands of fragments. This cave contained fragments of several hundred works, biblical and non-biblical.

In order to purchase the manuscripts that the Bedouins had taken large sums of money were required. An appeal was made to the educational institutions of the world. Besides almost $45,000 contributed by the· Jordanian Government, sums were received from such interested institutions as McGill University in Montreal, the Universities of Heidelberg and Manchester, McCormick Theological Seminary in Chicago, and the Vatican Library. Most of the material is now in the Palestine Archaeological Museum in Jerusalem (Jordan).

SUMMER, 1952:

Fragments of Greek New Testament works dating from the fifth to the eighth century were found. These included parts of the Gospels of Mark and John as well as the Acts of the Apostles. Other fragments of the Gospels of Luke and John, Acts, and Colossians written in the Syro-Palestinian language were found. The Bedouin campaign of 1953 claimed that all these fragments came from Khirbet Mird, the ruins of a Byzantine monastery located north-east of the Mar Saba in the Wadi-en-Nar. The monastery is that of Castellion, on the site of ancient Hyrcania, the stronghold of John Hyrcanus (134-104 B.C.)

SPRING, 1953:

Major Lippens and Father de Langhe of Louvain, Belgium, excavated Khirbet Mird. They worked in an underground chamber where they discovered fragments of Greek New Testament texts, as well as Arabic and Christian Palestinian Aramaic ones.

SPRING, 1954-1955:

More archaeological campaigns were conducted at Khirbet Qumran and in the outlying farm and industrial area of the Dead Sea community located at Ain Feshka. During the Spring of 1955, four more caves were found in the side of the terrace where the ruins of Khirbet Qumran are located. Also in 1955 nearly 600 coins were discovered in three pottery containers unearthed in a room of the main building. Some of these are from the time of Antiochus VII (138-129 B.C.), others are of Tyrian origin and date from about 9 B.C. Only one coin was from the time of Herod the Great (36-4 B.C.). The cemetery at Khirbet Qumran yielded about 1,000 graves laid out in parallel lines extending north and south. The simplicity of the graves indicated the austerity of the sect. All the skeletal remains were those of adults.

SPRING, 1956:

Early in 1956 Bedouins discovered Cave XI, from which they took several scrolls. The known contents of the cave, all seemingly from the first century A.D. and before 68 A.D., comprise: a Psalm manuscript with 34 Old Testament Psalms and 8 non-canonical pieces; a Leviticus scroll, incomplete, in the old Hebrew script; a written Targum (Aramaic translation) of Job; and Hebrew texts regarding an ideal or heavenly Jerusalem, as well as Hebrew blessing formulas having to do with the fruits of the field. Since this discovery, which included one or more manuscripts not yet seen by scholars, there have been no further manuscript finds in the Khirbet Qumran region.

SUMMARY

Milik gives the following summary:

> The discoveries of manuscripts in the Judaean Desert can be divided into three groups on the basis of their date and their provenance: (1) Manuscripts coming from the caves in the Qumran area, in the vicinity of the community settlement at Khirbet Qumran, dating, broadly speaking, from the second century B.C. to the first century A.D. (2) Documents from Murabbaat and another unidentified site, found in caves in wadis that are hard of access and remote from all centres of habitation, in the southern part of the Judaean Desert. These caves served as refuges in all periods, but were especially so used during the Second Jewish Revolt. (3) Manuscripts found in the ruins of a Byzantine monastery Hirbet Mird. This lay not far from Jerusalem, in the middle of the 'monks desert', which knew its greatest days in the fifth and sixth centuries of our era.[2]

The Israeli discoveries of 1960 and 1961, in the wadies west of Engeddi, all belong to the class of documents which Milik includes in group 2. They include military and family records in several languages (Hebrew, Jewish Aramaic, Greek, and Nabatean), but nothing pertaining to the community of Khirbet Qumran. The "unidentified site" mentioned by Milik is now known to be in Israeli territory, and is the principal source of the documents recovered, which amount to nearly 100 in all.[3]

---

[2] J. T. Milik, *Ten Years of Discovery in the Wilderness of Judaea* trans. J. Strugnell (London: SCM Press; Distributed in the U.S.A. by Allenson's, Naperville, Illinois, 1959), p. 19.
[3] See Yigael Yadin, "New Discoveries in the Judean Desert," *The Biblical Archaeologist,* XXIV (May, 1961), 34-50; (September, 1961), 86-95.

II. THE AGE OF THE MANUSCRIPTS[4]

The following criteria are available for the study of the age of the texts found in the area of the Dead Sea:

1. The linen in which the scrolls found by the Bedouin in 1947 were wrapped, has been tested by a radio-carbon process called the Carbon 14 process, developed by Dr. W. F. Libby at the Institute for Nuclear Studies of the University of Chicago. Carbon 14 is a radioactive form of carbon (atomic weight 14) which is present in all organic matter. Its rate of decay can be measured, and thus the age of the organic matter can be determined. The linen found at the Dead Sea was subjected to the test and the results showed that it was produced in the year 33 A.D., plus or minus 200 years. Therefore, the linen originated sometime between 168 B.C. and 233 A.D. The "atomic calendar" used for dating ancient objects has now been made more accurate through a redetermination by the National Bureau of Standards of the decay rate of radioactive carbon. The newly determined value for carbon 14's half life places the age of the scrolls at 1,983 years. This would date them about 20 B.C.

2. Since the work of Sir Flinders Petrie, the English archaeologist of the early twentieth century, pottery has become the key by which the historical periods of the past are opened. In the caves a type of ceramic jar was found which is similar to those discovered within the monastery building at Qumran. Using a "ceramic index," i.e. shape, ware, color, etc., archaeologists have determined that the jars belonged to the first century B.C.

3. The discovery of a *scriptorium,* a writing room, and inkwells in the monastery also establishes the connection between the monastic colony and the texts discovered in the caves. Thus the archaeological findings from the excavation of the monastery ruins establish a conclusive chronological determination of the time when the texts were hidden in the caves. Archaeological arguments, which are very detailed and have to be studied in order to appreciate fully the weight of the evidence, show with certainty that this monastery was destroyed in the year 68 A.D. That year is the *terminus ante quem* for the writing of the texts.

4. Another criterion for judging the age of the scrolls is paleography, the study of writing forms and styles used by copyists. Until recently the only material available for comparison was the Nash Papyrus, a fragment containing the Ten Commandments and the beginning of the Shema, the prayer based on Deuteronomy 6,4.

[4] The antiquity of the Dead Sea texts has been established by careful and reliable methods. Scholars are now in agreement that their dating is roughly between the second century B.C. and the first century A.D. Serious consideration is no longer given to the view of S. Zeitlin, editor of the *Jewish Quarterly Review,* who holds that the texts are medieval forgeries.

In the course of excavations at the Wadi Murabbaat, about ten or eleven miles south of Khirbet Qumran, texts were found dating from the time of Simon bar Kokhba (132-35 A.D.) which can be surely dated. The present texts present a form of script which is later than that of the Qumran texts. The paleographical argument substantiates the one based on archaeology.

5. Examination of the content of some of the texts shows that they describe a time before the year 80 B.C. They speak of the Teacher of Righteousness (or Legitimate Teacher), the founder of the sect who led the members away from Jerusalem during the rule of the "Wicked Priest" who is best identified with Jonathan (160-143 B.C.). The Teacher died during the rule of John Hyrcanus as High Priest (134-104 B.C.).[5]

III. THE CONTENTS OF THE SCROLLS[6]

It is common knowledge that ancient Jewish writings have been turning up in large numbers since 1947 in places south of Jericho, overlooking the northwestern part of the Dead Sea. Most, though not all, of these writings are in Hebrew; most, though not all, of them are very fragmentary. Some people have said they are fakes. Others assert that from them we can learn new and vital things about the origins of Christianity.

The "fake" idea is still held to by a very-small minority. Enough has been published by now to make it clear, however, that these documents are not fakes, and that while the earliest of them are datable in the second century B.C., most of them cannot be dated later than the destruction of Jerusalem in 70 A.D. The greater part of them are, in fact, from the first pre-Christian century, and the books of which these are the remains were composed (except for the Old Testament ones) in the second and first centuries B.C. Since they are texts of a group of Jews organized into a religious body during this time, they have of course much to tell us about the people among whom Christ our Lord preached the Gospel: ways they thought and prayed, their hopes and fears, and their understanding of the message of the Old Testament prophets. They present us with ceremonial customs in religion like those, familiar to the Apostles, out of which our Lord established His sacraments. Not always new, and not really vital to those who already have the Christian faith, their news value will probably diminish as the extent of their publication advances; but they will be studied by scholars for a long time to come, before they end up as stereotyped footnotes to the history of religion.

---

[5] The question of the dates of the "Teacher of Righteousness" is discussed in Milik, *Ten Years of Discovery,* pp. 64-83.

[6] This section was written by Monsignor Patrick W. Skehan, S.T.D. of the Department of Semitic and Egyptian Languages of the Graduate School of Arts and Sciences at The Catholic University of America, Washington, D. C. Monsignor Skehan is currently engaged in editing for publication a part of the Biblical manuscripts found in the fourth cave at Khirbet Qumran in 1952.

Not too many years ago it was fashionable in some circles to question the testimony of the Gospels as to what the Jewish people were expecting and hoping for during the teaching years of our Lord's life on earth. "Who do men say that I am?" He had asked. And the Apostles are said to have told Him, "Some say John the Baptist, others Elia, or one of the prophets." When they were asked what they, themselves, had to say about it, St. Peter spoke for them and said, "Thou art the Christ." Before all this, John the Baptist had been asked, "Why then do you baptize, if you are not the Christ, nor Elia, nor the prophet?" But, we used to be told, first century Judaism was not like that: the picture in the Gospels is an artificial one.

One of the documents from a cave near the Dead Sea ordains that the members of the pre-Christian Jewish group "shall judge by the first judgments according to which the men of the community began to be disciplined, until there shall come a prophet, and the Messiahs of Aaron and Israel." So now the hue and cry is off in another direction. All the language of Christian theology is read into holes in the leather where these documents are fragmentary, and even before they are published some make claims for them that amount to finding in them all of Christianity before Christ.

"In the fulness of time," our Lord came; and the Jewish people had better than a thousand years of preparation by Moses and the prophets for His coming. He took their confused hopes and aspirations and fulfilled the worthiest of them in Himself. He took also bread and wine, and, with a blessing, gave them to become the greatest of His sacraments. He took also 12 men, whom He made the rulers of His Church. Time after time, it is the thing foretold, and familiar thing of daily life, the traditional number, the expected pattern to which He gave new meaning. The community which left its manuscripts in caves by the Dead Sea knew of a banquet in which the "Messiahs of Aaron and Israel" would share, and in which, after a blessing, they would be the first to partake of the bread and the wine; their community meals were ordered on a similar pattern, with a presiding priest. They had a council of twelve for important decisions, though they complicated this by adding a group of three men of priestly family to make fifteen. They had a supervisor whose ruling functions sound in some respects like those of a bishop. Resemblances, on big points and on small, can be multiplied as the texts continue to be published. The Christian who has studied the Gospels and understood our Lord's teaching methods has no reason to be surprised.

Resemblances are easy to describe, and easy to exaggerate. It is regrettably true that some of those making pronouncements on the significance of the Dead Sea manuscripts are much more interested in finding in them plausible counterparts to Christian teaching than in evaluating what the documents themselves say. One test of this is the extent to which the Old Testament books are given their proper place in the discussion. The general public is repeatedly told that this or that phrase or teaching is used in the same way by the Dead Sea texts and in the New Testament, without being told that it is an Old Testament text or doctrine that is in question. Any Jew of our Lord's time would have known this and would have been able to employ it to similar effect. Unfortunately, many readers of today who have a deep interest in the beginnings of Christianity do not have a ready acquaintance with much of the Old Testament. Students of pre-Christian Jewish documents presumably do; and it is a disappointing lack of candor or of proper concern for an uninformed audience which allows some of them to deal out as noteworthy resemblances between texts, items whose common source in the Old Testament is in no way indicated.

On certain points, however, the informed Christian will be rather surprised if real similarities are discovered. He will remember that when our Lord, for the last time, though not the first, told His twelve followers, "Behold, we are going up to Jerusalem, and all things that are written by the prophets, concerning the Son of Man shall be fulfilled: for He shall be given over to the Gentiles and mocked and reviled and spit upon, and they shall scourge Him and put Him to death, and the third day He shall rise again," St. Luke goes on to say, "But they understood none of these things; and this word was hidden from them, and they did not understand what was said." The Christian of today knows that among the prophecies of Isaia there was one regarding a suffering servant of God, which Christ fulfilled in the events of Holy Week. But he will remember also that after the resurrection, on the road to Emmaus, Jesus Himself had to propose to two of His disciples the question, "Ought not Christ to have suffered these things, and so to enter into His glory?" and to explain the prophecies they had never before understood. Christ suffering to redeem the world is a whole system of theology for which the Jewish contemporaries of our Lord, even those chosen to be His followers, were almost completely unprepared.

Yet the claim has been made lately that the sufferings of our Lord for the sins of others had been anticipated in the death of a community leader known as the "teacher of righteousness" of the Dead Sea group. The name "teacher of righteousness" is prepared for by two or more passages in the Old Testament and was understood by St. Jerome as applying to our Lord. It is possible, though by no means certain, that the Jewish group in the Dead Sea neighborhood thought of the leader in question as one, perhaps even the principal one, of the various divine messengers in messianic time, to whom their literature refers. That they expected him to rise again from the dead at the end of time, along with all the just, after the manner described in the Book of Daniel, is likely enough, though not demonstrable from any text. But what of the circumstances of his death?

The death of the "teacher of righteousness" is chiefly remarkable for how little anybody can claim to know about it. There are five published texts which have been supposed to refer to it; only two of them certainly do. The first refers to an interval "from the day the teacher of the community was gathered in, until a messiah shall arise from Aaron and from Israel"; the second speaks of a period of 40 years "from the day the teacher of the community was gathered in." The words "gathered in" are the ones used in the Old Testament for the deaths of the patriarchs Abraham, Ishmael, Isaac, and Jacob. It creates a strong presumption in favor of natural death as opposed to death by violence (despite 1 Mc 14,30). Two other texts are in comments on the second chapter of the prophecy of Habacuc. These have in fact to do with the conduct and punishment of a "wicked priest" who made difficulties for the "teacher of righteousness" and his followers. It is the "wicked priest" who is quite clearly said to have suffered punishment, described as divine punishment, apparently by fatal illness, for his opposition to the "teacher." Nothing in these texts connects the opposition to the "teacher of righteousness" with any direct attack on his person; and in a commentary on Psalm 36 (37), which alone among the Dead Sea texts portrays the "wicked priest" as "seeking to slay" the "teacher," the tenor of the comment makes it plain that the effort was unsuccessful.

This situation has not been changed by any of the unpublished materials which have lately been drawn into the discussion. There is no text extant anywhere which specifies the manner of death of the "teacher of righteousness." There is no suggestion in any text that any value for the salvation of anybody was seen in that death. Those who have seen all the material are most anxious that it appear in print as soon as possible, in view of the untenable claims that have been made for it.

One such claim is that there was nothing in the idea of a crucified master, atoning for the world's sin in his suffering, and expected to rise again in glory as Messiah, which would have seemed out of place in the experience and most cherished hopes of the sect by the Dead Sea. This wholesale "reading in" of Christian doctrine into what we know of the group whose "Dead Sea Scrolls" are now under study is false at practically every turn. Atoning for the world's sin is a concept these people did not have. They used the law of Moses and the instructions of the "teacher of righteousness" as a way of atoning for their own sins, and left the rest to God. They do not discuss a salvation extending beyond the elect within the Jewish people itself. The "teacher of righteousness" was not their only master—a term with Christian connotations which is never applied to him in the texts. It has already been said that the manner of his death is not described, and no value is anywhere attributed to it. The hopes that were cherished by the Dead Sea group had to do with a divine intervention at the end of time, during which more than one Messiah should be present. The same document which speaks of the "gathering in" of the "teacher of righteousness" speaks also of a "period of wickedness, until arises the messiahs of Aaron and Israel," after the death of the teacher of righteousness. A discipline of waiting for God's redemption is imposed for this period, and there is a complete absence of any hint that anything the "teacher of righteousness" has suffered or done has changed the status of his followers in any respect. The ritual of the community is carried out, and its discipline observed, with no suggestion that the person of the "teacher" is in any way central to what is done. "As often as you do this, do it in commemoration of me," said Jesus of Nazareth. No such personal loyalty was asked for by the "teacher of righteousness," nor did either he or any of his followers ever make the tremendous claim that his mission from God was such that "not with the blood of goats and bullocks, but with his own blood he entered once and for all the holy place, having obtained eternal redemption." Even apart from the personal claims made by our Lord and for Him there is not in all the Dead Sea literature an evaluation of the sufferings of the past and of their significance before the coming of the Messiah that can be compared with the eleventh chapter of the Epistle to the Hebrews.

IV. SOME CONCLUSIONS

1. The similarities between certain ideas in the New Testament and in the Qumran literature surely are not to be denied. It is true that in some alleged instances the similarities do not exist, but erroneous exaggerations are relatively easy to apprehend and dismiss. Similarity itself allows of degrees, and the most deceiving of these is verbal similarity. The same words may be used, but have a quite different meaning in Christianity than they had in the framework of the Qumran doctrine.

Milik concludes his study with the following:

> However, there are numerous similarities between Essene and the authentic early Christian doctrine. Both hold the eschatological concept of the true Israel ruled by twelve leaders; both believe that they have already in this life a foretaste of the blessedness that the end of days will bring about; both believe that the spirits of good and evil are engaged in struggle both in the cosmos and in the soul of each man, and in both systems, the believer shares already in the life of the angels. In early Christianity, however, all these features, and many others too, are taken up into a new doctrinal structure and the integration of these elements with the central beliefs of the new faith transforms each one of them. Sometimes the transformation is merely qualitative, certain elements being more stressed and assuming a greater importance in the new system. For instance, both groups believe that the call to salvation is addressed to all men, without ethnic or social limitations, and that men are brothers, and God a Father to every man; both Communities of the Elect live in an atmosphere impregnated with forgiveness and love. But in other cases the adoption of Essene beliefs into an organic unit with the new doctrines completely transforms them. So, for instance, the period of the End has for the Christian already been in-

augurated with the coming of the Messiah. Further, the sense of the
sinfulness of human nature is so radicalized that a merely human media-
tion of the New Covenant and a merely human Messiah would no
longer seem effective. God must become Man and make the covenant
by atoning himself for our sins. God meets man in the intimacy of his
being, and this meeting bears its fruits in a "rebirth" where a "new
creature" is "born from on high."

Accordingly, although Essenism bore in itself more than one element
that one way or another fertilized the soil from which Christianity was
to spring, it is nevertheless evident that the latter religion represents
something completely new which can only be adequately explained by
the person of Jesus himself.[7]

2. Practically all scholars agree that there is no direct literary dependence
of the New Testament upon Qumran literature. In the New Testament we
find clear allusions to some apocryphal works, as was recognized long before 1947, for example, the *Assumption of Moses* and *Book of Enoch* in the
Epistle of Jude (vv. 9-15), and we know that these apocryphal works were
popular among the Essenes. However, there is no specific Qumran source
that is imitated or quoted in the New Testament.

3. There can be no doubt that Jesus and the New Testament writers were
acquainted with the Qumran teachings. It is difficult to determine the manner
in which they came into contact with the Qumran doctrine. Some scholars
would hold that St. John the Baptist and his former disciple, St. John the
Evangelist, were members of the Essenes. There is no evidence for this,
despite the clear influence which the Qumran teachings exerted on both men.
Other scholars have proposed that the Essenes were among the early converts
to Christianity; this is entirely probable in view of the aspirations of these
Jews. Their noble ideals, their asceticism, and their Messianic consciousness
would have rendered them particularly susceptible to the appeal of Christianity.
It is very likely that the influence of Qumran upon Christianity was largely
indirect. The Essene teachings were part of the general religious milieu in
which Christianity was born.

4. The Qumran point of view was most likely a climate more in accord
with Christian ideals than was the official Judaism which outlawed the Essenes.
Being part of the religious heritage of the first generation of Christians, it
contributed to their fund of religious languages and ideas. The Christians
could have adopted Qumran phraseology and practice without even being
conscious of the fact that these "belonged" to that sect. The Essene teaching
was so much a part of first century Judaism that it is as natural for Christianity to be affected by it as by the Old Testament religion in general. Moreover, it was just one of the many currents, one tributary in the entire flood of
religious ideas in the first century. It would be a mistake to forget that the

---

[7] Milik, *Ten Years of Discovery*. p. 143.

contemporary influences on Christianity were on a broader basis than Qumran Essenism.

5. Resemblances that exist between the Qumran texts and the New Testament can often be explained by the fact that the Old Testament was the source for the texts or doctrines in question. This fact is not always remembered in discussions on this subject.

MANUSCRIPTS AND VERSIONS
OF THE BIBLE

I. INTRODUCTION

WE DO NOT possess any autographs, original manuscripts, of the Books of the Bible. This is not odd if we consider the ages that separate us from the time in which the originals of the books of the Old Testament were written. Moreover, the materials that were used to write the books, usually papyrus and parchment, were relatively fragile. Thousands of copies exist; their value varying according to their time of origin and the care taken in their composition. Until the invention of printing, the written word had to depend on the pens of copyists. Each copy meant the possibility of new dangers, for example, the carelessness of the scribe, confusion of sounds when the text was dictated to the copyists, confusion of letters which resembled one another, inversions and repetitions. At times, individuals tried to restore the text to its original purity but succeeded only in making matters worse. Therefore, it is the task of scholars to collect all the available evidence and to determine the wording of the original.[1]

The interval between the appearance of the Biblical books and the extant copies is comparatively small when we consider the same problem in relation to ancient classics. For example, except for some copies on papyri from the early centuries A.D., most of the manuscripts that contain the works of authors like Sophocles, Aeschylus, Aristophanes, Thucydides, Euripides, Plato, and Demosthenes, are dated twelve to sixteen hundred years later than the time when they were first composed.

But until recently, the earliest Hebrew manuscript of the Old Testament was from the ninth century A.D. In 1947, the discovery of the Dead Sea

---

[1] The study of the history and criticism of the text of the Bible is known as Textual Criticism. The following are helpful introductory works concerning it: E. Tisserant and M. J. Lagrange, "The Transmission of the Text," *Guide to the Bible,* I, 587-620; G. Bardy and A. Tricot, "The Versions," *ibid.,* pp. 621-64; Frederic Kenyon, *op. cit.,* pp. 19-154.

Scrolls changed the situation. Now we have thousands of fragments of varying sizes of the books of the Old Testament in Hebrew which are 1000 or more years older than the previous copies.[2]

Since we do not have the original Hebrew manuscripts of the Old Testament, we must work from the indirect approach. We must use copies and translations which help us to reconstruct the text as it came from inspired authors.

Aside from the Dead Sea Scrolls the following are some of the Biblical translations and versions which are invaluable in the work of ascertaining the state of the original text.

II. HEBREW MANUSCRIPTS

There are numerous copies of these manuscripts. It is known that in 1780 there were more than 600 copies available; during the nineteenth century a collection in Leningrad contained almost 1600 volumes on parchment and about 750 on paper. None of these, however, is older than the ninth century A.D. The discovery in the late nineteenth century of manuscripts in the Geniza of the Synagogue in old Cairo added more than 100 ancient fragments. A Geniza was a room reserved for the "burial" of non-usable Biblical manuscripts. Some of the manuscripts date back to the sixth century A.D.[3]

A great deal of care was exercised in copying the manuscripts. Once a manuscript was copied and verified it was accepted as authentic and of the same value as the earlier copy. However, as time went on some changes appeared in the texts. During the sixth century A.D. Jewish scribes and rabbis, known as Massoretes, began the work of standardization. These men, whose name comes from the Hebrew word *Masora*, "tradition", collected the mass of traditional learning which had been handed down and with it they embellished the manuscripts of the Old Testament. They produced a "fence or hedge," around the text, made up of the accumulated traditions. The Massoretes were most anxious that nothing that had come down from the past should be lost. Between the eighth and tenth centuries the work was carried on laboriously and meticulously. Once the text of the Old Testament was fixed and standardized by the Massoretes, all earlier copies were hidden or destroyed. It is because of this fact that there are practically no copies available from before the ninth century A.D. Present Hebrew Bibles contain the text produced by the Massoretes; it is known as the *Massoretic Text*.

III. THE SEPTUAGINT TRANSLATION (LXX)

The Septuagint is the most important translation of the Old Testament. It was produced in Egypt during the second or third century B.C. Its history is a very complicated one and there are still some unsolved problems connected

[2] See pp. 243, 247-49.
[3] See Paul E. Kahle, *The Cairo Geniza* (London: Frederick A. Praeger, Inc., 1960).

with it. However, we can say that the translation was the answer to a very practical problem—the need of the large number of Jews who had settled in Alexandria and acquired its language, which was Greek.[4]

Legend has it that 72 old men were sent from Jerusalem to Alexandria to translate the Biblical books into Greek. They are said to have finished their work in 72 days; that is the origin of the name given to the translation, *Septuagint,* "Seventy." The fact is that the fall of Samaria in 721 and Jerusalem in 587 B.C. caused many Jews to settle outside Palestine. Thus began the great dispersal, which is referred to as the Diaspora. During the fifth century many Jews settled in Egypt, and the conquests of Alexander the Great in the fourth century encouraged even greater numbers to go there. The city of Alexandria became the greatest Jewish metropolis outside Palestine. There the Jews acquired the language and customs of the land. The need for a Greek version of the Old Testament was soon felt, and the translation was made by Alexandrian Jews long familiar with Greek.

The Septuagint is of great importance, and sometimes it is a better witness to the original text than the Hebrew version. It is a witness which is almost 12 centuries older than the Massoretic Text. Its quality is inconsistent, however, because it was the work of several individuals of varying abilities.

The Septuagint, at least in its final form, contains seven books which are not in the Hebrew Bibles: Tobia, Judith, 1-2 Maccabees, Wisdom, Sirach (Ecclesiasticus), and Baruch. A few additions appear in the books of Esther and Daniel. The Church adopted the Septuagint. This explains why Catholic editions of the Old Testament have more books than the Hebrew Bibles; the Protestants use the Hebrew Canon as the basis for their translations and relegate the seven books to a section of their editions which they call the *Apocrypha,* a name indicating that the books are not considered part of the Word of God.[5]

The most important copies of the Septuagint are the following codices, volumes which were formed by fastening together leaves of parchment: (1) *Codex Vaticanus,* from the fourth century A.D., found at present in the Vatican Library; (2) *Codex Sinaiticus,* also from the fourth century, discovered in the Monastery of St. Catherine on Mt. Sinai. Part of the text is in Leipzig, the other part is in the British Museum. (3) *Codex Alexandrinus,* from the fourth-fifth century A.D., located in the British Museum. Other

---

[4] Bardy, *op. cit.,* pp. 622-31; also Kenyon, *op. cit.,* pp. 97-134.

[5] The word *Apocrypha* is used by Catholics to refer to works which purport to be inspired Scripture but which are not part of the canon of the Bible. Non-Catholics refer to such works as *Apocryphal,* thus restricting the use of the word *Apocrypha* for the books which are in the Catholic Canon but not in theirs. We refer to these latter books as the *Deuterocanonical* ones; in general, these are the seven books which were included in the Canon after some discussion. The books of the Bible, exclusive of the seven, are called *Protocanonical.* For a study of this matter see: A. Tricot, "The Canon of the Scriptures," *Guide to the Bible,* I, 67-87, 103-12; also R. J. Foster, "The Apocrypha of the Old and New Testament," *A Catholic Commentary on Holy Scripture,* pp. 121-26.

libraries and museums throughout the world have large and small parts of the Septuagint, many of which are ancient papyri fragments.[6]

IV. OTHER TRANSLATIONS

The LXX is not the only Greek translation from antiquity. In the second century A.D. important translations were made by Aquila, Theodotion, and Symmachus. Besides these there are extant copies of translations in Ethiopic and Syriac, which were made in the fifth century. Origen, in the third century, produced the *Hexapla,* a work in which he gave, in parallel columns, the Hebrew text as well as the various versions current in his day.

V. LATIN VERSIONS

The original language of the primitive Church was chiefly Greek. There is evidence which warrants the view that the Septuagint version was the text used by the authors of the books of the New Testament when they quoted the Old Testament; at least the text they used was closely related to the LXX. As time went on, there was a need for Latin copies of the Bible because many converts in the Roman world did not understand Greek, and Latin was gradually becoming the vernacular.

There are evidences of early Latin versions from about the end of the second century and the beginning of the third. Further study is necessary before we can be certain about these versions. However, one thing is certain; by the end of the fourth century there were so many Latin versions that problems arose regarding the public reading of the Scriptures during the Liturgy and also in catechetical instructions. The need was for a uniform text to be used in the Latin Church; two men set out to produce it, St. Augustine (354-430) and St. Jerome (347-420). Since Augustine's work was not as extensive as that of Jerome, only the latter's will be considered here. It is commonly called the *Vulgate.*[7]

Pope Damasus (366-384) encouraged Jerome to produce a new Latin translation of the Bible. The work was begun in 383; within a year the Gospels were ready, and by 405 many of the Old Testament books were completed. Although there are some faults in the work, it does show that Jerome was a master of Latin prose.

His work did not meet with success at first. Many refused to accept it because it would mean a change in their habits regarding the reading and chanting of Scripture in liturgical worship. Its use, therefore, spread very slowly, and widespread acceptance did not take place until the reign of Charle-

---

[6] See Kenyon, *op. cit.,* pp. 113-27.

[7] *Ibid.,* pp. 141-44, 242-46, 250-64; also A. Tricot, "The Vulgate of Saint Jerome," *Guide to the Bible,* I, 645-64. A very useful collection of essays about the life and works of St. Jerome is Francis X. Murphy, C.SS.R. (ed.), *A Monument to Saint Jerome* (New York: Sheed & Ward, 1952).

magne in the eighth century. The name *Vulgate,* "the common text," was given to the work but it was not until the thirteenth century that this name was used generally. The Council of Trent in the sixteenth century adopted the Vulgate as the *authentic* Catholic version. This meant that the Council declared it to be free of all errors in matters of faith or morals.

The text of the Vulgate has suffered during history; various groups have been attempting to produce a critical edition. In 1907 a Pontifical Commission, composed of Benedictine scholars, was organized to study all the available manuscripts and to make available such an edition of the Vulgate. Since 1933 this work has been carried on by the Benedictines at the Abbey of St. Jerome in Rome.

There are innumerable quotations and long verbatim extracts from the Bible in the writings of early Christian authors, particularly the Fathers of the Church. Some of these are from as early as the second century, and all testify to the state of the text of the Bible in their respective ages.

appendix two

ENGLISH TRANSLATIONS
OF THE BIBLE

VERSIONS OF THE BIBLE

THE FOLLOWING list presents the principal English versions of the Bible from the Anglo-Saxon attempts during the Early Middle Ages to the present. Non-Catholic works are preceded by an asterisk.

670	Caedmon's Paraphrase of the Bible
709	Aldhelm's translation of the Psalms
735	Bede's translation of the Gospel of St. John
890	King Alfred's translation of parts of the Bible; Psalms
950	Alfred's paraphrase of the Gospels
990	Aelfric's translation of parts of the Old Testament (Pentateuch, Josue, Judges, Kings, Esther, Job, Judith, and Maccabees)
1215	The Ormulum, a metrical version of prayers, including portions of the New Testament
1250-1350	Several versions of the Psalter
1382	*The Bible of John Wycliffe
1525	*The Bible of William Tyndale (Pentateuch, Jona, New Testament)
1535	*The Bible of Myles Coverdale; the first English translation of the whole Bible
1537	*Thomas Matthew (John Rogers) published Tyndale's Bible and added several books (Josue to Chronicles) as well as the rest of the Old Testament from Coverdale
1539-41	*The Great Bible; a revision of Matthew's Bible

1539	*The Bible of Richard Taverner
1557-60	*The Geneva Bible; contained controversial (and anti-Catholic) notes
1568	*The Bishop's Bible
1582	The Rheims New Testament
1609-10	The Douay Old Testament
1611	*The King James Bible; known as the Authorized Version
1749-52	The Bishop Richard Challoner Revisions of the Rheims-Douay Bible
1849-61	The Revision of Archbishop F. P. Kenrick
1881-85	*The Revised Version
1901	*The American Standard Version
1913-35	The Westminster Version of the Sacred Scriptures
1937	The Spencer New Testament
1939	*The Complete Bible: An American translation
1941	The Confraternity of Christian Doctrine; New Testament
1944-50	The Monsignor Ronald Knox Translation
1946-52	*The Revised Standard Version
1952	The Confraternity of Christian Doctrine: Genesis to Ruth
1955	The Confraternity of Christian Doctrine: Job to Sirach
1961	*The New English Bible: New Testament
1961	The Confraternity of Christian Doctrine: Prophetic Books

READINGS IN THE BOOKS
OF THE OLD TESTAMENT

BOOK	CHAPTERS	CONTENTS
GENESIS	1-50	Creation to the death of the patriarch Joseph
EXODUS	1-15	Deliverance from Egypt: the Passover
	16-18	Wonders in the desert
	19-24	The Covenant
	34	Renewal of the Covenant
LEVITICUS	17-26	The Holiness Code
NUMBERS	11-14	Events during the years in the desert
	16-17	Rebellion against Moses
	20-24	Journey to the plains of Moab
DEUTERONOMY	1-6	Movement of Israelites on eastern side of the Jordan
	9-11	Recapitulation of the wanderings
	32-34	Song of Moses
JOSUE	1-10	Entrance into Canaan: early victories
	23-24	Final words of Josue: reminder of Divine goodness and renewal of Covenant
JUDGES	1-2	Infidelities of the Israelites; theological explanation of reverses and victories
	3-16	Epic-like stories of early national heroes
1 SAMUEL	1-2	Birth of Samuel; Canticle of Anna
	10	Saul, first king of Israelites
	16	David anointed king

BOOK	CHAPTERS	CONTENTS
2 SAMUEL	1-8	Death of Saul; David, king of all Israel
		The Dynastic Oracle
	11-12	David's sins of adultery and murder
	22	David's hymn of thanksgiving
3 KINGS	1-11	Death of David; reign of Solomon
		Building of the Temple and Palace
		Introduction of pagan practices
		Death of Solomon
	12-14	Schism: the sin of Jeroboam
	17-19	The Elia cycle
AMOS	3-9	Punishment of Israel for its infidelities
		Condemnation of social injustices
OSEE	1-6	Punishment of Israel for its infidelities
		Symbolism of the unfaithful wife
	11	Love of the Lord for His people
4 KINGS	2-13	The Eliseus cycle
		Weal and woe in the kingdom
ISAIA	6	Call of the prophet
	7-9	The Emmanuel Prophecies
4 KINGS	18-19	Reign of Ezechia
		Siege of Jerusalem
	22-23	Reform of Josia
DEUTERONOMY	6	Love of the Lord
		Observance of the Law
4 KINGS	24-25	Destruction of Jerusalem
		Exile in Babylon
JEREMIA	1	Call of the prophet
	21-23	Judgment against the unfaithful leaders
	31	The New Covenant
	50-52	Prophecy against Babylon
LAMENTATIONS	1	Elegy over Jerusalem fallen to the Babylonians
	4	

BOOK	CHAPTERS	CONTENTS
PSALM	136	Song of the people in Exile
EZECHIEL	2-3	Call of the prophet
	33-34	Replacement of the evil shepherds by the Shepherd
	37	Vision of the dry bones: symbol of the restoration of Israel
	40-43	The New Temple
DEUTERO-ISAIA	41	Encouragement for those in Exile
	43	Return from Exile; the New Exodus
	49	Restoration of Jerusalem
	52-53	The Servant of Yahweh
EZRA	1-6	Edict of Cyrus Return from Exile Rebuilding of the Temple
NEHEMIA	1-6	Rebuilding of the walls of Jerusalem
	9	Renewal of Covenant
JONA	1-4	Parable of religious universalism
JOB	1-2	The test of a man of wealth and piety
	3	Job's plaint
	19	Complaint followed by an act of faith
	38-41	The speech of the Lord
	42	Act of contrition and restoration
1 MACCABEES	1-3	Revolt of the Maccabees
2 MACCABEES	5-7	Persecution by Antiochus Epiphanes
DANIEL	7	Vision of the four beasts; the Son of Man
2 MACCABEES	8-10	Success of Judas Maccabeus Death of Antiochus Epiphanes Dedication of the Temple
WISDOM	5	Reward of the just after death
	7	Dignity of Wisdom
	9	Prayer for Wisdom

BIBLIOGRAPHY

I. EDITIONS OF THE BIBLE

The Holy Bible. New York: Benziger Brothers, Inc., 1961.
La Sainte Bible de Jerusalem. Paris: Les Éditions du Cerf, 1956.

II. DOCUMENTS OF THE MAGISTERIUM

Pope Pius XII, *Divino Afflante Spiritu.* Encyclical on the Promotion of Biblical Studies. Washington, D. C.: National Catholic Welfare Conference, 1943.

Pope Pius XII, *Humani Generis.* Encyclical Concerning Some False Opinions Which Threaten to Undermine the Foundations of Catholic Doctrine. Washington, D. C.: National Catholic Welfare Conference, 1950.

Rome and the Study of Scripture. A Collection of Papal Enactments on the Study of Holy Scripture Together With the Decisions of the Biblical Commission. St. Meinrad, Ind.: Grail Publications, 1958.

III. BASIC REFERENCE BOOKS

* Anderson, Bernhard W., *Understanding the Old Testament.* Englewood Cliffs, N. J.: Prentice-Hall, Inc., 1957.

* Crudens, Alexander, *Complete Concordance to the Old and New Testaments.* Philadelphia: John C. Winston Company, 1949.

DeVaux, Roland, *Ancient Israel. Its Life and Institutions.* Translated by John McHugh. New York: McGraw-Hill Book Company, Inc., 1961.

Ellis, Peter, *The Men and the Message of the Old Testament.* Collegeville, Minn.: The Liturgical Press, 1962.

Glanzman, George S. and Joseph A. Fitzmyer, *An Introductory Bibliography for the Study of Scripture.* Westminster, Md.: The Newman Press, 1961.

Pagano, Sebastiano, *Chronological Table of the Books of the Old Testament.* Ottawa: University Seminary, 1959.

Robert, A. and A. Feuillet (eds.), *Introduction a la Bible.* 2d ed., 2 vols. Tournai: Desclée & Cie, Editeurs, 1959.

Robert, A. and A. Tricot (eds.), *Initiation Biblique.* 3d ed. Tournai: Desclee & Cie, 1954. This work is available in English: *Guide to the Bible.* Translated by Edward P. Arbez and Martin McGuire. 2 vols. New York: Desclee Company, 1960.

IV. GENERAL WORKS

Auzou, Georges, *The Word of God.* Translated by Josefa Thornton. St. Louis: B. Herder Book Co., 1960.

Beaucamp, Évode, *La Bible et le Sens Religieux de l'Univers.* Paris: Les Editions du Cerf, 1959.

Bouyer, Louis, *The Meaning of Sacred Scripture.* Translated by Mary Perkins Ryan. Notre Dame: University of Notre Dame Press, 1958.

Bouyer, Louis, *The Word, Church and Sacraments in Protestantism and Catholicism.* Translated by A. V. Littledale, New York: Desclee Company, 1961.

Brillet, Gaston, *Meditations on the Old Testament. The Narratives.* Translated by Kathryn Sullivan, R.S.C.J. New York: Desclee Company, 1959.

Burgard, Charles, *Scripture in the Liturgy.* Translated by J. Holland Smith. Westminster, Md.: The Newman Press, 1960.

* An asterisk indicates a non-Catholic author

266

Castelot, John, *God So Loved the World*. Notre Dame, Ind.: Fides Publishers, Inc., 1962.

Castelot, John, *Meet the Bible*. 2 vols. Baltimore: Helicon Press, 1960.

Charlier, Celestin, *The Christian Approach to the Bible*. Translated by Hubert J. Richards and Brendan Peters. Westminster, Md.: The Newman Press, 1958.

Congar, Yves, *The Mystery of the Temple*. Westminster, Md.: The Newman Press, 1962.

Coppens, J., *The Old Testament and the Critics*. Translated by Edward Ryan and Edward Tribbe. Paterson, N. J.: St. Anthony Guild Press, 1942.

Daniélou, Jean, *Advent*. Translated by Rosemary Sheed. New York: Sheed & Ward, 1950.

Daniélou, Jean, *The Bible and the Liturgy*. Notre Dame: University of Notre Dame Press, 1956.

Daniélou, Jean, *Holy Pagans of the Old Testament*. Translated by Felix Faber. New York: Longmans, Green and Company, 1957.

Daniélou, Jean, *The Presence of God*. Baltimore: Helicon Press, 1959.

Daniel-Rops, H., *What Is the Bible?* Translated by J. R. Foster. New York: Hawthorn Books, Publishers, 1958.

Dannemiller, Lawrence, *Reading the Word of God*. Baltimore: Helicon Press, 1960.

Demann, Paul, *Judaism*. Translated by P. J. Hepburne-Scott. New York: Hawthorn Books, Publishers, 1961.

Dheilly, J., *Le Peuple de l'Ancienne Alliance*. Paris: Les Editions de l'Ecole, 1955.

* Dodd, C. H., *The Bible Today*. Cambridge: University Press, 1960. (Paperback edition).

Dougherty, John J., *Searching the Scriptures*. New York: Hanover House, 1959.

Fargues, Marie, *The Old Testament*. London; Darton, Longman & Todd, 1960.

Gelin, Albert, *The Religion of Israel*. Translated by J. R. Foster. New York: Hawthorn Books, Publishers, 1959.

Hunt, Ignatius, *Understanding the Bible*. New York: Sheed & Ward, 1962.

Johnson, Leonard, *Witnesses to God*. New York: Sheed & Ward, 1960.

Jones, Alexander, *God's Living Word*. New York: Sheed & Ward, 1961.

Jones, Alexander, *Unless Some Man Show Me*. New York: Sheed & Ward, 1951.

The Liturgy and the Word of God. Papers given at the Third National Congress of the Centre de Pastorale Liturgique. Collegeville, Minn.: The Liturgical Press, 1959.

McNally, Robert E., *The Bible in the Early Middle Ages*. Westminster, Md.: The Newman Press, 1959.

Monro, Margaret T., *The Old Testament and Our Times*. London: Longmans, Green and Co. Ltd., 1960.

Moriarty, Frederick, *Foreword to the Old Testament Books*. Weston, Mass.: Weston College Press, 1954.

Moriarty, Frederick, *Introducing the Old Testament*. Milwaukee: The Bruce Publishing Company, 1960.

An Old Testament Study Guide. Edited by Members of the Boston College Theology Department. Chestnut Hill, Mass.: Boston College Press, 1961.

Paulist Press Pamphlet Bible Series. New York: The Paulist Press, 1960-

* Richardson, Alan, *The Bible in the Age of Science*. Philadelphia: The Westminster Press, 1961.

* Rowley, H. H., *The Growth of the Old Testament*. London: Hutchinson University Library, 1950.

* Rowley, H. H. (ed.), *The Old Testament and Modern Study*. London: Oxford University Press, 1961. (Oxford Paperback Edition).

* Rowley, H. H., *The Unity of the Bible*. Philadelphia: The Westminster Press, 1955.

Steinmann, Jean, *Biblical Criticism*. Translated by J. R. Foster. New York: Hawthorn Books, Publishers, 1958.

Stuhlmueller, Carroll, "The Living Word of God: The Old Testament," *Worship*, XXXIII (June-July, 1959), 421-30

Sullivan, Kathryn, *God's Word and Work*. Collegeville, Minn.: The Liturgical Press, 1958.

Sutcliffe, Edmund, *The Old Testament and the Future Life*. 2d ed. London: Burns, Oates & Washbourne Ltd., 1947.

Tresmontant, Claude, *A Study of Hebrew Thought*. Translated by Michael F. Gibbon. New York: Desclee Company, 1960.

Tresmontant, Claude, *Toward the Knowledge of God*. Baltimore: Helicon Press, 1961.

The Word of Life. Essays on the Bible. Westminster, Md.: The Newman Press, 1960.

* Wright, G. Ernest (ed.), *The Bible and the Ancient Near East: Essays in Honor of William Foxwell Albright*. New York: Doubleday & Company, Inc., 1961.

* An asterisk indicates a non-Catholic author

V. THE BIBLE AND CHRISTIANS

Ahern, Barnabas M., "Gathering the Fragments: Bible Study in the U.S.," *Worship,* XXXVI (January, 1962), 101-06.

Ahern, Barnabas M., "Gathering the Fragments: Of Fear and Scholarship," *Worship,* XXXV (February, 1961), 160-65.

Ahern, Barnabas M., "Sacred Scripture," *The Critic,* XXI (August-September, 1962), 27-30, 79.

Baum, Gregory "Approaches to Scripture," *The Commonweal,* LXXIV (April 14, 1961), 71-73.

Bea, Augustine, "Biblical Studies Today," *Theology Digest,* III (Winter, 1955), 51-54.

Bea, Augustine, "Progress in the Interpretation of Sacred Scripture," *Theology Digest,* I (Spring, 1953), 67-71.

Coleran, James, "Current Theology: the Study of Holy Scripture," *Theological Studies,* V (March, 1944), 86-98.

Cushing, Richard Cardinal, "The Bible and Faith," *Friar,* XIV (November, 1960), 36-39.

Daniélou, Jean, "Holy Scripture: Meeting Place of Christians," *Cross Currents,* III (Spring, 1953), 251-61.

Dougherty, John J., "Liturgical Orientation in Scripture Study," *Worship,* XXXIII (November, 1959), 642-45.

Gleason, Robert W., "New Trends in Scriptural Interpretation," *The Catholic Mind,* LVIII (August, 1960), 299-304.

Gruenthaner, Michael, "Pope Pius XII and the Scriptures," *The American Ecclesiastical Review,* CXX (March, 1949), 233-38.

MacKenzie, Roderick A. F., "Present State of Biblical Studies," *Perspectives,* IV (September, 1959), 4-11.

McEleney, Neil J., "What's Happening to the Bible?" *The Catholic World,* CLXXXIX (May, 1959), 106-12.

McKenzie, John L., "The Bible in Contemporary Catholicism: Modern Scholarship vs Fundamentalist and Modernist Positions," *The Catholic World,* CXCI (July, 1961), 225-32.

McKenzie, John L. (ed.), *The Bible in Current Catholic Thought.* New York: Herder and Herder, 1962.

McKenzie, John L., "How to Read the Bible," *Ave Maria,* LXXXV (March 2, 1957), 12-15, 30.

Moeller, Charles, "Is it Possible, in the Twentieth Century, to be a 'Man of the Bible'?" *The Liturgy and the Word of God,* pp. 119-56. Collegeville, Minn.: The Liturgical Press, 1959.

Moriarty, Frederick J., "Bulletin of the Old Testament," *Theological Studies,* XII (September, 1951), 320-42; XIV (September, 1953), 402-29.

Pagano, S. "Readings From the Bible," *The Catholic Biblical Quarterly,* XVI (January, 1954), 20-32.

Siegman, Edward, "Use of Sacred Scripture in Textbooks of Dogmatic Theology," *The Catholic Biblical Quarterly,* XI (April, 1949), 151-64.

Vawter, Bruce, "Biblical Interpretations and the Positive Sciences," *The Homiletic and Pastoral Review,* LXI (September, 1961), 1127-38.

Vawter, Bruce, *The Bible in the Church.* New York: Sheed & Ward, 1959.

VI. BIBLICAL THEOLOGY

* DeDietrich, Suzanne, *God's Unfolding Purpose.* Translated by Robert McAfee Brown. Philadelphia: The Westminster Press, 1960.

Gelin, Albert, *The Key Concepts of the Old Testament.* Translated by George Lamb. New York: Sheed & Ward, 1955.

Giblet, J. (ed.), *The God of Israel, The God of Christians.* Translated by Kathryn Sullivan, R.S.C.J. New York: Desclee Company, 1961.

Guillet, Jacques, *Themes of the Bible.* Translated by Albert LaMothe, Jr. Notre Dame: Fides Publishers Association, 1960.

Heinisch, Paul, *Theology of the Old Testament.* Translated by William Heidt. Collegeville, Minn.: The Liturgical Press, 1950.

* An asterisk indicates a non-Catholic author

* Jacob, Edmond, *Theology of the Old Testament.* Translated by Arthur W. Heathcote and Philip J. Allcock. New York: Harper & Row Publishers, Inc., 1958.
Leon-Dufour, Xavier, *et al. Vocabulaire de Théologie Biblique.* Paris: Les Éditions du Cerf, 1962.
MacKenzie, Roderick A. F., "The Concept of Biblical Theology," *Proceedings of the Catholic Theological Society of America* (1955), pp. 48-66.
McKenzie, John L., *The Two-Edged Sword.* Milwaukee: The Bruce Publishing Company, 1956.
McKenzie, John L., "The Word of God in the Old Testament," *Theological Studies,* XXI (June, 1960), 183-206.
* Wright, G. Ernest, *God Who Acts.* London: SCM Press Ltd., 1952.

VII. SALVATION-HISTORY

Barrosse, Thomas, "Christianity: Mystery of Love," *The Catholic Biblical Quarterly,* XX (April, 1958), 137-72.
Daniélou, Jean, *Christ and Us.* Translated by Walter Roberts. New York: Sheed & Ward, 1961.
Daniélou, Jean, "The Sacraments and the History of Salvation," *The Liturgy and the Word of God,* pp. 21-32. Collegeville, Minn.: The Liturgical Press, 1959.
Dheilly, Joseph, "The History of Salvation in the Bible," *Lumen Vitae,* X (January-March, 1955), 31-44.
Hassveldt, Roger, *The Church, A Divine Mystery.* Translated by William Storey. Chicago: Fides Publishers Association, 1954.
Journet, Charles, "The Mysterious Destinies of Israel," *The Bridge,* II (1956-57), 35-90.
Jungmann, Joseph A., "Liturgy and the History of Salvation," *Lumen Vitae,* X (April-September, 1955), 261-68.
Kugelman, Richard, "Central Theme of the Old Testament," *The Homiletic and Pastoral Review,* L (April, 1950), 631-35; "Sacred History," *ibid.,* (May, 1950), 727-32; "Unfolding God's Plan," *ibid.,* (June, 1950), 816-21.
Liege, P. A., "The Mystery of the Church," *Theology Library.* Edited by A. M. Henry. V, 311-415. Chicago: Fides Publishers Association, 1958.
Norris, Frank B., *God's Own People.* Baltimore: Helicon Press, 1962.
Rochford, Vincent, "The Plan of God," *Pattern of Scripture,* pp. 23-69. New York: Sheed & Ward, 1959.
Vagaggini, Cyprian, *Theological Dimensions of the Liturgy,* pp. 3-12. Translated by Leonard J. Doyle. Collegeville, Minn.: The Liturgical Press, 1959.
Vawter, Bruce, "Our God is the God of History," *Worship,* XXXII (March, 1958), 225-33; (April, 1958), 287-300.

VIII. BIBLICAL INSPIRATION AND LITERARY FORMS

Benoit, Pierre, "Inspiration," *Guide to the Bible,* I, 9-52; also "Scriptural Inspiration," in Paul Synave and Pierre Benoit, *Prophecy and Inspiration,* pp. 84-168. Translated by Avery Dulles and Thomas Sheridan. New York: Desclee Company, 1961.
Fisher, J. A., *Jonas and the Whale.* Paterson, N. J.: St. Anthony's Guild, 1959.
Forestell, J. Terrence, "The Limitation of Inerrancy," *The Catholic Biblical Quarterly,* XX (January, 1958), 9-18.
Giblin, Charles H., "As it is written . . . A Basic Problem in Noematics and Its Relevance to Biblical Theology," *The Catholic Biblical Quarterly,* XX (July, 1958), 327-53.
Jones, Alexander, "Biblical Inspiration: A Christian Rendezvous?" *Theology Digest,* VIII (Winter, 1960), 13-14.
Lauer, Quentin, "The Genius of Biblical Thought," *The Bridge,* II (1956-57), 191-211.
LeFrois, Bernard J., "The Semitic Thought-Pattern in Sacred Scripture," *The American Ecclesiastical Review,* CXXXIV (June, 1956), 374-94.
MacKenzie, Roderick A. F., "Some Problems in the Field of Inspiration," *The Catholic Biblical Quarterly,* XX (January, 1958), 1-8.
McKenzie, John L., "The Social Character of Inspiration," *The Catholic Biblical Quarterly,* XXIV (April, 1962), 115-24.
Rahner, Karl, "The Inspiration of Scripture," *Theology Digest,* VIII (Winter, 1960), 8-12.

* An asterisk indicates a non-Catholic author

Stanley, David M., "The Concept of Biblical Inspiration," *Proceedings of the Catholic Theological Society of America* (1958), pp. 65-89.
Vawter, Bruce, *The Bible is Different*. Paterson, N. J.: St. Anthony's Guild, 1959.

IX. BIBLICAL HISTORY

* Albright, William F., *From the Stone Age to Christianity*, 2d ed. New York: Doubleday Anchor Books, 1957.
* Albright, William F., *The Biblical Period*. Pittsburgh: Biblical Colloquium, 1950.
* Bright, John, *Early Israel in Recent History Writing*. London: SCM Press Ltd., 1956.
* Bright, John, *A History of Israel*. Philadelphia: The Westminster Press, 1959.
Daniel-Rops, H., *Israel and the Ancient World*. Translated by K. Madge. London: Eyre & Spottiswoode, 1949.
Heinisch, Paul, *History of the Old Testament*. Translated by William Heidt. Collegeville, Minn.: The Liturgical Press, 1952.
Montjuvin, Jacques, *Panorama of Biblical History*. Translated by Terence W. Gervais. Paris: Les Editions de l'Ecole, 1958.
* Noth, Martin. *The History of Israel*, 2d rev. ed. New York: Harper & Brothers, 1960.
Ricciotti, Giuseppe, *The History of Israel*, Translated by Clement Della Penta and Richard T. A. Murphy. 2 vols. Milwaukee: The Bruce Publishing Company, 1955.
* Wright, G. Ernest, "Bringing Old Testament Times to Life," *The National Geographic Magazine*, CXII (December, 1957), 833-64.
* Wright, G. Ernest, "The Last Thousand Years Before Christ," *The National Geographic Magazine*, CXVIII (December, 1960), 812-53.
* Wright, G. Ernest, *The Old Testament Against Its Environment*. London: SCM Press Ltd., 1950.

X. DOCUMENTS RELATED TO THE OLD TESTAMENT

* Pritchard, James B. (ed.), *The Ancient Near East. An Anthology of Texts and Pictures*. Princeton: Princeton University Press, 1958.
* Pritchard, James B. (ed.), *Ancient Near Eastern Texts Relating to the Old Testament*. 2d ed. Princeton: Princeton University Press, 1955.
* Thomas, D. Winton (ed.), *Documents From Old Testament Times*. New York: Harper & Row, Publishers, Inc., 1961.

XI. BIBLICAL ARCHAEOLOGY

* Albright, William F., *Archaeology of Palestine*. Baltimore: Penguin Books, 1960.
* Albright, William F., *Archaeology and the Religion of Israel*. 3d ed. Baltimore: Johns Hopkins Press, 1953.
* Albright, William F., *Recent Discoveries in Bible Lands*. Pittsburgh: Biblical Colloquium, 1955.
* Burrows, Millar, *What Mean These Stones?* New York: Meridian Books, 1957.
DuBuit, M., *Biblical Archaeology*. Translated by Kathleen Pond. New York: Hawthorn Books, Publishers, 1960.
* Finegan, Jack, *Light From the Ancient Past*. 2d ed. Princeton: Princeton University Press, 1959.
* Glueck, Nelson, *Rivers in the Desert. A History of the Negev*. New York: Grove Press, Inc., 1960.
* Gray, John, *Archaeology and the Old Testament World*. New York: Thomas Nelson and Sons, 1962.
* Kenyon, Kathleen M., *Archaeology in the Holy Land*. New York: Frederick A. Praeger, Publishers, 1960.
* Pritchard, James B. *Archaeology and the Old Testament*. Princeton: Princeton University Press, 1958.
* Pritchard, James B., *Gibeon: Where the Sun Stood Still*. Princeton: Princeton University Press, 1962.
Steve, M. J., *The Living World of the Bible*. Translated by Daphne Woodward. Cleveland: The World Publishing Company, 1961.

* An asterisk indicates a non-Catholic author

* Wooley, Leonard, *The Art of the Middle East*. New York: Crown Publishers, Inc., 1961.
* Wright, G. Ernest, *Biblical Archaeology*. Philadelphia: The Westminster Press, 1957.

XII. BIBLICAL GEOGRAPHY

DuBuit, M., *Geographie de la Terre Sainte*. 2 vols. Paris: Les Editions du Cerf, 1958.
Grollenberg, L. H., *Atlas of the Bible*. Translated and edited by Joyce M. H. Reid and H. H. Rowley. New York: Thomas Nelson and Sons, 1956.
Grollenberg, L. H., *Shorter Atlas of the Bible*. Translated by Mary F. Hedlund. New York: Thomas Nelson and Sons, 1959.
* Kraeling, Emil G., *Bible Atlas*. New York: Rand McNally, 1957.
* May, Herbert G. (ed.), *Oxford Bible Atlas*. New York: Oxford University Press, 1962.
* Wright, G. Ernest and F. V. Filson, *The Westminster Historical Atlas of the Bible*. 2d ed. Philadelphia: The Westminster Press, 1956.

XIII. THE PENTATEUCH

Ahern, Barnabas M., "The Exodus, Then and Now," *The Bridge*, I (1955), 53-74.
Albertson, James, "Genesis I and the Babylonian Creation Myth," *Thought*, XXXVII (Summer, 1962), 226-44.
Arbez, Edward P., "Genesis I-XI and Prehistory," *The American Ecclesiastical Review*, CXXIII (August, 1950), 81-92; (September, 1950), 202-13; (October, 1950), 284-94.
Arbez, Edward P. and John P. Weisengoff, "Exegetical Notes on Genesis 1:1-2," *The Catholic Biblical Quarterly*, X (April, 1948), 140-50.
Asselin, David T., "The Notion of Dominion in Genesis 1-3," *The Catholic Biblical Quarterly*, XVI (July, 1954), 277-94.
Burghardt, Walter J., "On Early Christian Exegesis," *Theological Studies*, XI (March, 1950), 78-116.
De Fraine, Jean, *The Bible and the Origin of Man*. New York: Desclee Company, 1962.
Dubarle, A. M., "History and Myth in Genesis," *Theology Digest*, VI (Spring, 1958), 95-99.
Glanzmann, George S., *The Book of Deuteronomy*. 2 parts. New York: The Paulist Press, 1960.
Hauret, Charles, *Beginnings: Genesis and Modern Science*. Dubuque, Iowa: The Priory Press, 1955.
Hennig, J., "First Chapter of Genesis in the Liturgy," *The Catholic Biblical Quarterly*, X (October, 1948), 360-75.
Hessler, Bertram, *The Bible in the Light of Modern Science*. Translated by Sylvester Saller. Chicago: Franciscan Herald Press, 1960.
Hunt, Ignatius, *The Book of Genesis*. 2 parts. New York: The Paulist Press, 1960.
Johnson, Humphrey J. T., *The Bible and Early Man*. New York: The Declan X. McMullen Company, Inc., 1948.
MacKenzie, Roderick A. F., "Before Abraham Was," *The Catholic Biblical Quarterly*, XV (April, 1953), 131-40.
MacKenzie, Roderick A. F., "Divine Soliloquies in Genesis," *The Catholic Biblical Quarterly*, XVI (April, 1955), 277-86.
Maly, Eugene H., "Worship in the 'Priestly Tradition'," *Bible, Life and Worship. Proceedings of the Twenty-second Annual North American Liturgical Week* (1961), pp. 247-54.
McKenzie, John L., "Divine Sonship of Israel and the Covenant," *The Catholic Biblical Quarterly*, VIII (July, 1946), 320-31.
McKenzie, John L., "God and Nature in the Old Testament," *The Catholic Biblical Quarterly*, XIV (January, 1952), 18-39; (April, 1952), 124-45.
McKenzie, John L., "Literary Characteristics of Genesis 2-3," *Theological Studies*, XV (December, 1954), 541-72.
McKenzie, John L., "Myth and the Old Testament," *The Catholic Biblical Quarterly*, XXI (July, 1959), 265-82.
Moriarty, Frederick L., *The Book of Numbers*. 2 parts. New York: The Paulist Press, 1960.
Moriarty, Frederick L. and W. G. Guindon, "Genesis and Scientific Studies on the Origin of the World," *The Catholic Biblical Quarterly*, XII (October, 1950), 428-38.

* An asterisk indicates a non-Catholic author

Murphy, Roland E., *The Book of Exodus*. 2 parts. New York: The Paulist Press, 1960.
* Neher, André, *Moses and the Vocation of the Jewish People*. Translated by Irene Marinoff. London: Longmans Green & Co. Ltd., 1959.
Stuhlmueller, Carroll, *The Book of Leviticus*. New York: The Paulist Press, 1960.
Vawter, Bruce, *God's Story of Creation*. St. Louis: Knights of Columbus, 1955.
Vawter, Bruce, *A Path Through Genesis*. New York: Sheed & Ward, 1956.
* Von Rad, Gerhard, *Genesis. A Commentary*. Translated by John H. Marks. Philadelphia: The Westminster Press, 1961.

XIV. THE PROPHETS AND MESSIANISM

* Anderson, Bernhard and Walter Harrelson, (eds.), *Israel's Prophetic Heritage*. New York: Harper & Row Publishers, Inc., 1962.
Bourke, Joseph, "The Wonderful Counselor," *The Catholic Biblical Quarterly*, XXII (April, 1960), 123-43.
Cerfaux, L., *et al.*, *L'Attente du Messie*. Paris: Desclee de Brouwer, 1954.
Chaine, J., *God's Heralds*. Translated by Brendan McGrath. New York: Joseph Wagner, Inc., 1955.
Chouraqui, André, "The Messiah of Israel," *Cross Currents*, XI (Fall, 1961), 331-43.
Coleran, James E., "Prophets and Sacrifice," *Theological Studies*, V (December, 1944), 411-38.
Crowley, Edward J., *The Books of Lamentations, Baruch, Sophonia, Nahum & Habacuc*. New York: The Paulist Press, 1962.
DeGuglielmo, Antonine, "The Fertility of the Land in the Messianic Prophecies," *The Catholic Biblical Quarterly*, XIX (July, 1957), 306-11.
Dheilly, Joseph, *The Prophets*. Translated by Rachel Attwater. New York: Hawthorn Books, Publishers, 1960.
Flanagan, Neal, *The Book of Jeremia*. 2 parts. New York: The Paulist Press, 1961.
Flanagan, Neal, "Messianic Fulfillment in St. Paul," *The Catholic Biblical Quarterly*," XIX (October, 1957), 474-84.
* Heaton, E. W. *The Old Testament Prophets*. Baltimore: Penguin Books, 1961.
Huesman, John E., *The Book of Isaia*. 2 parts. New York: The Paulist Press, 1961.
MacKenzie, Roderick A. F., "The Messianism of Deuteronomy," *The Catholic Biblical Quarterly*, XIX (July, 1957), 299-305.
Maly, Eugene H., "Messianism in Osee," *The Catholic Biblical Quarterly*, XIX (April, 1957), 213-25.
McKenzie, John L., "Royal Messianism," *The Catholic Biblical Quarterly*, XIX (January, 1957), 25-52.
Moriarty, Frederick L., "The Emmanuel Prophecies," *The Catholic Biblical Quarterly*, XIX (April, 1957), 226-33.
Moriarty, Frederick L., "The Prophets: Bearers of the Word," *The Bridge*, III (1958-59), 54-83.
Murphy, Roland E., "Notes on Old Testament Messianism and Apologetics," *The Catholic Biblical Quarterly*, XIX (January, 1957), 5-15.
Peifer, Claude, "Anointing in the Old Testament," *Worship*, XXXV (October, 1961), 577-86; "Jesus the Anointed of Israel" *ibid.*, (December, 1961), 26-35; "The Anointing of the Christian," *ibid.*, (March, 1962), 234-42.
Siegman, Edward F., *The Book of Ezechiel*. 2 parts. New York: The Paulist Press, 1961.
Strange, Marcian, *The Books of Amos, Osee & Michea*. New York: The Paulist Press, 1961.
Stuhlmueller, Carroll, *The Books of Aggai, Zacharia, Malachia, Jona, Joel, Abdia*. New York: The Paulist Press, 1961.
Vawter, Bruce, *The Conscience of Israel*. New York: Sheed & Ward, 1961.
Vawter, Bruce, "In Many Fragmentary Utterances; the Use of Messianic Prophecy in Apologetics," *Proceeding of the Catholic Theological Society of America* (1959), 97-119.

XV. THE WISDOM LITERATURE

* Baumgartner, W., "The Wisdom Literature," *The Old Testament and Modern Study*, pp. 210-35. Edited by H. H. Rowley. London: Oxford University Press, 1961.
Bourke, Myles M., *The Book of Job*. 2 parts. New York: The Paulist Press, 1962.

* An asterisk indicates a non-Catholic author

Forestell, J. Terrence, *The Book of Proverbs*. New York: The Paulist Press, 1960.
Hessler, Bertram, "Koheleth: the Veiled God," *The Bridge*, I (1955), 191-203.
Hennig, J., "Book of Wisdom in the Liturgy," *The Catholic Biblical Quarterly*, XIV (July, 1952), 233-36.
Maly, Eugene, *The Book of Wisdom*. New York: The Paulist Press, 1962.
Murphy, Roland E., *Seven Books of Wisdom*. Milwaukee: The Bruce Publishing Company, 1960.
Murphy, Roland E., *The Book of Ecclesiastes and The Canticle of Canticles*. New York: The Paulist Press, 1961.
Siebeneck, Robert T., "The Midrash of Wisdom 10-19," *The Catholic Biblical Quarterly*, XXII (April, 1960), 176-82.
Skehan, Patrick W., "Borrowings from the Psalms in the Book of Wisdom," *The Catholic Biblical Quarterly*, X (October, 1948), 384-87.
Skehan, Patrick W., "Isaia and the Teaching of the Book of Wisdom," *The Catholic Biblical Quarterly*, II (October, 1940), 289-99.
Stanley, David M., "Israel's Wisdom Meets the Wisdom of God," *Worship*, XXXII (April, 1958), 280-87.

XVI. THE PSALMS

St. Augustine, *On the Psalms*. Translated by Dame Scholastica Hebgin and Dame Felicitas Corrigan. *Ancient Christian Writers: Numbers* 29-30. Westminster, Md.: The Newman Press, 1960-61.
Arbez, Edward P., "Recent Publications on the Psalms," *The American Ecclesiastical Review*, CXIX (August, 1948), 105-14; (September, 1948), 187-95.
Bea, Augustine, "New Psalter: Its Origin and Spirit," *The Catholic Biblical Quarterly*, VII (January, 1946), 4-35.
Bouyer, Louis, *Liturgical Piety*, pp. 229-42. Notre Dame: University of Notre Dame Press, 1955.
Fischer, Balthasar, "Christ in the Psalms," *Theology Digest*, I (Winter, 1953), 53-57.
Gelin, Albert, *The Religion of Israel*, pp. 43-63. Translated by J. B. Foster. New York: Hawthorn Books, Publishers, 1959.
Gelin, Albert, "The Prayer of the Biblical Man," *Worship*, XXXVI (February, 1962), 151-63.
Guichon, P., *Les Psaumes Commentés par la Bible*. 3 vols. Paris: Editions du Cerf, 1958.
Kissane, Edward J., *The Book of Psalms*. 2 vols. Westminster, Md.: The Newman Press, 1953-54.
McKenzie, John L., *The Two-Edged Sword*, pp. 265-85. Milwaukee: The Bruce Publishing. Company, 1956.
Merton, Thomas, *Bread in the Wilderness*. New York: New Directions, 1953.
Merton, Thomas, *Praying the Psalms*. Collegeville, Minn.: The Liturgical Press, 1956.
Murphy, Roland E., *Seven Books of Wisdom*, pp. 28-52. Milwaukee: The Bruce Publishing Company, 1960.
Sorg, Dom Rembert, *God's Love Songs*. 2d ed. revised. St. Louis: Pio Decimo Press, 1954.
Sorg, Dom Rembert, *Hesed and Hasid in the Psalms*. St. Louis: Pio Decimo Press, 1953.
Stuhlmueller, Carroll, "The Psalms and Spiritual Formation," and "Learning the Psalms Through Community Worship," *Bible, Life, and Worship. Twenty-second Annual North American Liturgical Week*, pp. 128-30, 255-69. Washington, D. C.: The Liturgical Conference, 1961.
Worden, Thomas, *The Psalms are Christian Prayer*. New York: Sheed & Ward, 1962.

XVII. THE DEAD SEA SCROLLS

Ahern, Barnabas M., "Gathering the Fragments: Of Qumran Literature," *Worship*, XXXV (November, 1961), 652-56.
Arbez, Edward P., "The Dead Sea Scrolls," *Guide to the Bible*, I, 113-23.
Briggs, Lyman J. and Kenneth F. Weaver, "How Old is It?" *The National Geographic Magazine*, CXIV (August, 1958), 234-55.
Brown, Raymond E., "The Messianism of Qumran," *The Catholic Biblical Quarterly*, XIX (January, 1957), 53-82.

* Burrows, Millar, *The Dead Sea Scrolls.* New York: The Viking Press, 1955.
* Burrows, Millar, *More Light on the Dead Sea Scrolls.* New York: The Viking Press, 1958.
Carmignac, Jean, *Christ and the Teacher of Righteousness.* Baltimore: Helicon Press, 1962.
* Cross, Frank M., "The Manuscripts of the Dead Sea Caves," *The Biblical Archaeologist,* XVII (February, 1954), 2-21.
* Cross, Frank M., *The Ancient Library of Qumran and Modern Biblical Studies.* 2d ed. revised. New York: Doubleday & Company, Inc., 1961.
Daniélou, Jean, *The Dead Sea Scrolls and Primitive Christianity.* Translated by Salvator Attanasio. Baltimore: Helicon Press, 1958.
DeVaux, Roland, *L'Archeologie el les manuscripts de la Mer Morte.* New York: Oxford University Press, 1961.
* Finegan, Jack, *Light From the Ancient Past,* 2d ed, pp. 263-97. Princeton: Princeton University Press, 1959.
Fitzmyer, Joseph A., "The Date of the Qumran Scrolls," *America,* CIV (March 18,1961), 780-81.
* Gaster, Theodor H., *The Dead Sea Scriptures in English Translation.* New York: Doubleday & Company, Inc., 1956.
Graystone, Geoffrey, *The Dead Sea Scrolls and the Originality of Christ.* New York: Sheed & Ward, 1956.
Guindon, W. J., "Radioactive Carbon and the Dead Sea Scrolls," *The Catholic Biblical Quarterly,* XIII (July, 1951), 268-75.
McCarthy, Dennis J., "Qumran and Christian Beginnings," *Theology Digest,* V (Winter, 1957), 39-46.
Milik, J. T., *Ten Years of Discovery in the Wilderness of Judaea.* Translated by J. Strugnell. London: SCM Press. Distributed in the USA by Allensons, Naperville, Illinois, 1959.
Murphy, Roland E., *The Dead Sea Scrolls and the Bible.* Westminster, Md.: The Newman Press, 1956.
Murphy, Roland E. "Insights into the New Testament from the Dead Sea Scrolls," *The American Ecclesiastical Review,* CXXXV (July, 1956), 9-22.
Murphy, Roland E., "The Dead Sea Scrolls and New Testament Comparisons," *The Catholic Biblical Quarterly,* XVIII (July, 1956), 263-72.
Oesterreicher, John M., "The Community of Qumran," *The Bridge,* II (1956-57), 91-134.
Skehan, Patrick W., "The Period of the Biblical Texts from Khirbet Qumran," *The Catholic Biblical Quarterly,* XIX (October, 1957), 435-40.
Sutcliff, Edmund, *The Monks of Qumran.* Westminster, Md.: The Newman Press, 1960.
* Tushingham, A. Douglas, "The Men Who Hid the Dead Sea Scrolls," *The National Geographic Magazine,* CXIV (December, 1958), 785-808.
Van der Ploeg, J., *The Excavations at Qumran.* Translated by K. Smyth. New York: Longmans, Green and Co., 1958.

XVIII. PERIODICALS

The Bible Today. Collegeville, Minn.: The Liturgical Press.	Bi-monthly
Bible et Terre Sainte. Paris: Maison de la Bonne Presse.	Monthly
Bible et Vie Chretienne. Paris: Castermann.	Bi-monthly
The Biblical Archaeologist. New Haven, Conn.: American School of Oriental Research.	Quarterly
The Bridge. New York: Pantheon Books.	Annually
The Catholic Biblical Quarterly. Washington, D. C.: The Catholic Biblical Association of America.	
New Testament Abstracts. Weston, Mass.: Weston College.	3 times annually
Theology Digest. St. Mary's Kansas: St. Mary's College.	4 times annually
Worship. Collegeville, Minn.: The Liturgical Press.	Monthly

*An asterisk indicates a non-Catholic author

INDEX

INDEX

AARON, 25, 103, 250, 252
Abel, 63-64
Abiam, 145
Abner, 127-28
Abraham:
  covenant with, 43, 73, 130
  death, 252
  journey to Canaan, 71
  origin, 71
  "our father", 69
  polygamy, 71
  receives Word of God, 68
  sacrifice of Isaac, 73
  virtues, 74
  wanderings, 47, 78
Abram, (see also Abraham), 21
Absalom, 129
Accadians, 71
Achab, 136-40
Achaz, 145, 148-49, 152
Actium, Battle of, 184
Acts of the Apostles, 246
Adam:
  Eve, 56
  fall, 59-62
  "image and likeness of God," 55-56
  life-span, 65
  name, 55
  New Adam, 92
  origin, 55-56
  original justice, 57
Adama, 118
Adar, Month of, 105
Adonai, 81
Adonia, 129
Aelfric, 8, 261
Aeschylus, 256
Agar, 71-72
Aggai, 167
Ahern, Barnabas M., 92n
Ahia, 134
Aialon, 119
Ain Feshka, 246
Ain Qadeis, 116
Albright, William F., 45, 46n, 51n, 53n, 69n, 80n, 81n, 87, 90n, 127n, 131n, 141n, 142-43, 161, 172, 184-85, 187n, 193n
Aldhelm, 7, 261
Alexander the Great, 174-76, 258

Alexander Janneus, 181, 191
Alexandra, 175, 183, 189
Alexandria, 42, 176, 258
Alfred, King, 261
Alt, Albrecht, 90, 90n
Amazia, 141, 147
Ambrose, St., 95
Amenophis I, 78
Amenophis IV, 78
Ammonites, 73, 129
Ammorites, 71
Amon, 154
Amos, 28, 141, 237:
  and God of Justice, 142, 197
  life and vocation, 142
  oracles, 142
  universalism, 142-43
Amphictyony, 123
Anathoth, 15
Anawim, 22, 153
Anderson, Bernhard W., 82n
Angels, 164-65, 178, 253
Anna, 22
Anthony, 184
Anthropomorphism, 50-51, 54-55
Antioch, 177
Antiochus III, 176
Antiochus IV (Epiphanes), 176-77, 179-82, 212
Antiochus V, 181
Antiochus VII, 181, 246
Antipater, 182
Aphek, 124
Aphorisms, 33, 76, 218
'Apiru, 71, 79
Apocalypse, 39
Apocalyptic Genre, 37-39
Apocrypha, 258, 258n
Apocryphal, 38, 254, 258n
Appolonius, 180
Aqaba, Gulf of, 117, 147
Aquila, 259
Araba, Valley of, 117
Arabia, 215
Arad, 116
Aramaic, 172
Arameans, 46, 136
Arbez, E. P., 83, 83n
Archelaus, 185

Aretas, 182
Aristobolus I, 181, 182
Aristobolus II, 182, 189
Aristophanes, 256
Aristotle, 175, 214
Ark of the Covenant:
  brought to Jerusalem by David, 128
  loss of, 166
  and professions of faith, 114
  in southern kingdom, 134-35
  taken by Philistines, 124
  and Yom Kippur, 105
Arnold, Franz X., 17n
Arnon river, 117
Artaxerxes I, 170, 174
Artaxerxes II, 170
Artaxerxes III, 170, 174
Asa, 146
Asamonaios, 181
Asaph, 229
Asherat, 115
Asheroth, 137, 140
Ashurbanapal, 153-54
Assyria:
  aid to Juda, 148, 200
  and defeat of Jehu, 140
  destruction of Israel, 134, 144-45
  end, 153-54
  invasion of Juda, 147
  rise, 136
Astarte, 114-15, 136-37, 164
Astruc, Jean, 10
Atargatis, 172
Athalia, 137, 146-47
Athanasius Yeshue Samuel, 242
Aton, 78
Augustine, St., 7, 89, 94-96, 109
Authors, Biblical (*see also* Inspiration, Genres):
  patrons, 230
Auvray, Paul, 3n
Avaris, 79
Azaria, 147

BAAL:
  cult under Achab and Jezebel, 136-37
  cult under Athalia, 146
  danger of confusion with Yahweh, 135
  end of cult in Samaria, 139
  pagan worship, 114-15
  sacrifice under Jehu, 140
Baalath, 114
Baasa, 136, 146
Babal, 68
Babel, Tower:
  Mesopotamian background of story, 67-68
  purpose of story, 68
Babylon:
  origin of empire, 154
  victory of Cyrus, 169
Babylonian Exile:
  beginning, 21, 161-62
  Biblical literature, 33, 44

book of Daniel, 178, 212
  devastation of Juda, 134, 161
  Diaspora, 171-72
  Ezechiel, 115, 164-68
  instrument of Yahweh, 210
  number of deportees, 162
  religious revival, 163-64
  return of Jews, 169-70
  social conditions during, 162-63
  Wisdom literature, 217
"Babylonian Job," 215, 219
Balaam, 108-10
Balac, 109
Baldah, 219
Ban, 115
Baptism:
  circumcision, 72
  prefigured by the Exodus, 95-96, 97 (*table*)
  prefigured by the Flood, 93, 96
Bardy, G., 256n, 258n
Bar Galgola, Joshua, 245
Bar Kokhba, Simon (Ben Koseba), 185n, 189, 245, 249
Baruch, 157, 216-17
Bathsheba, 129
Bede, 7, 261
Bedouins, 247
Benedict XV, Pope, 12
Ben Gurion, David, 83, 83n
Ben-Hadad I, 146
Benoit, Pierre, 29, 29n, 31n, 32n
Berith, 77
Berosus, 65
Bethel, 119, 135, 140:
  conquest, 119
Bethlehem, 209, 242
Beth-shan, 127
Beth-shemesh, 141
Beth-zur, 180
Bettenson, Henry, 8n
Bible:
  Christians and, 1-17
  early Church, 4-5
  historical-literary criticism, 9-11
  liturgy, 5-6
  Persian Period, 173
  Reformation, 7-8
  Renaissance, 6
  Tradition, 2-4
  vernacular, 8-9, 261-62
Biblical Commission, 12-13, 13n, 49-50, 50n, 229
Biblical Institute, 12
Biblical theology, 19-20
Biot, René, 58n
Bitter Lakes, 84
Boismard, M. E., 92n
Bossuet, Jacques, 10, 24
Bourke, Myles M., 62n, 81, 219n
Bouyer, Louis, 3n, 7n, 142n, 143
Bright, John, 66n, 83n, 84, 85n, 90n, 117, 121n, 127n, 141n, 163n, 170, 171n, 187n
Brinton, Crane, 7n

Brown, Raymond E., 178n, 212n
Brunet, Achille, 178n
Burghardt, Walter, 3n

CADES, 116
Caedmon, 7, 261
Caesar, Julius, 175, 183
Cain and Abel:
  purpose of story, 63-64
Cainan, 65
Calvin, John, 7
Canaan:
  conquest and settlement, 21, 76, 102, 120
  literary influence, 53-54, 215
  promised to Patriarchs, 47
  religion, 102, 114-15, 140
Canon, 29, 194, 217, 258
Canticle of Canticles, 216-17
Carchemish, 155
Castellion, 246
Catholic Biblical Association of America, 12, 12n
Causes, Kinds of, 30-31
Caxton, 8
Cazelles, H., 172n
Chaeronea, Battle of, 174
Chaldeans, 154
Challoner, Richard, 262
Charlier, Celestin, 6n, 33n
Chemosh, 115, 136
Christ (*see* Jesus)
Christian Faith:
  meaning, 17
  reasonableness, 17-18
  and Revelation, 16-18
Chronicles, Books of, 126, 170-71
Church:
  and Bible, 1-18
  Kingdom of God, 23
  Mystical Body, 23
  New Israel, 25
  sign and witness of God's presence, 17
  Tradition, 2-4
Circumcision:
  sign of covenant, 72
  forbidden by Antiochus IV, 177
Clarkson, John, 57n
Clement, St., 4
Cleopatra, 175, 184
Codex Alexandrinus, 258
Codex Sinaiticus, 258
Codex Vaticanus, 258
Collin, Remy, 58n
Commandments, Ten:
  Catholic, Lutheran, and Jewish division, 89 (*table*)
  explanation, 88-89
  original form, 89
  our response to love of God, 24
"Confessions of Jeremia," 157
Coppens, J., 10n
Core, Sons of, 229
Corte, Nicolas, 54n, 57n

Cosmogony, Semitic:
  explanation, 51 (*figure*)
Council of Jerusalem, 188
Covenant:
  with Abraham, 43, 69-72
  compared with marriage, 143
  cosmic, 47
  and Essenes, 191
  Ezechiel and New, 166
  Jeremia and New, 157-60
  observance under Jeroboam II, 141
  Old prepared for New, 88, 92-93, 201
  parity and suzerainty, 87-88
  renewal under Ezechia, 149
  renewal under Josia, 154
  at Sinai, 21, 43, 77, 87-88
Coverdale, Miles, 7, 261
Creation:
  Assyrian myths, 154
  Babylonian myth, 57
  cosmic and human, 20-21
  days, 55
  Genesis account, 43, 53-57
  monotheism vs. polytheism, 53-54
  Priestly Tradition, 54, 168
  Yahwist Tradition, 55
Credo, Hebrew, 46-47, 77, 113-14, 171
Cyril of Jerusalem, St., 95
Cyrus, 126, 169, 198
Cyrus cylinder, 169

DAMASCUS, 136, 140, 148
Damasus, Pope, 259
Dan, 135, 140
Daniel, Book of, 177-179, 251
Daniélou, Jean, 24n, 63n, 67n, 92n, 92-93, 93n, 94
Dante, 36
Darius I, 174
Darius II, 174
David:
  Ark of the Covenant, 128, 189
  "blessings of Jacob," 76
  "court history," 125
  defeat of Philistines, 128
  Dynastic Oracle, 130, 209
  edition of Biblical works, 33
  Goliath incident, 127n
  "ideal king," 129, 199
  Moses, 129
  Psalms, 228-30, 237
  "David redivivus," 199
  rule, 128-30
  Saul, 127-38
  Servant of Yahweh, 129
  Yahwist Tradition, 44, 55
Davis, Charles, 17n
Day of Atonement, 105-06
"Day of the Lord," 38
"Day of Yahweh," 197
Dead Sea Scrolls:
  age of manuscripts, 248-49
  carbon 14, 248

Dead Sea Scrolls (*cont'd.*)
  ceramic index, 248
  Christianity, 249-55
  contents, 243, 245-47, 249-53
  diary related to findings, 242-47
  Essenes, 190-91, 242, 253-55
  paleography, 248
  "scriptorium," 248
  "Teacher of Righteousness," 190, 249, 251-
    53
Debir, 141
Decalogue (*see also* Ten Commandments),
    88, 197
De Fraine, Jean, 13n, 56n, 58n, 59n
Deism, 9n
Dejaifve, G., 3n
De Langhe, Father, 246
Demetrius I, 181
Demetrius II, 181
Demetrius III, 182
Demosthenes, 256
Determinism, 191
Deuterocanonical Books, 258n
Deuteronomic Reform, 111, 126, 154-55, 160
Deuteronomic Theology of History, 45, 111,
    117, 121, 140, 155
Deuteronomic Tradition, 44-45, 89, 104,
    111-15
Deuteronomy, Book of:
  basic elements, 45
  "Book of the Law," 154
  compilation, 11
  content, 43, 111
  cultic credo, 113-14
  Dead Sea Scrolls, 245
  freedom of divine election, 69, 112
  origin and spirit, 111-12
  pagan places of worship, 114-15
  prayer, 113
  "Second Law," 43
  style, 112
  temptations of Jesus, 93
  theme, 111-12
De Vault, Joseph, 120n
De Vaux, Roland, 82n, 103n, 104n, 131n,
    233n
Dheilly, Joseph, 17n, 193n
Diaspora, 171-72, 188, 258
Digges, Sr. M. Laurentia, 121n
Divine Election, 69, 112
"Divino Afflante Spiritu," 3n, 13-15, 28n,
    32n, 35n, 36, 36n, 38n, 231, 231n
Domitian, 185
Drioton, Etienne, 54n, 80n
Dubarle, A. M., 61n
Dupont, Jacques, 13n
Dynastic Oracle, 130, 209
Dyson, R. A., 10n

ECCLESIASTES, BOOK OF,   216, 222-23
Ecole Biblique, 12
Eden, Garden of, 57
Edom, 74, 84, 116-17, 129, 147-48, 215

Egypt:
  defeat at Paneas, 176
  Exodus events, 42, 77-78, 81-85
  Hebrew bondage, 79
  Hyksos rule, 75
  Joseph, 74-76
  Moses, 80
  Plagues, 81-82, 138
  Typology, 93, 95-99
  Wisdom literature, 214-15, 219, 221
Ela, 136
Elamites, 71
Elephantine, 171-72
Elhanan, 127n
Elia, 137-38, 192, 208
Eliphaz, 219
Eliseus, 137, 139, 192
Eliu, 220
Elohim, 44, 228
Elohist Tradition:
  Abraham, 73
  Exodus, 81 (*table*)
  Feasts, 104
  Genesis, 75-76
  Joseph, 75
  meaning, 44
  Numbers, 107, 109
  Psalms, 228
Emmanuel, 151, 208-209
Emmaus, 180, 251
Engeddi, 247
Enoch, Book of, 254
Enos, 65
Enuma elish, 53-54, 54n, 57
Ephraim and Manasses, Tribes, 76
Ephratha, 209
Epic of Gilgamesh, 66, 66n
Epithalamium, 235
Esarhaddon, 153
Esau, 74
Esdras, Fourth Book of, 38
Essenes, 190-91, 242, 253-55
Ethan, 148
Euphrates River, 78, 129, 172, 174
Euripides, 256
Eve:
  fall, 59-62
  formation from rib of Adam, 56
  promise of salvation, 62-63
Evolution:
  definition and types, 58
  Genesis, 58-59
  position of Church, 58-59
Ewer, William Norman, 112
Exodus, Book of:
  Commandments, 88-89
  contents, 42, 47-48
  covenant at Sinai, 86-88
  images and golden calf, 90
  literary form, 78-79, 86-87
  name, 77
Exodus, Event of:
  bondage in Egypt, 79, 138

Exodus, Event of (*cont'd.*)
    central point in history and faith of Israel, 21, 77-78
    crossing the sea, 84-85
    date, 83-84
    evidence for event, 78
    feast of Passover, 104
    manna and quail, 85-86
    Moses, 80, 90-91, 138
    name, 77
    number who left Egypt, 82-83
    plagues, 81-82
    Prophets, 77, 92, 158
    Psalms, 78
    route, 86 (*map*)
Exodus, Typology of:
    books of New Testament, 93-94
    Christian Patrology, 94-96
    Liturgy, 96-100, 98-99 (*table*)
Exultet, 61, 97
Ezechia:
    Emmanuel Prophecy of Isaia, 208
    king of Juda, 149-151, 152
    praised by Deuteronomic historian, 125-26
Ezechiel:
    allegory of the faithless wife, 166-67
    arrival in Babylon, 164
    "Father of Judaism," 168
    influence, 33, 167-68
    and New Covenant, 166
    parable of the Shepherds, 167
    personality and mannerisms, 164
    priest, 167
    Priestly Tradition, 168
    prophet of the Exile, 102, 164-68
    prophetic call, 164-65
    Temple, 167-68
    "Torah of Ezechiel," 167
    vision of dry bones, 167
    warnings concerning responsibility of people, 165-66
Ezion-Geber, 147-48
Ezra, 168, 170-71

FALL, THE, 57n, 59-63
Fathers of the Church, 2, 4, 62, 94-97
Faulkner, William, 36
Feasts in Israel:
    Hannukka, 105
    Harvest, weeks, first fruits, 104
    Passover, 21, 78-79, 98-99 (*table*), 104
    Pentecost, 105
    Purim, 105
    Rosh Hashanah, 105
    Sukkoth, Tabernacles, Tents, 105
    Unleavened bread, 104
    Use of Psalms, 237
    Yom Kippur, 105
Fertility, Pagan Cult (*see also* Astarte, Baal), 60, 60n, 114-15
Finegan, Jack, 79n
Fitzmyer, Joseph A., 87n
Flanagan, Neal M., 87n

Flood:
    Babylonian accounts, 64, 66
    Biblical account, 66-67
    generation before and after, 64-65
    purpose of account in Genesis, 67
    typology, 92-93, 96
Forms, Literary (*see* Genre)
Foster, R. J., 258n
Franzelin, Cardinal, 29

GABAON:
    battle of Josue, 119
    the "sun-miracle," 119-20, 120n
Gabriel, Angel, 178
Geiselmann, Joseph R., 3n
Gelin, Albert, 178n, 198n
Genealogies, Genesis account of, 64-66
Genesis, 42
Genesis, Book of:
    Abraham, Isaac, Jacob, 69-74
    anthropomorphism, 50-51
    Cain and Abel, 63-64
    contents, 47
    cosmogony, 51-52
    creation accounts, 54-55, 168
    days of creation, 55
    Dead Sea Scrolls, 243, 245
    evolution, 58-59
    flood, 66-67
    Garden of Eden, 56-57
    genealogies, 64-66
    Joseph, 74-76
    monotheism vs. polytheism, 53-54, 57
    origin of mankind, 55-57
    Original Sin, 59-62
    Patriarchal Period, 68-69
    promise of salvation, 62-63, 212
    purpose, 49
    Tower of Babel, 67-68
Geniza, 257
Genre, Literary:
    apocalyptic, 37-39, 179
    definition, 36
    historical, 39-41
    kinds, 37-41
    poetic, 37
    Pope Pius XII, 35, 231
    Psalter, 230-37
Gerizim, Mount, 185
Gesen, 75
Gibeah, 127
Gibeon (*see* Gabaon)
Giblet, J., 87n
Gilson, Etienne, 6n
Gleason, Robert W., 82n
"Glory of the Lord," 108, 166
Glueck, Nelson, 69n
God (*see also* Covenant, Yahweh):
    acts in history, 20
    Biblical Inspiration, 27-32
    choice of Abraham, 21, 69, 112
    choice of Israel, 21, 92, 112
    choice of Prophets, 194-196

God (*cont'd.*)
  Hebrew belief, 53, 82
  interest in mankind, 68, 77
  plan, 19-26
  response by individuals, 16-18, 24-25, 45
  revelation, 16-17, 138, 195-96
  teachings in Psalms, 239-40
  teaching of Prophets, 196-98
Gods, Pagan (*see* Astarte, Baal, Chemosh, Moloch)
Golden Calf, 90, 135
Golding, William, 36
Goliath, 127
Gomorra, 72
Gordon, C. H., 72n
Goshen, 75, 82
Graf, K. H., 10
Grollenberg, L. H., 79n, 84, 84n, 119n, 131n, 140n, 141n, 150n, 171n
Grossouw, W., 24n
Gruenthaner, M. J., 54n
Guardini, Romano, 17n
Guillet, Jacques, 52n, 92n
Gutenberg, Johann, 8

HABACUC, 243, 252
Habiru, 71
Haering, Bernard, 18n
Haggadah, 188
Hai, 118-19
Halakhah, 188
Hallel, 238
Hammurabi, 66-67:
  Code, 106, 106n
Hannukka, 105, 181
Haran, 69, 154
Harland, J. Penrose, 72n
Hartmann, Louis F., 59-60, 60n
Hasidim, 180, 182, 189
Hasmonean, 181, 183, 184, 190-91
Hazael, 147
"Heart of the Pentateuch," 114
Hebron, 128
Heilsgeschichte, 20, 40, 47
Heinisch, Paul, 52n, 54n, 82, 83n, 91, 91n, 113n, 129-30, 130n, 132n, 155n, 187n
Hellas, 214
Hellenization:
  Book of Daniel, 177-79
  Books of Maccabees, 179-80
  Maccabean Revolt and consequences, 180-82
  process, 176-77
Henoch, 65
Henoch, Book of, 38
Henry VIII, 8
Hercules, 177
Herem, 115, 140
Herod the Great, 183-85, 189, 246
Herod Antipas, 185
Hesed, 87, 143, 158, 160
Hexapla, 259
Hieropolis, 172

"High Places," 114-15, 125-26, 146, 153
"History of Salvation" (*see also* Sacred History, Salvation History), 168, 178, 223
Hittite treaties, 87-88
Hodayot, 243
Hokmâh, 216
Holy of Holies, 105, 131, 151, 183
Homer, 175
Horeb, 138
Horemheb, 78
Huesman, John E., 152n, 209n
Hughes, Philip, 8n
"Humani Generis," 13, 16, 50n, 58-59
Hyksos, 75, 78-79
Hyrcania, 246
Hyrcanus II, 182-84, 189
Hyrcanus, John, 181, 246, 249

'IBRI, 79
Iliad, The, 175
Inspiration, Biblical, 28-32
Iron age, 63, 123
Isaac, 47, 69, 73-74, 252
Isaia (*see also* Second Isaia), 151-53, 243:
  anthology, 152
  Assyria, Yahweh's rod of correction, 149
  Emmanuel Prophecy, 208-09
  God of Holiness, 151, 197
  "remnant," 152-53, 211
  vocation, 151
  warning to Achaz, 148
Ishbaal, 128
Ishmael, 252
Israel:
  conquest of Canaan, 115-17, 120-21
  covenant at Sinai, 87-88
  descent from Jacob, 74
  dry bones, 167
  Egypt, 75, 79, 138
  Exile, 161-68, 169-71
  Exodus, 21, 77-78, 90-91
  faithless spouse of Yahweh, 143, 166-67
  Feasts, 104-05
  Messianism, 198-202
  New Covenant, 158, 160
  New Israel, 25, 93, 167
  periods in which Biblical books were produced, 33
  Prophetic movement, 192-94, 196-201
  Psalms in worship, 237-38
  religion, 163
  "remnant," 152-53, 211
  Roman occupation, 22
  rule by Judges, 121-22
  sacrifices, 103-104
  schism, 134-60
  Servant of Yahweh, 210-11
  shepherds, 167
  threat from Canaanite religion, 114-15
  Wisdom literature, 218-26
  Wisdom movement, 214-18
Issus, 175

JABBOK RIVER, 117
Jabesh-Gilead, 127
Jacob, 44, 47, 69, 74, 76, 84, 91, 171, 252
Janneus, Alexander, 189, 191
Jared, 65
Jashar, Book of, 119
Jason, 177, 179
Jaubert, Annie, 191n
Jebel Musa, 86
Jebusites, 128
Jehovah, 81
Jehu, 139-40, 146
Jeremia:
    "Confessions," 157
    contents of book, 157-58
    deportees to Babylon, 162
    "the Gospel before the Gospel," 158
    influence, 157
    New Covenant, 158, 160
    persecution, 155-56
    reproached Joakim, 155
    symbolism, 158
Jericho, 118, 118n, 120, 242, 249
Jeroboam I, 134-35, 137, 140
Jeroboam II, 141-44
Jerome, St., 3-4, 211, 251
Jerusalem:
    capital of Juda during schism, 134-35
    conquest by Antiochus, 177
    destroyed by Yahweh to punish the
        nation, 210
    destruction by Babylonians foretold by
        Jeremia, 156-57
    Essenes disappear after its destruction, 191
    gymnasium built by Jason, 177
    incorporation in Persian empire, 171
    made capital by David, 128
    rebuilding of walls, 170
    reform under Josia, 154
    returning exiles prosperous, 163
    ruin reflected in Psalms, 234
    travel prevented by Kings of Israel, 134
    unique place in hearts of Jews, 171
Jerusalem Temple:
    building, 131, 132 (*figure*)
    destruction by Babylonians, 162, 166
    destruction by Romans, 183, 185-86
    Ezechiel, 167-68
    Feasts, 104-105
    pagan practices, 148, 153, 164, 177
    pillaged by Shishak, 125
    Psalms, 227, 237-38
    rebuilding after Exile, 22, 170
    Seleucid influence, 176-77
Jesus Christ:
    chronology of last week, 191n
    Church, 3, 23-26, 130
    Dynastic Oracle, 130
    Emmanuel prophecy, 208
    Exodus, 92-100
    Faith, 18
    High Priest, 106
    Messianism, 205-13

mystery of salvation, 22, 62, 202
    New Adam, 92
    New Moses, 93, 97
    Person, 253-54
    prophets, 195, 202-204, 236
    Revelation, 16-18
    Sacraments, 24
    salvation-history, 22-26
    Scriptures, 4
    Servant of Yahweh, 210-11
    Shepherd, 168
    Son of David, 130, 236
    Son of Man, 178, 212-13
    Torah, 42
    Typology, 92-100
    Wisdom, 223-26
Jethro, 80
Jews:
    Babylonian Exile, 161-64, 169-70
    Diaspora, 171-72
    Elephantine Community, 171
    end of Jewish State, 185-86
    Hellenism, 174-80
    Maccabean Rule, 180-82
    parties and sects, 187-91
    Persians, 171-73
    Ptolemies and Seleucids, 175-76
    rebirth of Community, 163-64
    revolt of Bar Kokhba, 185n, 245
    Roman rule, 183-86
Jezebel, 136-37, 140, 146
Jezreel, 140
Joachaz, 140, 154-55
Joachin, 156, 164
Joakim, 155-56
Joas, 140-41, 146-47
Joatham, 145, 147-48
Job, Book of, 219-21
John the Baptist, St., 138, 250, 254
John Chrysostom, St., 4
John the Evangelist, St., 93, 254
John XXIII, Pope, 14n
Joiada, 147
Joly, Eugene, 17n
Jonathan, 127, 249
Jones, Alexander, 60n
Joram, 137, 139-40, 146
Jordan river, 118
Josaphat, 146
Joseph the Patriarch, 47, 74-76
Josephus, 89
Josia, 102, 126, 149, 154-55, 162, 200
Josue, 25, 33, 117-20
Josue, Book of, 117-18
Jubilees Calendar, 191n
Juda:
    Babylonian destruction, 134, 161
    Blessing, 76
    Ezechiel, 164-68
    Isaia, 151-53
    Jeremia, 157-60
    Kingdom, 135, 145-57
    Kings, 159 (*table*)

Judas Maccabeus, 179-81
Jude, Epistle of, 254
Judges, Book of, 121-22
Judges, Function of, 121
Jungmann, Joseph, 5n
Justin Martyr, St., 94

KAHLE, PAUL, 257n
Kardesh, 116
Karnak, 146
Keifer, William J., 206n
Kenrick, F. P., 262
Kenyon, Frederic, 8n, 256n, 258n
Kenyon, Kathleen, 69n, 118, 119n, 123n, 131n,
    258n
Khirbet Mird, 246
Khirbet Qumran, 245-47, 249 (*see* Dead Sea
    Scrolls)
King, Philip J., 40n, 121n
Kingdom:
    establishment, 123-26
    Israel and Juda, 159 (*table*)
    schism, 134-60
    sources of information, 124-26
    united, 126-33
Kings, Books of, 124-25, 136-37
Kirjath-Jearim, 124, 128
Kisleu, 105
Kissane, Edward, 212n
Kittim, 243
Klausner, Joseph, 198n
Kraeling, Emil, 172

LACHISH, 147
Lagrange, Pere Marie-Joseph, 12, 29, 256n
Lamech, 65, 106n
Larsa, 64
Law, 42, 126, 163, 201, 215
    and Moses, 47, 217, 252
Legitimate Teacher (*see also* "Teacher of
    Righteousness"), 249
Leipzig, 258
Leningrad, Hebrew Manuscripts in, 257
Leo XII, Pope, 11-12, 29, 29n
Leonard, William, 2n
Le Troquer, René, 58n
Levie, Jean, 3n, 16n, 17n, 36n, 40n
Leviticus, Book of:
    Christians, 106
    content, 43
    Feasts, 104-106
    historical background, 101-103
    Laws, 43, 101, 103
    Priestly Tradition, 101, 104, 168
    Sacrifices, 103-104
    style, 101
"Lex Talionis," 106
Libby, W. F., 248
Lippens, Philippe, 243, 246
Literary Forms (*see* Genres)
Loisy, Alfred, 10
Lot, 73

Luke, St., 28, 251
Luther, Martin, 7
Lyonnet, Stanislaus, 61n
Lysias, 180

MACCABEES, BOOK OF, 179-80
Maccabees, 171, 180-82, 189-90, 230
MacKenzie, R. A. F., 10n, 111n, 230n
Malachia, Book of, 138
Manasses, 151, 153-54
Manna, 85-86, 93-94, 99-100
Maqqabhah, 180
Marathon, Battle of, 174
Marcozzi, Vittorio, 58n
Marduk, 53, 57, 65, 67, 166, 233:
    and creation, 53, 57
Mari, 69
Mariamne, 184
Mark Antony, 175
Mar Saba, 246
Mashah, 80
Mashal, 218-19, 221
Masora, 257
Masseboth, 115, 137
Massoretes, 257
Massoretic Text, 243, 257-58
Mattathias, 180
Matthew, St., 93
Matthew, Thomas, 261
Matthusale, 65
McEleney, Neil, 44n
McKenzie, John L., 29n, 40n, 54n, 60n, 62n,
    121n, 187n, 205, 205n
Medes, 154, 169, 177, 212
"Mediator Dei," 14, 241n
Megiddo, 131, 154
Melanchthon, Philip, 7
Menahem, 143-44
Mendenhall, George E., 87n
Menelaus, 177
Mentelin, 8
Merari, 79
Merneptah, 83
Merom, Lake of, 120
Mesha, 115, 115n, 136
Mesopotamia, 46, 66-67, 215
Messiah (*see also* Messianism), 198-200, 252-
    54
Messianism:
    apologetics, 205-13
    personal, 198
    real, 198
    summary, 200-202
Meyer, Eduard, 39
Mezuzah, 113
Michael, Angel, 178
Michol, 128
Midianites, 80
Midrash, 126
Milik, J. F., 191n, 245n, 247, 247n, 249n,
    253, 254n
Miller, B. V., 57n
Mirabilia Dei, 24, 88, 93, 114

Moab, 115-17, 129, 136
Moabites, 73
Modernism, 11, 11n
Modin, 180
Mohammad Ed-Di'B (Mohammad the Wolf), 242
Mohel, 72
Moloch, 149
Mommsen, Theodor, 39
Monitum of the Holy Office, 13
Monogamy, 57, 71
Morality, Old Testament, 115, 115n
Moran, W. L., 13n
Moriarty, Frederick, 119n, 121n, 131n
Moses:
  background, 80
  character, 90-91
  death, 43, 117, 178
  Exodus, 42, 80, 90
  law, 43, 102, 171
  Pentateuch, 45-46
  plagues in Egypt, 81-82
  sin, 108
  Sirach's praise, 91
  vocation, 21, 47, 171-72
Mosheh (*Mashah*), 80
Mouroux, Jean, 17n
Mount Gilboa, 127
Mount Sinai, 21, 80, 86-87, 93, 138
Murashu, 163, 163n
Murchland, Bernard, 25n
Murphy, Richard, 12n
Murphy, Roland E., 82n, 208n, 217n, 221n, 222n
Mystical Body of Christ, 16, 18, 23-25
"Mystici Corporis," 14, 23n

NAAMAN, 139
Nabateans, 182, 182n, 183
Nabi (*see also* Prophets), 192-94
Nabopolassar, 154
Nabor, 69
Nabuchodonosor, 155-56, 162, 166, 169
Nadab, 136
Nash Papyrus, 248
Nathan, 130, 197, 210, 235
Naturalism, 9n
Necho, 154-55
Necromancy, 153
Nehemia, 168, 170-71
Nephesh, 56
New Covenant (*see also* Covenant):
  Essenes, 191
  Ezechiel, 166
  Jeremia, 158, 160
  Old prepared for New, 88, 92-93, 200-201
New Testament:
  books, 93-94
  Dead Sea Scrolls, 249-55
  Exodus, 92-94
  Original Sin, 60-61
Ninive, 154
Nippur, 162

Noe (*see also* Flood), 65-67
Nominalism, 6
North, Robert, 84n
Noth, Martin, 90, 90n
Numbers, Book of, 42-43, 107-10
Nuzu Tablets, 71-72

O'CALLAHAN, ROGER T., 72n
Ochozia, 139-40, 146
O'Doherty, E., 121n
Old Covenant (*see* Covenant, New Covenant)
Old Testament (*see also* Covenant, New Covenant):
  angels, 178
  books, 173
  Dead Sea Scrolls, 252
  Essenes, 254
  prefigured New Testament, 92-93
Omri, 136, 139-40
Orchard, Dom Bernard, 2n
Origen, 259
Original Justice:
  Church's teaching, 57n
  Man and Woman created in, 57
Original Sin, 59-62
  consequences, 63, 66-68
Ormulum, 261
Osee (King of Israel), 145, 150
Osee (Prophet), 112, 143, 152, 166, 197
Osty, E., 172n

PACTS   (*see* Treaties)
Palestine:
  origin of name, 185n
Paneas (Panium), Battle of, 176
Paralipomenon, Books of, 126, 170
Parente, Pietro, 11n
Parousia, 25, 39, 93
Parthenos, 208-209
Parties, Jewish:
  Essenes, 190-91
  Pharisees, 188-89
  Sadducees, 189-90
  Sanhedrin, 188
  Scribes, 187-88
Pascal, Blaise, 222
Passover, 21, 78-79, 98-99 (*table*), 104
Patriarchs:
  circumcision, 72
  origin of Old Testament, 45-46
  period, 68-69
  promises and Exodus, 77
Paul, St., 3, 27-28, 93, 221
Peka, 144-45, 147-48
Peloponnesian War, 174
Pentateuch:
  authorship, 45, 88-89
  contents, 42-43
  "heart," 114
  meaning, 42-43
  name, 42
  outline, 147-48

Pentateuch (*cont'd.*)
  purpose, 43
  theme, 46-47
  thesis, 46-47
  traditions, 44-45
  unity, 45-46
Pentecost, Feast of, 104-105
Persepolis, 171
Persians, 171-75, 212
Peter, St., 23
Petrie, Flinders, 248
Phacea, 144
Phaceia, 144
Pharisees, 182, 188-89
Phasael, 183
Philip of Macedon, 174-75, 212
Philistia, 129
Philistines, 84, 120, 127, 148
Phillips, R. P., 30n
Philo, 89
Phinehas, 79
Phoenecia, 136, 175
Phylactery, 113
Pieper, Joseph, 3n
Pilate, 185
Pillars, Sacred, 114-15
Pithom, 79
Pius XII, Pope, 14n, 16n, 19, 23n, 35, 50, 56, 59, 241
Plagues (in Egypt), 81-82
Plato, 214, 256
Plumpe, Joseph C., 4n
Poelman, Roger, 17n
Polack, A. I., 198n
Polygamy, 71-72
Polygenism, 59, 59n
Pompey, 182
Praetorium, 185
Priestly Tradition:
  Exodus, 81 (*table*), 89
  Feasts, 104
  Genesis, 54, 64, 74
  Leviticus, 101
  meaning, 45
  Numbers, 107
  origin at time of Babylonian Exile, 168
Pritchard, James B., 13, 54n, 66n, 120n
Prophecies, Messianic, 205-13
Prophets (*see* names of various prophets):
  Christian relationship, 202-204
  Golden Age, 137
  kinds, 193-94
  meaning, 192-93
  messianism, 198-213
  monotheism, 196-97
  morality, 197-98
  requirements, 194-96
  sin, 143, 157-58, 160, 165-67, 197-98
  and typology, 92
  work, 196
  and worship, 103-104
Protocanonical, 258n
Protoevangelium, 62-63

Proverbs, Book of, 214-15, 218-19, 221-22
"Providentissimus Deus," 29n
Psalms, Book of:
  authorship, 228-30
  genres, 230-37
  teachings, 239-40
  use in worship of Israel, 237-39
  value, 240-41
Psalter (*see* Psalms)
Ptolemies, 175-76, 212
Pul (Phul), 144
Purim, Feast of, 105

QUMRAN (*see also* Dead Sea Scrolls), 190-91, 242-55
Qohelet, 222-23
Quasten, Johannes, 4n

RABBI, 187
Raguel, 80
Rahner, Karl, 29, 59n
Rama, 146
Rameses II, 78-79, 84
Rameses III, 123
Raphael, Angel, 178
Rationalism, 9n
Rebecca, 74
Red Sea, 84-85, 93, 96
Redaction, 155
Reed Sea (*see* Red Sea)
Reformation, Protestant, 7, 7n
Remnant, 22, 33, 92, 142, 210-11
Renaissance, 6
Renan, Ernest, 10
Retribution, Temporal, 52n, 215, 219-21, 222, 240
Rezin, 145, 147-49
Ricciotti, Giuseppe, 66n, 83, 83n, 84, 84n, 181n
Richardson, Alan, 17n
Rigaux, B., 62n
Robert, A., 8n, 54n, 215n
Roboam, 134, 137, 145
Rodin, Auguste, 30
Rogers, John, 261
Rosh Hashanah, Feast of, 105
Rowley, H. H., 69n, 120n

SACRAMENTS, 24, 93-94, 98-99 (*table*)
Sacred History (*see* "History of Salvation" and Salvation-History), 20, 68, 77, 93, 168
Sacrifice, human, 82
Sacrifices (in Israel), 103-104
Sadducees, 189-90
Sages:
  in Israel, 215-16
  pagan, 214-15
  Wisdom literature, 216-18
Salvation-History (*see also* "History of Salvation," Sacred History), 20-26
Samaria, 134, 150
Samaritans, 170
Samson, 122

Samuel, Books of, 124-25
Samuel (Prophet), 124
Sanhedrin, 182, 188, 212
Sara, 72
Sargon, 80, 145
Satan, 178, 219
Saul, 126-28
Schnierla, William S., 13n
Scribes, 187-88, 216
Scriptorium, 248
Second Isaia, 33, 102, 152
Sects, Jewish (*see* Parties)
Sedecia, 156-57
Seleucia, 175
Seleucid, 175-76, 179-82, 212
Seleucus, 175
Sennacherib, 150, 153
Septuagint, 42-43, 175, 208, 227, 257-59
Servant Songs, 201, 210-11
Sethos I, 79, 84
Shallum, 144
Shalmaneser III, 140
Shalmaneser V, 145, 150
Shechem, 135
Shekinah, 94, 107-108, 108n
Shema, 113, 248
Sheol, 52, 190, 219-20
Shiloh, 124, 128
Shishak, 125, 145-46
Shophet, 121
Shophetim, 122
Shunem, 127, 139
Sichem, 76
Siegman, Edward F., 13n, 164n
Siloam tunnel, 150
Simeon, 22
Simon, Richard, 10-11, 11n
Sin:
    Day of Atonement, 105
    nature, 75
    Original Sin and consequences, 20-21,
        59-63, 66-68
    Prophets, 142-43, 157-58, 160, 165-67,
        197-98
    sacrifices offered for forgiveness, 103
    scapegoat ceremony, 105
Sinai:
    covenant, 21, 43, 77, 87-88
    location, 86-87
Sirach, 216-17, 224
Skehan, Patrick W., 8n, 40n, 191n, 249n
Socrates, 214
Sodom, 72
Solomon, 21, 33, 44, 102, 125, 129-32, 167,
    216-17, 236
"Son of Man," 178, 212-13
Sophar, 219
Sophocles, 256
Suhard, Celestine Cardinal, 13, 50n
Sukenik, E. L., 242
Sukkoth, Feast of, 105
Sullivan, Mother Kathryn, 87n, 111n

Sumerians, 66, 71
Sutcliffe, Edmund F., 52n
Symmachus, 259
Synave, Paul, 29n
Syncretism, 137, 145, 155
Synod of Oxford, 8
Spinoza, Baruch, 9-10
Stanley, David M., 29n
Steinmann, Jean, 11n
Strange, Marcian, 142n
Stuhlmueller, Carroll, 11n, 101n, 208n

TAMMUZ, 164
Targum, 247
Tavard, George, 3n
Taverner, Richard, 261
Taymans, Francois, 82n
"Teacher of Righteousness," 190, 249, 251-53
Tehillim, 227
Temple (*see* Jerusalem Temple)
Tertullian, 95
Tetragrammaton, 80
Thales of Miletus, 214
Thebes, 78
Theocracy, 47, 126
Theodore of Mopsuestia, 211
Theodoret, 96
Theodotion, 259
Theophany, 87, 138, 164
Therapeutae, 191
Thomas, D. Winton, 54n, 136n, 140n, 145n,
    169n
Thomas Aquinas, St., 6n, 18n, 56
Thothmes, 78
Thucydides, 256
Tiamat, 53
Tiglath-Pileser I, 123, 144-45
Tiglath-Pileser III, 148, 150
Tigris river, 172
Tishri, Month of, 105
Tisserant, E., 256n
Titus, 185
Tobia, Book of, 217
Torah, 42, 117, 177, 187-88, 190, 227
"Torah of Ezechiel," 167
Tradition and Bible, 2-4
Traditions in Pentateuch, 44-45
Transjordan, 107, 128, 135
Translations of Bible, English, 7-8, 261-62
Treaties:
    Parity, 87
    Suzerainty, 87-88
Trent, Council of, 11
Tresmontant, Claude, 56n
Tricot, A., 8n, 187n, 256n, 258n
Tutankhamon, 78
Tyndale, William, 7, 261
Typology (*see* Exodus, Typology of)
Tyre, 177, 215

UR, 67-68, 71
Utnapishtim, 66

VAN CASTER, MARCEL, 20n
Van Imschoot, P., 87n
Vatican, Council of, 11-12
Vawter, Bruce, 9n, 13n, 17n, 52n, 59n, 178n, 202n, 208n
Vespasian, 185
Vincent, A., 10n
Vollert, Cyril, 61n
Voltaire, Francois, 9-10
Von Rad, Gerhard, 47n, 117
Von Ranke, Leopold, 39
Vulgate, 220, 259-60

WADI MURABBAAT, 245, 247, 249
Wellhausen, Julius, 10, 117
Whealon, John J., 11n
Wisdom:
    Israelite sages, 215-16
    literary forms, 218-19
    Old Testament literature, 216-18
    pagan, 214-15
Wisdom, Books of:
    Ecclesiastes, 222-23
    Job, 219-21
    literary form, 218-19
    Proverbs, 221-22
    Psalter, 227-41
Wisdom Incarnate, 218, 223-25
Woolf, Virginia, 36
Wright, G. Ernest, 56n, 112n, 117n, 150n
Wycliffe, John, 7-8, 261

XERXES, 174

YADIN, YIGAEL, 247n
Yahu, 172
Yahweh (*see also* God, Feasts, Prophets, Servant Songs):
    anthropomorphism, 50-51

Babylonian Exile, 163-64
covenant with Abraham, 69-71
covenant with David, 130
covenant at Sinai, 21, 77
Day of the Lord, 38, 197
Deuteronomic viewpoint, 125
heavenly court, 164-65, 178
infidelity of kingdoms, 125-26
King, 126
meaning of name, 80-81, 81n
mentioned on Stele of Mesha, 115
persecution of followers, 136-37, 177
prohibition of images, 90
sanctuaries in Israel, 135
Shekinah, symbol of presence, 121
Shepherd of Israel, 167
source of wisdom, 216
use of name in Psalms, 228
worship in Jerusalem, 128, 131
Yom Kippur, 105
Yahwist Tradition
    Exodus, 80-81, 85
    Feasts, 104
    Genesis, 55-57, 63-64, 69-72, 74-75
    meaning, 44
    Numbers, 107, 109
    Psalter, 228
Yehud, 172
YHWH, 80
Yom Kippur, Feast of, 105

ZACHARY, 22
Zacharia, 144, 147, 167, 200
Zadok, 189-90
Zealots, 185
Zeitlin, S., 248n
Ziggurat, 67-68
Ziglag, 127
Zimri, 136
Zwingli, Ulrich, 7

NOTES